W9-ACL-321

Paul A. Herbig

Handbook of Cross-Cultural Marketing

Pre-publication
REVIEWS,
COMMENTARIES,
EVALUATIONS . . .

"**P**rofessor Paul Herbig's handbook provides a truly 'user-friendly' and pragmatic approach to cross-cultural marketing. This book is not only interesting but also easy to follow. The author does an excellent job of introducing traditional marketing concepts and providing current applications. As such the book is a good resource for basic cross-cultural marketing information and discussion.

Perhaps the most important aspect of this book is the inclusion of recent trends and developments in international marketing. Where many books often lag behind in introducing current issues on cross-cultural marketing, Herbig does otherwise. As such, readers are going to find many segments to be insightful and informative."

Alma Mintu-Wimsatt, PhD
Associate Professor of Marketing,
Department of Marketing
and Management,
College of Business and Technology,
Texas A&M University,
Commerce, Texas

More pre-publication
REVIEWS, COMMENTARIES, EVALUATIONS . . .

"**T**his is an exciting, highly useful, and practical handbook in the discipline of international marketing and a must read for managers and academics in the changing global marketplace. Paul Herbig's work is a thoughtful, comprehensive, and refreshing mixture of insightful ideas in the domain of cross-cultural marketing, which at present is in dire need of sound and constructive works. The book will be extremely beneficial to multinational and cosmopolitan managers who want to compete efficiently and effectively in the worldwide markets."

Syed Tariq Anwar, DBA
*Professor of Marketing
and International Business,
T. Boone Pickens College of Business,
West Texas A&M University,
Canyon, Texas*

The International Business Press
An Imprint of The Haworth Press, Inc.

NOTES FOR PROFESSIONAL LIBRARIANS
AND LIBRARY USERS

This is an original book title published by The International Business Press, an imprint of The Haworth Press, Inc. Unless otherwise noted in specific chapters with attribution, materials in this book have not been previously published elsewhere in any format or language.

CONSERVATION AND PRESERVATION NOTES

All books published by The Haworth Press, Inc. and its imprints are printed on certified ph neutral, acid free book grade paper. This paper meets the minimum requirements of American National Standard for Information Sciences–Permanence of Paper for Printed Material, ANSI Z39.48-1984.

Handbook
of Cross-Cultural Marketing

INTERNATIONAL BUSINESS PRESS
Erdener Kaynak, PhD
Executive Editor

New, Recent, and Forthcoming Titles:

Handbook of Cross-Cultural Marketing

Paul A. Herbig

The International Business Press
An Imprint of The Haworth Press, Inc.
New York • London

Published by

The International Business Press, an imprint of The Haworth Press, Inc., 10 Alice Street, Binghamton, NY 13904-1580

© 1998 by The Haworth Press, Inc. All rights reserved. No part of this work may be reproduced or utilized in any form or by any means, electronic or mechanical, including photocopying, microfilm, and recording, or by any information storage and retrieval system, without permission in writing from the publisher. Printed in the United States of America.

Cover design by Marylouise E. Doyle.

Library of Congress Cataloging-in-Publication Data

Herbig, Paul A.
    Handbook of cross-cultural marketing / Paul A. Herbig.
       p.   cm.
    Includes bibliographical references and index.
    ISBN 0-7890-0285-X (alk. paper).
    1. Marketing—Cross-cultural studies. 2. Export marketing—Cross-cultural studies. I. Title.
HF5415.H393   1997
658.8'48—dc21
                                           97-10774
                                             CIP

I dedicate this book to my siblings: John Robert William Cracken, my brother-in-law but brother in spirit, for all of his help to us when we needed it most; Phillip Herbig, Merrie Herbig Rockwell, and Marty Herbig, who have put up with me all these years. And to my own bunch: Rachel, Robert, and William, who tolerated me during the long months of writing, especially when I became intolerable. I love you all.

ABOUT THE AUTHOR

Paul A. Herbig, ABD, is Professor in the Management and Marketing Department of the Graduate School of International Trade and Business Administration at Texas A&M International University in Laredo, Texas. Prior to his career in academia, he worked in marketing management and product management for AT&T, Honeywell, and Intermec. He is the author of *Innovation Matrix* (Quorum, 1994), *Innovation—Japanese Style* (Quorum, 1995) *Marketing—Japanese Style* (Quorum, 1995), and *Cross-Cultural Negotiations* (Quorum, 1996). In addition, he has published more than 200 articles in journals such as *Industrial Marketing Management,* the *Journal of Product Innovation Management, Management Decisions,* the *Journal of Business Research,* and the *International Journal of Commerce and Management.* A frequent participant in national and international conferences, Professor Herbig has taught at the University of Hawaii–Manoa, as well as in Panama City and London. His research interests include reputation and market signaling and cross-cultural negotiations.

CONTENTS

Foreword

The charm of culture lies in its being at once inherently qualitative and complex. This makes the lack of definition and organization a formidable one. Paul Herbig is successful on both scores. Even in his introduction, the author identifies ten aspects of culture of special relevance to cross-cultural practitioners. And commendably, the organization of the book is focused on hands-on marketing impacts.

Clearly, there is two-way interaction between marketing and culture. From a human ecology viewpoint, the role of marketing is the dual one of reflecting ever-changing culture *and*, in turn, changing the culture. This is true of the domestic and multinational company as well as at the macro and public policy levels. At the macro level, marketing has a crucial role to play in stimulating growth in the developing countries.[1] Herbig rightly points out that we should never assume transferability of cultural concepts. This applies to public policy regarding marketing as well as private policy. Sweden and the United States are probably world leaders in the development of consumer policy. Yet, the transferability of public policy measures has proven limited due to differences in underlying culture. In the United States, consumer legislation is rooted in the notion that public policy should be shaped as "help to self-help" of the individual, whereas Sweden has long had the philosophy that all consumers are basically "underprivileged" and in need of state assistance.[2]

At the firm level, marketing's role as a cultural change agent raises fascinating ethical issues.[3] The promotion of powdered milk in developing countries as a baby food "superior to" breast milk has been questioned, and a special international code of ethics now effectively constrains excessive promotion. Similarly, the use of advertising not only to capitalize on prevalent smoking habits in export markets, but also to increase the number of smokers, has been challenged on medical grounds. On the other hand, this writer wholeheartedly agrees with observers who claim that family planning is "the world's most urgent marketing challenge."

Real or would-be ethical issues may also arise when a product new to a culture is introduced to it. C. Northcote Parkinson relates the example of pepper, introduced in England by the East India Company a few centuries ago. Critics labeled the sale of pepper a shameful waste and termed the product an unnecessary luxury. But in a country where refrigeration was all but nonexistent, pepper became not a luxury, but an urgent necessity in the course of but a few years.

The country of origin literature illustrates another interesting aspect of cross-cultural marketing. Most people will have perceptions of the quality, price, durability, etc., of products made (or assembled) in other countries. When in doubt which brand of a given product to buy, research has demonstrated that many consumers will be influenced by their ideas about the country of origin of the various brands.

Herbig's observation that we are still far from a homogeneous global culture is certainly correct, the visions of Levitt, Ohmae, and others notwithstanding. In the United States, we have abandoned the melting-pot tradition in favor of recognizing the cultural identity of Cubans, Mexicans, other Hispanics, and Vietnamese, as well as an array of other immigrant groups. The breakup of the communist dictatorship resulted in a fragmentation of the former Soviet Union along ethnic lines. In the European Union, "Brussels" stands for the notion of Europeanization, at the cost of the dozen component national states. But, paradoxically, we are also seeing a concomitant *intranational* cultural fragmentation along ethnic, religious, and other conventional lines in most of these countries (proceeding further in Southern than in Northern Europe). There seems to be no good reason to assume that the cultural fragmentation trend will be broken this side of 2005. Of course, not all cultural differences call for marketing adaptation. The differences in a given case may be trivial (at least from a marketing point of view) relative to the similarities, the market niches implicitly defined by the differences may be too small, and so on. Nevertheless, increasing fragmentation will call for increasing adaptation. Herbig does a fine job of developing the details of cultural adaptation strategy in international marketing.

A given country's overall culture may be classified into subcultures on other than conventional criteria such as ethnicity, religion, and (in the case of immigrant groups) country of origin. Intercultural variations of relevance to international marketing may also be reflected by demographic characteristics such as age and education. A potentially significant, but largely neglected source of distinction of marketing relevance is information-seeking behavior of consumers. It turns out that all highly industrialized countries have in common at least two groups which we have labeled "information seekers" (IS) and "average consumers." IS consult a far greater number of information sources than average consumers, and spontaneously mention availability of information as a buying criterion significantly more often than average consumers.[4] Among other relevant characteristics is that IS have cosmopolitan values, while average consumers are the protagonists of local culture. IS tend to be opinion leaders, average consumers do not. IS, then, is the avant-garde "global" consumer segment.

While IS do not constitute more than 10 to 15 percent of the aggregate number of (adult) consumers in the highly industrialized countries, an MNC bent on introducing "exciting" products might well consider a standardized marketing strategy to this "cross-cultural culture."[5]

Paul Herbig is a man in pursuit of culture with a passion, but he loves culture not for its own sake. He loves it because of the challenge that culture presents to international marketing operations. This challenge is a dual one: the cross-cultural similarities which hold promise of standardized strategy with economies of scale and scope, and the differences which call for detection, adaptation, and heightened customer orientation. His work will command the attention of globally oriented marketing executives and students alike.

Hans Thorelli

Acknowledgments

Four distinguished gentlemen are responsible for this book. Dean Khosrow Fatemi, Dean of the Graduate School of International Trade and Business Administration at Texas A&M International University in Laredo, Texas, took a chance on me when the rest of academia would not. I am in his debt forever. His constant encouragement in my writing and editing has challenged me to take on new endeavors. Few citizens of this world are such that if they said jump, one would jump without question, whether one is leaning over a cliff, peering out the open hatch of a plane 10,000 feet up in the sky, or at the top of the Empire State Building. Dean Fatemi, I am proud to say, is one of those few. For him, I would jump. It has been a pleasure working for him and I hope to do so for many more years.

The second is Dr. Erdener Kaynak, editor of the International Business Press division of The Haworth Press. I have known Dr. Kaynak for many years, as the editor for many of the numerous journals to which I have contributed. He has been supportive and professional to me in all my endeavors for him. He has been and continues to be a fine friend, esteemed colleague, outstanding academician, writer, and editor. I am hopeful that this will be only the first of many future collaborations with Dr. Kaynak and IBP/Haworth.

Dr. Hans Thorelli and Dr. Joe Miller from Indiana University complete the foursome. Dr. Thorelli honored me by writing the foreword to this book. Both Dr. Thorelli and Dr. Miller have been constant sources of support during and after my time at Indiana University. Through the darkest days when I felt the skies would never clear and daylight and better times would never arrive, they supported me and gave me both assistance and encouragement. I thank both of you.

Many others were contributors to this work. Dr. Rama Yelkur of TAMIU assisted me with Chapter 1 on culture. Nacho Zabaleta, an outstanding MBA/IBK student at TAMIU, provided me with assistance for Chapter 2 and Chapter 14. Dr. Danny Butler from Auburn University reviewed Chapter 3 on marketing research and provided significant input for that chapter. Dr. Carol Howard worked with me on Chapter 5. Dr. Alan Shao provided many valuable comments for international advertising within Chapter 6. Dr. Fred Palumbo from Yeshiva University help me considerably with international trade show information in Chapter 7 and Chapter 8 on international sales promotion. Drs. Jackie and Milton Mayfield assisted me with the preparation of Chapter 4 on cross-cultural negotiations. Dr. Brad O'Hara of Southeastern Louisiana University helped me with sales and sales management information in Chapter 9. Dr. Ken Day helped me with Chapter 10 as did Joe Miller from Indiana University. Dr. Arch Woodside from Tulane assisted me with the international pricing portions of Chapter 11. Dr. Laurence Jacobs from the University of Hawaii-Manoa assisted me by reviewing and commenting on Chapter 12. Dr. Alain Genestre, also from TAMIU, provided insights for Chapter 14. Terry Ang, a graduate assistant from TAMIU, previewed Chapters 13 and 15 for me. I wish to thank all of you for your collaborative efforts.

Other thanks go to those who assisted me in the general preparation of this manuscript: to my wife, Rachel, and my father-in-law, Bill Cracken, who reviewed earlier drafts of this project; to my secretary, Alma Rodriguez; to my colleagues Barry Carr and Cindy Houser, for their encouragement during the course of this project; and to the countless students who served as sounding boards for the ideas used in this book.

Introduction

The growth in international trade since 1970 has seen unparalleled increases: $314 billion in trade in 1970 versus $5 trillion in 1995, a threefold increase in real terms (annual increases of 5 percent). Annual increases during the 1990s averaged 11 percent. Trade exceeds 25 percent of total global GNP; experts indicate that this percentage will continue to increase in the decades to come. Many European countries have total trade volume (imports plus exports) that surpasses 70 percent of their GDP. Considerably smaller, the United States' trade component has been traditionally low due to its geographical isolation and resource self-sufficiency. Yet, DRI/McGraw-Hill estimates American exports (manufactured goods and services) will exceed $1 trillion by 1998. Worldwide Foreign Direct Investment (FDI) in 1995 was up 46 percent from 1994 to $325 billion; Americans accounted for a record $95 billion of this. Growth not only continues, but escalates. Interactions between countries are growing exponentially. If a company is not going global, it is either buying or selling to foreign firms or American subsidiaries of foreign firms. In the United States, the last bastion of parochial beliefs, even small companies are realizing they have but three options: go global, get out of the business, or go broke. International marketing must exist for the survival of the firm.

Many definitions of marketing abound. The most succinct definition for marketing is one that "seeks to fulfill wants and needs of one's customers." Marketing in the simplest form attempts to understand customers in terms of what they buy, when they buy, why they buy, how much they buy, where they buy it, and with what they buy. The relationship with culture comes into play with the realization that each of the descriptors noted above varies from culture to culture. Americans find it peculiar that the Chinese believe a dog is a delicacy to be savored at dinner, while the Chinese find it peculiar that Americans buy packaged, processed dog food and keep dogs as pets. Meanwhile, the French take their dogs with them to the finest restaurants where the dogs, too, are served at the table. One must remember that logic is relative: global consumers show astonishing resourcefulness in finding ways to buy what really matters to them. The poorest slums of Calcutta are home to 70,000 VCRs. In Mexico, homes with color televisions outnumber those with running water. No self-respecting Cantonese would accept any less than a 29-inch TV with flat screen technology. One cannot gauge another's wants and needs by one's own standards![1]

Cultural misunderstandings may not just be dangerous but also fatal: Bata sandals caused a riot in Bangladesh which resulted in over 50 people being wounded; fundamentalist Muslims demonstrated because the logo on the sandals resembled the Arabic characters for Allah, "God" in Arabic. The logo was intended to be a stylish drawing of three bells. As a result, the government banned the sale of the sandals. Other times, misunderstandings prove only embarrassing to the company: Betty Crocker attempted to capture the British cake mix market by offering U.S.-style fancy cake mixes with frosting; the company discovered that British consumers ate their cake at tea time and preferred a dry, spongy cake that is suitable for being picked up with one hand while the other manages a cup of tea. Only when the company produced and marketed British-style cake mixes did it prosper. United Airlines, upon acquiring Pan Am's Pacific routes, inaugurated their Pan-Pacific flight service by handing out white carnations to each passenger; white is the Oriental symbol of death.

Being ethnocentric in one's thinking (i.e., if it plays in Peoria, it should play in Beijing) has led many a company down the path to unexpected, painful, and sometimes overwhelming failure. Federal Express showed its ethnocentric tendencies when it entered the European marketplace: all company brochures, promotional materials, and shipping bills were in American English. To keep arrival times constant, package pickup deadlines were set for 5:00 p.m. in the evenings, even though many Europeans have workdays that normally end later; for example, 8:00 p.m. for the Spanish. Federal Express had assumed that lifestyles and work schedules were the same in Europe as in the United States. Federal Express tried to put a round peg in a square hole and, not surprisingly, failed as a result.

Naivete and carelessness have also been disastrous. Classical examples abound. Jolly Green Giant was translated into Arabic as "Intimidating Green Ogre." Ford introduced a low-cost truck, the "Feira," into some of the less-developed countries of Latin America; the name means "ugly old woman" in Spanish. Ford's top-of-the-line automobile was introduced in Mexico as "Caliente"; this is slang in Mexico for a street walker. A food company advertised its giant burrito as "Burrad." Colloquially, this meant "big mistake." Olympia's Roto photocopier did not sell well because "roto" refers to the lowest class in Chile; "roto" in Spanish means "broken." Americans are not the only ones who err: In Japan, a soft drink called "Pocari Sweat" was a success. To the Japanese, this name conveyed a positive, healthy, thirst-quenching image. Japanese consumers react to brand names strictly based on its foreign name, not the content or meaning. This product's name, however, did not transfer well to the American consumer.

The classic 1990s example of how not to do cross-cultural marketing comes from EuroDisney. Walt Disney Company had successfully launched Tokyo Disneyland years before. However, it was only a licenser, garnering but a small fraction of the revenues as the price for its name and mystique while another company owned the park. Two mistakes in the company's sparkled past would not be repeated in Europe: it would own and control the park and it would own enough land for its own hotels. Disney was fanatically intent on bringing Americana to the Europeans. After prolonged negotiations with a variety of European countries, Disney passed on a site in sunny Spain for a location twenty miles east of Paris, which it believed projected a more central location. Of the final $4 billion price tag for the project, Disney invested only $160 million; the French Government assumed the bulk of the financial risk,[2] including the construction of two adjoining freeway exits and a connecting suburban train line to Paris.

Why should Disney have worried? It had been successful in Tokyo; why shouldn't it be successful in Paris as well? Tokyo has more than three times as many inhabitants as Paris with a per capita income 50 percent higher than the Parisian native. Tokyo Disneyland is only six miles from downtown Tokyo while EuroDisney is 20 miles outside Paris. Europeans can be in Florida within a matter of hours, a geographic luxury the Japanese do not have. Disney World competed directly with EuroDisney for the Europeans' entertainment dollar while Tokyo Disneyland had no such competition. Winter temperatures in Tokyo, while cold, are still bearable, while French winters are cold and snowy and unbearable. Attendance at EuroDisney in winter could have been anticipated to be four to six times less than Tokyo Disneyland.[3]

Early on, omens were unambiguous. The cultural elite in Paris lambasted the project as an affront to French cultural traditions. (Responding to their concerns, Disney decided French would be the official language at EuroDisney.) Farmers protested the manner in which the French government had condemned their land so that it could be sold to Disney. The rigid legal approach was offensive to the French, who consider depending on lawyers to be a last, not first, resort.[4] The firm found itself defending its conservative dress codes (Disney prohibited facial hair and limited the use of makeup and jewelry), regimented training practices, and plans to ban alcohol from park facilities. Enhancements were added and the park, originally budgeted at $2 billion, ended up costing nearly $4 billion, pushing EuroDisney's break-even parameters sharply higher and perhaps far beyond its ability to deliver.[5]

Disney had worked hard to adapt EuroDisney to European tastes. Fantasyland focused on the Grimm Brothers fairy tales and Alice in Wonderland. Discoveryland exhibits drew attention to Jules Verne, H.G. Wells, and Leonardo da Vinci. EuroDisney's castle is called *Le Chateau de la Belle au Bois Dormant* (Sleeping Beauty's home). A theater featured a movie on European history. The Visionarium showed a 360-degree movie about French culture. Signs are in multiple languages. Pirates of the Caribbean played pirate songs in three languages: English, French, and Dutch. A multilingual staff was available (the reservations center had separate phone lines for each of twelve different languages). EuroDisney had Mickey Mouse and Donald Duck with French accents. Basically, however, the Disney strategy was to transplant the American park to Paris. The American management system was exported in total; Disney knew it would work because it was Disney and it had always worked in the past. This arrogance worsened relations with the local French.

In April 1992, EuroDisney opened its doors. A preopening party provided spare ribs without providing the silverware; French visitors were perplexed. Start-up problems abounded. Disney planners presumed hotel guests would stay an average of three to four days as they do at Disney World in Orlando; the actual average was closer to two days. (Many guests arrive early in the morning, rush to the park, come back late at night, and check out the next morning before heading to the park for the second day.) Disney thought Monday would be a light day with Fridays heavy and allocated staff accordingly; the reality was the reverse.[6] These shorter stays lowered occupancy rates and placed an unanticipated burden on the hotel's operations because of the unexpectedly high volume of check in and check out activity.

Attendance was highly seasonal and peaked during the summer months: Europeans typically take one long vacation in the summer instead of short visits typical of Americans.[7] (Their family vacation budgets are more modest than Americans, and more carefully rationed to sustain the longer vacations.) Disney executives believed incorrectly that they could change French attitudes of not wanting to take their children from school during the school year and to take shorter breaks many times a year rather than one long vacation in the summer.[8] The dismal Central European winter inhibits attendance for one-third of the year. Visitors spent 12 percent less on food and souvenirs than expected. Instead of riding the expensive trams, Europeans preferred walking. The high American service level available at Disney World and Disneyland was not easily exportable: EuroDisney's youthful French employees did not see the need to cut their hair, dress uniformly, smile incessantly, and provide world-class service to the park attendees.[9] For a European who had visited the Disney parks in the United States, the experience was second-rate and often not considered worth the high prices charged.

Alcohol was not served since Disney felt a family theme park should not do so; Disney failed to consider the European penchant for drinking wine and beer with meals. The park did not offer sufficient restaurant seating for its European customers, who enjoy a leisurely meal and expected to sit down at the accustomed dinner hour. Breakfast was erroneously initially downplayed (Disney ended up trying to serve 2,500 breakfasts in a 350-seat restaurant); instead of croissants and coffee, full breakfasts were desired. Instead of jammed parking lots, bus lots were jammed with insufficient facilities for bus drivers. Food prices were too high inside the park, and hotel prices were too high outside of it. (Why stay at a Disney hotel when one could stay in Paris where rooms were abundant and inexpensive?)

The Disney team again and again disregarded the advice of locals. They did not adequately take into consideration the cultural factors that differed between Disneyland, Disney World, Disney World Japan, and the European marketplace. Europeans wanted more local content in their parks. Whereas the Japanese are fond of American pop culture, the Europeans wanted their own. To them, detail and craftsmanship were more important than heart-stopping rides. The Magic Kingdom concept alone was not compelling enough to entice Europeans to extend their stay beyond one or two days.[10] The solution was to have been the now delayed adjacent MGM movie theme park, which was then put on indefinite hold.

EuroDisney's first year resulted in a loss; forecasted attendance was nearly 12 million visitors the first year; although actual attendance was substantial (9.5 million), it was far below the operating break-even level of 11 million. Fewer French came than were predicted (although French nationals were still the largest group of visitors, accounting for 29 percent of all attendance).[11] What went wrong? EuroDisney's high admission price (30 percent higher than Orlando's park, even though conditions in Europe—lower disposable income, recession, conservative vacation, and spending habits—suggested the opposite) made visitors keen to take as many rides as possible and perform less shopping.[12] Visitors' average length of stay was well below plan.[13]

In retrospect, Disney, although adapting the park itself, failed to take the time to understand its potential customers better and, in essence, assumed the unassumable, the Self-Reference Criterion: they had a formula that had succeeded in the United States and (presumably) Japan, they saw no reason to tamper with it, and it should also work in France. Arrogance and poor planning led to a tarnishing of the Disney mystique, which is still being fixed. On March 15, 1994, Disney and its partners announced a restructuring agreement. The Euro prefix was intended to provide the theme park with a pan-European branding; that this did not work out was indicated when the name of the park was changed during 1995 to Disneyland Paris. As of 1996, the park was still losing money, albeit at a smaller rate.

It is admirable to learn from one's mistakes; it is yet more fruitful not to make them in the first place. Right on the throes of Disney's EuroDisney disaster, Disney proposed an American historical theme park planned for Virginia. Disney failed to learn its lesson about harmonizing with the host community by demanding the community put up $160 million or it would go elsewhere. And again, it was surprised by a controversy it had failed to anticipate (the potential desecration the park's sprawl might cause to the Bull Run Civil War battlegrounds nearby).[14] Disney has since withdrawn its proposal from Virginia.

This book was written expressly with the intent to assist all companies, not merely American companies, to increase their likelihood of success in international markets by better understanding, relating to, and working with those from different cultures. In the United States, foreign culture is not the exclusive domain of foreign citizens. In this new multicultural age, American citizens could be of Vietnamese, Mexican, Haitian, Russian, Bosnian, Native American, or Indian ethnic descent, just to name a few. They could be born in the United States or in their homeland. Many still carry their culture with them. Unlike 100 years ago, assimilation into the American culture is not a sure bet. Therefore, understanding of culture is of major importance, even to those who deal domestically with only domestic plants and domestic customers. To those who do deal with foreign customers, suppliers, and bankers, understanding culture becomes not merely important, not just critical, but mandatory, if one's organization is to succeed in the international marketplace.

PART I:
PREMARKETING

Chapter 1

Culture Impacts of Markets: Pitfalls and Potentials

AN INTRODUCTION TO CULTURE

Over 450 definitions of the word culture exist.[1] Culture is a system of communications that makes a human society possible that incorporates the biological and technical behavior of human beings with their verbal and nonverbal systems of expressive behavior. Culture is the sum total of a way of life, including such things as expected behavior, beliefs, values, language, and living practices shared by members of a society; it is the pattern of values, traits, or behaviors shared by the people within a region.

Some catalyst must exist that is capable of transforming private meanings into public meanings so they become understood by other (future, unborn) members of the society; culture is that catalyst. Culture consists of both explicit and implicit rules through which experience is interpreted. It is the instrument by which each new generation acquires the capacity to bridge the distance that separates one life from another. The function of culture is to establish modes of conduct, standards of performance, and ways of dealing with interpersonal and environmental relations that will reduce uncertainty, increase predictability, and thereby promote survival and growth among the members of any society.

Human societies create a hierarchy of codes for regulating human interaction which offers order, direction, and guidance in all phases of human problem solving by providing "tried and true" methods of satisfying physiological, personal, and social needs. Shared cultural norms give the people of any society a sense of their common identity and a means of relating to one another. Culture provides standards and "rules" regarding when to eat and what is appropriate to eat for breakfast, lunch, dinner, and snacks, and what to serve to guests at a dinner party, a picnic, or a wedding.

Culture influences behavior and explains how a group filters information; cultural meanings render some forms of activity normal and natural and others strange or wrong. In the process of social evolution, people find certain behaviors and values to be adaptive and helpful; others are found nonadaptive and even harmful. Helpful practices are shared and rewarded; harmful practices are discarded and discouraged. Over a period of time, useful behaviors, values, and artifacts become institutionalized and incorporated as part of the cultural traditions. The individual internalizes these institutionalized practices and often forgets their origin. Shaking hands, a characteristic form of greeting in many Western cultures, may have originated in the primitive practice of strangers clasping each other's weapon arm, both as a sign of friendship and as protection from attack. Its original function had considerable usefulness and was therefore institutionalized as a social tradition; now, thousands of years later it is functionally obsolete but it still survives as a valued custom. Likewise, many of any society's cultural behaviors and traditions have outlived their original purpose and survive as symbolic acts—a form of "cultural baggage." These societal norms have led to the development and pattern maintenance of institutions in society with a particular structure and way of functioning. These include the family, education systems, politics, and legislation.

Institutions (schools, social clubs, churches, unions) reinforce the societal norms and the ecological conditions that led to them. In a relatively closed society (as that of the Japanese), such a system will hardly change at all. Institutions may be changed, but this does not necessarily affect the societal norms; and when these remain unchanged, the persistent influence of a majority value system patiently smoothes the new institutions until their structure and functioning is again adapted to the societal norms. Cultural beliefs, values, and customs continue to be followed so long as they yield satisfaction. However, when a specific standard no longer fully satisfies the members of a society, it is modified or replaced, so that the resulting standard is more in line with the current needs and desires of the society. Thus, culture gradually but continually evolves to meet the needs of society.

These norms differ between cultures. One culture may focus on different aspects of an agreement (e.g., legal, financial) rather than another (e.g., personal, relationships). Some cultures focus on the specific details of the agreement (documenting the agreement), while other cultures focus on how the promises can be kept (process and implementation). Americans may negotiate a contract while the Japanese may negotiate a personal relationship. Culture conditions people to view and to value differently the many social interactions inherent in fashioning an agreement. For example, a study found that the Chinese would choose decision alternatives involving greater face saving, longer term repayment of obligations, more authoritarian and less consensual decision process, and greater focus on pan-ethical viewpoint than Anglos.[2] The Chinese tend to accept their environment rather than seeking to change it. They seek to fit or harmonize with the environment while Westerners seek control of their environment. These behaviors, deeply rooted in their respective cultures, have immense implications for business behaviors and marketing practices.

One example lies in the differences of the importance of the individual to the group (individualism versus collectivism). In Japan, the impulses and needs of the individual tend to be subordinated to the good of the group; in the United States, any intrusion by the group on the rights of the individual is regarded as unwarranted (if one is the land of the big "WE," the other is the land of the big "I"). In Japan, predominant values are for minimizing differences, preserving harmony, and reinforcing group loyalty; these customs are derived from ancient Japan where a nation short on resources but long on people required the participation of all its members in an orderly manner if survival were to result—hence, a heavily collectivist tradition evolved. In the United States, the prevailing customs tend for maximizing difference, confrontation, and compromise. This individualistic approach may be derived from the frontier days when one's nearest neighbor was miles away and one had to be very driven, self-oriented, and individualistic to survive.

The aim of decision making in one culture is to avoid discord in pursuit of consensus, while in the other culture, it is to promote competition in ideas in pursuit of objective truth—vastly different philosophies but equally reasonable based upon their own respective geographical limitations and history.

Few humans are consciously aware of their own culture. This is analogous to a fish in water. The fish is at home in, and comfortably unconscious of, its environment, the water. The last thing a fish would discover would be water. It becomes uncomfortable and aware of its environment only when it is out of the water and exposed to air. Similarly, mankind, throughout most of history, has been only vaguely conscious of the existence of culture and has owed this lack of consciousness to contrasts between his tribe's own customs and those from another tribe with which he happens to be in contact. This results in culture shock when humans find themselves out of their natural cultural environment.

The following provide a set of characteristics for culture:

1. *Functional:* In every society, the culture of that society has a functional purpose that provides guidelines for behavior that are crucial for the survival of the group.
2. *A social phenomena:* Culture arises out of human interaction, is a human creation, and is unique to human society.
3. *Prescriptive:* Culture defines and prescribes acceptable behaviors.
4. *Learned:* Culture is not inherited genetically but is rather the result of acquired behavior learned from other members of the society.
5. *Arbitrary:* Cultural practices have a certain arbitrariness since behaviors acceptable in one culture are not acceptable in other cultures.
6. *Value laden:* Culture provides values and tells people what is expected of them.
7. *Facilitates communications:* Verbal and nonverbal.
8. *Adaptive/dynamic:* Culture is constantly changing to adapt to new situations and new sources of knowledge; it changes as society changes and evolves.

9. *Long term:* Contemporary cultures have resulted from thousands of years of accumulated experience and knowledge.
10. *Satisfies needs:* Culture exists to satisfy the needs of the people within a society. Culture takes on new traits and discards the old, useless ones according to the society's needs. However, the core values remain the same.

CULTURE AND MARKETING

One of the most difficult, but also most important aspects of doing business in a foreign country is to understand the differences in cultural perceptions and values, the differences in needs within a society. Within a cultural context, a firm's products and services can be viewed as offering appropriate or acceptable solutions for individual or social needs. Since marketing is based upon satisfying the varied needs or wants of a firm's customers, and the needs and wants are very much culturally based, a successful international marketeer seeks to understand the cultural mores of the country to which he/she is attempting to market. If a product is no longer acceptable because a value or custom related to its use does not adequately satisfy human needs or fails to satisfy or address adequately the particular cultural values of the society, the firm producing it must then be ready to adjust or revise its product offering. The need to address a potential market from a cultural point of view prior to marketing to the foreign country or transact a business deal with another society separates the successful firm from the unsuccessful one. Culture and cross-cultural differences can be seen in a variety of human interactions, including but not limited to language, nonverbal communications, religion, time, space, color, numbers, materialism, manners and customs, aesthetics, status consciousness, and food preferences. Any of these interactions are potential pitfalls for the unweary or careless, as many companies, both American and otherwise, have discovered to their dismay. An interesting example is filter-tipped cigarettes. Filter-tipped cigarettes often sell poorly in less developed countries. Consumers in wealthier countries are more aware of the health risks and willing to pay more for the filter tip. In poor countries where the life expectancy rarely exceeds 40 years, threats from cancer are much less real and can be more easily ignored. For these consumers, the extra cost involved in the filter becomes the critical issue.

Language

Eskimos have many words to describe the concept of snow because the difference in the forms of snow plays a much more important role in their daily life than say, a native of Bermuda or Haiti. A country's language is key to its culture. Language expresses the thinking patterns of a culture; what is important and what is not important to a particular culture can be ascertained by what is present and what is not present in its language. The words of the language are merely concepts reflecting the culture from which it is derived. It is the spoken language that dominates as it changes more quickly and reflects the culture more directly. The Sapir-Whorf hypothesis suggests that language is not merely a mechanism for communicating ideas, but is itself a shaper of ideas.

Regional dialects can produce substantial differences in the same language (note natives from Minnesota, Mississippi, and Massachusetts may not be able to easily understand each other). For example, former West Germans and former East Germans have difficulty communicating. The language of West and East Germans diverged for 45 years since they were divided in 1945 and until their reunification in 1990. The *Wessi* (as a West German is called in East Germany) have different words and different meanings for the same word than their cousins in the East.[3]

Cultures are proud of their native tongue. In today's modern world, concerns exist in many countries that one's language is becoming obsolete. France passed a law in February 1994 which became effective in 1996 that French radio stations have to devote at least 40 percent of their prime-time music programming to songs in French. This ignores the fact that English is the language of choice for the hip in France. The law also indicates every second French song has to come from so-called new talent; the law does not require that the artists show talent, simply that they haven't made any hits. Critics complain that the 40 percent quota is too high, citing the mediocrity and uniformity of French music production. France is seeking to protect its culture against what it considers the perfidious influence of the English language.[4] Disney was taken to court because merely seven out of 5,000 items in its Paris retail store did not have French labels. (Parisian law requires all labels be written in French.)

French consumers prefer American television and tune out French programs. American films account for over 70 percent of all box office receipts in the European Union. (*Jurassic Park* had lines that stretched for blocks; meanwhile, the high-budget French film, *Queen Margot* was moderately successful in France and flopped abroad.) The French government considers this invasion American cultural imperialism. France spent $16 billion to produce cultural products in France in 1994, three-quarters of which came from the government. The European Union demands that 51 percent of all television programming be European. French moviegoers pay an 11 percent tax so the government can provide most of the funding for the French film industry. French language must be used on television and radio, in all advertising, and in schools and work-places. The use of an English term is forbidden if an adequate French word is available.[5]

The major blunders in language come from mistranslation, lack of understanding of slang or idioms in the native language, and use of the wrong dialect. Exxon's Japanese brand name, *Esso*, meant stalled car when pronounced phonetically in Japanese. Exxon's replacement of *Enco* referred to a sewage disposal truck. A Spanish translation for Budweiser: King of Beer used the wrong gender; Beer (*cerveza*) is a noun of the feminine gender in Spanish, and therefore cannot be the King, but must be the Queen of Beers. "Cue" toothpaste was introduced in France by Colgate-Palmolive who did not realize that *Cue* in French is a pornographic word. When the American film *City Slickers* went to France, its title was changed to *Life, Love, and Cows*.[6] Brown sugar is referred to differ-ently according to Hispanic locales and backgrounds; in New York (*azucar negra*), Miami (*azucar prieta*), California (*azucar cafe*), South Texas (*azucar morena*), and elsewhere (*azucar pardo*).[7] Americans are not the only ones who make translation errors. *Creap* (Japanese coffee creamer) and *Super Piss* (a Finnish product for unfreezing car locks) were products introduced into the United States which, not surprisingly, did not prosper.

The solution to avoiding such faux pas is backtranslating: having one translator translate a document or ad from the original language to the intended language and having a second translator independently translate the message back to the original language. If the incoming and outgoing messages agree, the translation is likely to succeed. If there is disagreement, analysis of the message must be made, the message changed, and backtranslated again until the two match. For example, the term "entree" means "appetizer" in Australia, but "main course" in Israel; if the product were labeled an entree, its price and market position would need to differ considerably in those two countries.[8] Although backtranslation will solve the problems of literal translation issues, it does not eliminate the problems of whether or not the "context of use" is the same.

Nonverbal Communications

Nonverbal behavior may be defined as any behavior, intentional or unintentional, beyond the words themselves that can be interpreted by a receiver as having meaning. Nonverbal behaviors could include facial expressions, eye contact, gestures, body movements, posture, physical appearance, space, touch, and time usage which are different from culture to culture. Nonverbal behaviors either accompany verbal messages or are used independently of verbal messages. They may affirm and emphasize or contradict spoken messages. Nonverbal behaviors are more likely to be used unconsciously because they are habitual and routine behaviors. Over 70 percent of the content of any message is not contained in the verbal but in the nonverbal portion of the message. People will tend to emphasize the nonverbal element and override the verbal if there is disagreement between the verbal expression and the body language.

Noise consists of the background distractions that have nothing to do with the substance of the message, and can derive from gestures, space (proximity), or behavior which seems overly or insufficiently courteous, or clothing or work surroundings that do not feel right for the occasion. Gestures and body postures that have a meaning in a certain culture can have a completely different significance in a different cultural environment. Sometimes the noise can be so great that little if any of the communication gets through.

Showing the sole of the shoe to an Arab or using the left hand when conducting business to a devout Muslim has cost many a business-person considerable business opportunities. (The right hand is used for eating; the left is reserved for toilet functions.)

The most irritating "noise" to Americans when conducting business with the Japanese is silence or the use of long pauses before responding. The Japanese often use little verbal activity, nod frequently, use silence, and even close eyes while others are speaking (this helps them concentrate in Zen Buddhist fashion). Silence to a Japanese means one is projecting a favorable impression and is thinking deeply about the problem. When in an impasse, the typical Japanese response is silence, withdrawal, or change of subject. Japanese politeness can at times come across as artificial and excessive to many Americans. American directness and overbearing manner may signal to Japanese a lack of self-control and implicitly untrustworthiness; at the very least, it signals a lack of sincerity (which means "truthfulness" to the Japanese). A Japanese will smile when he/she is amused, as it is customary for a servant to smile when he/she is scolded by his/her master. A servant will also smile when he/she is forced to report an unfortunate event, a polite gesture that the servant does not wish to burden his/her master with personal tragedies; the smile indicates that it is not necessary to take the tragedy too seriously.

An American attributes an unwillingness to engage in a frank conversation with an Indian who does not look the American directly in the eye; the Indian attributes to the American an attempt to control and dictate by means of direct physical confrontation. To look away is a sign of respect to Indians, while in the United States, respect is shown by looking directly at the speaker. In India, older people are automatically given respect due to their age. Touching an older person's feet is not an uncommon practice in India, a practice that shows respect for one's seniors.

In contrast, the French have direct and intense eye contact that the Americans will attribute to aggressiveness and stubbornness. The French person meanwhile is likely to attribute weakness, casualness, and insincerity to the American when the intense gaze is not returned or it is avoided. Americans also unknowingly create noise: slouching, chewing gum, using first names, forgetting titles, joking, wearing too casual clothing, being overtly friendly toward the opposite sex, speaking too loudly, being too egalitarian with the wrong people (usually lower class), working with one's hands, carrying bundles, tipping too much. Such noise in one's conduct, although perfectly natural in communication with another of one's own culture, may have the unintended effect of derailing the message when in a cross-cultural setting.

Religion

Religion has profound influences on the beliefs and practices around the world. Coca-Cola printed country flags on its cans in Spain; McDonald's did the same for its carry-out bags for its children's meals in Britain—both in an effort to capitalize on the World Cup soccer games in 1994. Muslims quickly became outraged. The green and white flag of Saudi Arabia featured an Arabic passage ("There is no God but Allah and Mohammed is his prophet.") that they felt should be treated with reverence, not commercialism, let alone to be thrown out in the trash. McDonald's printed 2 million of the bags for the promotion while Coca-Cola had produced 270 million cans bearing the flags of the 24 World Cup nations participating in the games. Both companies immediately ceased production of the offending products.[9]

However, a smart marketer can also take advantage of religion. Historically, camera sales in Saudi Arabia were quite limited because of Islamic traditions. However, Polaroid instant photography allowed Arab men to photograph their wives and daughters in the privacy of their homes without the need for strangers to handle the film in a processing lab. Consequently, sales boomed there. Beef is taboo for Hindus: McDonald's in India sells vegeburgers (made of soybeans) and lamb. Animism, in which spirits and ancestors are thought to have an ongoing interest in the behavior of the living, is not an unusual rite. Thus, the smart businessman might want to consult an oracle or soothsayer about the propriety of making a deal.

Time

Time, how we define it in our lives, how it affects our work, and the role it plays in our worldview, is a universal aspect of all cultures. A culture's attitude toward time determines the importance placed on the development of personal relationships in business. In a culture where everyone is busy, when there never seems to be enough time to get everything done, little chance or importance is given to building long-term, solid personal relationships. In those cultures where time is less of a constraint, a certain valuing of personal relationships exists, if no other reason than there is time for them. While Americans might expect a meeting to begin and end at a certain time, with a series of important points discussed in between (linear logic), Latins typically arrive later than the time stated, expect to discuss a great many items not on the Americans' agenda, and keep the meeting going long beyond its stated end-time (circular logic). Latins set schedules based not on points on a clock, but rather on a series of events: first, do this; then when it is finished, they then move on to the next task. They give each task the time needed to complete it. Their schedule is not deadline oriented. Similarly, Indonesians have "rubber time"; to them, time is elastic and qualitative. If something comes up that is more important than business—such as a festival or a wedding, business gets postponed.[10]

Americans schedule; the clock "runs" for them; everything must be organized, compartmentalized, have a beginning and an end. The Chinese, with over 5,000 years of cultural heritage, have a different perspective on time. When Mao Tse Tung was asked what he thought of the French Revolution, he replied (only half-joking), "It is too soon to tell." Producing a satisfactory agreement in as short a time as possible may be one of the least concerns of the Chinese. The Chinese generally believe that a considerable amount of time should be invested in establishing a general climate of understanding, trust, and willingness to help in matters quite apart from the issues brought to the table. They do not view time as a constraint or as a set of limits in which a particular task must be completed.

International deals take longer to conclude than purely domestic transactions. McDonald's negotiated for nearly ten years to open its first hamburger restaurant in Moscow. IBM needed almost two years to secure an agreement to build a computer plant in Mexico. Negotiating a joint venture in China takes an average of two years. The organization of most European and Japanese businesses, and their modes of operation, usually require considerably more time to negotiate than is the case in American firms. In the case of European firms, it usually takes at least twice as much time, and up to six times as long is often required for Japanese firms. The extent to which American expectations of the duration of a negotiation can differ from those of a foreign foe was demonstrated at the Paris peace talks to end the Vietnam war: the American negotiators checked into the Ritz Hotel while the North Vietnamese leased a villa for two years.

Cultures can differ in time conception, time perspective, and time experiencing. A preferred temporal perspective (toward the past, the present, or the future) exists in each culture, and provides the foundation for behavior. An orientation toward the future implies an expectation of advancement or progressive development; one is able to predict, plan for, and change forthcoming events and conditions. An orientation toward the present implies a predominance of the state of the moment; one's only concerns are those that are happening now. An orientation toward the past implies a belief that everything that is or will be has also existed or taken place in a period before the present. Temporal perspective influences overall strategy, especially issue formulation and decision making.

For Americans, a 10 a.m. appointment typically means arriving five minutes early and engaging in business at 10 o'clock or shortly thereafter. In Japan, failure to arrive on time is viewed negatively. For Germans, punctuality is next to godliness—10 a.m. means 10 a.m. precisely. In Nigeria, the same 10 a.m. starting time is only an approximation, and tardiness is not negative. The attitude toward time is less rigid for Latin Americans than North Americans; delays of 30 minutes or more are not surprising. When setting times for appointments, one should ask, "*La hora inglesa, o la hora espanola?*" or "The English hour (promptly at the time specified) or the Latin hour (30 minutes or more late)?" Much business in Spain is conducted over the evening meal, which seldom begins until 9 p.m. and is often closer to midnight. No business is conducted in the afternoon during siesta (2 to 4 p.m.) when lunch is commonly held. This is not at all uncommon in many Latin American countries.

Cultures also have different ways of organizing and using time. Monochronic (linear) time emphasizes schedules, segmentation, and promptness; these cultures compartmentalize events and concentrate on one thing at a time. In these cultures, only a limited number of events are permitted within a given period and scheduling provides for priority setting. The future can be altered, an implication of expectation of advancement or progressive development. Monochronic cultures are concerned with causality. In such cultures, communication and argument are based on the need for logic. Monochronic cultures are "doing-oriented," as they concentrate on the future.

Polychronic (circular) time stresses involvement of people and completion of transactions rather than adherence to a preset schedule. Time is not limited; it is endless with no beginning or end. Time exists beyond humanity, external to the control of human beings. The future is not solid or firm and cannot be planned. Appointments are frequently broken and important plans may be changed right up to the minute planned. Because polychronic time is nonlinear, many things happen at once, a simultaneous use of time. Traditional societies, nonindustrial cultures, are typically polychronic. Polychronic societies are concerned with equilibrium; communication and argument are based on the need for balance. Polychronic cultures are "being-oriented," viewing the here and now as the focus.

The monochronic nature of Germans and Americans (ranking activities by priority and impact and doing one thing at a time) frustrates a polychronic culture's tendencies to do more than one thing at a time and be open to inevitable disruptions. The Japanese, because of their circular polychronic sense of time, stress end results and are less concerned about how long the process takes to get there; thus, they are less concerned about adhering to time schedules, instead preferring to focus on the end result. Time is not as important to a Japanese as it is to one from the West. Not being hasty is a sign of wisdom and sincerity. Japanese value high quality over immediate gain and they wait patiently for the best possible result. Americans are most comfortable discussing items in an orderly (linear) fashion while Latin Americans wish to discuss many points at the same time, talking over and louder than others when attempting to emphasize a point. Since life is unpredictable, punctuality is not emphasized; delays occur frequently, especially when other, more important concerns take priority. Polychronic cultures do not necessarily place their faith in tomorrow; tomorrow is unknown. Monochronic cultures are future-embracing while polychronic cultures tend to be future-suspicious but present-embracing: Those cultures feel that if we cannot control tomorrow, let us make the best of today.

Monochronic cultures' preference for linearity and logic appears to polychronic cultures as one-dimensional and sterile. Monochronic cultures, on the other hand, find polychronic cultures illogical and unproductive. Polychronic cultures view monochronic cultures as being without concern for human reality and applicability. For monochronic cultures, the mighty oak is the strongest tree while for polychronic cultures, the flexible willow is symbol of strength.

Different cultures value the amount of time devoted to the goal pursued in different ways. Americans want to make a deal quickly, reduce formalities to a minimum, and get down to business. For relationship-oriented cultures, a need exists to invest time in the process so that the parties can get to know one another well and determine whether they wish to embark on a long-term relationship. The Japanese view time as a continuum and are long-term oriented; they are conservative and patient. In the West, time is a commodity in limited supply; it can be saved, wasted, controlled, or organized. In the Near East, time is not scarce. In Arab cultures, it can be foolish to plan, for "Only Allah can know the future." *Ansh'Allah* it is said, "God Willing." In Ireland, time is less important as, "God made so much of it."

For the French, traditionally, concern is not on time but on precision and quality. While Americans typically opt for the deadline, the French will opt for taking what they consider a reasonable amount of extra time to get the product or project to the level of quality they believe necessary. Americans see the deadline, the schedule, as more important, while the French view the quality as their primary concern.

Space

While Americans feel comfortable with a space distance of three feet (and very little touching), Mexicans, Italians, and Arab men typically get extremely close to their counterparts: space is close, people stand close to each other, sit close to each other, and regularly touch and embrace each other. These cultures believe in virtual eyeball-to-eyeball contact. The Japanese and English prefer greater distances. Mexicans use some physical contact to signal confidence, such as a hand on the upper arm. Americans who are standoffish from the *abrazo* (Latin American embrace) have signaled a certain coolness to their hosts. Mexicans communicate with hand movements, physical contact, and emotional expressions.

Right and left can take on different connotations: the Arabic and Hebrew languages are read from right to left while most Western languages are read left to right. This affects the flow of logic. A three-panel advertisement for a laundry detergent showed dirty clothes and the soap in one panel followed by a busy washer in the second and the third, on the far right, showing clean clothes. The ad was printed unchanged for an Arabic insert: to one familiar with the Arabic language, it appeared that clean clothes went in the washer with the detergent and after washing the detergent made them dirty! In Spain, Denmark, Holland, and Germany, Catholic women wear the wedding ring on the right hand, not the left as is common in the United States. The right-handed motor in an English mill is the same as a left-handed motor in an American mill. Americans views the production run from the downstream and thus see the motor differently from the British who look at things from the start of the production run.[11]

In France, supervisors are placed at the center to watch and control the subordinates all around them. In Japan, where no separate offices exist and the work area is one large, open space, supervisors sit at one end of a room from where they can see and hear everything that is going on in the room. While window offices are of high status in the United States, the Japanese expression "sitting near the window" refers to employees who have been retired on the job.

Another variant of space is the value placed upon history within a culture. To Americans, any building older than 50 years is worthy of being called a National Historic Shrine. Yet, many Americans have no regrets about demolishing an old building and replacing it with a modern office tower. In Europe, cultures are proud of their millenniums of history and the shrines they have. Conflict naturally results. In June 1996, McDonald's wanted to put a restaurant in a 150-year-old building in Paris that Picasso and other famous artists once frequented. Even though other franchises are located on the Champs Élysées, Parisians have declared the city's historic Mont-parnasse district off limits. McDonald's quickly capitulated.

Color

Vendors in Hong Kong dunk white eggs in tea to change the naturally white color to brown. In most parts of Asia, white repre-sents death, and must be avoided. New England brown eggs, which come from Rhode Island Red hens, therefore have a natural advan-tage in the Hong Kong market ($25 million in 1994).[12] Green denotes adventurousness in the United States and Japan but trust-worthiness in China and Korea.[13] In Taiwan, a man wears green to signify that his wife has been unfaithful. In China, the most popular color is red; it denotes happiness. Black also elicits a positive response because it denotes power and trustworthiness. For decades, Darkie Toothpaste was among the best-selling brands in Asia, with a package featuring a minstrel in blackface. Due to protests from African Americans, both the brand name and package have been changed. Although blue is thought to be the most mascu-line color to most Americans, in France and Britain, it is red. Amer-icans think pink is feminine, while most of the world considers yellow to be the most feminine color. In China and Japan, grey is associated with inexpensive products; however, in the United States, grey is associated with expense as well as high quality and dependability.

Numbers

The number 7 is considered bad luck in Kenya, good luck in the Czech Republic, and has magical connotations in Benin. The use of the number 4 should be avoided in Japan, since the word for 4, *sfrih*, sounds like the Japanese word for death; merchants do not sell packs of four in Japan. In Hong Kong, the number 8 is lucky. A million million is a billion for the Japanese and British, but not for Americans.

A careless American manufacturer once requested critical parts from an European supplier. He designated the required date as April 7, 1995: 4/7/95; he received the urgent parts nearly three months later on July 4—unlike American month/day/year, Europeans use day/month/year.

Manners and Customs

An American awards ceremony is characterized by humor and a joyous, fast-paced tempo—all of which is directly opposite from what would be acceptable and understandable in Japan. When awards are given to a Japanese group, the participants rarely come forward when called to receive their awards, they clap at the wrong times, and do not react when they should. The Western practice of opening a speech with a good joke falls flat in the Orient. John Condon gave an excellent example in a speech in 1974: "If this were an all-U.S. audience, I might begin with a joke. If this were an all-Japanese audience, I might better begin with an apology. Since we are a mixed group, let me begin by apologizing for not making a joke."[14]

Status Consciousness

The English language has one form of address; all persons are addressed with the pronoun "you." In the Germanic and Romance languages, two forms exist, the personal and the formal. In Japanese, three forms exist, depending upon whether one is speaking to a superior, subordinate, or a peer. Different forms exist for male and female, and even to distinguish between an older brother and a younger brother. Not indicating the proper form can alienate foreign partners. Americans may have difficulty playing the high social status role that goes with important position in societies such as Mexico. There is an art to being waited on and deferred to while at the same time being protective of the personal dignity of people in lower social positions. Most Latin parents would prefer their children to enter a high-status occupation such as law, architecture, or medicine. In general, business is thought of as low in prestige. Latin society is fairly rigid by American standards; Latins are raised to have a strong sense of social place. Respect for rank and hierarchy is instilled in children at a very young age.

To an egalitarian society (such as the United States), status differences may not just be difficult to understand and to adjust to, they also may be dangerous; for example, Korean copilots are conditioned to keep quiet, being subordinate to the pilot. Providing information to a superior or asking too many questions is regarded as disrespectful, while confessing ignorance is a loss of face in a highly status-prone society such as Korea's. This situation has more than once caused near misses in the airways.

Food Preferences

Next to language, food and drink are the most culturally sensitive and grounded topic. Examine the differences inherent in eating breakfast. Traditionally, Germans eat bread with cheese or meat in the mornings, while the Japanese eat primarily rice-based breakfasts. The instant orange juice drink, Tang, was difficult to market in France because the French drink little orange juice and almost none at breakfast. Tang instead repositioned the drink as a multifavored refreshment, good anytime. Kellogg's has sold its cornflakes in France since 1935 with minimal success. The French have not traditionally eaten corn; 80 percent of the corn harvested in France is fed to pigs and chickens.

Japanese traditionally have considered breakfast cereals a children's snack. As health-conscious Japanese began to eat cereal for breakfast, new cereals were demanded that contained bran, granola, whole rice, and even vegetables. Kellogg's Genmai Flakes is made from ground whole rice. Nestlé's Vegetable Time is a salty cornflake cereal with vegetable powder, in three colors: green for spinach, orange for carrots, and yellow for pumpkins. Many Japanese suffer from lactose intolerance, which complicates the promotion of a breakfast consisting of cereal and milk.

Unlike Japan, India is an ideal market for Kellogg's to introduce its cereal, since breakfast is a well-established daily meal in India; since milk is already a staple in most Indians' diets, fewer cultural changes will be necessary. Even though most Indians eat a hot breakfast with traditional foods such as *chapatis* (an unleavened bread) or *dosas* (a fried pancake), Kellogg's is targeting India's vast 200 million middle-class consumers. Nonetheless, it faces an uphill battle, as Indians are unaccustomed to waking up to Western-style breakfast cereals. Just 3 percent of Indians eat breakfast cereal; most prefer cooked breakfast. The lifestyle of Indians (polychronic) allows them plenty of time to cook and consume a leisurely hot breakfast. Kellogg's assumes that people will pay a premium for convenience and speed (120 rupees for a box of Kellogg's Cornflakes compared to 30-40 rupees for an Indian brand). Kellogg's is still optimistic.[15]

General Foods introduced American-style Jell-O to Great Britain, but the British were not interested in the powdered substance; in Great Britain, the product is sold in its jelled form; if it does not jiggle and look ready to eat, it isn't proper.

CROSS-CULTURAL IMPLICATIONS FOR MARKETERS

The following guidelines are suggested to minimize cross-cultural marketing mistakes:

1. Be sensitive to do's and taboos. Develop cultural empathy.
2. Recognize, understand, accept, and respect another's culture and differences.
3. Be culturally neutral . . . different is not necessarily better or worse.
4. Never assume transferability of a concept from one culture to another. Just because local businesspeople in developing countries tell you they don't like Americans, it does not mean they don't want to buy American goods. It simply means they are expected to say certain things in public, but that they may operate differently in private.
5. Use the following steps to avoid the Self-Reference Criterion (SRC). SRC is the concept that if I like and use a product, everyone should; if it sells well in Peoria, it should likewise in Bejing. As an example, examine marketing Texan Iced Tea to the United Kingdom:

   a. Examine those cultural and environmental attributes of the product you wish to market that make it a success in your

home market (e.g., iced tea in Texas: hot, dry climate; preference for sweetness; caffeine).
   b. Compare these attributes to those found in the target market (e.g., hot, dry climate versus cold, wet climate; less sweetness desired).
   c. Note those particular attributes where substantial differences exist (e.g., hot, dry Texas versus cold, wet England)
   d. Changes in the product or promotion must be made to account for the differences noted. In some cases, differences are too great, and the best option is not to enter. This is not a hypothetical example.[16]

An example of SRC and the failure to follow the above rules is Snapple fruit drinks. Snapple sales fell in Japan to 120,000 bottles a month (in April 1996) from 2.4 million bottles a month the previous year. The Quaker Oats company stopped shipping Snapple to Japan altogether. Why? Japanese consumers loathe some of the very traits that made Snapple popular in the United States: the cloudy appearance of the drinks, the sweet fruit juice flavorings, and floating stuff with a taste too sweet for the typical Japanese. Yet, Quaker would not change its drinks to suit local tastes. Quaker also skimped on marketing research and marketing. In the beginning, sales were strong, as Snapple's unusual-shaped bottle and its American image had initially attracted millions of curious buyers, but they did not become repeat purchasers.[17] Other products that were SRC failures in Japan include Ruffles and Cheetos: Ruffles chips were too salty for Japan; Cheetos were too cheesy and Japanese didn't like their fingers turning orange. However, unaltered Snickers bars and M&Ms sell well in Japan.

Chapter 2

The Standardization versus Adaptation Debate: Wherefore Art Thou Now?

STANDARDIZATION (GLOBALIZATION)

Ever since the creation of the first multinational business entity around the time of the Sumerians, the ideal world environment for any merchant from any country was one that demanded only one product, designed only one way, priced one price, distributed and promoted the same way throughout the known world. This desire is universal, getting the most for the least effort. However, throughout most of history, this was not possible. Even the Romans understood that what was desired by the Gauls would not necessarily work for the Nubians or the Greeks and vice versa. This was the final synopsis for most of the ensuing two millenia. However, the times are changing. And according to many business prophets, the world is finally becoming one with itself.

With the advent of the wide availability of fast jet aircraft service and the opening of most countries' borders, one can practically be at any point on the globe within a day, certainly within two days. Satellite dishes have made communications almost instantaneous, even to the most remote parts of the world. Therefore, according to Levitt,[1] the world is undergoing a "globalization," a converging of all cultures toward one common global culture. Levitt was not the first to argue for standardized marketing, Perlmutter[2] and Wind, Douglas, and Perlmutter[3] described a similar concept they called geocentric orientation. Levitt's classic article espouses that different cultural preferences are the vestiges of the past, that the peoples of the world are becoming more and more alike, and, in general, needs and wants are becoming homogenized. Levitt stated that consumers throughout the world are increasingly motivated by the same desires to modernity, quality, and value: they all want a quality product at a low price. New technology and standardized methods of production have made global marketing programs feasible. Says Levitt: "Only global companies will achieve long-term success by concentrating on what everyone wants rather than worrying about the details of what everyone thinks they might like" (p. 5). Levitt believes that market segments in a particular market are not unique, but share commonalities with other segments elsewhere: "Everywhere, everything gets more and more like everything else as the world's preference structure is relentlessly homogenized" (p. 6). Companies must learn to operate as if the world were one large market, ignoring superficial regional and national differences and selling the same products in the same way throughout the world. According to Levitt, companies need to look for similarities instead of differences in the markets in which they operate. Examples Levitt provides include: McDonald's, Coca-Cola, Pepsi-Cola, Marlboro, Revlon, Sony, and Levi's.

Modern marketers, just like their brethren in Sumeria or Rome, wish to believe in this, as it would indeed make all their marketing efforts easier—sell a Coke or McDonald's hamburgers the same way all around the world. If we are indeed converging toward one global culture, then this book would have no purpose, since eventually (and the supporters of the argument say sooner than later), the global culture will dominate and no separate cultural attributes between societies will exist. The evidence supporting Levitt's globalization proposition (hereafter referred to as standardization, as globalization or globalizing is a vague term that has been previously defined in many other ways) is considerable. Russian youngsters rollerblade by the Kremlin; Moscow subways are filled with English language ads. Shelves of Russian stores are filled with Coca-Cola.[4] P&G promotes Pampers diapers worldwide with the same slogan for all 56 countries: "Even when they're wet, they're dry." Three-fourths of movie tickets sold in Europe in 1995 were for U.S.-made movies, up from 56 percent in 1985. Seventy percent of all films shown on European television are from Hollywood. In 1995, for the first year ever, international box office receipts surpassed domestic gross; Hollywood is expecting 20 to 25 percent annual growth in revenue per film in Asia over the next five years.[5] Kenici Ohmae argues that customers in the Triad (the three industrialized areas of the world: Western Europe, North America, and Japan) are becoming increasingly so much alike (with similar incomes, educational achievements, lifestyles, and aspirations), that expensive customization of the marketing mix by country is less necessary.[6] This is true since Western markets offer many commonalities: nuclear family dominates, most consumers are highly educated, have high incomes, and are similar economically, politically, and culturally.[7]

Basketball is quickly becoming an American global product. Throughout the world, name recognition exists, uniforms are sold, and fans root for their favorite NBA and college teams. The NBA opened the first of 15 NBA global retail stores in Seoul in June 1996 and it plans to open 60 retail establishments worldwide within several years, selling NBA licensed products and NBA branded goods manufactured in South Korea by early 1997.[8] American pop culture dominates the global youth and young adult markets: the sportswear, the sneakers, the sweat shirts, the entertainment, and the music are all American.

Michael Porter[9] identified the forces that allow standardization to exist:

1. Growing similarity of countries in terms of available infrastructure, distribution channels, and marketing approaches.
2. Fluid global capital markets: national markets are growing into global markets because of the large flow of funds between countries.
3. Technological restructuring: the reshaping of competition globally as a result of technological revolutions such as microprocessors.
4. The integrating role of technology: reduced cost and increased impact of products have made them accessible to more global consumers.
5. New global competitors.

Global companies view the entire world as one big market. This theory is based upon the belief that boundaries among countries do not effectively separate different target markets; customers are similar. The global company is more centralized, with the corporate headquarters deciding the overall strategy and the subsidiaries deciding among the tactics to be used to achieve these strategies. A global company seeks to standardize its operations. Some marketing practices are easier to standardize than others. (Brand name, positioning, service standards, warranties, and ad themes are easier to standardize across countries while distribution, personal selling, sales training, pricing, and media selection are more difficult to standardize.)[10]

ADVANTAGES AND DISADVANTAGES

The alternative to standardization is adaptation. Multinational companies which adhere to the adaptation strategy believe that each country should be approached separately as a different market. These companies have subsidiaries in each country in which they operate. The power to make decisions is decentralized with the branch in that specific country having a great deal of independence in its activities. When using a multinational strategy, a company enters a foreign country with no presuppositions about the market. A company either buys or conducts its own research to find out exactly what the target market wants. Finally, the company develops the marketing strategy,[11] which is typically customized for that particular market. Arguments for standardization are based on economies of scale and enhanced product quality and assume homogenized world markets and decreased costs result in lower prices and increased sales volumes. Arguments for adaptation are based upon price discrimination and the theory of friction underlying the relations between headquarters and local representatives, and assume diverging markets and importance of segments.[12]

Whether a company should standardize or adapt its marketing mix has become one of the most burning strategy issues for managers around the world. Companies using a standardized strategy can achieve the benefits of cost reductions, improved quality of products and programs, enhanced customer preference, and increased competitive leverage.[13] Global marketing strives for efficiencies of scale by developing a standardized product of dependable quality to be sold at a reasonable price to a global market. This strategy emphasizes cultural similarities regardless of the geographic locations of consumers. This strategy results in higher profits, lower real costs, global sourcing, homogeneity of consumer behavior, political and legal environmental compatibility, global corporate orientation, economies of scale, and a global corporate philosophy and orientation.[14]

Companies can achieve economies of scale by creating a standard product that will sell worldwide.[15] Polaroid claims to have achieved economies of scale by entering foreign markets. McCann-Erickson claims to have saved $90 million in production costs for the advertising program it developed for Coca-Cola by carrying over certain elements of the program on a global basis over a 20-year period. Colgate-Palmolive introduced its Colgate tartar-control toothpaste in over 40 countries, each of which could choose one of two ads. For every country where the same commercial runs, Colgate-Palmolive saves $1 to $2 million in production costs alone. The company has also saved millions by standardizing the look and packaging of certain brands. A standardized strategy uses fewer products. This reduction in the product line allows a company to improve the products that it offers by specializing in how to make the product better more efficiently.

A consistent company's image across boundaries can increase customer preference, since the image that the customer has of the company is reinforced. Advantages of standardization exist for those products that appeal to mobile users, tourists, or businesspeople. These customers enjoy the consistency of standardized product offerings from companies such as Gillette, Kodak, and Hilton as they move from country to country. A strong standardized and consistent American image can also be advantageous overseas and lead to a standardization strategy; examples include Levi's, Wrigley's, KFC, McDonald's, Coca-Cola, Burger King, and Pizza Hut. The marketing mix of such companies is essentially the same, with few distinctions as required by the different environments. A standardized strategy also provides more points from which to attack competitors. By entering markets in the home market of the competitor or in other markets, companies can weaken competitors. The strategy can also be used in order to prevent competitors from entering a market if a company is able to enter early and effectively because it strengthens itself in that particular market.

The main problem with standardized strategies is that they are very difficult to implement; an unsuccessful standardized strategy could lead to catastrophic results for a company. The main difficulties that a global corporation will face are cultural differences, legal differences, language and communication problems, geography, parallel imports, and hedging. Ford attempted to create a world car, only to find even creating a pan-European car was not possible, as needs (e.g., air conditioning versus heating) differed tremendously across that one small continent. The international differences in buyer behavior, rather than the similarities, which poses stumbling blocks to successful international marketing. Thus, the differences must receive disproportionate attention from the marketer. As it has been remarked, an American and a Japanese are 95 percent similar and 5 percent different in everything that matters. Disadvantages of a standardization strategy are that a company becomes less responsive to local needs, distances itself from market/customer, reduces adaption to local behavior, and often becomes less competitive locally.[16]

As noted previously, cultural differences abound. To not be aware of or take cultural differences into account has been fatal reasoning for many organizations. Tyson Foods customizes more than 5,000 products to satisfy local taste preferences in 57 countries. Nestlé instant coffee is produced in 200 different blends globally. Even where the basic American concept plays well abroad, the programs often require a good deal of adapting or reshooting. Five different versions of the game show *The Price is Right* exist, each with local participants and local hosts. Series such as the *Honeymooners* are licensed and then translated into the local language, cast using local actors for the voices, and sold to local networks. The award-winning Budweiser commercial using frogs to croak out the brand name, used *coqui* (clams) in Puerto Rico (the Puerto Rican mascot) rather than frogs because Puerto Ricans view frogs as unclean.

Coca-Cola introduced the two-liter bottle in Spain without realizing that Spanish refrigerators are smaller than in other countries.

The outcome was that the bottles did not fit in the refrigerators, and Coca-Cola had to design another bottle. Sales were lost over the period when the bottle was redesigned. Coca-Cola simply cannot be promoted the same way on a global basis, since it is not perceived the same way by consumers across the globe. For example, Spanish Coke enthusiasts see Coke as an excellent mixer; Italians replace wine with Coke as a dinner drink, and the Chinese view Coke as a refined luxury drink for only the most fortunate.

The different laws that govern countries are important for the global company simply because they inhibit companies' capability to standardize. For example, according to Islamic law, financial interest is considered as usury, and is therefore illegal. When dealing with countries following the Islamic code, banks will buy shares in the company's corporation with the agreement that after a certain period of time, the corporation will buy the shares back at the price of the loan plus the interest for the period. Even countries that have the same legal system will have differences in the particulars of the law. As an example, England and the United States base their systems in common law, but comparative advertising in England is illegal, while it is frequently used in the United States.

Communication is one of the biggest barriers that a company has to face when it becomes global. When advertising, global companies need to know what message they are trying to convey and what message they are actually conveying. When American Airlines translated the commercial "Fly in leather" to Latin American countries, the output sent was to encourage people to fly naked. Chevrolet kept the American name for the model Nova to sell it in Mexico: *Nova* in Spanish means "does not go." Parker made a fool of its brand when their ball-point advertising, "Use Parker and avoid embarrassing situations" was translated in Spanish improperly: consumers heard that using Parker pens reduces the possibility of pregnancies. Four different ways exist to say tire in Spanish, depending on where one is: Spanish call it *neumatico*; Peruvians, *caucho*; Mexicans, *llanta*; and Argentineans, *goma*. Concepts and the way that they are expressed differ between cultures.

For another example, the concept of affection is universal, but the form in which it is expressed is different across cultures. Kissing, an expression of affection in the West, is alien to many Eastern cultures, and even taboo in some.[17] In English-speaking Canada, chocolate snacks are considered kid stuff but in French-speaking Canada, chocolate snacks are considered as serious snacks for all ages. Meanwhile, Koreans find American chocolate bars too sweet. Not unexpectedly, studies have found that the most important reason for companies not to standardize were due to differences in consumer tastes and habits and competition.[18] Although Hollywood seems to be the source of universal entertainment, refreshments differ considerably across borders: Chileans like sweet popcorn, while coffee accounts for 10 percent of concession sales in Mexico; Samoans like Mochi Crunch (a rice cracker) and dried squid chunks, while Polynesians prefer packaged betel nut flavored with lime.[19]

The distribution of products is probably the hardest task for a company to be able to standardize. The physical terrain and climate of a country are important environmental considerations. Altitude, humidity, and temperature are climatic features that affect the uses and functions of products and equipment. Products need to be modified to work properly in different environments. Rolls-Royce found that cars from England required extensive body work and renovations after a short time in Canada; it was not the cold that damaged the cars, but the salted sand spread to keep the streets passable throughout the four or five months of virtually continuous snow. The fenders and doorside panels corroded and rusted, and the oil system leaked.

Another important feature of geography is the distribution of products. For instance, Colombia is made up of vast mountains, and the cities are connected by roads on which going 25 miles per hour seems like a heroic task.

Table 2.1 summarizes when to use standardization and when adaptation is preferred.

STANDARDIZE OR ADAPT?

A full decade has passed since Levitt's globalization proposition was issued. How have the multinationals reacted? Have they standardized or adapted? In general, industrial goods are the most likely to be successful in any globalization strategy as are modern technologically advanced consumer durables. Traditional consumer non-

TABLE 2.1. Standardization versus Adaptation: When to Use Which

When Standardization Is Preferred
• high costs of adaptation • primarily industrial products • convergence and similar taste in diverse country markets • predominant use in urban environments • marketing to predominantly similar countries • centralized management • scale of economies in production, R&D, and marketing • meeting competition when competitors produce standardized products • consumer mobility • if positive home country image (country of origin) effect exists
Where Adaptation Is Advantageous
• differences in technical standards • primarily consumer and personal use products • variations in consumer needs • variations in conditions of use • variations in ability to buy, differences in income levels • variations in technical sophistication, skill levels of users • strong cultural differences • local environment-induced adaptation, differences in raw material availability, government requirements and regulations • use by competitors • variations in national habits (e.g., clothes are worn longer between washings than in the U.S.; in some European countries, boiling water is used for washing; washing by stream)

durable products are most likely to require customization due to national tastes and habits.[20] Consumers' perceptions of product preference, brand recognition, and price for a consumer nondurable brand product in diverse countries differs and consumer differences do exist in diverse countries with regard to their perception of a consumer nondurable product.[21]

One splendid example comes from Japan. Gillette has a 10 percent market share in Japan (65 to 70 percent worldwide); Schick has 62 percent. Schick stresses its Japanese way of marketing (adapt), while Gillette is emphasizing its American roots (standardize) by airing the same ads it runs in the United States and selling Sensor in the same packages with the brand names in bold English letters and a Japanese version of it only in tiny letters in a corner. The only difference in the TV ad is that the narrator says "the best a man can get" in Japanese. Schick on the other hand, has not used a foreigner in its ads for the past decade. The TV ads for Tracer blades show a young Japanese actor shaving before taking his dog to the beach. The product is called FX in Japanese because Schick says it is easier for the Japanese to pronounce. Schick sells razors through Seiko and 150,000 wholesalers. Gillette tried to sell razors through its own salespeople, a strategy that failed because Gillette didn't have the distribution network available to Japanese companies. It later doubled its salespeople and entertained wholesalers.[22] The outcome still has not been decided but Schick has the edge.

Cisco sells a computer networking product, an industrial product. Supposedly, it should be able to globalize easily. However, Cisco discovered customer requirements varied from country to country. In Japan, office buildings lack the space for installing the company's electrical equipment; Japanese managers place the network routers on office desks. The Japanese also needed smaller routers with noiseless cooling systems that could fit under desks. German customers had specific requirements. French regulators insisted something French be in the product and demanded that Cisco test products at French-based facilities. Twenty-five core categories were finally decided upon for 40 key countries.[23]

Many reasons exist for a standardization strategy. The homogenization of world cultures support this strategy. Savings in the costs of developing unique products and marketing them justify standardization. The integration of international markets and the emergence of strong worldwide competition also justifies such a strategy. The Parker pen company provides ample ammunition that the opposite may be just as true. Parker had marketing efforts in 154 countries and, traditionally had decentralized operations to the individual countries with more than 40 ad agencies responsible for each market niche the company was active in. During the 1980s, a centralization strategy was formulated whereupon all of the countries' marketing activities would be brought under a global umbrella, and all aspects of the marketing mix would be standardized from Parker's headquarters. Parker believed in the globalization gurus, that cultural and competitive differences were less important than the similarities. Parker chose a single ad agency and decided to use the motto, "Make your mark with a Parker" on a global basis. Graphic layout and photography was identical throughout the world. In the end, the advertising "tried to say something to everybody, and it didn't say anything to anybody."[24] The disastrous campaign resulted in the sale of the writing division, the resignation of the CEO, and the restoration of the decentralization approach.

Are we in fact globalizing? If we are, one ought to see a convergent effect of many cultural indexes. Of the many cross-cultural studies that have been conducted, several have been longitudinal in nature. Hofstede's[25,26] analysis of IBM managerial value survey data is the most classic. The results from his work have been replicated and confirmed many times over. In more than 20 years since the original study was made, the replications (and even the later duplicate IBM study done by Hofstede) indicate very clearly that (1) no convergence is taking place; that is, values of the indexes are not collapsing toward a common mean; and (2) if anything, there is a divergence occurring; that is to say, values among member countries of the same cluster are becoming even more distant—slowly but certainly. Americans, British, Canadians, Australians, and New Zealanders, although from the same Anglo background with less than 250 years spread, are diverging; it is not only with humor that one speaks of the Americans and British as two nations divided by a common language.

A second argument against the globalization is the increase in ethnic awareness that is becoming almost universal around the world. This can be seen in Native Americans' efforts to regain tribal lands, African Americans' heritage pride (the rise of popularity and availability of Black Studies courses in many American colleges), the rise in interest among the assimilated Americans in their own family heritages, the breakup of the "republics" within the Soviet Union, and the aggressive campaign in Hawaii to restore Hawaiian native rights. The interest among Americans in knowing their ethnic backgrounds and celebrating "home country" traditions is another supporting plank among this resurrection of ethnic pride.

Why should this be? For over two hundred years, America has been the melting pot, the country of assimilation of immigrants from widely diverse countries and cultures. Why should we now see a rejection of the assimilation? (For example, this can be seen in the Southwest and in South Florida by the Hispanic-Americans who are seen by many as clinging to the native culture and not even attempting assimilation as did the immigrants of the past.) Why the sudden crisis in the Balkans or Russia where it appears every ethnic group wants to secede and form their own nation? Why now? Why at this point in time?

Obviously, if cultures were converging, were globalizing occurring as predicted, the opposite reaction would be seen. What actually is occurring is to have been expected if it is a divergent world. An explanation which would seem to fit the facts is that the global age has caused most of the peoples of the world to realize how small the world really is and to instill fears of what it means to them. The return to ethnicity can be thought of as a means of seeking a self-identity much as a Texan deepens his/her drawl when he/she goes to the Northeast or a Bostonian does likewise in Texas. One must have a terra firma to cling to. In a crowd, an individual seeks to reaffirm his/her own particular identity. And it appears that in this age of global information and travel, a return and a deepening of ethnic awareness and values (hence culture) provide the self-awareness and sought-after identity to the problem of the ever-increasing closer world: "I am not a citizen of the World; I am a Hawaiian (or German or Scot); a citizen of Earth has no cultural history yet I do, so I must be something." This is not contradictory. One can have jet aircraft, faxes, personal computers, and satellite dishes and still not yield one's own culture. Cultures assimilate institutions into their own environments. Baseball in Japan, although being played by the same (on the surface anyway) set of rules as in America, has been thoroughly Japanized.[27]

Naisbitt understood this seemingly contradictory state of affairs. On one hand, English has become the language of the international youth culture and American music and entertainment its official logo. Even most of the slang is American English: "rap music," "computer hacking." The trend of a global culture through transportation and communications advances have resulted in an unexpected backlash. As Naisbitt comments appropriately: "The more homogeneous our lifestyles become, the more steadfastly we shall cling to our deeper values—religion, language, art, and literature. As our outer worlds grow more similar, we will increasingly treasure the traditions that spring from within." Naisbett calls this cultural nationalism.[28] By threatening the cultural integrity, smaller tribes have begin to reassert their cultural nationalism.

A globalization of values is not generally occurring; the opposite appears to be taking place. Cultures are diverging in their attitudes while still modernizing. This is not the first time this phenomenon has occurred: the Meiji Japanese managed to modernize their country in the latter half of the nineteenth century without sacrificing their own cultural values; they called this "Western technology with Eastern morals." If this is the case, understanding of different cultures will become even more critical to marketeers in the years to come. This thesis has considerable usage in that differences between cultures do exist and will continue to exist if not widen.

Therefore, standardization does not appear to be a realistic strategy in many cases. Yet, the pure adaptation strategy is costly and inefficient. Does a middle ground exist? Yes, a grey area exists between the two extremes. It is called Glocalization.

GLOCALIZATION

Due to the difficulties that a globalization strategy faces, another term has developed in recent years called glocalization.[29] Glocalization realizes that perfect standardization at every possible level is practicably impossible due to the constraints discussed above. Instead, glocalization seeks uniformity, especially in elements that are strategic such as positioning where the tactical approaches are localized. It is a "think global, act local" strategy.[30] For instance, Sony sets the long-term strategy from Tokyo, while regional managers make their own product decisions locally. Just as it is not safe to say that all groups of people are the same, consumers are beginning to adopt some of the same lifestyles. However, culture and traditional values do not disappear. Marketers must consider these differences when creating effective ads and relevant messages. A review of how American multinationals (many of which were used as examples of globalization by Levitt) have actually adapted their operations overseas would be instrumental in conveying the concept. Camel is a well known company for its standardized approach. In most countries, Camel cigarettes are promoted as a Turkish blend of cigarettes; but in Greece, the promotion is changed to an American blend of cigarettes. Camel's global campaign was adapted to different geographic areas: One part of the campaign was based on wilderness, different types of jungle, or local wildlife areas[31] according to cultural preferences.

The commercial from Coca-Cola that showed 1,000 singing children on a hilltop was edited 21 different ways for broadcast overseas.[32] Coca-Cola's award-winning commercial with Mean Joe Greene giving his jersey to a young boy who had offered him a bottle of Coke after a tough game could not be used outside of the United States, since few foreigners understood football nor knew who Joe Greene was. The theme remained, but the boy, the language, and the star were changed to accommodate local interests; for example, advertisements in South America used popular Argentinean soccer star Diego Maradona and those in Asia used Thai soccer star Niwat.

Nike created a worldwide advertising program which it tailored to each overseas market. The basic ad was "Bo Knows" with Bo Jackson, where recognizable players (internationally) exclaimed that Bo knows various sports (in local languages without subtitles). Reebok created different localized commercials for many country markets and still uses different advertising themes. American Express launched a $100 million campaign in 1994 that covered 30 nations; and 60 ads focused on "places you want to go, people you want to see." All spots around the world followed the same formula: Merchants expound on their business philosophies, then talk about the American Express card.[33]

McDonald's offers a standardized menu, but adapts to local environments. A berry-based drink is offered in Brazil; a fruit-based shake is offered in Malaysia, Singapore, and Thailand. McDonald's introduced McChao, a Chinese fried rice, in Japan. It also uses mutton pot pies in Australia and McSpaghetti in the Philippines. McDonald's serves coconut, mango, and tropic mint shakes in Hong Kong. Donald McDonald represents McDonald's in Japan because the Japanese have difficulty pronouncing the letter R. Wendy's serves shrimp cake sandwiches in Japan. The company adjusted its menu in Quebec to include poutine, a French-Canadian dish consisting of fried potatoes covered with cheese curds and brown gravy.

Levi's allows local managers to make decisions about adapting products to suit local tastes. In Brazil, these decisions involve distribution. There, Levi's established a chain of 400 Levis' Only stores, many in small, rural markets. These stores accounted for as much as two-thirds of Levi's Brazilian sales. James Dean is the central figure in all Levi's ads in Japan. Indonesian ads show Levi's-clad teenagers driving around Dubuque, Iowa in 1960s convertibles. Levi's advertising generally uses English language and American music. Levi's represents casual wear in the United States while wearing them is an upscale fashion statement in Europe. Levi's Jeans are made in Japan to satisfy the tighter fit desired by Japanese consumers. Levi's developed its Femina jeans featuring curvaceous cuts that provide the ultratight fit traditionally favored by Brazilian women.

Campbell's Soup company is the king of adaptation. Campbell's discovered that the English prefer a more bitter taste than Americans. The British complained that Campbell's soups were too thick (the British did not dilute it, as they were used to eating the soup without adding water). The Japanese are anti-can (most Japanese walk to the market and don't like to carry heavy cans). Irish and Italians prefer creamy tomato soup, Germans want rice, and Colombians want spice. Australians prefer cream of pumpkin soup. Campbell's advertises its 15 varieties of soup to Argentineans as the Real Soup, stressing its list of fresh ingredients. It advertises to Polish working mothers by emphasizing its convenience. In Poland, Campbell's introduced eight varieties of condensed zupa and flaki, a peppery tripe soup. The average Pole consumes five bowls of soup a week—three times the American average, and 98 percent of Polish soups are homemade.

Campbell's sells soup in Mexico in large cans with enough soup to serve four or five because Mexican families are generally large.[34] In Mexico, Campbell's sells Crema de Chile Pablano. In China, watercress and duck gizzard soup, scallop broth, radish and carrot soup, and pork, fig, and date soups are popular. Campbell's opened the Hong Kong kitchen in 1991 to adapt and create recipes for soup to reach the 2 billion Asian consumers. The Chinese average one bowl of soup per day, among the highest per capita soup eaters in the world. Campbell's offers corn and chicken soup in East Asia. However, dog soup and shark's fin are out.

The favorite Domino's pizzas in Australia are those with prawns and pineapples. Domino's Pizza in Japan offers such toppings as grilled chicken, spinach, onion, corn, squid, tuna, and corn salad. Pizza Hut offers its Japanese customers barbecued chicken, burdock root, potato, and macaroni salad.

PepsiCo created a global brand of Lay's Potato Chips to enter the annual global market of $17 billion. American consumers partake of more than 20 pounds of salty snacks a year, eight times the world average. Foreign eaters tend to go more for local fare; for example, Asians prefer pellet snacks (processed chunks of corn or wheat). After interviewing 100,000 consumers in more than 30 countries in 1995, PepsiCo determined that the potato chip was the most popular snack, with a worldwide market of $4 billion. PepsiCo is marketing all its brands of potato chips under the uniform Lay's brand name. PepsiCo also has installed new equipment to its foreign operations to provide quality and consistency similar to that seen in the United States. Having a unified brand allows the company to buy raw materials in bulk and will cut costs by more than $200 million per year. Nonetheless, local tastes still differ: in Europe, the most popular flavor for potato chips is salt and vinegar; Poles and Hungarians go for paprika flavoring; in Asia, fish flavors top the list. PepsiCo has a shrimp chip venture in Korea and a squid/peanut snack for Southeast Asia. PepsiCo introduced cheeseless Chee·tos in China because the Chinese do not like cheese; 100 million bags were sold in 1995. PepsiCo has launched a seafood-flavored style of Chee·tos and is planning to build a new $30 million plant in China to meet the growing demand.[35]

Unilever's TV commercials for Dove soap used the same themes and were identical, but the actors were local as was the language used. Mars candy company abandoned successful European brand names in the pursuit of standardized global brands: Raider was renamed Twix; Britain's Marathon became Snickers; and France's Bonitos became M&M's. Unfortunately, the path is not as easy with Milky Way and Mars candy bars. Both bars are sold worldwide, but they refer to different products in different countries. In the United States, Milky Way has caramel and chocolate; in Europe, it has no caramel. The European version of the Mars bar has no almonds. Europeans view nuts as something you feed horses. To them, Hershey chocolate bars taste bitter.[36]

not true

Some products have certain core technologies, subassemblies, or components that can be standardized on a worldwide basis, while other parts require adaptation to local conditions. Whirlpool washing machines sold in Europe or the United States were not suited to wash the traditional saris worn by Indian women. Whirlpool, in response, created a Western-style automatic washing machine that is compact enough to fit into Indian houses and that incorporates specifically designed agitators that will not tangle saris. These machines handle only half the capacity (11 pounds) of the typical U.S. model. Most of the machine is built from standardized components. Whirlpool has designed a World Washer, a small, stripped down, automatic washing machine targeted to meet the needs of developing nations such as Brazil, Mexico, and India. This, although being a standardized product, must be customized as local needs arise.[37] Whirlpool must have regional manufacturing centers due to varying size and varying consumer preferences around the world. Even though the features, dimensions, and configurations of machines may vary from market to market (the French want top-loading washing machines; the British want front-loading ones; the Germans want high-speed machines, while Italians prefer slower spin speeds), much of the technology and manufacturing processes involved are similar. Even though the products that come out of the Italian and German plants are totally different, the insides of the machines do not vary and both can be standardized and simplified into a common platform. Glocalization, therefore, is the use of a global theme with the adaptation as necessary around the globe to accommodate local tastes and requirements.

CONCLUSIONS

The issue of whether to adapt or to standardize a company's operations is one of the most important issues in international marketing. Standardization is a philosophy that views the world as one market. This philosophy provides serious advantages that can improve a company's competitive edge. Although standardization can substantially increase a company's productivity and profits, the risks incurred if the standardization process is not done correctly can outweigh the benefits. Marketing a single product one way everywhere can scare off customers, alienate employees, and blind a company to its customers' needs. Successful companies state that international marketing works only with some brands, some places, sometimes, and will never replace brands and ads geared to the locals.[38] The concept of standardization is only a philosophy, one that cannot be used in general in the real world. Glocalization is the working arm of standardization. It realizes that some degree of adaptation is necessary in the real world.

Kustin's[39] study indicates that over the last 20 years, there has been a slow progression of standardization across product categories; however, he indicates the potential for standardization is a function of the product category and the group of markets involved. Child's[40] research is extremely illuminating: most of the studies noted that conclude convergence focused on macro issues and the structure and technology of the organizations themselves. Most of the studies that concluded divergence focused on micro level issues and the behavior of people within. He concludes that organizations worldwide are growing more similar while those within organizations are maintaining their cultural uniqueness.

The applicability of a universal approach for consumer goods appears to be limited to products that have certain characteristics such as universal brand name recognition, minimal product knowledge requirements for consumer use, and product advertisements that demand low information content. Two constraints make globalizing food products especially difficult. The first is recognizability. People want to know what their food is made of and they usually want to know how it is processed. They require recognizability in the appearance, taste, and texture of foods. Consumers impose no such requirements for durables. This usually means that a food or beverage product will not sell in countries where the people are not familiar with its ingredients. Coffee is a good example; instant coffee is unpopular in Germany, France, and Italy, where people drink a lot of freshly brewed coffee. The second constraint is age.

The more a product is associated with long-standing usage habits, the less internationally marketable it usually is. The more recent the product, the more likely it can be globally marketed. Europeans have definite tastes regarding shoes and suits; but casual jeans tend to be universal.[41]

Consumer products used at home (food and beverages) are often more culturally grounded than products used outside the home (e.g., autos). Products tend to be less culturally grounded if they are used by young people whose cultural norms are not ingrained, people who are well traveled, and ego-driven consumers who can be reached through myths and fantasies shared across cultures.[42] The target market for standardization is most often the upper segment of the market (income or education) rather than with the average consumer—consumers with low status concern, low dogmatism, high education, who are white-collar workers, who have high incomes, and have fewer cross-cultural differences than other consumer groups.[43] Only certain products can be marketed similarly, in some places, and only after variables such as marketing mix and culture have been analyzed.[44] For example, low-priced products (e.g., McDonald's hamburgers) and luxury products (e.g., Rolex watches) can typically be internationalized. Global campaigns appear successful for the following product categories:

- status durable goods (e.g., BMW, Mercedes-Benz)
- nondurable goods with prestige image (e.g., Perrier water)
- global services with status (e.g., American Express Gold Card)
- global retailers that cater to the elite (e.g., Tiffany jewelry).

Products in between tend to be more culturally grounded and require varying levels of adaptation to local tastes.

However, a worldwide culture with common norms does exist. This group has grown up accustomed to worldwide communications and transportation. The teenage culture shares a youthful lifestyle that values growth and learning with appreciation for future trends, fashion, and music. Teenagers are very self-conscious about the way they look. Role models act as an important influence on their choices[45]; MTV has become the cable company for youth and broadcasts its English language programming throughout the world. Levi's has become the clothing of choice among youth while running shoes and printed T-shirts (usually with English slogans) complete the global youth's uniform. McDonald's restaurants represent the gathering place for youth anywhere around the globe. Coke and Pepsi are engaged in a global battle for the thirst of the world's youth population.[46] It is projected that in the 1990s, the size of the global teenage market will reach 1.37 billion.[47] Marketers have been quick to take advantage of this huge and homogeneous market: Benetton introduced colorful Italian knitware based on a global advertising campaign ("The United Colors of Benetton") to global teens; Sony introduced "My First Sony" line of audio products for youth.[48]

The youth market is remarkably stable around the world; teens in Tokyo, Chicago, Paris, and Sydney have more in common with each other than they do with their parents. The older generations have withdrawn into their shell. Naisbitt called this cultural imperialism. The youth, raised in this first truly world culture, have adopted it and are being marketed to in a global way (alas, still with some adaptations such as language). Perhaps Levitt was right after all, but two generations too soon.

Chapter 3

Cross-Cultural Negotiations

A PRIMER ON CROSS-CULTURAL NEGOTIATIONS

Negotiation is the process by which at least two parties try to reach an agreement on matters of mutual interest. The negotiation process proceeds as an interplay of perception, information processing, and reaction, all of which turn on images of reality (accurate or not), on implicit assumptions regarding the issue being negotiated, and on an underlying matrix of conventional wisdom, beliefs, and social expectations. This becomes more apparent when the negotiation process is international, when cultural differences must be bridged. Negotiations involve two dimensions: a matter of substance and the process. The latter is rarely a matter of relevance when negotiations are conducted within the same cultural setting. Only when dealing with someone from another country with a different cultural background does process usually becomes a critical barrier to substance; in such settings, process first needs to be established before substantive negotiations can commence.[1]

When one takes the seemingly simple process of negotiation into a cross-cultural context, it becomes even more complex and complications tend to grow exponentially. It is naive indeed to venture into international negotiation with the belief that "after all, people are pretty much alike everywhere and behave much as we do." Even if they wear the same clothes you do, speak English as well as (or even better than) you, and prefer many of the comforts and attributes of American life (e.g., food, hotels, sports), it would be foolish to view a member of another culture as a brother or sister in spirit. That negotiation style you use so effectively domestically can be inappropriate and when dealing with people from another cultural background; in fact, its use can often result in more harm than gain. Heightened sensitivity, more attention to detail, and perhaps even changes in basic behavioral patterns are required when working in another culture.[2] One should not be surprised to be invited to take a sauna right in the middle of an intense negotiating session with a Finnish client; Finns often resolve important issues and solidify relationships in the sauna (five million Finns and 1.5 million saunas in Finland).

Different cultural systems can produce divergent negotiating styles—styles shaped by each nation's culture, geography, history, and political system. Unless you see the world through the other's eyes (no matter how similar they appear to you), you may not be seeing nor hearing the same. No one can usually avoid bringing along his/her cultural assumptions, images, prejudices, or other attitudinal baggage into any negotiating situation.[3]

In cross-cultural negotiations, many of the rules taught and used domestically may not apply—especially when they may not be culturally acceptable to the other party. For most Western negotiators, this includes the concepts of give and take, of bargaining, and even of compromise. The common Western ideal of a persuasive communicator—highly skilled in debate, able to overcome objections with verbal flair, an energetic extrovert—may be regarded by members of other cultures as unnecessarily aggressive, superficial, insincere, even vulgar and repressive. To another American, the valued American traits of directness and frankness show evidence of good intentions and personal convictions. To an American, it is complimentary to be called straightforward and aggressive—not necessarily so, however, for members of other cultures. To describe a person as "aggressive" is a derogatory characterization to a British citizen. To the Japanese, those very same traits indicate lack of confidence in one's convictions and insincerity. Instead, terms such as thoughtful, cooperative, considerate, and respectful instill positives in the Japanese and other Asian cultures.

Even the concept of negotiations has different meanings for different cultures. In negotiations with the Japanese, the word "negotiate" and its usual translation *kosho* have different meanings. *Kosho* has nuances of fighting, conflict, strategy (*senryaku*), and verbal debate (*iiau*), whereas Western-style negotiation lacks these overtones and usually suggests discussion, concession, and conference.[4] To the Japanese, negotiation is like that between father and son. The status relationship is explicit and important. The son (seller) carefully explains his situation and asks for as much as possible because he will have no chance to bicker once the father (buyer) decides. The son (seller) accepts the decision because it would hurt the relationship to argue and because he trusts the father (buyer) to care for his needs.

Throughout the Middle East, the word "compromise" connotes a negative meaning as in the phrase, "her virtue was compromised." An Arab fears loss of manliness if he compromises. The word for "mediator" in Persian means "meddler," someone who barges in uninvited. To the Mexicans and many Latins, compromise translates into a matter of honor and giving in means yielding dignity and integrity, which is held in high regard. To Russians, an offer of compromise is a sign of weakness. To give up a demand once presented, even a minor or formalistic point, implies losing control of one's own will and becoming subjugated to another's will. The natural impulse of many Russians when provided an offer of compromise is to go on the offensive, seeking to exploit and to establish dominance. An unreciprocated concession reeks of weakness and invites attack. To the typical Russian, a weak individual chooses compromises; a strong person with self-esteem who commands the respect of his/her fellow peers forces his/her will on others and does not avoid confrontations.

Domestically, the study of negotiation tends to encompass business relationships between parties, tactics, bargaining strategies, contingency positions, etc. However, in a cross-cultural context, besides the usual rules of negotiation, one has to be wary of fine nuances in relationships and practices and how they are perceived and executed by members of other cultures.

A CROSS-CULTURAL PERSPECTIVE OF THE NEGOTIATIONS PROCESS

The classical view of the negotiation process undergoes four stages: Nontask, Task, Persuasion, and Agreement.[5] Although all negotiations include these four aspects, the strategies, tactics, content, duration, and sequence spent in each phase, as well as the emphasis and importance of each phase may differ substantially between the two cultures at the bargaining table.

Nontask sounding focuses on establishing a relationship among the negotiating parties. During this stage, information specific to the issue under negotiation is not considered; rather, the parties seek to get to know each other. The first stage includes all those activities that might be described as establishing a rapport or getting to know one another, but does not include information related to the "business" of the meeting. A fundamental difference between Americans and Japanese is that the Japanese rely much more heavily on personal relationships in business and spend a disproportionately higher amount of time on the rapport (nontask) stage than do Americans.[6] This philosophical difference tends to create inherent conflict between firms from these two cultures and heightens the probability of failure.

The Japanese negotiation process usually starts with an introduction from a reference, a go-between, a *shokaisha* (third-party introducer), who has arranged the initial meeting. It is preferred that the *shokaisha* have a strong relationship with the buyer and thus be influential; the buyer does not want to damage the harmony and relationship with the *shokaisha* by rejecting the proposal. The buyer usually attends the first meeting as well as the last meeting, the signing ceremony. Before the first meeting, he/she is a prime source of information for both parties. In case of an impasse in the talks between the two sides (either during the negotiations or afterward during the normal conduct of business), the buyer is often asked to become involved to settle their differences, to become a *chukaisha* (mediator).

In the view of the Japanese, emotion and personal relations are more important than cold facts in business relations. The key issue is, "Can I get along with these people and their company and do I want to sell (or buy) their products?" It is not, "Can I make money on this deal?" The Japanese are particularly interested in the sincerity of those they are negotiating with. They are typically unwilling to do business with someone who they think may prove to be arrogant or unpleasant, or who they think does not like them as individuals, as a company, or as a nation: "I do not do business with someone who does not like us!" The Japanese do not separate personal feelings from business relationships.[7] If the Japanese feel that their relationships are not yet anchored and may drift, they will stall and hesitate to do business until they are comfortable with the other party.

Task-related exchange of information focuses on providing information directly connected to the issue under negotiation. During this stage, the negotiators consider the information exchanged regarding the parties' needs and preferences or the parties' subjective expected utilities of the various alternatives open to the participants.[8] The most important stage to a Japanese negotiator is the information gathering stage. Only after those on the buying side feel that they have established a trustworthy relationship will business be brought up.

Japanese negotiators are concerned with understanding the other side's point of view. Exchanging information and asking for more information are constants with the Japanese. A complete understanding is imperative to the Japanese; they ask endless questions to identify the needs and preferences of both parties while offering little information and ambiguous responses. The reasons for needs and preferences are critical data for Japanese, who seek to place information within an interpretive context. Each phase of the discussion process may generate more questions that must be answered. The emphasis is on exchanging extensive detailed information.

Many times, the Japanese use the initial meeting merely to gather information, which is then fed back to their superiors and peers for deliberation and a carefully prepared response. The Japanese strongly believe it is folly to make an offer until one knows what the other side wants. This explains the slow start, the lack of an initial proposal, the emphasis on information gathering, and the long drawn-out preliminary groundwork that is usually encountered when negotiating with the Japanese. The Japanese need detailed information to build the foundation for whatever decision they intend to put forward. No one is blamed or rebuked for shortcomings in the deal or for the failure of the venture or the negotiations, as all concerned managers participated in the negotiating and final decision making.

Persuasion focuses on efforts to modify the views of the other parties and sway them to "our" way of thinking through the use of various persuasive tactics. This stage of negotiations is often inter-twined with other stages (i.e., persuasion goes on while exchanging information and making concessions). This third stage, compromise and persuasion, is the stage in which most American companies will overcompensate compared to the Japanese. If not handled properly, failure becomes almost certain. Americans see persuasion as a kind of conquest whereas the Japanese look on it as a meeting of the minds. The Japanese verb "to persuade" (*fukumeru*) also means "to include." Persuasion will often be conducted behind the scenes, not during a formal negotiating meeting.

For Japanese managers, there is not a clear separation of informa-tion seeking and persuasion. The two stages tend to blend together as each side more clearly defines and refines its needs and preferences. So much time is spent in the task-related exchange of information that little is left to discuss during the persuasion stage. Maintaining harmony, avoiding loss of face, and gaining the agreement of all involved are most important. For the Japanese, it is more important to maintain the harmony in the relationship than to be frank and open. The Japanese believe that little persuasion should be necessary if the parties have taken the time to understand each other.

The first Japanese proposal is carefully drafted and reasonable, reflecting the Japanese preference for well-informed, best solutions and consensus building. The Japanese offer what they feel is correct, proper, and reasonable. If the initial trust building was carried out successfully, cost may not be bargained on at all. Japanese negotia-tors often find themselves with no contingency or fallback plans, few officially authorized concessions, and an absence of clear policies on some questions. They react negatively to open disagreement and aggression. Japanese avoid confrontations and respond the threats by changing the subject, keeping silence, or withdrawing.[9]

What an American may consider normative, positive behavior (negotiating and reaching a compromise with an enemy), a Russian perceives as showing cowardice, weakness, and unworthiness; the word "deal" has a strong negative connotation, even in contem-porary Russia. A negotiation is treated as a whole without con-cessions. At the Strategic Arms Limitation Talks (SALT), the Americans thought they had an agreement (meaning conclusive commitment), while the Soviets said it was an understanding (meaning an expression of mutual viewpoint or attitude). When the Americans thought they had an understanding, the Soviets said it was a procedural matter, meaning they had agreed to a process for conducting the negotiation.

Concessions and agreement is the culmination of the negotiation process at which an agreement is reached. To reach an agreement that is mutually acceptable, each side frequently must give up some things; concessions by both sides are usually necessary. Depending upon cultures involved, promise breaking is tolerated, expected, or even desired. In some cultures, the negotiations process effectively ends when the contract is signed; elsewhere, it may not be so. Members of one culture may focus on different aspects of an agreement (e.g., legal, financial) than do members of another culture (personal, relational). The implementation of a business agreement may be stressed in one culture, while the range and prevention of practical problems emphasized in another culture. In some cultures, the attention of people is directed more toward the specific details of the agreement (documenting the agreement), while other cultures focus on how the promises can be kept (process and implementation). Americans negotiate a contract; the Japanese negotiate a personal relationship.

Cultures force people to view and value differently the many social interactions inherent in fashioning an agreement. The French prefer to begin with agreement on general principles while Americans tend to seek agreement first on specifics. For Americans, negotiating a deal is making a whole series of compromises and trade-offs on a long list of particulars. For the French, the essence is to agree on basic general principles that will guide and determine the negotiation process afterward; these principles become the framework, the skeleton upon which the contract is built. In the Arab world, a person's word may be more binding than many written agreements; thus, insistence on a contract may be insulting to them. A Greek sees a contract as a formal statement announcing the intention to build a business for the future, the negotiation is complete only when the work is accomplished. Mexicans treat the contract as an artistic exercise of ideas and do not expect contracts to apply consistently in the real world. Mexicans appear to be more concerned with the general wording of the agreement, while Americans appear to be more focused on the specific wording of the agreement itself.

CONTEXT IN CROSS-CULTURAL NEGOTIATIONS

The amount of information in a given communication is called context. Context includes both the vocal and nonvocal aspects of communication that surround a word or passage and clarify its meaning—the situational and cultural factors affecting communications. In verbal communications, information is transmitted through a code that makes meanings both explicit and specific. In nonverbal communications, the nonverbal aspects become the major channel for transmitting meaning. The verbal factors include the rate at which one talks, the pitch or tone of one's voice, the intensity or loudness of the voice, the flexibility or adaptability of the voice to the situation, the variations of rate, pitch, and intensity, the quality of the voice, the fluency, expressional patterns, or nuances of delivery. Nonverbal aspects include eye contact, pupil contraction and dilation, facial expression, odor, skin color (e.g., blushing), hand gestures, body movement, proximity, and use of space.

The greater the contextual portion of communication in any given culture, the more difficult it is for one to convey or receive a message. Conversely, it is easier to communicate with a person from a culture in which context contributes relatively little to a message. In high-context cultures, information about an individual (and consequently about individual and group behavior in that culture) is provided through mostly nonverbal means. It is also conveyed through status, friends, and associates. Information flows freely within the culture although outsiders who are not members of the culture may have difficulty reading the information. Northern Europe (low context), with its Protestant tradition and indoor culture, tends to emphasize the technical, the numerical, the tested, the quality. Southern Europe (high context), with its Catholic background and open air lifestyle, tends to favor personal networks, social context, innovation, and flair. Meetings in Southern Europe are often longer, but the total decision process may be faster.

In a low-context communication, information is transmitted through an explicit code to make up for a lack of shared meanings—words. Americans tend to be low-context, focus on substantive issues, on what is being said: "Just the facts, ma'am." In low-context cultures, the environment, situation, and nonverbal behavior are relatively less important and more explicit information has to be given. A direct style of communications is valued and ambiguity is not well regarded. Relationships between individuals are relatively shorter in duration, and personal involvement tends to be valued less. Low-context countries tend to be more heterogeneous and prone to greater social and job mobility. Authority is diffused through a bureaucratic system that makes personal responsibility difficult. Agreements tend to be written rather than spoken; they are treated as final and legally binding. Insiders and outsiders are less closely distinguished; foreigners find it relatively easier to adjust, and immigration is more acceptable. Cultural patterns tend to change faster in low-context societies. In low-context cultures, initial relationship creation may be passed over fairly rapidly, while in high-context cultures, this is a very important function throughout the process; the decision whether or not to sign may depend on the relationships established. Low-context countries include the Anglo countries and the Germanic and Scandinavian countries.

German culture is low context, therefore specific terms and concepts are very important. They balance between their own profit and the satisfaction of their client. The Germans are people of their word; a handshake is as good as a written contract. However, they are very concerned with the precision of the written word. Since Germans believe friendships and personal relationships can complicate negotiations, they prefer to keep a distance between themselves and the other team of negotiators; they therefore appear to be distant and impersonal. Since Germans tend to be detail oriented, having technical people as part of the negotiation team is important. Being punctual is expected. German negotiations are planned and well organized, direct in their approach. German protocol is formal. Germans tend to be very conservative. Correct posture is a sign of inner discipline. Manners are of utmost importance to Germans. German society is quite paternalistic. Corporate decisions are made at the top, but with a great deal of detail from workers. Quality is important, and decisions are pondered and carefully scrutinized to be sure such quality exists in any projects they undertake.[10] The

Germans do not appreciate emotional gestures; hands should never be used to emphasize points. They believe in remaining calm when under pressure.

In high-context cultures, the external environment, situation, and nonverbal behavior are crucial in creating and interpreting communications. Members of these cultures are programmed from birth to depend heavily upon covert clues given within the context of a message which is delivered verbally. In languages spoken in those high-context cultures (such as Arabic, Japanese, or Chinese), subtlety is valued and much meaning is conveyed by inference. The Japanese talk around a point, believing that the point should be discovered from the context. *Haragei* (belly language) is the Japanese expression that implies being able to communicate without words. High-context communication is faster, more economical, more efficient, and more satisfying, but if common programming does not exist between sender and receiver, communication is incomplete. High-context individuals seek information on many levels in addition to the spoken word, but when dealing with low-context cultures, the spoken word is primarily all they get. On the other hand, low-context individuals are quite confused by the ambiguity contained in the spoken or written answers of high-context individuals. By reading inaccurately, misinformation and miscommunication results.

When an American says "Yes," it usually means "I accept the terms." However, "Yes" in many Asian countries may mean one of four different items. It may mean that the other side recognizes that one is talking to them, but not necessarily that they understand what is said. Second, it could mean that what was said was understood and was clear but not that it was agreed to. Third, it may mean that the other party has understood the proposal. Last, it may mean total agreement.[11] The actual meaning must be inferred from the context of the message.

In high-context cultures, relationships between individuals are relatively long lasting and individuals feel deep personal involvement with each other. These cultures place great importance on personal relationships. Members from such cultures will focus energies and time on developing an understanding and trust of the other person and less attention to the specifics of the deal. Only when convinced of the other's integrity, reliability, and sincerity, and only when comfortable doing business with the other party, will a member of a high-context culture negotiate in earnest. The need for confidence and trust in the other party is particularly strong in countries where a businessperson is unable to depend upon a strong and independent legal system to settle his/her conflicts and hence is forced to depend heavily on personal relationships. Mainland Chinese always hesitate to negotiate unless they know much about the individuals with whom they are contemplating doing business.

Italians tend to be extremely hospitable, but are often volatile in temperament. When they make a point, they do so with considerable gesticulation and emotional expression. Impressed by style, they tend to dress well themselves. Moreover, they enjoy haggling over prices.[12] Italians often exhibit a calculated nonchalance. A common tactic is to unexpectedly close a negotiating session, pretending the whole thing is of minor importance. Urgency on the part of the negotiator might send a signal that one is desperate to complete the deal.

In high-context societies, those in authority are personally responsible for the actions of subordinates, which in turn creates super loyalty by subordinates to their superiors. Agreements tend to be spoken rather than written. Insiders and outsiders are clannish. Actual cases exist of entire communities (Sicilian) able to carry on whole conversations by gestures alone. High-context cultures can be found in East Asia (Japan, China, Korea, Vietnam), Mediterranean countries (Greece, Italy, Spain, and to a lesser extent, France), the Middle East, and to a lesser extent, Latin America and South America.

In high-context countries, negotiators require sufficient knowledge of the culture to communicate understandably and acceptably. It is only if they are in a position to share the assumptions of the people with whom they are dealing that they can build up relationships and have highly satisfactory interactions. These assumptions will embrace the cognitive structures of the people concerned and the worldview that they hold, which are derived from culture. In high-context cultures, the external environment, situation, and nonverbal behavior are crucial in understanding communications. In a low-context culture, a much greater portion of the meaning in a given communication comes from the spoken word, which is more literal and detail oriented. High-context cultures such as Mexico look at their North American counterparts as more structured, rigid, and direct. Mexicans are often unable to speak frankly about some matter due to the desire to save face. To the low-context culture, the written word is binding, regardless of what evolves later; to the high-context culture, the contract is a sign of good faith and the relationship between the two parties, not the contract, is what matters; the contract is a symbol of the bond between its drafters. For high-context cultures, the human side of the negotiation process is more important than the technical aspects.

The Russians are considerably higher context. Issues involving authority, risk, and control and how they affect the relationship among the negotiating parties are so important to them that it may be difficult for a Russian negotiating team to get to the subjects on the agenda until those issues are resolved. Form and substance are inextricably linked. For Russians, silence should not be taken as consent but rather as disapproval. Silence leaves them with their options completely open. They can either say nothing, implying acquiescence and approval, or later express disapproval and state that they had never agreed to any such thing. Or they can do both at different times, depending on their interests at the moment. Russians negotiate by moving upward through the hierarchy; each level must involve a concession of some kind. Russians also typically make concessions late in the process. They begin by making large demands and offer very little in return; this is counter to most American experiences.

CONTRACTUAL IMPLICATIONS

Americans tend to be bound by law, not by relationships, tradition, religion, or culture. The objective of American negotiators is usually to arrive at legalistic contracts, and therefore the dominant concern is with getting the details right, and to use all relationships to facilitate the achievement of unambiguous understandings. A legal advisor is often included in the team to reduce the level of misunderstanding and conflict after signing. The action of signing a contract symbolizes an intention to fulfill the stated terms. An

American would not hesitate to sign a contract with his or her own worst enemy if it were sufficiently endowed in legal terms. Americans will honor a contract to the letter, whatever circumstances later arise.

With the Chinese, the contract may not represent finality but a starting point. Rather, the Chinese approach is to negotiate the process to establish a human relationship, often one of an essentially dependent nature, and therefore to create the bonding of "friendship." Consequently, they negotiate to do business with each other, often leaving the specific terms to be determined in the future based on the circumstances which occur. To a Chinese, a drafted legal contract is seen as inappropriate or irrelevant because it carries no sense of commitment. The business clauses might form a useful agenda, but obligations come from relationships—not pieces of paper. A contract is viewed as worthwhile only as long as it is necessary or convenient: McDonald's 20-year contract for a site in a central Beijing building did not keep it from being evicted after a mere two years.[13] When the Chinese suddenly find themselves in a situation where honoring a particular term in the contract will be difficult, they may turn to their partners, expecting not only understanding, but support and help in getting them out of their dilemma by changing the terms in the agreement. Americans often react with disbelief when this occurs. In response, the Chinese feel abandoned and deceived by a trusted business partner, who is unwilling to help them in their hour of need.

From the American perspective, a contract represents the culmination of a series of negotiations, the result of an arrangement, the development and delineation of procedures, rules, regulations, and standards by which all parties agree to behave with each other from this point forward until the exact state stipulated as the termination date of the contract. Under the terms of the developed contract, there can be no variation, no modification unless so indicated and agreed within the contract. That is why American contracts are lengthy; every contingency must be carefully anticipated and thought through ahead of time. The contract becomes a contract of objectively verifiable and predictable action between two parties.

The American expectation of contractual finality is foreign to the Japanese way of thinking. The Japanese do not view the signing of a contract as the end of negotiations, but merely as an indication of the direction to be taken; adjustments and modifications can be made as conditions and circumstances warrant it. (If contractual language is necessary, a phrase such as the following is often used: "All items not found in this contract will be deliberated upon in a spirit of honesty and trust.") The Japanese prefer that the contractual obligations be left as vague as possible in order to provide for a maximum amount of flexibility; Japanese contracts are always considered open for renegotiation. Japanese negotiators do not mind suggesting major changes even after a contract is signed. The traditional Japanese view is that a contract is secondary in a business transaction, which should be premised on an ongoing, harmonious relationship between two parties who are committed to the pursuit of similar objectives; relationships, not contracts, are negotiated.[14] The Japanese do not believe that a contract alone can ensure the success of a venture. According to Japanese thought, a truly wise person would not absolutely commit himself or herself, since human interactions are so indeterminate.[15]

RECOMMENDATIONS FOR SUCCESS

Over two-thirds of U.S.-Japanese negotiation efforts fail even though both sides want to reach a successful business agreement. Barriers to a successful agreement are often of a cultural nature rather than of an economical or legal basis. Since each side perceives the other from its own ethnocentric background and experience, often neither side fully comprehends why the negotiations failed. It is precisely this lack of knowledge concerning the culture and the "alien" and "unnatural" expectations of the other side that hinders effective negotiation with those from another culture. When Ford agreed to acquire the production side of Ferrari and use the Ferrari name in the United States, the deal was made on handshakes. Soon thereafter, Ford's attorneys arrived with contracts and accountants came to take inventory—normal business practice to Americans. Ferrari, the owner, was upset; he had an understanding with gentlemen, not with attorneys and accountants, and the deal fell through.

International business negotiators are separated from each other not only by physical features, a totally different language, and business etiquette, but also by a different way to perceive the world, to define business goals, to express thinking and feeling, and to show or hide motivation and interests. The way one succeeds in cross-cultural negotiations is by fully understanding others, using that understanding to to realize what each party wants from the negotiations, and to turn the negotiations into a win-win situation for both sides.

1. The path to success in negotiations is "prepare, prepare, prepare." Preparation is essential if one is to be proactive rather than reactive. Counterpunching only works when you are prepared before the blow is thrown. Preparation is difficult enough in domestic negotiations, but when the many multifaceted cross-cultural aspects are added, the problems and time necessary for adequate planning rise exponentially. Planning means coming prepared technically as well as culturally. Many foreigners come to the negotiating table well prepared technically and operationally and expect you to be likewise. Poor preparation, in addition to being a major obstacle to your success in achieving an agreement, can also have adverse cultural considerations—in the Orient, not having the answers or being sloppy may be a reason to lose face. The Chinese (as well as the Japanese and Russians) are usually meticulous in their preparation and well briefed on technical uses. Any sloppiness in the preparation of their opponent will be used against them. Meetings tend to fail in inverse proportion to the time spent in preparation and in direct proportion to the time spent meeting. Cross-cultural negotiations can often take anywhere from two to six times as long to reach an agreement as domestic negotiations. It would be appropriate to take the time to learn about the culture and language of the society you are to meet with. Set aside at least a week for such a study or even a month if it is a major commitment. Another reason for preparedness is to learn about and be able to counter negotiating tactics that may be peculiar to the culture you intend to visit and may have the effect of harming your efforts. Forewarned is forearmed.[16]

2. Extensive preliminary work by subordinates or cross-cultural brokers (go-betweens) is often necessary for a successful outcome

of a negotiation. It usually pays to spend what you consider to be an excessively large amount of time upfront with the other side's subordinates and aides to get them on board and in agreement before the CEOs get together. This is especially true and required if one is working with the Japanese—their *ringi* consensus (decision-making system) demands this decision from middle management upward. It is necessary to know who are the key gatekeepers and decision makers, where they are located in the organization, and what their authority and impact and involvement on the upcoming negotiations will be. In many cultures, behind-the-scenes actions are more important than the actual meeting—so the actual negotiating meeting can become a mere formality.

3. It is advantageous to know the language of the other team. Even if you decide not to use it at the bargaining table, knowing it can be handy. A foreign language can be an awesome barrier. Words have different or multiple meanings. Perceptions and concepts starkly differ across cultures. If any doubt whatsoever exists to the meaning of a word or action, ask questions. For your part, paraphrase your response, go slowly, and recap your position often. Eliminate, if possible, the use of jargon, idioms, or slang. Speak clearly, audibly, and slowly. Explain each major point in several different ways, but do not be condescending. Expressions and gestures may be useful in making a point with foreigners and bridging the gap between two foreign languages. In most cultures, it is advisable to always maintain a pleasant disposition and not show signs of anger. Meaning may be further modified by gestures, tone of voice, and cadence, which are important to the message sent but are not found in straight translations. A truly bicultural interpreter offers multiple benefits. If you do know the language, he or she can offer you more time to think and more time to prepare your response and next statement. Even if you do know the language, chances are you may not understand fully the culture and the particular nuances and implied meanings involved. Often, equivalent concepts do not exist between cultures. Detailed probing and illustrations, examples, and explanations must be given to provide complete understanding. A truly bicultural interpreter can help you phrase responses with just the correct shades of meaning and decisively impact the entire negotiation process.

4. Since language barriers will always exist in any cross-cultural negotiations, pictures are worth more than a thousand words. One should plan to support presentations with instructive visuals whenever possible. Photographs, drawings, diagrams, copies of key documents, catalogs, books, even samples of products should be brought if they will help state your case. Bringing an English copy to the meeting is fine if that is all that is available. Many members of other cultures can read English better than they can speak it. But beware: certain colors, symbols, subjects, or models can be taboo or distasteful to members of the other culture. Using them can be hazardous to the health of the agreement. Check out your visuals with your bicultural interpreter or an ethnic member of your company's local office to check for any faux pas before you present them. You can always redo them; but once you have presented them, it may have caused irrevocable damage to the negotiating effort.

5. The side that uses time most effectively usually wins. Americans are, in the eyes of foreigners, notoriously impatient, always seem to be in a hurry, and usually must come back with a signed agreement to show the boss the trip was eventful and not just a boondoggle. They can be driven into an agreement they really do not want just to take home a signed document. It is therefore a good strategy not to let the other side know your return plans, to prepare for the long term, and to be patient. The Chinese value patience and will freely use all sorts of stalling tactics and delays. This behavior can also stem from lack of experience, sluggish bureaucracy, subordinates having fear of criticism from above, or just plain slowness in decisions coming down from above. In any case, negotiations cannot be rushed, nor should they be.

6. Most agreements have long lasting implications. In many cultures, a written agreement is therefore not the culmination of the talks, but considered only the start of a longer relationship. To the Chinese, for example, the signing of a contract is not the termination of the negotiations, but a prologue to a longer, continuous relationship. It sets the stage for a growing relationship in which it will be proper for the Chinese to make increasing demands on the other party. You can expect a Chinese negotiator in the post-agreement implementation phase to continue to press to further his/her objectives; closure is never fully reached. In Japan and Greece, a

contract is considered valid only as long as it serves both parties' interests. The Russians interpret a contract strictly or loosely according to whether or not it is in their best interests to do so. Get the specifics on paper. If you are working with a culture that likes such general, broadly worded agreements, it would be useful to agree on the details and get them on paper. Otherwise, the other party could come back to you later on with an interpretation of dubious merit that is advantageous to their position and not to yours.

7. *Know your bottom line.* Benjamin Franklin said, "Necessity never made a good bargain." What is your BATNA (Best Alternative To a Negotiated Agreement)? What is your walking away point? At the point when an agreement no longer benefits you, you must be able to walk away without a deal, no matter how disappointed you are. Have a predetermined point where it becomes preferable not to make a deal and stick to it. Too many executives, having made the decision to do business, are so anxious to conclude a deal that they proceed despite the poor agreement reached. Amounts already invested and effort already expended should be irrelevant to a decision maker. The deal itself should not be the objective. If the deal cannot justify itself, the best alternative is to walk away, no matter how great your disappointment.

Chapter 4

Cross-Cultural Dimensions of Marketing Research

INTERNATIONAL MARKETING RESEARCH

The use of marketing research as business intelligence has the same utility to marketers as does military intelligence for the general staff of the armed forces. A review of anecdotes in this book indicates that the majority of the mistakes could have been avoided if the marketer had had better knowledge of the marketplace. The usage of marketing research in a cross-cultural context is a necessary facet to assist a marketer in minimizing potentially fatal errors, especially those problems that might arise in cross-cultural research when testing the role that certain sociological constructs play in buying behavior. The goal in this chapter is to examine marketing research as it pertains to culture and cross-cultural research issues.

Temptation all too often exists to use the Self-Reference Criterion. Little if any market research is done before the fact and any research that is performed is either as a postmortem or after a product has bombed in an attempt to restore it. Unilever introduced a superconcentrated detergent version of Surf to the Japanese market, only to find out that the premeasured package didn't dissolve in the wash; the product was not designed to work in a new, popular low-agitation washing machine, and the "fresh smell" was not relevant in Japan since most consumers hung their wash outside to dry in the fresh air.[1] Mattel also fell victim to ethnocentricity: Mattel attempted without much success to market its classic Barbie doll to the Japanese market. Mattel, in desperation, licensed Takara, a Japanese company. Takara's research revealed that most Japanese girls thought the doll's breasts were too big and the legs unrealistically long. Japanese Barbie was thoroughly made over, including brown eyes and hair. Within two years, Takara had sold over 2 million Barbie dolls.

Generally, the tools for research remain the same; however, the environments and the inferences from the research output could change drastically, depending upon the cultural venue. Marketing research, in essence, refers to gathering, analyzing, and presenting information related to a particular problem. The problem must be clearly defined in order to provide any meaningful data; the questions asked must relate to the problem specified. CPC International wanted to introduce Knorr dehydrated soups to Americans. They initiated market research by taste test comparisons. Americans indicated their preference for the taste of Knorr. Knorr even reformulated its European product to make sure the soups appealed to American tastes. Upon positive receipt of the extensive tests showing strong preference for the Knorr product, CPC decided to go ahead, straight into a disaster. All the taste tests were performed with already made soups. When American consumers discovered that the soups had to be prepared and were not ready to eat (requiring 15 to 20 minutes cooking time versus the heat-and-serve benefit of canned soups), failure resulted. The taste panel tests did not simulate the actual market environment for the soup. The questions asked did not reflect the true scenario.

Market research can be either primary data (newly obtained data) or secondary data (previously acquired data). Primary data can be obtained from either personal interviews, surveys, focus groups, observation, or experimentation. Each has distinct cultural influences and potential dangers when used in an international setting. For example, telephone surveys work poorly and give poor results when used in countries with low telephone penetration, such as most of Africa and Bangladesh; mall-intercept interviews may provide biased results because of the skewed demographics of mall users in many countries; only the affluent upper class are able to afford products in malls in developing countries (if malls exist at all there).

Secondary data gathering tends to be less culturally sensitive. Potential errors when using secondary data include source quality (who collected the data, the purpose of the data, and how the data were collected) and data quality. Data quality refers to the relevance of the data to the researcher's information requirements. Does the data provide responses to the particular questions asked? Concerns here include compatibility and comparability (when comparing different sets of data from different countries, are similar units of measurements and definitions used?), accuracy and reliability of the data (has the data been consciously distorted, or was the data collection of the original data flawed?), the recency of the data (is the data infrequently and unpredictably updated?), and the availability of the data. For example, the term "urban" varies from market to market. In Japan, an "urban" area has a population of 50,000 or more; in India, it includes centers with only 5,000 or more inhabitants; in France and Germany, any community with over 2,000 inhabitants qualifies as urban, while in Norway or Sweden, as few as 200 may be listed as urban. Obviously, comparing the number of urban centers between these countries would be misleading, providing worthless results. PepsiCo found age categories varied tremendously among countries it markets to. PepsiCo also found the local market definitions of consumption differed so greatly that no international comparisons could be made.

A fundamental issue with cross-cultural research is whether the similarities or differences noted in the market analysis are in fact real. Researchers must always question if it is a problem in the measurement method or instrument that has caused the erroneous result and indeed not the actual cultural differences.[2] Additionally, culture has proven notoriously difficult to define, and this difficulty has hindered empirical research. Delimiting a cultural group is often impossible; the unit of analysis is not necessarily a nation-state. (The Kurds do not have a state of their own, residing in parts of Iran, Iraq, and Turkey. On the other hand, the Jewish culture prospered for nearly two millennia without a land they could call their own.) Thus, any marketing research that is cultural or cross-cultural in nature has major constraints even before it has begun.[3]

CULTURAL INFERENCES
OF MARKETING RESEARCH

Each of the five primary data-collecting techniques have potential cultural pitfalls that could create erroneous results.

Interviews, especially when in person, could be the bearer of a host of problems. Not the least of these is translation: one interviewer requested to speak to the "madam of the house" rather than the "lady of the house." India has 14 official languages spoken in different parts of the country; knowing which one to use where is a major concern. Every language has multiple dialects and its own slang and idioms; idioms in each Spanish-speaking country can be significantly different from its neighbors; one should not blindly use the same translation of a questionnaire for all countries, even if people in those countries speak the same language. An unwary interviewer could create belligerent or nonresponsive respondents by saying the wrong phrase at the wrong time. For instance, considerable difference exists between "High" and "Low" German; the use of the wrong form could nullify the results of an otherwise worthwhile interview. Problems with translation have led to severe difficulties at the United Nations Conference for Women in Cairo in the fall 1994. It seemed that the French have no term for the word "empowerment." Neither do the Chinese or the Russians. United Nations translators for all five of the conference's official languages besides English (Arabic, Chinese, French, Spanish, and Russian) were attempting to comprehend the American buzzwords and idioms; for example, family leave and reproductive rights.[4]

Problems with responsiveness of respondents abound. Many culture-bound reasons exist why one would be responsive or would provide inaccurate or misleading responses. Respondents may be unwilling to share information because they feel the interviewer may be a government agent, a state of affairs most often found in newly freed countries in areas such as Eastern Europe or any states of the former Soviet Union. Respondents may be unwilling to share their true feelings with interviewers because they suspect the interviewers may be tax agents of the government. (In Italy, it is said that each company kept three sets of accounts: one for the tax authorities, one for the shareholders, and one for the owners.) In Poland, the interviewer and interviewee should be of the same sex. There, one should be careful about asking about the political past of a person, discussing the church, or asking women about their age. Since the crime rate in Poland has skyrocketed in recent years, great reluctance also exists in letting a stranger into one's home.[5]

The cooperative respondent sometimes gives responses that he/she believes will please the interviewer rather than state his/her true opinions or feelings. This is often viewed in a variety of cultures as being polite; Latins tend to go overboard and tell you what they think you would like to hear rather than what they really think—especially if it is negative. This is called the "courtesy effect" (also known as hospitality bias or social acquiescence). This phenomenon is particularly common in Asia, but also present in countries such as Poland. When Japanese consumers are asked directly for their opinions about a new product being tested, they are much more reluctant to criticize the new product than are consumers in the West. To the Japanese, right and wrong are relative values. A tradition of courtesy makes for cooperative respondents; however, these statements do not give an accurate account of the subject being investigated. Another potential respondent bias is "sucker" bias, when the outsiders (in this case, the foreign researchers) are fair game for deception.[6]

Nonresponse is critical. A respondent may not be able to answer meaningfully, being illiterate or uneducated. Terms used by the interviewer may not be known to respondents, even in their own language; this is "technical illiteracy." Respondents may be asked to think in a way foreign to their normal thought patterns, perhaps asked to reason analytically rather than intuitively. The question, therefore, is not meaningful to them. Consumers may be unwilling to talk to strangers; respondents may be more reluctant to discuss personal consumption habits than Americans and thus not answer questions: a French Canadian woman does not like to be questioned and is more likely to be reticent in her responses. In some cultures, a man would consider it beneath his dignity to discuss shaving habits, personal clothing, or other personal items. In many cultures, preferences for hygiene products are too personal to share with strangers.

Respondents in the Netherlands or Germany are reluctant to divulge information on their personal financial history; it is said that the Dutch are more willing to discuss sex than money. Privacy issues abound, especially in Europe. One of the European Union's directives on data privacy states that respondents cannot be asked sensitive questions without prior written permission. The European

Union also has legislation in place restricting the use and sale of consumer research data in Europe. This limits what can and cannot be asked.

Infrastructure limitations also dictate interviewing. To use mail surveys, a particular country's postal service should be relatively inexpensive, flexible, convenient, and efficient. This is not the case in Italy. The respondents also must be receptive to mail; many Japanese will not read a letter that is not written in longhand—a typed or mass addressed envelope indicates the sender is not sincere about the relationship. In addition, mail surveys presume a degree of literacy and education, facets that are not always available in many developing and undeveloped countries. In Poland, useful address directories still do not exist, and due to housing shortages, people often do not live at the address at which they are registered. The Polish postal system has a long transit time with a huge mis-carry rate. Although mail surveys are used by researchers because of their relatively low costs, geographical flexibility, ability to reach dispersed samples, and ability to code data easily into a common format, cross-cultural mail surveys have numerous major problems including low response rates, nonavailability of sampling frames, poor mail service, and high levels of illiteracy among respondents.[7] Response rates also differ significantly across nationalities.[8]

Phone surveys (telemarketing) also require infrastructure to succeed. Telephone books or directories are not available for many cities in the developing world. In Latin America, Russia, and China, telephone interviews are impractical because few people have phones; less than 10 percent of the population have phones in the Philippines. Using the telephone in China for marketing research is not very appropriate because it is not an acceptable means to obtain information. Chinese do not like to talk over the phone, but would rather arrange meetings to talk with researchers personally.[9] It is almost impossible to perform phone surveys in Mexico since at most, telephone penetration in Mexico City is 60 percent; elsewhere in Mexico, it is much less. This means house-to-house research must be conducted. Even then, Mexican consumers are not accustomed to someone calling on the phone or knocking at the door and asking for an opinion. The Polish telephone system had one of the lowest coverages in Europe in 1990 (8.6 phones per 100 people), with thousands of villages without a phone line and millions of people on the waiting list. In Japan, the increase of working women means fewer women remain at home during the day. Use of door phones or intercoms has also increased, as fewer people will open their doors to strangers.[10] The Japanese home is much more private than American homes. (It is standard courtesy to offer tea but not to invite people into one's house, even if you have known them for years.)

The Japanese prefer face-to-face discussions instead of telephone or mail surveys. Latins also prefer face-to-face interviews. They like to physically see and interact with the person they are talking to. Mexican corporate culture believes in personal contact rather than distant voice: "Please call my secretary to set up an appointment" is the most common answer inquirers get when trying to interview someone in corporate Mexico by phone.[11] Even to obtain written publicly assessable data, it is often necessary to personally pay a visit to the venue where the document was issued. Therefore, interviewing in some cultures takes more time due to the need for in-person interviews than in other countries.

The personal interview mode is the least successful in Saudi Arabia; Saudis consider their homes off limits to strangers. Only very trusted friends are allowed to enter their homes. The very private and reserved nature of Saudis is not conducive to personal interviews; they consider their beliefs, values, personal orientations, and their family attributes as private information. The independent and free nature of Saudis blocks them from answering a barrage of questions; placing them in a position in which they would be justifying or explaining their actions to strangers would not be tolerated.[12] Telephone interviewing can be difficult; daytime calls to Saudi households would not work because social norms require Saudi women not to respond to calls from strangers, especially a nonrelated male. It is possible to get cooperation if female telephone operators were used; however, women interviewers are not easily available because it is not common practice for women to work outside the home. Saudis prefer face-to-face relationships.

Japanese market research tends to be personal interview oriented. Japanese managers believe that soft data (qualitative) obtained from visits to dealers and other channel members reflect the true behavior and intentions of real consumers. The Japanese managers use hard data (quantitative data such as shipments, inventory levels, and retail sales and other information that show the items' actual movement through the channels) to compare their products to those of their competitors. Japanese managers also visit channel members at both the retail and the wholesale levels to analyze any sales and distribution coverage reports, all monthly product movement records (weekly for some key stores), plant-to-wholesaler shipment figures, syndicated turnover, and shipment statistics on competitors.[13]

This hands-on gathering of data gives the managers a distinctive feel for the market, something they believe surveys or quantitative research methods cannot supply. The soft data approach appears to lack the methodological rigor of scientific market research, but it is by no means haphazard or careless. Results can be more meaningful because managers actually observe how consumers behave in buying situations and how salespeople actually respond.[14] Japanese managers try to track changing customer tastes closely and quickly. This approach provides them a deep and focused understanding of the marketplace and enables them to fine tune their marketing rapidly.

Japanese companies rely heavily on personal observation as a means of obtaining information. They expect their personnel to spend time in the field talking to customers in order to keep up to date on needs. Company personnel are also expected to learn about the market firsthand, not just from reading research reports or sales analyses. Watching or imitating their competitors is another source of learning.[15] When Canon cameras were losing ground to Minolta, Canon decided that its distributors were not giving adequate support. Canon did not use data from a survey of consumers or retailers to make the decision. It did, however, send three senior managers to look into the problem. Acting like customers, they would note how the cameras were displayed and how the clerks served customers; these senior managers concluded that the dealers were not enthusiastic about Canon cameras. Thus, they learned critical information that conventional surveys would not have covered. Seiko has its watch designers spend up to half their time outside of Japan talking with distributors, retailers, and consumers. The purpose is to keep the designers' fingers on the pulse of changing consumer preferences.

Another reason for the preference for personal observation and interviews over preferred Western methods such as phone calls or mailings could be the lack of telephone usage for socializing in Japan. The cultural acceptability of the telephone is not the same in Japan as in the United States. Even among Japanese youth, the phone is used not to chat with friends, but to arrange meetings to get together face to face and converse. A greater emphasis is placed on direct, interpersonal relationships, and, as a result, the Japanese are usually hesitant to give a direct "No" to a personal request.

Despite this, observation by the culturally naive could provide inaccurate information. Observers viewing Dutch shoppers might notice that Dutch grocers stock milk in containers no larger than one liter. They might also observe that most Dutch shoppers buy several containers at a time. They might infer from this a latent demand that is being unmet for larger containers. In fact, Dutch consumers demand freshness, shop every day, and own only small refrigerators.

FOCUS GROUPS

Focus group market research—interviewing a group rather than individuals—is a well-acknowledged source of market information. Major cultural differences exist in focus group research; one cannot simply take the same materials used to conduct focus groups in the United States and send them to a foreign country and expect to get comparable or even reliable results. One major difference is time; the researcher must spend approximately double the time spent in the United States setting up focus groups to do likewise overseas. In some countries, participants can simply be asked to show up at a later date at a location where they will join the focus group. In other countries, such as those of Eastern Europe, participants have to be brought into the group immediately because commitments made for a future date have little meaning; consumers cannot predict what they will be doing in a few days; thus, planning ahead is difficult.[16]

Compared to the eight to ten people in an American focus group, most foreign groups consist of only four to six participants. However, length of group discussion outside the United States can be long by U.S. standards, up to four hours.[17]

In some places, providing a payment to participants is sufficient motivation for them; in other countries, one first needs to host a luncheon or dinner for the group so that members get to know each other and are willing to interact. Not all societies encourage frank and open exchange and disagreement among individuals. Status consciousness may be result in the opinion of one participant being reflected by all others. Disagreement may be seen as impolite. Certain topics may be taboo. The group interactions may be completely misread if the culture is not completely understood by the focus moderator. Focus groups in Latin America often disappoint; as many as nine out of ten respondents will not show up even if they have promised and you have reminded them: they simply cannot say no.[18] When they do show up, unless explicitly told otherwise, participants tend to bring friends and relatives who have not been screened.[19] The Polish will participate in focus groups, but strong leftover resentment from their years as a Soviet satellite still exists against their being questioned. If the Polish focus group contains a clergyman, it is likely that all other participants will be very hesitant in putting forward views which conflict with those of the clergyman.[20] Foreign moderators tend to be much less structured and authoritative, feeling it necessary to make group members feel comfortable with each other and build rapport.

The main advantage of the focus group method is that it engages respondents interactively: One respondent's remark stimulates another's thought. In the United States, focus groups are primarily composed of strangers; Americans do not hesitate to speak their minds when they do not know the others in the group and will probably never see them again. Conversely, in Japan, in a room full of strangers, the Japanese will not speak up; instead, they tend to follow more strict rules concerning when to be quiet and when to be talkative. The Japanese do not care to embarrass the presenters if they do not know the answer or to ask a question if it is of less value to the other participants; therefore, few questions are ever raised by the Japanese when invited to do so.

Instead, a successful Japanese focus group consists of friends, relatives, or a similar in-group (one with demographic homogeneity, those of equal status who know each other well). The Japanese are more likely to speak their real feelings to those they know. In such a grouping, there will be more responses, less superficial agreement, and more healthy differentiation. Mixing users and nonusers is not recommended when any social judgment is attached to the art of using or not using the product. The Japanese pay close attention to the relationship between people and inanimate objects. The Japanese do not want to upset the people who are attached to the object. They are concerned with who owns it or what interest people have in it rather than with the thing itself. Therefore, negative comments must be not only encouraged but also pulled out by the facilitator. The Japanese will not comment negatively if they think the facilitator represents the company making the product. Increasing the distance between the speaker and the issue helps get varied opinions from Japanese respondents. Status is important in Japan. The oldest person (male if in a mixed group) with higher social status has the authority to speak first and more often than others. Having social equals in the focus group eliminates the status problem.

Unlike the format of an American focus group, where one question posed by the facilitator is followed by an average of three to five comments by different respondents, a Japanese focus group facilitator's utterances are typically followed by only one or two respondent statements. In Japan, the facilitator stands in the middle, and after one respondent has answered, the facilitator must take control and ask another respondent for his or her opinion on the previous comment. The Japanese respect the group leader and place on him or her all the responsibility for directing the discussion.[21]

Often, the facilitator will get only short answers, superficial and tentative nods of the heads, or simply guttural noises from the Japanese respondents, indicating that they have understood the question, but have no particular follow-up answer to present. This is because the facilitator has posed the question in a way that is incompatible with the Japanese. The facilitator must not use an aggressive communication style. A challenge will be perceived as rude, manipulative, insincere, or simply stubborn and ignorant. Educating the participants by inviting them to express their opinions and having the facilitator be native helps solicit comments and feedback in a Japanese focus group. A tendency to conform among Japanese group members may initially suppress varying opinions. The Japanese need to be coaxed slowly to express opinions that differ from others in the group. The nonverbal must be carefully observed since just 7 percent of the total impact of a message is conveyed verbally, 38 percent paralinguistically (through voice tone, pitch, amplitude, inflection), and 55 percent through body language.[22]

Surprisingly, the Japanese are better respondents in a group than in a one-to-one interview. No matter how skillful the interviewer may be, he or she is still a stranger, and the Japanese are not prone to open their hearts to a stranger. On the other hand, in a group situation, the Japanese are with others like themselves. A great amount of interpersonal trust can be developed, and very candid views can be exchanged without any animosity. That is why those with similar lifestyles and backgrounds and ages must be chosen. The Japanese are great in groups because they are attentive and interested in what others have to say. Since opinions are not immediately expressed, the opening part of a session is typically slow. When an idea is introduced, a respondent typically expresses a very tentative reaction. However, another respondent may pick up on some nuances of the comments and add some of his or her own. Gradually, the idea will be positioned and a consensus formed.

Betty Crocker attempted to market its cake mixes in Japan only to find customer obstacles. After numerous focus groups, it was found that the essential problem was psychological; making the cake mix in the rice cooker raised the danger of contaminating the rice, and, hence, homemakers hesitated to use the product. Yet, conclusions drawn from focus groups must be carefully weighed against the existing cultural inertia: Frito-Lay found that prawn is the favorite flavor of Thai focus groups. Thais said they thought an American snack with a native flavor (*tom yam*) was inappropriate. Frito-Lay decided to market American flavors for an American snack.[23]

CROSS-CULTURAL MARKETING RESEARCH

Potential cross-cultural errors in international marketing research include:

Definition Error: The way the problem is defined by each culture. A 1963 *Reader's Digest* study reported that French and German consumers ate significantly more spaghetti than did Italians; the study had concerned itself with only packaged spaghetti and not total spaghetti consumption (many Italians prefer to buy in bulk).

Frame Error: Different populations being sampled from different cultures.

Selection Error: How the actual sample is selected from the population. Saudi Arabia has neither street names nor house numbers. Street maps are frequently unavailable in parts of South America. This lack of infrastructure complicates sampling procedures. In many Third World countries, only a small percentage of the population may own phones and it also may be nearly impossible to access rural areas if adequate transportation is not available. It is therefore, in these situations, often extremely difficult to obtain a proper random sample.

Construct Equivalence: Consists of conceptual equivalence, functional equivalence, and instrument equivalence.[24]

Conceptual Equivalence: Does the concept express similar attitudes or behaviors across cultures? The word "family" has different connotations in different parts of the world and thus may be inappropriate. In the United States, it generally means the nuclear family of parents and children. In many Latin countries, it means the extended family including grandparents, aunts, uncles, and cousins. Concepts often have totally different meanings in different cultures and are thus inappropriate for use on an international scale. Care has to be exercised to ensure that the words used to elicit responses carry similar meanings to individuals in different cultures.

Functional Equivalence: Does the concept or construct serve the same function in different cultures? While refrigerators are used to store frozen foods in some countries and to chill water and soft drinks in others, in certain markets, they serve as status symbols and are prominently displayed in the home, often in the living room, not the kitchen; the typical Asian refrigerator size ranges from 6 cubic feet to 10 cubic feet and may be only 4 feet high with the top of the unit typically being used to hold something else such as a lamp or plant. As such, the prominent placement leads to a demand for stylish colors and finishes; in India, it is not uncommon to find refrigerators sold in bright red or blue.[25]

If similar products have different functions in different societies, their parameters cannot be used for comparative purposes. Beer is not considered an alcoholic beverage in Northern Europe; neither is wine in Mediterranean countries. Both would be regarded as kin to soft drinks in their respective countries. A researcher was thus surprised (but should not have been) when the survey reported Italians hardly ever drank alcohol (all the while with respondents routinely sipping wine while answering the questionnaire!).

Instrument Equivalence: Errors arising from questionnaire and interviewer: are the scale items, response categories, and questionnaire interpreted identically across cultures? This measures the validity and importance of the research questions. An instrument that measures a phenomenon uniformly in different cultures is absolutely essential for comparative evaluation of market characteristics. Any survey questionnaire is susceptible to considerable bias in cross cultural applications. Dominant cultural traits tend to affect the nature of response: The Japanese as a group tend to be more humble, which often leads them to undervalue assets, while the Middle Eastern respondent is more prone to exaggerate.

A major dimension of instrument equivalence is metric equivalence: the scoring or scalar equivalence of the measure used. The desired effect is to achieve a similar likelihood between cultures. While the five- or seven-point balanced differential scale is commonly employed in the United States, in other countries, consumers are much more familiar with 10- or even 20-point scales, while in some, a three-point scale is the norm. Westerners tend to take extreme positions and work inward; Germans are more extreme than English. U.S. respondents exhibit greater tendencies toward extreme response than non-U.S. respondents, especially Asians and Latins. The Japanese tend to take a neutral position and then work outward, seldom reaching the extremes. Thus, the range of Japanese scores is generally more limited than that of Westerners, making use of such scales problematic. Latin Americans are more likely to use the extreme points on a scale to express their individualism, while Indians may express similarly intense opinions using points near the middle of the same scale. In Northern Europe, a four-point scale is preferred to a five-point scale, to force a choice: people do not want to stand out from the crowd and tend to give average opinions otherwise.

A group of outstanding international business professors from a major Midwestern research university taught in a faculty exchange program at an East Asian sister school. Used to receiving between

4.5 and 5 (with 5 being outstanding) on their student evaluations, they were astonished to receive a score of 3 (average). The mystery was cleared up after discussions with some of the students: the students had expected an outstanding program and had received the same; therefore, they gave a score of 3, as performance had equaled their expectations.

Other potential problems in conducting cross-cultural marketing research include:

Definitional Equivalence: In France, fragrance is measured on a hot-cold continuum; in the United States and the UK, this is not so. In the UK and United States, beer is considered an alcoholic beverage; in Latin Europe, it is not. In Japan, supermarkets usually occupy multistory structures and sell non-foodstuffs and usually even have restaurants—not the same definition as found in the United States.[26]

Social Desirability: Does an item or questions in a given cultural or social context reflect the proper way in the respondent's culture that they should answer? For instance, sex is a taboo subject in India. Latins will not readily admit to drinking alcohol. Researchers need to determine if topics are socially acceptable or not. Such topic bias must be eliminated, as it only muddies the picture.

Interpretation Problems: Complexities of cultures render interpretation hazardous. Italians, Spanish, and Latin Americans may seem to be effusive and to overstate their answers. Germans and English often understate their enthusiasm.

Measurement Equivalence: Includes calibration, translation, and metric equivalence. Both calibration and translation equivalence seek to assure that measurement instruments mean the same thing after translation. Translation equivalence implies that the same questionnaire items measure the same latent constructs in different populations (differences in currencies and units of weight). It implies that a construct can be measured by the same questionnaire items in different countries (translation equivalence) and whether or not the units of measure are the same in different countries (calibration equivalence). Metric equivalence is when the subjects respond to the measurement scales in the same way. Two threats exist for metric equivalence: scalar inequivalence and inconsistent scoring across populations.[27] Before 1989, Eastern European countries did not apply the international standards and classifications for statistics laid down by the UN; others that had been used were notoriously biased.

CONCLUSIONS

Considerable culture bias occurs in marketing research; what may be viewed undesirable in one culture may be viewed as an accomplishment in another. Researchable problems within one culture may not be researchable within another because of societal taboos and different levels of abstraction. Major problems regarding cross-cultural marketing research include unwilling respondents, unwilling to provide current and truthful information; locating knowledgeable sources; discussion of personal or family matters taboos; private matters not discussed with strangers; are you with the government? hesitancy to answer; limitations of infrastructure; sampling problems; language, slang, idioms, or dialects; literacy rates; and education levels.

Success stories underscoring the value of research exist. P&G's market research indicated that Japanese mothers are very concerned with keeping their babies clean and as a result, change their children's diapers far more often than Americans do. In response, P&G devised Ultra Pampers, a more absorbent diaper that keeps the child drier and makes frequent changing a less messy task. In its research effort, P&G also discovered the value of storage space in the average Japanese's home; the company made the diapers thinner to fit in a smaller space and take up less of the valuable home space; Ultra pampers is now the market leader in Japan. P&G had to adapt Cheer to fit Japanese market requirements, since many Japanese consumers washed their clothes in cold tap water or used leftover bathwater.

Kentucky Fried Chicken customized its American product and strategy to suit the tastes of the Japanese consumers. By using indirect Japanese market research techniques, it promoted the restaurants as trendy and high class, not as fast-food restaurants. After consulting directly with customers, French fries were substituted for mashed potatoes, the sugar content in the coleslaw was reduced, and fried fish, cold corn salad, and smoked chicken were added to the menu.

Domino's initial market research in Japan indicated that home delivery of pizza was not feasible. The Japanese emphasized such foods as raw fish, rice, and seaweed in their diets and dislike such pizza staples as tomato and cheese. Pizza is considered a snack food rather than a meal, which makes it difficult to justify the high prices necessary to make the home delivery business profitable. The consumers who like pizza the most are teenage girls, the segment of the Japanese population with the least disposable income. Those most likely to pay a premium for a meal would prefer to eat out in a spacious restaurant than in their own cramped residences. Finally, Domino's guarantee of speedy delivery was perceived to be impossible in Tokyo's traffic. Domino's did not give up. It made the pizzas smaller (10- and 14-inch pies rather than 12- and 16-inch versions favored in the United States), added optional toppings preferred by the Japanese (corn, squid, and tuna), and had its employees use motor scooters (with customized roof design and Domino's logo) instead of cars to move around Tokyo to deliver pizzas. In addition, the company retained the 30-minute delivery promise by concentrating on populous, affluent neighborhoods of big cities and limited the delivery radius to two kilometers.

In the Middle East, Singer learned that husbands were the buyers and that they were not interested in saving their wives' personal effort; Singer changed its pitch to Arab men that sewing machines would make their wives more useful and better able to attend to a husband's needs.

How can one succeed when conducting cross-cultural marketing research? One should use short, simple sentences while also using a limited vocabulary and familiar words. Employ active rather than passive words. Repeat nouns rather than using pronouns. Avoid metaphors and colloquialisms. Avoid possessive forms. Avoid words which indicate vagueness.

Any research instrument must use categories which are tested for relevance and this often implies searching out other people's categories in their own language. At a minimum, the survey instrument must be backtranslated. A far more aggressive strategy recommended to minimize any of the errors noted earlier in this chapter is decentering: successive iteration process of translation and retranslation of an instrument each time by a different translator. The versions are sequentially compared. If the two versions are dissimilar, the original is modified and the process is repeated until both show the same or similar wordings. The original instrument itself undergoes a change and the final version and its translation have equally comprehensive and equivalent terminologies in both the languages.

In addition, one must beware of response bias. Other suggestions include to heavily pretest, consider equivalence problem in design state, utilize and understand the local infrastructure, use an experienced firm or individuals from the local country, if available, and be open and flexible. As a last note of importance, the interpretation of results should be done with local advice so that explanation of reason is not biased by one's home culture.[28] International market researchers, when involved in cross-cultural research, must understand and expect that such research will be more costly, take longer than expected, and that researchers must be more careful than in similar domestic research, especially in viewing and analyzing the results.

PART II:
MARKETING

Chapter 5

Cross-Cultural Aspects of Products

PRODUCTS

A product is a bundle of utilities, a cluster of value satisfactions. Products can be classified as either goods (physical) or services (intangible). (Services will be examined in more detail in Chapter 11.) A customer attaches value to a product in proportion to its perceived ability to help solve problems (resolve wants or meet needs). A product has three major elements: the core product, the physical entity; the tangible product (packaging, brand name, features, quality, and styling); and the augmented product (installation, delivery and credit, training, after-sale service, and warranty). This chapter will examine the cross-cultural aspects of the first two elements of goods. The augmented product will be examined in detail in the chapter on aftermarket.

The importance of the entire product (all three elements) cannot be overstated. Coca-Cola or Pepsi-Cola is selling more than a carbonated water in their cans of cola. Sold with the can are the aspects of refreshment, enjoyment, and entertainment, as well as being thirst quenching. For Coca-Cola and Pepsi-Cola, the tangible product takes on more importance than the core product. The customer buys the total product, the combination of the three elements; each element would not succeed on its own. Different colas have different attributes, and each brand is intended to meet the demands of a particular set of target customers. The customers are buying satisfaction, which is derived from a product's attributes, various features, and characteristics.

As another example, Gillette often has to sell the idea of shaving before it can sell its blades. In some countries, facial hair is removed with a machete or a sharp edge of glass. To persuade these men that shaving can be easier and more comfortable (without losing its macho qualities), Gillette sends a van from village to village carrying its salesmen who are equipped with all the essentials. (Free razors are given; however, in classic Gillette fashion, blades must be purchased.) In those cases where shaving is common, other factors (primarily economic) take precedence. To counter the discovery that few Mexican men who shave used shaving cream, Gillette introduced plastic tubes of shaving cream that sold for half the price of its aerosol cans. The product *Prestobarba* (Spanish for quick shave) was an instant success.

The effect of culture upon a product can be directly tied to the total product concept. As cultures vary, these differences are noted in tastes. The core product is often the same. (It is the tangible product and augmented product set that typically differ.) Any product has a bundle of psychological features just as important as its physical features. These psychological features are instrumental in providing customer satisfaction. Different cultures provide different values to different psychological features. Adoption and potential adaptation of products can be affected as much by how the product concept conflicts with the norms and mores of the culture as much as it is by its physical features. For example, Lever Brothers attempted to introduce its packaged frozen food line into developing countries, where refrigerators rarely existed in the home. Realizing the futility of such an effort at this stage of the countries' economic development, the company developed and marketed successfully a line of dehydrated vegetables. The company will continue to track development of countries and will introduce the packaged frozen food line at an appropriate time when the infrastructure (markets with freezers) and the required complimentary items (freezers in the home) are more widely available. Pop-Tarts proved to be a failure in England; they were considered too sweet for the English palate. Even more detrimental, though, was the fact that most potential buyers did not have toasters.

In another example, automobile styling shows distinct cultural patterns. German taste is rooted in nature and its slow changes and enduring quality. Thus, Mercedes designs change slowly and must be carefully balanced to last as long as they do. Nothing stands out on a

Mercedes. All elements are carefully balanced. Conversely, the Japanese tend to put their cars in front of a wall whereas Westerners are apt to use nature as a backdrop. In Japan's tight streets, cars are most often viewed close up; thus, the Japanese like those visual elements attractive to the eye when viewing the car in segments. Americans design cars to look their best from 20 to 30 feet away; it is the whole picture rather than details which is desired. When Westerners conjure up an image of a car, it is from the side view. With the Japanese, it is a frontal view. The Japanese read personality and expression into the "face" of a car. Their concerns are whether a car's "eyes" are too sleepy or awake and whether its "mouth" is appropriate (a reference to shape and size of headlights and grill). Westerners are drawn to a muscular smoothness in cars, while the Japanese reject animalist traits in their cars and cannot accept the Western world's attraction to leather (historically connected with horseback riding). When market pressures induced the Japanese to use leather upholstery, the Japanese at first removed the smell—the very thing Westerners tend to find most appealing about leather interiors. While Westerners are attuned to remodeling, reworking, and changing a bit at a time, the Japanese are used to starting with a clean slate.

The Japanese have a holistic view of products. The Japanese concept called *kansei* involves the oneness of the product and the user and takes into account all the intangible things that make a customer feel both confident and at home with when using the product. The Japanese word *keihokutanshoka* (lighter, slimmer, shorter, and smaller) implies that less expensive items are more useful products because they are economical to purchase, use, and maintain.[1] Smaller versions of standard products follow the Buddhist concept that small is better. Japanese consumers are quite fastidious when it comes to the quality and performance of products. If a purchased product turns out to possess even the slightest blemish, Japanese consumers will complain to the retail store and manufacturer.[2]

Japanese companies historically launch multitudes of new products and use the total consumer marketplace as their test market; if a product succeeds, the companies make more of it; if it fails, it is dropped. Coca-Cola, like many Western companies, would stay with a product and try to make a go of it, fearing bad public relations if it were to acknowledge defeat: In the 1960s, a fortified tomato juice called VI-ProMin was kept on the shelves for several years without success. After finally adapting to local practices, the company is now releasing as many as 50 new beverages annually with launch times as little as 30 days. The company has learned to get in and get out of the Japanese market with ease and to shrug off the inevitable failures: it launched a "lactic-based" drink called Ambasa Whitewater that initially sold millions of cases, but faded after 18 months and was then pulled off the shelves.[3]

CULTURAL VARIANCES: EXAMPLE OF THE HISPANIC MARKET

Over 20 Spanish-speaking nationalities make up the U.S. Hispanic population, and each has its own national holidays, cultural characteristics, foods, traditions, and values.[4] The marketer is well advised to distinguish between the subcultural differences among the major Hispanic groups (such as Mexican, Cuban, or Puerto Rican).[5] For example, Tang, the instant breakfast drink, bills itself as *jugo de china*, which is the Puerto Rican idiom for orange juice. But to all other Hispanics, the phrase was meaningless; *jugo de naranja*—the juice of oranges—would have been a better generic choice. The word for peanut butter is *mantequilla de mani* for Hispanics from the Caribbean and *crema de cacahuate* for those from Mexico.[6] In 1988, Campbell's Soup acquired a Puerto Rican company-owned brand of canned beans called *Casera* ("home cooked" in Spanish) and heavily marketed the products in Miami and New York. However, Campbell's found that culinary preferences differed widely among the Hispanic population: *Casera*'s canned beans were pinto beans, popular among Puerto Ricans; most Hispanics in Miami are Cubans who prefer black beans.

Bud Light made two different commercials for its Hispanic thrust. "Caribbean," featuring salsa music and a tropical environment, was designed for Puerto Ricans, Cubans, and Central and South Americans; the actors sounded Cuban and were more fair skinned. The second ad showed men wearing cowboy hats in a bar environment with Mexican ranchera music; darker-skinned actors with Mexican-American accents reigned.

Gerber designed *The Tropical Line* for the Hispanic market with snazzy hot pink and yellow packaging. The product line offers a variety of tropical fruits such as mango, papaya, guava, banana, and pineapple. The line includes three fruit juice combinations, nine fruit desserts, and two cereals. The chicken and rice entree is seasoned with garlic, onion, and tomato puree. Gerber advertised the product on Spanish language TV and radio, outdoor and subway billboards, print advertising, and direct mail. It is being distributed to areas with large Hispanic populations (New York, Florida, California, Texas, and Chicago).

Kraft created a new 15-member ethnic marketing division and launched a brand of fast-melting white cheese and rich cream called *Valle Lindo* (beautiful valley) especially for Hispanic consumers. Ads aired on Spanish language television and radio stations in Houston. Kraft increased its ethnic marketing spending by 60 percent during 1996 to $24 million. This differs from Proctor & Gamble's approach: P&G adopted a centralized ethnic marketing system then scrapped it and returned to the individual brand management approach. Frito-Lay treats Hispanic Americans as a single market because the company tries to project a consistent national image. It advertises on Spanish language television and local advertisements occasionally address local populations but in general, aims at broadest possible target. Linking the attributes of a product with the benefits of the community will be a most efficient promotional strategy for the Hispanic market.[7]

Mexican homemakers seek to make the meal a moment of affection and family togetherness; the primary responsibility for keeping the family happy and securing its integration falls to the homemaker, and the meeting around a delicious meal is an important element. The purchase of ready-to-eat food and fast food goes against a Mexican woman's image of being a mother who looks after her children and who is zealous in her responsibilities. Hispanic consumers also do not like being told they are targeted because they are different, they already see themselves as minorities, as outsiders; they don't want to do anything that strengthens that stereotype.

A review of the Hispanic market indicates that cross-cultural marketing does not necessarily mean cross-border marketing. Even within one's own borders, an understanding of a subgroup or different ethnic group could lead to the need for different products for different needs.

FEATURES AND SPECIFICATIONS

Features include a host of attributes. Some of the most obvious, and most important, are dimensions, size, capacity, and volume. A major cultural problem is the American system of weights and measures versus the rest of the world's metric system. But other problems also abound for the unweary. Different physical characteristics of consumers often influence product designs. GE Medical Systems designed a product specifically for Japan; the unit is smaller because Japanese hospitals are smaller and the typical Japanese patient is smaller. Swiss watchmakers make smaller watches for Japanese consumers, reflecting the fact the wrists of the Japanese are smaller than those of most Westerners. Although Germans buy over 500,000 pairs of cowboy boots annually, U.S. companies get little of the business: toes in U.S. boots are not pointy enough. American heels are perceived to be too wide. Non-American shoe manufacturers have also had to reciprocate to be successful in the United States.

Local cultural tastes often have forced many international companies to modify components, and possibly the entire product, to be successful. Italians dislike grapefruit-flavored Gatorade, while Germans love it. Many Europeans think Hershey chocolate bars taste bitter. General Foods introduced Jell-O in the UK only to find that the British consumers prefer a solid, not Jell-O's wavering form. Heinz modifies its ketchup by adding spices, curry, or peppers, depending upon the local market tastes. Heinz developed a special line of rice-based baby foods for the Chinese market and a fruit-based drink for children called Frutsi for the Mexican market.

General Foods blends different coffees for the British (who drink their coffee with milk), the French (who drink their coffee black), and for Latin Americans (who prefer a chicory taste). Nestlé and Coca-Cola entered a joint venture to convince Koreans that canned coffee (warm or cold) is an alternative to soft drinks. Two versions were introduced: rich and regular (creamier). Coca-Cola already has its Georgia brand and Nestlé has Nescafé canned coffee drinks in Japan. Koreans drink only one-fourth the amount of coffee that the Japanese do.[8] Nestlé tried to sell instant coffee to England; the company found that most English prefer a light, almost blond coffee; as British coffee habits had been developed during the Second World War and heavily influenced by American troops, British taste in coffee is similar to that of Americans.

Sometimes the taste is unknown and must be acquired. In this case, a major educational effort is often needed.[9] Heinz is teaching the rest of the world how to use ketchup: advertisements in Greece show potential consumers how ketchup can be poured on pasta, eggs, and cuts of meat. Heinz also sponsors cooking lessons in Tokyo to Japanese homemakers on using ketchup as an ingredient in Western-style foods such as omelets, sausages, and pasta. Americans prefer a relatively sweet ketchup, but Europeans prefer a spicier, more piquant variety.

Campbell's soup found that Brazilian housewives determined their self-esteem by their homemaking abilities: the importance of making soup from scratch eliminated any value of a soup from a can. Interestingly, Campbell's soup company, recognizing that selling in America is akin to selling internationally, has divided the United States into 22 distinct markets based on unique cultural and ethnic tastes and preferences. Special brands have been created to cater to the particular regional needs determined in Campbell's research. Examples include spicy ranchero beans and nacho cheese soup in the Southwest, Creole soup in the South, red bean soup in Hispanic markets, pepper pot soup for Philadelphia, and zesty pickles for the Northwest.

Adaptation sometimes is necessary to succeed. Trivial Pursuit had to adapt in order to be successful overseas. In Britain, questions on cricket are preferred to that of baseball. The French love questions on nightlife, art, and literature. Forty international editions have been prepared.[10] The Blue Diamond brand of almonds was an unknown commodity in East Asia until Blue Diamond launched its campaign of exotic new almond-based products that catered to local tastes: almond tofu, almond miso soup, and Calmond, a nutritional snack concocted from a mixture of dried small sardines and slivered almonds. Television ads featured educational messages on how to use almonds in cooking, the nutritional values of almonds, and the versatility of almonds as a snack; Japan is now the largest importer of almonds. Blue Diamond exports to over 100 countries and assumes no two markets will react the same. For most Westerners, milk-based products are usually consumed at meals and bedtime for their sleep inducing, soothing, relaxing properties. In Thailand, the same products are consumed on the way to work and often away from home for their invigorating, energizing, stimulating properties. In the UK and Holland, people prefer tablets; in France, suppositories are preferred; and in Germany, an injection will do.

The marketing philosophy of Japanese enterprises is to discover ways to match technology with the traditional lifestyle and culture of Japan: For example, having Japanese language word processors with handwriting typefaces, noiseless washing machines, rice cookers designed to change cooking time automatically to match the type of rice being cooked, and high-tech *kotatsu* (traditional Japanese heaters).[11] A high value is placed on retaining the Japanese culture and making technology serve the user. The introduction of a new product is often accompanied by demonstrations in numerous homes as well as new product shows held at large hotels in the major cities.

Sometimes, culture becomes secondary to politics and is used as a nontariff barrier. Even after 1992, protectionist practices linger in Europe. Italy allows only products made from durum wheat—Italy's predominant type—to be called pasta. France bans Coca-Cola from using aspartame (NutraSweet) as an artificial sweetener in Diet Coke. Gatorade had to add extra vitamin B1 to sell its product in France.[12]

BRANDS

Brand names performs many key functions:

1. A brand name identifies the product or service and allows a customer to specify, reject, or recommend brands.
2. A brand name communicates messages to a consumer. Information provided could include statements regarding the product users' style, modernity, or wealth.[13]

3. A brand name functions as a piece of legal property in which the owner can invest and through law is protected from competitor trespass. Brand names convey the image of the product; "brand" refers to a name, term, symbol, sign, or design used by a firm to differentiate its offerings from those of its competitors, to identify a product with a particular seller. Branding adds value to products and services. This value arises from the experience gained from using the brand: familiarity, reliability, and risk reduction, as well as from association with others who use the brand.

Brands have staying power due to the promotional efforts expended by companies to create awareness and image for their brands. Standardization of both the product and brand are not necessarily consistent; a regional brand may have local features or a highly standardized brand may have local brand names. As a result of separate marketing, Unilever sells a cleaning liquid called Vif in Switzerland, Viss in Germany, Jif in Britain and Greece, and Cif in France; it would be very difficult to standardize the brand name for all European markets since each brand name is well established in each local market.

Brand names often are difficult to standardize on a global basis. Johnson's Pledge furniture cleaner is called Pronto in Switzerland and Pliz in France while retaining its American brand name in the UK. Translation problems could render the translated version obscene or with a negative connotation (due to local slang or idioms). The brand name could already have been registered with another local or international company. Yet, many brand names are worth their weight in gold. Anyone's list of the top ten global brands would have many of the same companies: Coca-Cola, Sony, Kodak, Disney, Nestlé, Toyota, McDonald's, IBM, and Pepsi-Cola.

Global brands carry instant recognition and especially for international travelers represent a risk avoidance strategy versus using local brands. European consumers buy American, for its quality, prestige, and American image. Goodyear sells its tires in Germany with advertisements of Indy cars. Budweiser has made a name for itself as a premium brand with an American ad campaign. Europeans also pay premium prices for American goods: $7 for a six-pack of Bud in the UK versus $2 in the United States. European teenagers wear baseball caps (backward of course) and wear football jackets over their basketball T-shirts. Jack Daniel's and Southern Comfort have prospered abroad, advertised and sold as American brands.[14] The Japanese lean toward pastoral names or names of girls for their car models: Bluebird, Bluebonnet, Sunny, Violet, and Gloria versus animal and power names for American car models: Mustang, Cougar, and Cutlass. The first sports car Nissan sent to the United States was named Datsun Fair Lady. Seeing a fiasco in the making, the name was changed to 240Z. However, branding is not a guarantee for success in the global market.[15] Some restrictions on brand names exist: "med" in France is limited to medical products, thus potentially causing firms to adjust brand names.

The lack of success of Suchard's entry into the UK market demonstrates that if a company is a powerful marketer in one country, it can't literally transfer those brands and still expect them to be successful. The UK chocolate company Thorntons experienced difficulties in France. Cadbury followed a fragmented branding approach, retaining the brand names on the various companies it has acquired in Europe.[16] Coca-Cola uses Coke Lite as a brand name instead of Diet Coke in France since the term "diet" is restricted due to medical connotations and suggests poor health. Coca-Cola changed Diet Coke to Coke Light in Japan; Japanese women do not like to admit to dieting and in Japan, the idea of diet implies sickness or medicine. Other name changes are not necessarily voluntary: In India, because of a ban on the use of foreign brand names, hybrid brand names are the norm; for example, Maruti-Suzuki, Dom-Toyota, Kinetic-Honda, and Lehar Pepsi.[17]

The Japanese worship brand names, the perfect solution in a society where individual preference is muted. Once a designer name or brand logo catches on, the scramble begins. As soon as consumers are confident the logo means status or prestige, they will snap up anything that sports the reassuring logo. The Japanese have taken this fanaticism a step further. They do not rush out and buy just any recognizable brand; they buy catalogs filled with photographs of accepted brand products. Before making a purchase, many consumers must consult a reference work to guarantee a brand's prestige. Different reasons for this brand loyalty exist according to age groups. The main reason the older Japanese rely heavily on brand names is that in their formative years (during the Second World War and the years of postwar poverty), goods were scarce and few opportunities existed; being unsure of exactly what they wanted, these older Japanese opted for the safety of a product's famous name. The youth tend to prefer brand names because of their fashion consciousness. Consumers associate product quality, safety, and reliability with the image of the company that produces it. Consumers need to see the company as trustworthy and reliable in order to evaluate a brand favorably.[18]

This hierarchical concern with brands can be seen in the way the various Suntory whiskey brands have clearly defined ranks and, therefore, occupy different positions in society. In the early 1960s, the best-selling Suntory brand was a light whiskey called Red; a few years later, Kaku was priced higher. The most premium brand was called Old. Later on, priced even higher for senior executives, came Suntory Reserve. When a Japanese salaryman selects a Suntory brand, he does so solely according to his position in the company. Suntory Old dominates the Japanese market in the middle level. Reserve is what you drink when you reach high management.[19]

When Nabisco went to Japan, consumers there found the Oreos too sweet, so the amount of sugar was reduced to give them a more bitter taste. Some consumers still found them too sweet and told Nabisco they just wanted to eat the base without the creme, so Nabisco added a modified Oreo without the creme, Petit Oreo Non-Creme Cookies, which consisted of single wafers without the creme.

Brand loyalty also can vary across cultures. Chinese consumers tend to be more brand loyal and tend to purchase the same brand or product other members of the group recommend; they tend to be members of a small number of reference groups. Hispanics tend to be more brand loyal, more likely to use familiar stores, and more likely to be conscious about prices and promotions than non-Hispanics. This could be due to relatively low income levels and large family sizes.[20] One explanation for greater brand loyalty and the corresponding lower tendency to buy private label brands could be that the purchase of prominent brands connotes the assimilation of ethnic consumers into the mainstream economy. Many new immigrants are familiar with many brands from their native experience and continue to use those brands from risk avoidance as well as the emotional experiences (of the homeland) they may be connected to. Colgate toothpaste holds a 70 percent market share due to its dominance in Latin America. However, Crest, though holding only 15 percent of new immigrants, has nearly twice as many of the acculturated Hispanics.

The cultural context of brand loyalty can be explained easily through the use of Hofstede's dimensions. Power distance is the willingness to accept that those with power are entitled to it and those without power ought to accept the way things are and just go along with it. This is an Asian cultural tendency. Big market share brands are the kings of their brand world and consumers from cultures with high power distance tend to believe in them implicitly: the dominant brand has achieved what it has because it is the best and one should not question it. The power dimension is related to uncertainty avoidance (risk). A third dimension is individualism-collectivism, the degree to which one's individual beliefs are submerged to fit in with the greater good of what is acceptable in society as a whole. Asian cultures tend to be highly collective. This collective orientation has implications for consumer attitude formation and brand loyalty and ensures the survival of the dominant brand.[21]

PACKAGING

Packaging considerations depend upon the market for the product: In the case of a product targeted at businesses, packaging is usually plain, bland, and functional in nature (safety, security, and delivery functions). For consumer products, the packaging becomes part of the promotional effort. As industrial products are far less culturally grounded, the majority of this discussion will deal with consumer products. However, consumer products can be marketed by self-service or over the counter. In cultures where over-the-counter predominates, promotional considerations for packaging takes on less importance.

Government requirements can also greatly influence a product's final design. U.S. law levies taxes on certain chemicals destined for toxic waste dumps. A law in Denmark requires that drinks be sold in refillable bottles. Canadian regulation requires deposits on beer bottles. German law requires that at most, 28 percent of all beer and soft drink containers be disposable. The law also insists that companies collect their used packaging for recycling. R. J. Reynolds reported needing more than 250 different packages to satisfy different brand styles and foreign government requirements. For example, in Australia, the number of cigarettes contained in a package must be printed on the front of the package. In Saudi Arabia, product names must be specific. Prices are required to be printed on the labels in Venezuela, but in Chile, it is illegal to put prices on labels or in any way suggest retail prices that should be changed.

Packaging can become an integral part of a product's success or failure. Lego's Bunny Set promotion, where the block toys reside in a bunny-shaped storage case—failed to impress the Japanese. The Japanese considered the bunny pack as superfluous and objected to the notion of being forced to waste money on unwanted products. On the other hand, Lego was slow to match Tyco's storage case buckets in the United States (Lego wanted its elegant see-through cartons standardized worldwide), and only did so after Tyco had severely eroded its market share. (After its introduction, American parents purchased more buckets than cartons; Lego has now introduced the bucket concept worldwide.)[22]

In France, Amora ketchup (a local brand) overtook Heinz by introducing plastic bottles resembling rocket ships, a move Heinz matched. In Panama, Aunt Jemima pancake mix and Ritz Crackers are sold in cans rather than in boxes because of the high humidity. Gillette sells Silkience shampoo in one-half ounce plastic bubbles in Latin America; it sells Right Guard deodorant in plastic squeeze bottles, the poor man's aerosol. Whereas Americans prefer to buy mayonnaise and mustard in glass containers, consumers in Germany and Switzerland buy these same products in tubes. Consumer image of packaging differs across cultures. Reactions to floral designs on soap packages were given a low value by Hong Kong consumers while Americans associated the same design with feminine products of neutral value.[23]

Packaging may not even exist in developing or undeveloped countries. In 1991, Andersen Consulting assisted the Moscow Bread Company in improving its distribution of bread in Moscow.

Andersen found as much as one-third of the bread was wasted. The consultants recommended plastic bags as a means of keeping the bread fresh, a novel idea at the time. Although 95 percent of the food in developed countries is packaged, only 2 percent of the food in the former Soviet Union was packaged. Russian consumers responded well; the bags guaranteed freshness and extended the shelf life of their bread, and were also able to be reused.

Companies that sell brand name packages are beginning to use symbols and not words on their labels. Frango Chocolates (candy sold by Marshall Field's in Chicago) did not go over well in Portugal: *frango* in Portuguese means chicken. The company consequently began using a symbol. When Scott paper products (e.g., Scott towels) are sold overseas, they feature a symbolic icon—a towel and arrow that suggests absorption. However, symbols too can have translation problems: Always feminine products packages feature a dove, which in the United States symbolizes peace and serenity; in Japan, however, the dove is the symbol of death. The swastika is associated with Nazi Germany for most Western societies; thus, it is a negative image; however, in many Asian societies, the swastika is a sign of good luck and perfectly acceptable to have on a package. Gerber found out the hard way that in low literacy countries, pictures and symbols are taken literally. When Gerber introduced baby food in jars to Africa with its standard picture of a baby on the label, the mostly uneducated consumers thought the jars contained ground-up babies. Marketers should avoid using triangular shapes in Hong Kong, Korea, or Taiwan, as the triangle is considered a negative shape in those countries.

In Hong Kong, Philip Morris changed the phonetic name of its cigarette from three syllables (*mo li see*) to four (*mor ha li see*) and in so doing, the company changed the value from a product associated with no luck to one in which touch conferred luck upon the consumer. Zaitun, a Malaysian toiletry, is packaged in predominantly green and white packs and has both Arabic scripts and Bahasa Malaysia on it. Its Islamic name is reinforced by the twin visual stimuli of Islamic colors and traditional Arabic script; a strong identity for its Malaysian customers has been established.[24]

Pepsi scrapped its traditional red, white, and blue colors in favor of electric blue in an effort to create awareness of its product and have it stand out on the grocery shelves. PepsiCo's Project Blue cost $500 million and revamped manufacturing (freshness standards and quality controls) and distribution to get a drink with a consistent taste throughout the globe as well as overhauling its marketing and advertising. Internationally, Coca-Cola outsells Pepsi three to one.[25]

Japanese consumers also place heavy emphasis on the packaging and overall appearance of products. The product must be wrapped and tied in the right way. Specific kinds of strings must be used for specific items; the presentation is as important as the product itself. The typical Japanese consumer will not purchase a product that is not well wrapped; a poorly packaged product conveys an impression of poor quality. To the Japanese, form is as important as function. Packaging must be beautiful and of high quality; it is expected to be aesthetically pleasing as well as functional. Packaging paper used for wrapping and bags are of excellent quality, and wrapping an item in three layers is standard practice. Lever Brothers sells Lux soap in stylish boxes because more than half of all soap bar purchases in Japan are made during the two gift-giving seasons (winter and summer). The packaging, how a company gives the message, and the execution cannot be overemphasized. The Japanese feel that if a company does not go to the trouble of presenting its ideas properly, then how can its products be any good?

COUNTRY-OF-ORIGIN EFFECT

The Japanese have developed extremely high standards for product quality, durability, and reliability. Japanese consumers view cosmetic anomalies as an indication of something wrong with the manufacturing process that could lead to more serious problems. Outward appearance is an important indicator of *anshinkan* (the peace of mind that comes from dealing with reliable and trustworthy persons). If a newly purchased car breaks down, for example, the buyer will probably refuse to make any payments until the dealer performs all the necessary servicing.[26] The word "quality" is used in Japan the way the word "excellence" is used in the West. In Japan, it is believed that the occupant of an untidy desk cannot think clearly; such a person's mind must be as disorganized as his or her desk. Japanese customers like to visit their suppliers' plants; a dirty plant usually leads to skepticism about the quality of the plant's output.[27] Output and process cannot be separated.

The country-of-origin effect is an influence that the country of manufacture has on a consumer's positive or negative perception of a product. The country, the type of product, and the image of the company and its brand, influence the magnitude of the effect upon the global consumer. Industrialized countries generally have the highest quality image. The Plymouth Laser and the Mitsubishi Eclipse are identical sport coupes built by Diamondstar Motors. The cars sell for approximately the same amount. However, Eclipses outsold the Laser and the Eclipses always received higher customer satisfaction ratings. The bottom line is that people perceive that the Japanese car is of better quality than an equivalent American car.[28]

This effect can also potentially cause the near extinction of local brands if they are deemed inferior. American and European consumer products have become so popular in China that they have eclipsed their Chinese counterparts. China has launched a "buy Chinese" campaign. Beijing is starting to demand foreign companies maintain the Chinese product lines they acquire instead of flooding the market with Western versions of the same product: Beijing recently vetoed Kodak's attempt to buy Chinese native Lucky Film Co., the number three film brand in China, and approved Germany's Benckiser's purchase of a competitive Chinese brand only after the company agreed to maintain the brand. In order to get Beijing's approval to build additional bottling plants throughout China, Coca-Cola entered a joint venture with a Chinese company to produce a fruit soda called *Tianyudi* (Heaven and Earth). Oftentimes, consumers can scarcely find Chinese brands in some categories such as carbonated beverages. Chinese consumers almost always prefer Western brands to Chinese brands after decades of buying shoddy goods from state-owned factories.[29]

Consumers have vague but definite stereotypes associated with various countries and products. Scotland is associated with Scotch whisky; France with perfume, wine and cheese; Italy with pasta; and America with cigarettes. Marlboro gains from its recognition as an American cigarette, while Chanel No. 5 gains by being a French perfume, and Johnnie Walker a Scotch whisky. An Italian whiskey or German wine or Scotch perfume would be negatively influenced by the effect. Products made in Germany are more highly regarded by American than French consumers. In countries where another country's image is high, a premium price may be charged for those types of products.

Typical Japanese consumers have an ethnocentric attitude. Oftentimes, they quickly reject foreign-made items, regardless of quality, in favor of locally manufactured goods. However, foreign products are thought to be appealing in terms of design and individuality. The European image is represented by Mercedes-Benz and Wedgwood. The American image is represented by colas, jeans, cigarettes, and chain restaurants. Most Japanese have an exotic image of foreign goods,[30] but still distrust products not made in Japan. As more Japanese travelers are introduced to foreign products, they tend to return home demanding these items.[31] The marketing strategy of most foreign companies in Japan is to get away from the image of foreignness through localized advertising and to have their products seen as Japanese products. Ads for Coca-Cola and McDonald's successfully use this Japanese imagery. A reverse ethnocentric effect occurs as well: at the Moscow Pizza Hut, consumers did not purchase the Moscva Seafood pizza with sardines and salmon; they did not want a seemingly domestic product. (If it is their own, it must be bad.)

CONCLUSIONS

To increase the likelihood of success when a company is proposing to market products into a new culture (whether or not it is a different country), backtranslating should be used to minimize the chance of a product or brand name being offensive to the host society. At the very least, marketers should understand and follow any special governmental regulations concerning packaging, labeling, and quality standards of products. (Europe's ISO 9000 is quickly becoming an industrial standard.) Market research should be performed to minimize the SRC. An understanding of how a product (or its substitute) is currently be utilized within the cultural norms will help marketers to recognize which aspects of a product must be adapted in order for any success to be realized.

With regard to brands, creation or maintenance of a global brand is highly dependent upon the existing status of the brand. If a company has maintained independent brand names for the same product for numerous countries, it becomes more difficult and chancy to implement a single global brand name. If a product has been adapted in various countries to accommodate local tastes, the creation of a single global brand is not recommended.

Variations in national habits force product adaptation. Clothes are worn longer between washings than in United States; in some European countries, boiling water is used for washing; washing in streams is a habit in less developed countries. Middle-class women in Spain rarely wash their own hair; British women rarely do not wash their own hair; and Japanese women are fearful of overwashing their hair and removing its protective oils. Erno Laszlo tried from 1982 to 1985 to sell its skin care products identically everywhere. However, fair-skinned Australian and delicate Asian women are not the same. Polaroid's first attempt to introduce slide copiers in Europe failed because its product could not handle European paper size. Rubbermaid has set a goal of generating 30 percent of its sales abroad by the year 2000, up from 18 percent in 1995. Most Americans like housewares in neutral blues or almond colors; Southern Europeans prefer red containers; customers in Holland want white. Americans bought millions of open-top wastebaskets; Europeans are picky about garbage peeking out of bins and wanted bins with tight lids that snap into place. European consumers prefer metal tool kits and wooden desks to plastic, which is perceived as cheap. The Rubbermaid name caused confusion in the UK, suggesting to many customers a maker of rubber dolls.[32]

Tupperware, in response to Rubbermaid's international endeavors, is retooling itself to focus on overseas sales by offering lunchboxes with chopsticks, stylish picnic items, ergonomic kitchen gadgets, and aims to introduce a steady flow of new products tailored for individual markets. In Japan, that means selling children's lunchboxes with chopsticks that pull apart and items such as chopstick rests, kimono holders, and rice dispensers. A different lunchbox with Mickey Mouse kicking a soccer ball is produced for Latin American customers under a partnership with Walt Disney Co. In Europe, Tupperware sells picnic sets featuring sleek styling to appeal to consumers who nibble on cheese and sip wine. Tupperware plans to build on its international strength by expanding into new markets. The company manufactured its first products in China in 1996. In India, Tupperware just received government approval for a wholly owned operation. By the fourth quarter of 1996, Tupperware will be in Turkey. Latin America has been Tupperware's fastest growing region, having formed a partnership with Walt Disney Co. to make lunchboxes and other kid's products for Latin consumers under the name "TupperMagic." The Mickey Mouse lunchboxes and other products were introduced in five Latin American countries between February and May of 1996. Within weeks, each country was sold out of a year's supply.[33]

Chapter 6

Cross-Cultural Influences on Advertising

ADVERTISING

Advertising is the most widely used promotional tool. Mass media advertising is especially effective when marketing consumer products. It is not unusual for consumer product firms such as Proctor & Gamble or Unilever to spend 10 percent or more of their annual revenues on mass media advertising. The multibillion dollar commercial television market is funded entirely on mass media advertising. (Advertising as a percent of GDP is 2.4 percent, or over $150 billion for the United States.) In the United States, entire industries rely upon advertising. Global advertising revenues are projected to reach $650 billion by the year 2000. (The United States accounts for nearly 50 percent of global revenues, with Japan second, and the UK third.)[1] Advertising expenditures in developing countries such as India and China have increased significantly and will increase much more so in the near future as such countries continue industrializing.

Advertising is used to pave the way for the sales force, to gain distribution, improve brand image, and create goodwill for a company. Advertising has four basic features: it is a paid presentation; it is a nonpersonal presentation; it promotes specific ideas, goods, or services through the mass media channels of communication designed to reach the general public (including but not limited to television, radio, newspapers, magazines, and billboards); and it must identify its sponsor—the individual or organization that pays for the advertisement. Advertisers must know who their customers are likely to be, develop effective communications with those customers, be aware of the constraints that affect the communication, use creativity to prepare the message they want to communicate, send the message through the proper channels, and combine all these steps into an advertising campaign. In every country, advertising is just one element of the marketing mix; its role depends upon the use of and preference toward the other elements of the mix within a country. Yet, advertising and promotion are not only the most visible but the most culture bound of the firm's marketing functions.

Standardization of Advertisements

A standardized advertisement is an advertisement that is used internationally, with virtually no change in its theme, copy, or illustration, except for translation when needed. Standardized advertising strategy becomes impossible if:

1. various national markets are in different stages of maturity;
2. an idea depends on a large budget which is unsupportable in some markets;
3. it defies local customs and regulations or ignores the efforts of its competition.[2]

Standardization is easier for new products. Products suitable for standardization include products for which audiences are essentially similar (e.g., urban, elite, teens) and those products that can be promoted via image campaigns (e.g., luxury products and high-tech products). The visual element in an advertisement is the element most amenable to standardization across cultures.[3]

John Deere promotes its products with a globalized single strategy advertising campaign because the nature of the product, the tractor, is such that it is perceived similarly in nearly all markets and standardization allows a uniform image worldwide.[4] Reebok spent $140 million to create a global brand strategy and consolidated all of its advertising under the Leo Burnett advertising agency. English language ads are quite common throughout the world, especially in Europe and Latin America, sometimes with full text, other times with only English brand name with the main information in the local language or even the two languages combined. In an effort to standardize, Levi's uses the sublingual, using 1960s rock music and nonspeaking actors in often amusing situations to promote the rugged American virtues of its jeans. Similarly, Levi's overcame Europe's obstacle of many languages by creating advertisements that consisted solely of visuals and music without any language references.

MTV Europe has 200 advertisers, almost all of whom run unified English language campaigns across its 28-nation broadcast areas. However, as much as MTV wishes to standardize, laws force the company to adapt: MTV Europe is required to black out pan-European low-alcohol beer commercials that appear in Norway, which prohibits them. In Poland, commercials' lyrics must be sung only in Polish.[5] Campaigns beamed to Brazil must be modified to include local content. Australia prohibits all imported advertising, so advertisers have to reshoot commercials with Australian film crews and actors.

Yet, pure standardization is rarely utilized. McDonald's uses a global strategy by offering its basic product line to all markets and consumers, yet adapts its line to suit tastes and preferences as required. Coca-Cola's theme of "can't beat the feeling" is the equivalent of "I feel Coke" in Japan, "unique sensation" in Italy, and "the feeling of life" in Chile. Dove soap went global by having a series of commercials, shot in one location, with the familiar line: "Dove contains one-quarter moisturizing cream," but with a succession of pretty thirtyish women from all parts of the globe praising in their own language Dove's skin-softening virtues. *Time* magazine has 133 editions across the globe.

Messages must be adapted according to local culture. To attempt to force standardized messages onto unreceptive audiences will only result in failure. Japanese advertisers suggest rather than persuade; vague and indirect messages are used. Comparative ads in Japan are not considered good taste, and testimonials are seen as pushy and phony. Cheer detergent was initially advertised in Japan using slice-of-life television commercials similar to those used in the United States; these ads were found to be among the most hated in Japan. The campaign was quickly replaced with a new series using a famous sumo wrestler as spokesperson.[6] Playtex attempted to create a global brand for its Wow bra. However, in South Africa, women are not allowed to be shown modeling bras and fully clothed models held up the bra on a hanger. Commercials in other countries had to be 29, not 30 seconds in length because some countries wanted one second of silence at the beginning of the ad. Adaptation becomes operationally imperative.

CULTURAL INFLUENCES ON ADVERTISING

The way cultures react to communications and messages differ. Advertisers that understand these differences succeed. Those that ignore them fail. Korea is a word-of-mouth advertising country: a customer's testimony is more effective than television or newspaper advertising; Koreans value the testimony of a friend, family member, or opinion leader.[7] Likewise, Chinese consumers tend to rely more on word-of-mouth communications. The concept of family is important to the Chinese and is thus played up in advertisements.

The content of ads within a society mirrors that of the society: ads in countries high in collectivism contain more group-oriented situations than found in individualistic societies. Cultures high on the power dimension have more ads with characters of unequal status than low countries.[8] Asian cultures get more information from contextual items than Europeans do.[9] Television commercials that play well in low-context cultures frequently seem cold and arrogant to those from high-context cultures. Similarly, commercials made specifically for high-context cultures confuse low-context cultures because in spite of all the ads' contextual richness, people in low-context cultures never seem to "get to the point."[10] Predominantly verbal ads (preferred by high-context cultures) tend to be too language dependent (which hampers their ability to cross cultural boundaries), comparatively poor at eliciting imagery (which attenuates their memorability), and generally boring (generate low attention, are not likable) when viewed by those from low-context cultures. Indian visuals contain a disproportionately high percentage of children; France uses the aesthetic visual proportionally higher; Korea includes the price 38 percent of the time, while other countries do so less than one-fifth of the time; and the United States has five to ten times more comparative advertising.[11] Obviously, these differences reflect cultural differences between countries.

Cultures with a nonlinear perception of time provide scattered information without explicit conclusions—more symbolic, more drama-lecture. Cultures with a linear perception of time are more likely to use a credible source that addresses the viewers directly, providing reasoned arguments along with visual information. American advertising is more informative than that of Japan, China, and South Korea. Information strategy is more likely to be used in individualistic, polychronic, and in cultures with low uncertainty avoidance. Argument strategy was more likely to be used in monochronic cultures with low power distance, high uncertainty avoidance. Motivation with psychological appeal is used in collective cultures with high power distance. Symbolic association is more frequently used in polychronic cultures with low power distance. Imitation is found in monochronic cultures with high power distance and uncertainty avoidance. Lecture format is more likely to be used by cultures with high power distance and uncertainty avoidance and to be particularly avoided by polychronic cultures which prefer a drama format. Those cultures with low uncertainty avoidance avoid drama.[12]

Nonverbal or visual advertising is most likely to satisfy a company's global market objectives.[13] However, it should be noted that body motions are interpreted differently among cultures. In Japan, pointing to one's own chest with a forefinger indicates that the person wants a bath. In India, kissing is considered offensive and not seen on television, in movies, or in public places. Symbols are not universal; for example, snakes symbolize danger in Sweden while they represent wisdom in Korea. In Saudi Arabia (and many Arab nations), it is against the law to publicly advertise symbols that contain Christian or Jewish connotations. (All neon lighting fixtures in a major hotel in Riyadh had to be scrapped because they were shaped like crosses.)

CROSS-CULTURAL ADVERTISING

Cultural differences can create problems when potential customers translate the message into their own cognition. The rugged cowboy image of the Marlboro Man was unsuccessful in Hong Kong where the urban population did not identify with horseback riding in the countryside. Philip Morris changed its ad to reflect a younger, better dressed, landed truck owner and success ensued. A cosmetics firm attempted to sell its lipstick in Japan using a television ad that depicted Nero coming to life just as a pretty woman wearing the lipstick strolled by; since Japanese women had no idea who Nero was, the commercial confused rather than amused or informed. African men were upset by a deodorant commercial that showed a happy male being chased by women; the men thought the deodorant would make them weak and overrun by women. Eastern Europeans still have difficulty getting used to advertising; years of Communist propaganda have led many Eastern Europeans to suspect that advertising is simply a way to promote products nobody wants to buy.

P&G found that its ads for Camay soap did not work in Japan because the ads featured men complimenting women on their appearance; the directness was not well received. In another Camay commercial, a Japanese husband was shown in the room while his wife was bathing, an invasion of privacy the Japanese consumers found distasteful. When the commercial was revised so that the man was removed from the scene, but with a male voice narrating, the commercial was very successful. For years, DeBeers ran ads (which were immensely successful when shown in the West) that showed Western couples in evening dress, reflecting the standard mentality that equates diamonds with grandeur, and the women smiling and kissing their husbands upon receiving diamonds as a present. These ads met with minimal success in the Japanese market because such a scene is not realistic in Japan; instead, a Japanese woman would shed a few tears and pretend she is angry at her husband for spending so much money. Subsequently redone, the ads showed a tired wage earner and his hard-working wife in their tiny apartment. Upon receiving the gift, she snaps angrily at her extravagant spouse. The ad was a remarkable success.

As always, when dealing with different cultures, translation problems can be, if not fatal, at least embarrassing. In Spanish, the very word for advertising poses a problem since the corresponding Spanish word means propaganda, which has other connotations in English. Estée Lauder decided not to export its Country Mist makeup to Germany when it discovered that the word "mist" is slang for manure there; the product was marketed under the name Country Moist. Parker pens had to change its advertising campaign: *bola* means "ball" in some countries, but "revolution" or "lie" in other Latin American countries. Its Jotter pen also did not prove to be a winner in Latin America; *jotter* there refers to a jockstrap. Maxwell House advertised its product as the "Great American coffee" in Germany; Germans, however, have little respect for American coffee. Thirty different dialects of Arabic exist; even the printed language is not uniform. This is also a problem in advertising.

Poor marketing research is a major source of cross-cultural advertising blunders. A McDonnell-Douglas ad for its aircraft in India showed an elephant that was an African, not Asian, elephant; even worse, the model in the commercial wore a turban in the style of Pakistan, not India. A toothpaste product's advertising in parts of Southeast Asia stressed that the toothpaste helped enhance white teeth: Since the local people deliberately chewed betel nut to achieve the social prestige of darkly stained teeth, the ad was ineffective. Owls have a negative effect when used in advertisements in India; the owl means bad luck there.

Misunderstanding or lack of understanding of differences between cultures also have led to a number of advertising mistakes: Ralston Purina used a toy bunny in Hungary in ads for its Eveready Energizer batteries; Hungarian consumers thought the ad was touting a bunny toy, not a battery. When a baby care company advertised soap to Hungarian consumers showing a young woman holding her baby, Hungarians saw an unwed mother: the model was wearing a ring on her left hand; Hungarians wear wedding bands on the right. Lipton's hot tea ads in Hungary showed Tom Selleck standing atop a mountain, holding a steaming mug; the commercial did not play well, as few knew who he was.[14] A Johnson and Johnson ad in Poland featured a woman in a hospital who just had a baby. Polish women only have babies in a hospital if they or their babies are seriously ill. AT&T's "Reach out and touch someone" advertising campaign was viewed as too sentimental for most European audiences.

Gulda Beer ads in Nigeria showed a large, rough-hewn man in a blue denim jacket, based upon the American movie character, Shaft. He was shown holding a mug with the brown glass Gulda bottle resting on the table. Research showed Nigerian beer consumers believed good beer only came in green bottles. After repositioning the advertising and repackaging, the brand was a success. In Thailand, Listerine attempted to directly transfer its well-known U.S. TV commercials, showing a boy and girl, one advising the other to use Listerine to cure bad breath. This did not work well; public portrayal of boy-girl relationships was considered objectionable to Thais. When the commercial was adjusted to show two girls talking to each other, sales exploded.

Culturally sensitive companies understand differences exist and make accommodations for them: Volvo emphasizes economy, durability, and safety in America; status and leisure in France; performance in Germany; safety in Switzerland; price in Mexico; and quality in Venezuela. Mars' U.S. advertisements for its Pedigree dog food used golden retrievers, while the use of poodles in advertising was more effective in Asia. Nike adapted the way it did business in Mexico. Instead of "Just do it," the motto is "Do it." J.C. Penney's marketing strategy for Mexico is geared toward Mexican consumers' greater fashion consciousness, concern with youthfulness, and family orientation. Its main messages are the same as in the United States: quality, customer service, and competitive prices. P&G's English language Canadian ads for Irish Spring soap stress the soap's deodorant value, while its Canadian French language ads focus on the soap's pleasant aroma.

Cultures in general do show distinct differences regarding tastes for their advertisements. French advertisements use more emotional appeals than American advertisements, but American advertisements contain more information cues. Sexual appeals are more frequently used in French advertisements than in American ones. A Nivea print advertisement was banned in the United States for indecent exposure, but the same message and image had been used in Germany without any controversy. The French use humor more frequently in advertising than Americans; puns and jokes predominate in French advertising. American commercials often feature a celebrity or credible source to provide testimonials or arguments in favor of the product, while French and Taiwanese advertisements are more likely to make explicit promises that are beyond the product's realistic capabilities.[15] American commercials are more information laden than British commercials, which tend to be more entertaining, have understated humor, and rely heavily on visual cues.[16] A typical British ad will almost always contain some element of fun, whereas the Germans tend to applaud technical perfection.

In Japan, self-assertive communication style—the direct style, the "hard" sell—is often seen as arrogant, insensitive, egocentric, disruptive, disrespectful, discourteous, impolite, and potentially embarrassing to a company. Indirect is nonconfrontational and better. It is better to offer a modest reward than an incredible promise. Japanese viewers dislike garrulous and argumentative sales talk; product information should be short and conveyed with music that sets a mood. Japanese advertisements are more likely to develop a story, describe the expression of people, and poetically enhance the mood of the product, emphasizing the affective rather than cognitive. The product message comes at the end of the commercial, almost as an afterthought to the rest of the commercial.

Advertising to the Hispanic Market

Two common mistakes are made when dealing with the Hispanic market. One is to try to adapt marketing strategies which were successful with non-Hispanics to Hispanics. Some marketers still tend to ignore the Hispanic market and think that they can just advertise as they do to the average Anglo consumer and still effectively reach Hispanics. AT&T tried to incorporate a Latin flavor in its commercials by employing Puerto Rican actors. In the ad, the wife says to her husband: "Run downstairs and phone Mary. Tell her we will be a little late." Two major cultural errors were in the message: Latin wives seldom dare order their husbands around and almost no Latin would feel it necessary to phone to warn of tardiness, since it is expected.

Since Hispanics tend to take pride in and keep their language, they have a different culture and beliefs than Anglos. When listening to the radio, Hispanics listen to many Spanish stations, and watch a lot of Spanish television. Most marketers must create different promotional campaigns to satisfactorily satisfy the two markets. Pizza Hut used a Spanish theme and saw higher sales in regions such as New York, Texas, California, and Florida. The company did not nationally advertise the specific campaign, only in the cities that had a large share of Hispanics.

The second and more subtle mistake is to believe that the same campaigns will work with all Hispanics, that all Hispanics are the same. Creating a generic ad that appeals to all segments of the Hispanic market can be difficult. Mexicans, Cubans, and Puerto Ricans speak different dialects and have considerably different tastes.[17]

Over 20 Spanish-speaking nationalities make up the U.S. Hispanic population, and each has its own national holidays, cultural characteristics, foods, traditions, values, and dialect.[18] The marketer is well advised to distinguish between the subcultural differences among the major Hispanic groups (such as Mexican, Cuban, or Puerto Rican).[19] Saturn learned the hard way that there are differences in dialect.[20] Countless other examples of dialect differences abound for the unweary marketer.

Mexicans and most Central and South Americans are avid soccer enthusiasts, while Cubans and Caribbean Hispanics follow baseball. Surf detergent fell into this trap by only using baseball themes in its Hispanic promotions. It sponsored activities at little league parks and demonstrations at discount stores nationally. Its success was well noted on the Eastern seaboard of the United States (home to most Cuban and Caribbean Hispanics), but had cool, limited success in Mexico, Central, and South America.

Regional companies tend to have advantage, they can usually target one specific group. Florida's Publix supermarket chain held a highly successful media campaign targeted at Cuban Americans: The ad, accompanied by Hispanic rhythms, featured shoppers loading their grocery carts with tropical fruits and interspersed shots of expansive blue skies, palm trees, and pastel motifs associated with the Caribbean. By way of contrast, Tianguis, a Los Angeles grocery chain, had a fiesta-like atmosphere to appeal to its mostly Mexican-American customers.

Yet, marketing to basic, fundamental similarities that exist among all Hispanics can provide the road to a national campaign. A Pepsi ad, espousing the Pepsi generation, took place at a *quinceanera*—the sweet 15 party, the coming of age for Hispanic girls—an event universal with Hispanics. Likewise, See's Candies took a family-oriented approach, showing an entire family sharing a box of their candies, emphasizing the Hispanic family values. Frito-Lay treats Hispanic Americans as a single market because the company tries to project a consistent national image. It advertises on Spanish language television and local advertisements occasionally address local populations, but in general, the company aims at the broadest possible target.

Bullfights are popular events among Hispanics, so Coca-Cola ran an advertisement that portrayed a bullfight. Coca-Cola theorized that Hispanics would view this as an everyday event in their Hispanic culture, and would respond by purchasing their product. To Anglos, however, this advertisement portrayed animal abuse. They would not see the ad for Coca-Cola, but instead see the pain the animal would be experiencing and therefore would more than likely not purchase the product for regular consumption.

Some types of advertisements are much more effective when trying to reach the Hispanic market; for example, the marketing of an official product of a sports group/event and, having the product endorsed by famous respected people is effective. Hispanics think official products of sports groups/events are credible. Anheuser-Busch, Campbell, and Coca-Cola were among the sponsors of Carnival Miami. AT&T uses the Major League Soccer circuit as a Hispanic marketing vehicle with television ads. Hispanics are taught to look up to their elders and to follow in their footsteps, so that is why they are more likely to respond to a famous and well-respected spokesperson.[21]

Japanese Advertising

Japanese advertising is designed to appeal to emotions, produce good feelings, and create a happy atmosphere. Japanese ads are visually attractive and eyecatching, featuring bright colors. This reflects Japanese sensitivity to aesthetics, color, and design. The Japanese often use symbols and strong gestures in their television commercials. Japanese ads may be humorous and appeal to the consumer's intelligence; however, they do not convey much product information. The vast majority of television spots are "mood commercials" designed to make consumers feel good about a product. Japanese ads seem to violate many of the American precepts for good advertising; it is sometimes hard to discern what the product is from viewing the ad.[22]

Japanese advertising is emotional, suggestive, and indirect, while Western advertising has a more verbal, direct message and is logical. Toyota created two versions of a Japanese ad for one of its automobiles. "Engine" was a straightforward, to-the-point presentation of the mechanical excellence of the new car. "Bird" had the same message, but superimposed on it a scene of an open road and the symbol of a bird. "Bird" was by far the more successful ad. Mechanical qualities are often taken for granted by the Japanese, so the emotional aspects are more important. The mobility of having a car affords the average Japanese consumer psychological escape and freedom, well symbolized by the open road and the bird.[23]

In Japan, differentiation among products consists not of explaining with words the points of difference among competing products, but of bringing out nuances and overall differences in tone. This is done by dramatizing those differences in the people appearing in the commercial, the way they talk, the music, and the scenery rather than emphasizing the unique features and dissimilarities of the product itself. Nonverbal advertising predominates; the key is the ability to communicate far beyond what is actually said or written in commercials.[24]

A Japanese from birth learns to actively complete ideographs, to complete sentences, and to fill in missing words in conversations. Thus, commercials are short (10 to 15 seconds) and can be left "incomplete," that is, without the final "successful application" shots that accompany virtually all American commercial messages.[25] The high-context, implicit Japanese are extraordinarily sensitive to how something is said or how a slogan or pitch is written. If the language is not exactly "right," the consumer will be rebuffed rather than attracted, regardless of the product being sold.[26]

Direct comparisons with the competition are almost never used in Japan; it is taboo for any company to acknowledge the existence of its rivals, let alone attack or put down a rival. The accepted Japanese industry norm is to avoid slandering, defaming, and attacking competitors. Polite lies are more acceptable than the expression of contradictory opinions. Although Japan's Fair Trade

Commission (FTC) during the late 1980s eased restrictions on comparative advertising, most Japanese companies and media networks have been reluctant to air them. Pepsi's ad with M.C. Hammer comparing Pepsi to Coke was an attempt to go against the cultural grain; although voted the second most popular commercial on the air during the time it was run, after considerable pressure from the networks, it was subsequently pulled by Pepsi.[27] Pepsi then ran full-page ads in major newspapers showing clips from the TV commercial; the text noted: "Unfortunately, we can't show you this on television. So, to answer your request, we are airing it in the newspaper."[28]

CROSS-CULTURAL INFLUENCES ON ADVERTISING REGULATIONS

The Malaysian government has a 41-page advertising code enforced by the Ministry of Information's Radio Television Malaysia. All commercial storyboards must be submitted to RTM for approval and then again after filming is completed. (Twenty-five other countries require preclearance of commercials in one form or another.) Malaysia is determined to protect its Islamic population from the excesses of Western advertising and marketing. Some of the bans include no pork, alcohol, or cigarette advertising; women in advertisements should be decently dressed. RTM requires all commercials be filmed in Malaysia and use only Malaysian models. Impulse deodorant had to overcome numerous obstacles to advertise in the Malaysian market. One of the company's commercials featured the male lead hastily buying flowers for a passing sweet-smelling girl, and consequently starting a relationship with her. In Malaysia it is considered very unrefined for a girl to accept such advances, so in the Malaysian version, the girl shows only a flattered smile. Seiko watch company ran an ad in Malaysia using the theme, "Man invented time; Seiko perfected it." The Malaysian network received a complaint from a Muslim holy man charging that the commercial should be withdrawn because God, not man, invented time. The new slogan developed was "Man invented time-keeping; Seiko perfected it."[29] Malaysia also outlaws ads showing women in sleeveless dresses and showing their underarms, pictures considered offensive by strict Moslem standards.

Advertising regulations range across the entire spectrum. Italian stations do not guarantee audience delivery when spots are bought. France and Italy ban all cigarette and tobacco advertising. France bans while Italy severely restricts alcoholic beverage advertising. (Both tobacco and alcohol advertising is partially or totally banned in most European countries, as well as in India and Argentina.) German companies have voluntary agreements not to advertise alcohol to young people. In Belgium, pharmaceutical advertising is illegal.[30] France has outlawed the use of foreign language in all advertising copy. (Forty countries regulate languages that can be used in advertisements.) Germany prohibits the use of superlatives and it is illegal in Germany to do comparative advertising among two brands (as many other countries do). Special taxes are also a consideration: In Austria, taxes of 10 to 30 percent exist on ad insertions; radio advertising carries a 10 percent tax, a uniform tax of 10 percent exists for television ads, and cinema ads have 10 percent tax in Vienna. In China, advertising has to be truthful; companies must provide proof to back up what is advertised.[31]

Comparative advertising is outlawed in many European countries such as Germany, Italy, and Belgium. Philip Morris in 1996 had an aggressive European ad campaign that cited scientific studies to claim that secondhand tobacco smoke wasn't a meaningful health risk to nonsmokers and suggested that inhaling secondary smoke is less dangerous than eating cookies or drinking milk. Furor over the campaign caused Philip Morris to pull the ads in France and Belgium and halt the ads elsewhere in Europe. Philip Morris made a major miscalculation by comparing tobacco with other products and thus entered into the realm of comparative advertising.[32] In addition, the French banned the campaign on the grounds that it was thinly disguised tobacco advertising. Television ads for tobacco in Europe have been illegal since 1989.

Kuwait's government-controlled TV network allows only 32 minutes of advertising per day during the evening. Commercials exclude superlative descriptions, indecent words, shocking shots, indecent clothing or dancing, revenge shots, and attacks or comparative ads on competition; it is illegal to advertise cigarettes, lighters, pharmaceuticals, alcohol, airlines, and chocolates or other candies. Benetton's advertisement of three little children sticking out their tongues was deemed pornographic and banned in Arab countries, where the depiction of internal organs is prohibited. Saudi Arabia prohibits advertisements or media of fortune telling and horoscopes, advertisements that frighten or disturb children, comparative advertising, or any woman in an advertisement.

A consumer affairs court in Helsinki banned a TV commercial sponsored by McDonald's and charged the fast food chain with using the advertisement to exploit the loneliness of a child. Coca-Cola's international theme of the 1970s, "Coke adds life," was refused in Scandinavia and Thailand because it was considered an overclaim. In Spain, advertising of toys should have the range of prices included so parents know in advance if they can afford to buy them.[33] On the positive side, some countries are loosening their regulations; for example, bidding on time slots is now the norm in South Korea.[34]

In some countries, commercial television is minimal. Instead of advertising revenues funding media, a TV owner pays an annual fee to the government for television viewing; governments then broadcast commercial-free programs. (Italy, Finland, Sweden, Germany, and Britain have such a practice.) Even when advertising exists, major changes must occur; Germany sells cinema space by the meter rather than by the second, so agencies have to create 43-second ads. TV advertising in Germany has historically been shown before and after programs. In the Middle East, some products are not allowed to be advertised on TV.[35]

Direct regulations are not even necessary to influence media content: in many undeveloped countries, the economy is largely state-controlled. Not following the government line can be fatal: In 1993, Uganda banned the leading critical and independent publication (*The Monitor*) from receiving advertising from government and state-run companies, thus causing it to lose nearly 50 percent of its revenues overnight.[36]

The media availability varies across countries. In certain parts of Africa, local advertising agencies are not even available. An agency that a company uses may not be in the country intended or the services that it provides may not be adequate for a company's purposes. Some countries restrict ownership of ad agencies; seventeen allow only minority foreign ownership, and Indonesia, Nigeria, and Pakistan allow none at all.[37] Traditionally, foreign businesses with an interest in Eastern Europe had to use one of the state advertising agencies . . . this led to a dearth of advertising talent which is just now being rectified.

OTHER FORMS OF MEDIA

The availability of other forms of media is another concern that marketers need to take into account before engaging in global advertising. In many parts of rural India, television does not exist. The only forms of advertising are ambulant theaters that show movies from village to village. In India, Wilkinson uses puppet shows.[38] Southern and Western Europeans like to watch TV while in Northern and Central Europe, radio is the most important medium. Newspapers are popular in Scandinavia and Germany (70 percent), whereas only 15 percent read a newspaper in Portugal. Unlike in the West, where advertising constitutes around 80 percent of newspaper revenue, in most of Africa, the ratio is reversed: most of revenue is derived from circulation.[39]

Media in most Communist Bloc countries were state owned and did not accept advertising. This has changed . . . even to the extent of the official Communist newspaper *Pravda* accepting advertising. In addition to carrying news, newspapers can also have a commercial element. Under Communism, the advertising emphasis in Eastern Europe was placed on being noncommercial, as that promoted generic demand for product categories by informing, persuading, and propagandizing. Even today, in Russia, much advertising is used to provide consumers with factual information about goods that are available for sale . . . rational user benefits rather than emotional approaches dominate.[40] A lack of media advertising tradition has led to an overall poor marketing/advertising infrastructure.

The average Japanese consumer is an avid television watcher and newspaper reader. The fold-in advertisement for newspapers (*orikomi*) is widely used. This allows even small stores to advertise to a limited area with a minimum outlay. "Transit advertisements" are printed advertisements that are displayed in public transportation areas such as railway cars and buses; they are very common in Japan because of the high reliance on public transportation and the long commutes for the typical worker. Major users of transit advertising include magazines and publishing companies, food companies, major retailers, cosmetic companies, hotels, and restaurants.

In Japan, over 200 new magazines are started annually, and more than half of these are either fashion oriented or related to consumer life. Japanese magazine advertising is more informative in nature. Because the themes of these publications provide psychographic information, it is possible for manufacturers and suppliers to utilize them strategically besides simply advertising in them.[41] *Newsweek* successfully launched a Japanese version of its magazine in 1986; its 150,000 copies sold out immediately, and numbers continue to grow. The Japanese version presented to readers a comprehensive international news magazine that took stories mainly from the U.S. domestic edition and placed emphasis on international news; the main targets were intelligent, business-oriented, white-collar workers, with business managers and college students as secondary targets.

In Mexico, billboards are effective and efficient advertising media, especially in crowded cities. With Mexico's traffic-clogged main arteries with slow moving traffic at nearly all hours of the day, billboards provide a large captive audience. Mexicans also enjoy being outside and are considerably more often outside than Americans. Rather than 2 percent of all spending by smaller and localized users, as in the United States, outside advertising represents about 5 percent of advertising spending in Mexico, with usage by all sizes of companies. Outdoor advertising is prevalent throughout Eastern Europe as well. Interestingly, since car ownership was relatively low, most billboards were positioned to reach pedestrians rather than motorists.[42] However, marketers can still make the same errors on billboards as they do in mass media advertising: Pan-American erected huge billboards in Japan showing a reclining Japanese woman in a kimono; in Japan, only prostitutes recline in such a manner. Where once it had encouraged outdoor advertising, the Vietnamese government is tearing down billboards it finds offensive.[43] In an extraterrestrial venture, Pepsi announced it was teaming up with two Russian bottling partners to invest $550 million in Russia over the duration of the decade. Most of the money was for 11 new plants and a new distribution system, but some of it is allocated to having cosmonauts build a "space billboard."[44]

Hundreds of hours of infomercials hit the airways weekly throughout Asia. These program-length advertisements feature celebrity endorsements and demonstrations of products. Sales in Asia were to be $200 million in 1995, this virtually without touching India or China.[45] In Britain, certain taxi cabs are completely painted with advertisements, interiors as well; the cab driver is given $3,000 in exchange for driving these corporate colors throughout the country for a year.

Meanwhile in Turkey, some buses are encompassed completely by advertisements. Throughout Europe, commuter trains are also being plastered, legitimately, with ads complementing the print campaigns of brands.[46]

CONCLUSIONS

Advertising is a key tool in international marketing. It involves a significant commitment of funds, it represents the sole international representative for many companies, and it is required to accurately position the product as desired for multinational companies. For an advertisement for foreign markets to succeed:

- the message must be meaningful in terms of the experience of the people;
- the message must appeal to some responsive chord among the desires and ambitions of the targeted audience; and
- the message must not offend sensitivities.

When advertising cross-culturally, the following must be adhered to:

- Understand local regulations and their effects upon advertising.[47]
- Do not assume that just because a commercial appeals at home it will also appeal to foreigners with equal effectiveness.

- Create a global theme, but localize to particular markets as necessary.
- Thoroughly do the research to minimize potential translation and usage problems.
- As advertising objectives vary from market to market, customize objectives for each target market designated and do so with the culture in mind.
- Clearly designate the target audience within the target market.
- Examine media alternatives and availability within the target market.
- Review local agency availability and capabilities.
- Hire a native speaker to translate the advertising message.

Chapter 7

Cross-Cultural Aspects of Trade Fairs

TRADE FAIRS AND SHOWS/EXPOSITIONS

Trade shows or expositions (American terms) or trade fairs (European term) are among the best ways to enter a market—or find it. Here, in one place, you can find products or services to buy, sell products you manufacture or represent, and investigate what the competition is up to. Trade shows offer an opportunity not just to obtain sales orders, but also to test product receptivity, research customer attitudes, acquire distributors and agents, circulate promotional material, capture leads, network with colleagues, and keep on top of the competition. Exhibiting has three unique advantages: inexpensive person-to-person contact (providing a company with leads at one-third the cost of an industrial sales call), information exchange between buyer and seller, and time compression in purchasing, or a shorter sales cycle. Trade shows cut the follow-up calls a company must make to book an order from five to one, and reduces the cost to book a new sale by four-fifths.[1]

By taking an exhibit booth, a company is essentially announcing its intention to enter the marketplace as a viable competitor. Trade fairs represent an excellent and cost-effective short-term method of market research and product introduction, domestically or internationally: Some international companies generate as much as 70 percent of their annual sales at international trade fairs. However trade shows can be a distraction and a tremendous waste of time and energy if a company does not know how to work them properly. The most logical way to meet a number of prospects face-to-face is to exhibit products at a trade fair that showcases one specific industry or several related industries.

There are two main types of shows/fairs: horizontal and vertical. A horizontal show exhibits a wide variety of products. An example of this type of event is the Hamburg Fair in Germany, which exhibits almost everything in both consumer and industrial goods. A vertical exposition is product specific; for example, it may be limited to medical products, computers, or electronics. Electronica, held in Munich, Germany, each year, is a typical vertical show. Comdex is an example of a vertical exposition held in many countries around the world. Its largest event is held each November in Las Vegas, Nevada, although smaller similar shows are held in strategic markets around the world (i.e., Europe, Japan, South America, etc.). The most logical way to meet a number of prospects face-to-face is for a company to exhibit at a trade fair that showcases one specific or several related industries. For example, a microbrewery could exhibit at a beverage show and/or at a specialty food event.

Expositions are further classified as either *Association shows* or *Independent shows*. Association shows are those which are sponsored by specific trade associations. Independent events are sponsored by organizations in the private business sector which specialize in show creation and management. It is very common to find a major magazine publisher involved in trade shows with an exhibit division as part of its organization. Conceptually, the advertisers in a magazine are the exhibiting companies while the readers represent the attendee base. Thus, there exists a great deal of synergy between the magazine division and the trade show division of many publishers throughout the world.

In the United States, trade shows are also differientiated between *business-to-business* and *consumer/public* events. While the former is almost exclusively restricted to the trade, consumer events are open to the general public where preregistration is not required but an entrance fee charged at the door. Business-to-business shows are usually by invitation with preregistration as a requirement. Boat, auto, and home improvement shows are good examples of public events.

Trade fairs/shows date back in history to the time when most trade was centered at markets or fairs. International trade fairs have been a primary vehicle for reaching potential buyers and introducing products since the sixteenth century. Among companies in Europe, they account for nearly 22 percent of media budgets.[2] The Frankfurt Book Fair, for example, has been held regularly since the thirteenth century. In the United States, trade events can trace their roots to the completion of the Chicago International Exposition building in 1872.

In today's international marketplace, trade fairs have emerged as "shop windows," where thousands of firms from many countries display their wares. For a company that is new to exporting, significant benefits can be gained from locating and using representatives, agents, or distributors in foreign countries. They are as familiar with their national marketplaces as a regional salesperson is with his or her territory in the United States. They understand local customs and regulatory procedures, and can introduce their clients to top executives, guiding them through the nation's business culture. Trade fairs can also be a fertile ground for cultivating new customers for small and midsized businesses; the entry time for exporting can be cut from six years to six months through wide usage of foreign trade fairs.[3]

While 60 percent of business visitors at U.S. trade expositions expect to purchase an exhibited product within two months, nearly 100 percent of businesspersons at foreign fairs are buyers with order books in hand or distributors looking for products that can be sold in the United States. European firms average 33 percent of marketing budget for trade fairs versus only 25 percent for U.S. firms. At overseas events, it is common to observe a larger number of chief executives in attendance than one might see at an event in the United States. This is because CEOs of foreign companies consider it part of their job to work the trade fair floors.[4] It is also due to the need of a company to reinforce its commitment to do business in that country or region of the world. And, decisions that can be affected at the trade fair can be made face-to-face with the international prospect or customer.

Internationally, trade fairs assume greater significance, and exhibiting at trade events can be an extremely effective way to promote export products. In 1991, nearly 2,000 trade shows took place in over 75 countries, with the number of trade shows doubling in the last ten years.[5] In North America, a total of 4,400 trade shows of 50 booths or more exhibited in 1996. Corporations now spend $3.6 billion per year to exhibit in trade shows, more than they spend on trade journal advertising.[6]

European trade fairs tend to be much larger than those found in the United States: the Cologne, Germany, trade fairs bring together 28,000 exhibitors from 100 countries with 1.8 million buyers from 150 countries. *Tradeshow Week* reports that even a small country such as Belgium is heavily involved in expositions as an effective tool to promote exports. In 1995, 34 trade fairs were held, primarily in Brussels, with 5,880 international companies exhibiting and attracting almost 500,000 attendees. Russia's Expocentr, which was privatized in 1991, organizes trade shows/fairs. In 1995, 90 shows were held with some 10,000 companies from 78 countries participating and which drew 3 million visitors.[7]

West German trade fairs attracted over 400 U.S. exhibitors. American attendees were estimated at over 80,000. Thousands of American companies participate in overseas trade fairs. American companies and exhibits are favored at overseas trade fairs because Americans are known to be on the cutting edge of technology and having an American firm with that technology at a trade show can attract large crowds. Most Trade Fairs in the United States run only three to five days. The Guangzhow (Canton) Fair in China is held semiannually and runs for a full month each half year. The Hannover Fair in Germany runs for nearly two weeks. The importance of Hannover Fair is that many companies budget 20 to 25 percent or more of their total marketing communications budget for trade fairs; it is not uncommon for 50 to 70 percent or more of that to be budgeted for the Hannover Fair. At the Hannover Fair, exhibitors can buy 12-year space contracts from the various trade associations that build exhibition halls on the fairgrounds (versus year to year as is common in the United States); about one-third of the stands stay in place year to year.

The advantages of foreign trade shows are that they allow exporters to meet buyers directly; they provide firsthand exposure and interest in overseas markets for their products; they allow firms to observe the competition; and they allow for the gathering of marketing research data.[8] Trade shows (fairs) have advantages over other promotional methods in that an exporter can gather critical marketing related data such as competitive reactions, product development and research, pricing structure, and distribution structures.[9] The trade show environment is also action oriented and ideal for product demonstrations. Seeing products in action attracts crowds at show booths and invites attendees to ask questions and engage sales personnel.

Potential exporters experience numerous difficulties at international trade shows. Reassigning domestic employees to man the international exhibit stand will not work since two types of export knowledge are required of a competent exporter, objective (general) knowledge and experiential knowledge.[10] While the former can be taught, the latter can only be learned. Thus, the international exhibits should be manned only by committed personnel who have such experiential knowledge.

Americans are known as being on the cutting edge of technology, and foreign fair managers favor U.S. exhibits because of the attention they attract. Yet because of their huge and homogeneous domestic market and the mixed reputation of trade shows in the United States, American companies have not been as aggressive as their counterparts abroad in venturing into foreign markets. Thus, they have not been as committed to international trade show marketing. Yet, trade shows can be fertile grounds for cultivating new customers for small and midsized businesses. In 1995, thirty-nine American firms participated in a seven-day electronics production equipment exhibition in Osaka, Japan, and came home with $1.6 million in confirmed orders and estimates for the following year of $10.1 million. Five of the companies were seeking Far Eastern agents and distributors through the show and each was able to sign a representative before the show closed. While typically, only 20 percent of those attending a U.S. trade show have traveled a distance greater than a day's drive, many foreign trade fairs attract 30 to 40 percent of their attendees from other countries.

Government Sponsorship

France is more directly involved in trade fair export event sponsorship than any other European nation. Through the French Committee for External Economic Events (CFME), France sponsors more than 200 trade events each year. The British equivalent, the

British Office of Trade Bureau (BOTB), picks up 5 percent of the costs to firms for establishing booths/stands at fairs; half of the BOTB marketing expenditures go to trade fair activities. During the 1989 to 1990 period, 8,000 individuals were subsidized to participate in nearly 350 fairs. Trade fairs are also Germany's principal method of providing opportunities for market exposures for small firms. The Confederation of German Trade Fair and Exhibition industries (AUMA) identifies, screens, and rates more than 2,500 trade fairs and exhibitions worldwide and, oversees German participation in them. Each year, AUMA helps organize and manage more than 100 fairs held each year within Germany, involving more than 100,000 exhibitors and drawing nearly 10 million participants. German states also are represented; NorthRhine-Westpahlia, for example, spends between 60 and 65 percent of its roughly $3 million annual export promotion budget on trade fairs and will cover nearly 50 percent of the costs of setting up and staffing exhibit booths. In the United States, several states, including Colorado, Indiana, Kansas, South Dakota, and Wyoming have established European-style trade fair subsidy programs often covering as much as 50 percent of a company's expenses at approved international trade shows.[11]

European trade fairs offer an excellent opportunity for U.S. exporters to develop contacts in Eastern Europe. In aggregate, the Cologne trade fairs bring together 28,000 exhibitors from 100 countries with 1.8 million buyers from 150 countries. Participation in a trade fair is one of the best ways to test the potential of Europe and may be the most important step in a U.S. exporter's European marketing plan. Ten of the 20 largest trade show venues in the world are in Germany. Hannover, with its CEBIT (information technologies) and its industrial fair (6,000 exhibitors for 600,000 visitors over a two-week period), is Germany's most important exhibition center. But Frankfurt, where the popular IAA car show is held every other year, draws more visitors than Hannover. The Federation of German Trade Fair and Exhibitions indicated the number of exhibitors at Germany's 102 major trade fairs during 1996 was 120,000, occupying 6 million square meters of exhibition space and having over 10 million visitors. In Cologne, 1 million visitors attended 24 trade fairs. Dusseldorf had 25 annual fairs. The annual Hannover Fair in Germany has over 5,000 exhibitors in 20 major categories. In 1990, 561,060 visitors attended; that same year, Amsterdam's 12-day Household Fair attracted more than 300,000 attendees.[12] The Paris Air Show is a biennial event. Over 2,000 exhibitors from over 40 countries displayed their products and services.

The new Tokyo International Convention Center, with its over 250,000 square meters of floor space, will attract many shows. However, Germany still leads, with two-thirds of the most important trade fairs and exhibitions. Even with that much space, the Tokyo center will rank no higher than third, less than the Hannover Fair (with 461,000 square meters) and Cologne fairgrounds (with 263,000 square meters).

CROSS-CULTURAL DIMENSIONS OF TRADE FAIRS

A trade show is another forum for selling. Cultural influences are just as important in the conduct of a trade fair as in a personal selling or advertising effort. For example, in Mexico, businesspeople will not do business until a good relationship has been developed. At Mexican trade shows, it is common to find high-level executives manning the booths/stands because a person's title carries a great deal of weight. A majority of booths are run by the general managers and owners. The intercultural, interpersonal contact that upper-level managerial peers form at these trade events can become long-term business relationships. Also, in Europe, because trade fairs are valued components of a firm's marketing strategy, the caliber of a company's staffing and its exhibit reflects its position in the industry.[13]

In essence, at trade fairs, companies are inviting people to dine at their homes, so they want to put their best foot forward. Attendees tend to be owners, partners, and buying professionals. Decision-making authority is more top centered in Mexico and Europe than usually is the case in the United States. However, a recent survey of 100 chief executive officers (CEOs) from 500 major U.S. companies found that 82 percent had visited at least one company exhibit in 1989.[14] When attending a Mexican trade show, one should bring high-level representation. Most events in Mexico begin late in the day and crowds tend to come toward the end of the show. Whereas U.S. attendees tend to program their visiting pattern from the directory of exhibitors, Mexican attendees proceed up and down the aisles in a methodoical manner. Mexican attendees like to see which companies are exhibiting first. They may pass up a booth or stand back and listen to a conversation that is going on and, if interested, they may come back to that booth/stand. Lists of attendees are usually not distributed at Mexican or European shows. Some American events provide partial lists or allow one to access attendee lists for a fee after the event.

While most U.S. shows run from 9 or 10 a.m. until 4 or 5 p.m., Mexican shows often do not open their doors until 2 or 3 p.m. and end at 8 or 9 p.m. The peak times for trade shows in Mexico tend to be 6 to 8 p.m. This is true throughout most of Latin America. Brazilian trade fairs usually start in the afternoon, sometimes even as late as 4 p.m. and run late into the evening hours, occasionally as late as 10 p.m. A typical Brazilian trade fair may have only 60 to 100 exhibitors, but it will attract buyers from throughout the world. While it appears the trade events are less formal, one should not be misled by the informality of a Latin businessperson.

In the UK, manufacturing firms spend almost one-fourth of their promotional budgets on trade fairs. It is not unusual for many European firms to spend up to 50 percent on fairs (versus less than an average of one-sixth for an American firm). The European style of exhibiting has been described as "listen and learn," in contrast to the American method, which is described as "show and sell."

One major difference between the attendees of European and American trade fairs is that nearly all Europeans go to buy whereas only about 60 percent of the visitors at American events expect to buy in the near future. Many visitors from the general public typically attend in the United States; abroad, most fairgoers are not just businesspersons but decision makers. Thus, trade fairs in the United States are not the major marketing tool that they are for European and Asian companies. The top 100 shows in Germany average 77,000 attendees versus 22,000 for the top 100 U.S. shows.[15] German trade fair industry benefits greatly from its networking, voluntary collaboration between organizations (*partnerschaft*). Trade associations are extensively involved with the trade fair organizer, which results in a close working relationship been associations that represent visitors and exhibitors.[16]

Asian trade shows have many unwritten rules. Many of the best products are not displayed by exhibitors, but are kept in a back room of a nearby hospitality suite in order to prevent competitors from copying new products. The only way to see the interesting products is to talk to a senior salesperson.[17] Companies must avoid pushing a prospect at Asian shows. Asians like to take time to know the people and the company with which they will be working. Asians prefer friendly conversations as a prelude to nuts-and-bolts business discussions. Japanese exhibits at trade shows differ from those typical in the West. A Japanese booth will be constructed on the floor before an exposition, displayed during the show, and typically destroyed at the conclusion of the show. Reusing booths is not a typical Japanese practice.

Most international shows are built on raised flooring or on a platform; many show managements in Europe require all exhibits to be constructed on raised flooring, with all electrical wiring, cables, and telephone lines running under the platform.[18] Carpet and tiles are covered with protective covering during booth construction. Since Europe still has a hodgepodge of electrical standards, transformers specific to each country must be used; for example, an electric cord from a German computer will not plug into electrical outlets in the United Kingdom.

Trade Fairs: Cross-Cultural Costs and Amenities

Space in European trade fairs is typically allotted on a first-come first-served basis. The regular routine (which is different than in the United States) is for a company to pay for space without being able to select where its exhibit will be in the exposition hall. Show space is at a premium at the most popular trade shows, and waiting lists of two or three years are common. Experienced exhibitors often buy space two years in advance and begin working one year before the show to develop the booth theme and promotions. Space costs at European shows can be high, as much as five times that of a comparable American trade show space. For example, the National Housewares Manufacturers' Association at Chicago's McCormick Place charges $4.75 per square foot, compared to $25 per square foot at a similar Ambiente Fair in Frankfurt, Germany.[19] Although trade shows in Europe can be a bargain when the dollar is strong against most European currencies, that usually has not been the case during recent years.

The biggest mistake for an American firm to make is to assume and budget as if it were doing business in America. To reduce costs in construction and shipping, many firms have booths constructed in Europe to take advantage of local craftsman's expertise and knowledge. In some cases, exhibits can be built and finished right on the exhibition floor. At the end of the show, the booth is then scrapped or its components sold to another exhibitor.

Trade show booths/stands in Europe often include more amenities than their counterparts in the states: they have more comfortable meeting space and a wide range of refreshments, even to the point of booth workers serving alcohol. The Paris Air Show—held every other year during odd calendar years—included hospitality chalets on the flight line. Typical chalets include top-notch restaurants and full working offices and hospitality rooms. European trade fair stands (booths) tend to be much larger and more elaborate than their American counterparts, sometimes having upper levels with private conference rooms and featuring comprehensive exhibits and product demonstrations. Serious business and negotiations can be conducted on the spot. Telecom '95 displayed over 100,000 square meters of exhibiting space and attracted 150,000 visitors from around the world for a week in Geneva during October 1995. Among the booths were some with two-story waterfalls and 200-seat theaters. Planeloads of customers were ferried in by exhibitors. Catered lunches, private concerts, and exclusive seminars were typical. Rent was $482 per square meter for ground level space and $164 for space on the first floor. It required 150-person crews to work a stand of 1,200 square meters. Some of the exhibitor booth personnel stayed two hours away by train.[20] In some locations in Europe, hotel rooms are scarce and many participants stay in alternative accommodations, including private homes and even on houseboats.

In France, companies must be prepared to conduct business in French; in other places such as Switzerland, English will suffice. It is very helpful to have translators on hand for those people who may be excellent prospects but cannot speak English. It is also important to provide sales and product literature in the country's language; translation slip sheets that can be inserted into English-language brochures. A company's representative at a show should notice and respect cultural differences in dress, formality, and the exchange of business cards. Name tags are a no-no at German trade shows. The use of badges is almost nonexistent throughout Europe.[21] In Europe, clothing is conservative. Manners are formal. It is best to refer to hosts by their titles. Do not address a stranger or new acquaintance by his or her first name. It is not offensive, but may be considered bad manners. Among Europeans, it is expected that a company's CEO or other senior executives be in attendance.

Trade fair venues in some parts of the world may be poorly equipped and semiskilled labor may be hard to find. Venues could even have dirt floors which wreak havoc with sensitive electronic equipment. In Egypt, the only way to get things done is by paying a gratuity. Promotional giveaways can cause near riots in less developed countries. Every exhibit in China has crowd restraints or railing enclosing it.[22] In Saudi Arabia, one has to learn to work around the seven 15-minute prayer breaks Moslems take daily.

Trade Fair: Booth/Stand Location and Display

It is essential to get the best possible space. Companies must find the spot where they will get the most traffic. Find out who is next to you. You don't want to be next to someone who will distract your intended audience. Try to stay away from competitive booths. Make certain that your booth is manned by the right people; certain people are excellent at trade shows and others are not. Time is one of the costliest and most valuable assets, and you do not want to waste it. You should find the most attractive way to display merchandise and tell your story. In planning show demonstrations, it is important to discover what power requirements exist in the country and arrange to obtain foreign equipment for live demonstration or multimedia presentation. For booth materials, you must know what materials are acceptable before your exhibit company begins the design process.[23] Again, before exhibiting, attend and audit the event to understand the marketing environment that you will be experiencing as as an exhibitor. You will save much time, money, and aggravation.

TRADE SHOW RECOMMENDATIONS

Trade shows are becoming increasingly specialized (they promote a single or related industry category to a unique audience; i.e., vertical shows).[24] A company must decide on what trade show it will attend or exhibit in about a year in advance in order to make all the necessary arrangements. It must check to see if its material should be translated into the language of the host country. The company must also determine price information on products delivered to that country and prepare sales materials and aids.

Trade shows are a terrific place for an American manufacturer that wants to test the export waters. If your company has a product that has been successful in the United States, has production capabilities that can expand, and knows that its costs will go down if it can find more distribution, you should go to a trade show on a fact-finding expedition to audit the show and gather information about the market's potential. You should find out what products are directly competitive with your company's. Then start talking to a few people about your product. Bring plenty of literature with you. Also make sure you either bring someone with you who really knows the language or arrange for a translator to travel with you. All major convention centers have translators for hire at rates that range from $10 to $20 per hour. The $75 or so a day is a smart investment.

Most importers also look for price quotes to find out what the item will cost at the closest port of entry—Rotterdam, Le Havre, and Naples, for example. It is wise to work in advance with a freight forwarder—usually the same one who ships a company's display to the fair—to develop a list of c.i.f prices for different ports.[25] Mailing lists of prospective distributors in a trade fair's country may be obtained from show organizers or the U.S. Department of Commerce. At the fair, an exhibitor should display a sign welcoming inquiries about distributorships.[26] A company thinking of having its own booth (stand) at an overseas fair should not make such a decision before having a company representative visit the fair and audit the event. The U.S. and Foreign Commercial Service of the U.S. Department of Commerce offers lists of potential agents for various products in a number of countries who can be contacted in advance. The Department of Commerce also has a number of programs that are useful to exporters seeking foreign markets. They include:

1. *Catalog Shows:* An International Trade Administration official will display a company's printed or video catalog at a foreign trade show and provide a marketing study on response to a firm's product/service offerings.
2. *Certified Trade Mission:* U.S. company officials participate in overseas meetings or technical seminars with senior government officials, as well as selected agents and distributors.
3. *Matchmaker Trade Delegations:* U.S. officials arrange a host of meetings, lasting from two to seven days, between U.S. companies and prospective agents, distributors, or joint venture partners.[27]

Finally, many of the larger trade fairs also have their own agents and distributor services. It is advisable to check with the Department of Commerce to see if the fair organizer has been certified by the U.S. government. This certification is in effect a seal of approval and indicates that the fair organizer is qualified to assist U.S. firms.

A series of direct mail pieces will help establish interest among potential attendees and provide the vehicle for communicating any on-site promotions. A preexhibition direct mail program can be sent to the decision makers a company wants to see at the convention, offering them a premium or show special as an incentive to encourage them to stop by its stand (booth). A large supply of press kits should be brought to the show's press room. The kit should have material pertinent to the show such as information on new products and technology introduced at a company's booth. As with booth information, the press kit should be in the language of the host country. Multiple kits are frequently the order of the day, as there may be more than one major language spoken by attendees (e.g., in Europe, French, German, and English).

Since the foreign trade show exposition is physically located elsewhere, and the majority of participants will be locals from the host nation, it is best to adapt to the cultural traditions inherent in exhibiting in the host country, to accept the physical limitations present, and to conduct business according to local customs.

Chapter 8

Cross-Cultural
Sales Promotional Techniques

SALES PROMOTION AND CULTURE

Sales Promotion consists of those promotional activities other than advertising, personal selling, and publicity. Common promotional tools include coupons, sweepstakes, games, contests, price-offs, demonstrations, point-of-purchase offers, cents-off deals, premiums, samples, cash refund offers, event sponsorship, and trading stamps. Differences in preferences for sales promotional tools are a direct expression of cultural differences; for instance, French consumers prefer coupons and twin-pack promotions unlike British consumers who, for the same brand, respond better to "x percent extra free."[1] Sales promotions are likely to be less effective where mass media coverage is poor. The use of promotions requires some sophistication on the part of the retailers in the targeted country. Price-offs tend to be ineffective in environments where prices are subject to bargaining and can be subject to trade misuse. Stamps tend to be ineffective where the target market is not amenable to delayed gratification, may be unfeasible in unstable economic conditions, and their handling and redemption both require stable and sophisticated channels. Promotional packaging tactics such as in, on, and near packs do not require literacy extensive media support or distribution channels, although they may require packaging adaptation.[2] Many of the sales promotional vehicles in the United States (particularly sweepstakes and contests) have been found to be more effective when targeted at lower income segments. By way of contrast, coupon usage in the United States is correlated with socioeconomic standing: in general, the higher one's level of education and income, the greater is his or her use of coupons.[3]

The international standardization of the sales promotion function is usually difficult because experience has shown that what is successful in the United States does not necessarily prove as effective overseas. Coupon distribution is an excellent example. The use of coupons and other promotional tactics in Europe, although low by U.S. standards, has been steadily increasing.[4] A 1991 study reported that the consumers in the United Kingdom and Belgium were the most active European Union coupon users. In 1990, an average of 17 coupons per household were redeemed annually in the UK and 18 per household in Belgium, compared to 77 per household in the United States and 26 in Canada for the same year.[5] In Italy and Spain, only three coupons per household were redeemed. Yet, market growth is uneven. Coupon distribution and redemption dropped in the UK between 1991 and 1992 (the emphasis lately appears more on quality than quantity), while growing elsewhere on the continent. Meanwhile, coupon distribution and redemption in both the United States and Canada has been declining.[6]

Fair trade regulations in Japan limit the value of premiums to a maximum of 10 percent of retail price and no more than 100 yen (about 80-90 cents). In highly fragmented retailing structures such as Japan's, small store size precludes the use of some promotional tools that occupy store space (e.g., in-store sampling) or slow down checkout traffic (e.g., coupons).[7] In the highly concentrated retailing systems of Northern Europe, the emphasis is on price-oriented trade deals and in-store consumer promotions. In high-inflation economies, consumer promotions that offer immediate return work best. However, they can sometimes work too well! As the first mass mailing of free samples in modern Poland, P&G mailed 580,000 bottles of Vidal Sasson Wash & Go shampoo to consumers in Warsaw. Poles wrecked mailboxes to steal them for personal use or for sale on the black market.

Money-back guarantees often make Hispanics believe that there must be a reason why the company is offering them. The Hispanics think that the product what is being offered with the guarantee must be a cheap product that will not last. Less than half of Hispanics view it as a credible promotional tool.[8] Mexico, for example, requires that special offers and cents-off deals be approved by a government agency before they can be used. Although the legal restrictions are bothersome, they have not stopped the use of sales promotions.[9] In France, premiums are called "sales with a bonus." In Belgium, they are called "linked offers," which is a totally different concept than that in French law.

Restrictions on sales promotions vary tremendously around the globe. The cross-national use of contests and sweepstakes can be complex due to differing legal requirements. Laws in other countries may restrict both the size and the nature of the sample, premium, or prize. The value of the item received free is often limited to a certain percentage of the value purchased. In other cases, the free item must be related to the product purchased. Germany's unfair Competition Law has been interpreted to prohibit items such as coupons, boxtops, and giveaway articles unless these will remain a consistent policy of the company throughout the year.[10] The choice of prize desired by the culture can drastically vary; the item must be attractive to the local consumer.

Corporate event sponsorships (tacking the company name onto an event) are big in Japan; it typically costs several million dollars for a tournament on the Japanese Professional Golfers Tour. Major tennis tournaments go for one-tenth of that amount. In addition, the title sponsor must generally buy two-thirds of the television advertising time. Japanese beer and spirits maker Suntory invites hundreds of distributors, customers, and other guests each September to a week-long retreat at its Suntory Golf Tournament. Most favored clients are paired with leading professional golfers in a pro-am charity match which precedes the tournament. Coca-Cola (Japan) spends over $2 million a year in Japan on community sports programs, with its independent bottlers spending half again as much.[11]

A packaged foods marketer in the Philippines must refrain from using high value on-pack premiums in consumer promotions, otherwise, the final price would be beyond the reach of most consumers. The great disparity in income throughout the world is an important obstacle to worldwide product standardization. To achieve market penetration, firms must either modify their product or produce a different, less costly one.[12]

COUPONS

By offering a rebate through coupons, a manufacturer can attract some consumers who are otherwise more inclined to buy a competing brand. Sending out coupons allows the sellers to separate market segments with different degrees of consumer brand loyalty. This kind of price discrimination is profitable for the seller when the cost of couponing is sufficiently low. Couponing increases competition and reduces profits.[13] The use of couponing is advised when considerable price sensitivity exists for the product category or when brand switching is common. Coupons provide a catalyst for consumers to choose one brand over another when homogeneity between brands is perceived. The use of coupons is often an effective way to gain new users for a brand and to stimulate repeat purchases.

Annually, over 300 billion coupons are distributed to American consumers with a redemption rate of 2.5 percent. (Twenty-five percent of the coupons accepted are misredemptions.)[14] This abysmally low rate of redemption and the inability to target successfully with coupons has American consumer goods manufacturers seriously questioning the continual usage of coupons as a promotional tool. Brand loyalty has diminished and many consumers use coupons only for products they would ordinarily buy anyway, thus negating the major function of the promotional tool. (Estimates are that three-quarters of coupon redemptions are made by current brand users.) Proctor & Gamble in December 1995 began to notify several selected markets that it was eliminating coupons. The company was investigating several other substitute marketing programs including "everyday low prices." P&G studies have indicated that for most customers, coupons are not an efficient promotional tool and they offer only limited benefits to manufacturers, distributors, and consumers.[15] Couponing elsewhere around the globe has seen variable results, even dying out in some countries. In France, a recently launched smart card may totally replace the endless special offer coupons that fill French mailboxes.[16]

Coupons or price discounting are not effective methods of promoting products to Hispanics, especially foreign-born Hispanics. The concept of coupons does not exist in many parts of Latin

America. In addition, since the Spanish word *cupones* is often associated with welfare or government handouts, many Hispanics perceive a stigma attached to using coupons.[17] Therefore, it is better for marketers to offer in-store promotions and free samples.

Newspapers and magazines are the most popular means of distributing coupons in the UK, while Spain and Italy rely heavily on in- or on-pack promotions. Door-to-door distribution of coupons is also very common elsewhere in Europe. In Holland and Switzerland, major retailers refuse to accept coupons, while it has only recently become legal in Denmark and the Netherlands. Belgians do not like to clip coupons in magazines or newspapers. In Germany, only full value coupons may be used in consumer promotions. (German law limits coupon discounts to 1 percent of the product's value.)[18] Door-to-door distribution is the more common distribution means than the freestanding newspaper inserts as found in the United States.[19]

Coupon distribution in Italy continues to grow with the average face value of coupons redeemed increasing slightly. Coupons distributed on a product package were still the media of choice for Italian manufacturers. In Spain, the coupon market continues to decline with distribution falling drastically over the past few years with an equivalent decrease in the average face value redeemed. The decline can be directly related to the strong Spanish economy that has resulted in little need to stimulate sales by use of consumer promotions.[20] Although advertising remains simple and relatively inexpensive in Eastern Europe, the use of promotional tactics such as coupons is on the rise there. However, usage is limited due to backward infrastructures, limited address lists availability, and obsolete or inaccurate lists.[21]

The Japanese FTC ruled that coupons were not illegal per se, but coupons must not be used as a vehicle to increase the circulation of the print medium; consumers should be buying the medium for its content, not because it offers coupons. Thus, coupon activities in Japan are still in the early stages of popularity. In 1990, the restriction on newspaper coupons was preferred; however, considerable reluctance on the part of retailers and consumers alike has kept the use of coupons stagnant. The maximum discount offered, however, was limited to 50 percent of normal price. Immediately thereafter,

SEIYO, Japan's number three grocery chain at the time, put coupon advertisements in all the major daily papers, placing between five and ten coupons (which were valid for one week and redeemable only at SEIYO stores) in each paper. Of the estimated more than 100 million coupons distributed in 1991, only 125,000 were redeemed (the average redemption rate was 0.12 percent, less than one-tenth the rate found in the United States; the highest rate was for a health and beauty aid at .29 percent). In March 1992, Japan's two largest newspapers, *Ashai Shimbun* and *Yomiuri Shimbum,* generated another campaign. Over 17,500 retail locations were reached. Subsequent campaigns were initiated in May and September of that year, distributing a total of 259 million coupons. The distribution of coupons by direct mail and magazines and by in/on-pack promotions and of retailer-sponsored coupons is very limited in Japan. Most coupons are redeemed through manufacturers or their appointed agents and redemptions are almost negligible. The coupon market in Japan is growing very slowly due to the low consumer interest in coupons and the lack of cooperation from major Japanese retailers.[22] Japanese consumers are still too embarrassed to be seen at a checkout line redeeming them. Japanese consumers will often object to the notion of "being forced to waste money on unwanted products," which they see as the result of couponing.

Europe is experimenting with alternative media. Image Products, an English company, introduced coupons on the back of supermarket receipts in 1992 and has had great success. Polygram records promoted new albums on the back of bus tickets, also in the UK, as has Rock Circus, another record company.[23]

In general, coupons require literacy and some sophistication on the part of retailers and consumers. Coupons also require a well-developed backward channel to handle their redemption. In markets where retailers are small, scattered, and highly disorganized, the logistics become difficult, expensive, and often cost-prohibitive. Coupons also require well-developed print media for new product introductions; social status perception can also affect coupons' effectiveness. In general, coupon distribution and redemption is related to the marketing sophistication of the culture; in those advanced cultures such as the United States and the UK, it appears that coupon usage is decreasing, while in cultures where marketing sophistication is relatively low but increasing, greater coupon usage can be found.

PUBLIC RELATIONS AND CULTURE

The Japanese have little concept of public relations in the American sense. Since the Japanese are very modest and self-effacing, they cannot understand self-promotion. They have little need for corporate public relations. The tendency of the Japanese to be closemouthed and even secretive about their business is a result of several cultural and economic factors. Traditionally, Japanese society has been closed—made up of exclusive groups and groups within groups. Each group is very sensitive about its existence, responsibilities, and privileges and is basically hostile to all other groups. To some degree, each group is in competition with the others as well. This system precludes the free and open exchange of information between groups since the primary motivation is to protect one's own group and outdo all others. In addition, Japanese managers and clerks generally do not have the authority to provide information or make offers on their own. A Japanese manager can either say no or do nothing—which is the same thing—but the manager as an individual cannot expose the company or commit the company to anything by himself.

Japanese weekly magazines (*shukanshi*) are often shamelessly sensationalistic. From scandals and muckraking trivia on politicians and celebrities, to entertaining and informative guides for job hunters, music shoppers, or club hoppers, the weeklies run stories on nearly all topics. The combined circulation of weeklies in 1993 was 1.65 billion copies. They are the ideal diversion for office workers making the long daily train commute to and from their various companies. Newsstands at train stations comprise nearly 70 percent of the weeklies' circulation. By using low-quality paper, these magazines can sell at relatively low prices. Japanese news reporters belong to press clubs assigned to cover a particular organization. This system places the journalists in a dependent position with the organization they cover, since they can be cut out of the information loop if they write something unflattering.

China generally lacks skills in public relations. China's Communist-led system is to blame with its principle that the center of power is identical with the center of truth. It is more important for the leaders in Beijing to show that they are in control, even when they are not, than to worry about the public relations consequences for their country.[24]

Public relations can be a major influence at the corporate level as well. The bad press and boycotts that come with doing business with dictators can outweigh the benefits. That is why PepsiCo sold its minority share in its joint venture bottling company in Burma to its Burmese partners. PepsiCo will continue to allow the bottler to use its syrup and trademark. In 1995, PepsiCo earned $8 million in profits from its 40 percent stake in the Burma venture. Student demonstrations at U.S. campuses cost it a $1 million food service contract at Harvard University and a Taco Bell outlet at Stanford.[25]

CULTURAL DIMENSIONS OF GIFT GIVING

The original meaning of gift giving in Germany, *schenken* (giving), meant "to pour, to give a drink," and as such was the oldest form of honor. On the other hand, it was also synonymous with the term "bond" because gifts were often directly bound or pinned to the body of the recipient, showing the idea of a tie established by the gift. In archaic societies, this idea serves as a basis for gift giving: everything is linked to its original owner. Giving away a personal object means giving away a part of one's spiritual essence and creates a bond between oneself and the recipient.[26]

Gift giving is an often overlooked after-sales function. Customs of giving gifts are complex and meaningful. In some countries, gifts are expected and the failure to present them is considered an insult; whereas in other countries, offering a gift is considered offensive. To the Chinese, the gift of a clock symbolizes that "time's up," i.e., death, and as such is not usually an appropriate gift. A gift of cutlery in Latin America conveys that you want to end a relationship; a handkerchief means that you wish the recipient tears; their guests should never give 13 of anything or give black or purple items as gifts.[27] Do not give handmade dolls to a Brazilian because these dolls are associated with voodoo. In Europe, chrysanthemums are associated with funerals and should not be given as gifts. Avoid the color purple when giving gifts in Italy, as it represents death. In Islamic or Arab countries, visitors should never give gifts of alcoholic beverages or photographs, paintings, or sculptures depicting women.

Gift giving is a common custom in Poland. In Hungary, small token gifts are acceptable at a first meeting, but once a business relationship has solidified or a genuine friendship has been established, more elaborate gifts can be given.[28] In many parts of the former Soviet Union, gifts are appropriate, especially for the most senior members of the organizations with whom one is dealihg. The Japanese cannot be outgiven, they lose face if they are outdone. One never gives an unwrapped gift in Japan or visits a Japanese home empty-handed. Proper etiquette requires that one should give the gift with both hands in Japan.

In Germany and Switzerland, local executives do not feel comfortable accepting gifts because they do not like to be obligated. Gifts are rarely exchanged in Germany and are usually not appropriate.[29] Gift giving is also not the norm in Belgium, France, Ireland, or the UK. In Denmark, modest, carefully thought-out practical gifts from one's own country are appropriate. One does not give gifts at the first meeting in Portugal and Greece, though business gifts are welcomed after the initial contact. In Italy, one gives a small gift to associates who have been particularly positive and helpful. Flowers are acceptable gifts in the Netherlands.[30]

In the United States, it is acceptable for a boss to give a secretary roses to express appreciation for helping to close a big deal; in Germany and in many Latin countries, such action would be seen as a sign of romantic attachment and therefore inappropriate. In Japan, one should not wrap the gift in white, but one must wrap it (not wrapping it is considered an offense). One must not unwrap one's own gift in the presence of the giver; one must also express appreciation for the gift at the next meeting.

The *shigarami*, or social obligation, is an intimate part of every Japanese life and is largely defined by consumer lifestyles and customs. This concept manifests itself in the customs of summer gift giving (*ochugen*) and winter gift giving (*oseibo*) and in client service (*settai*). Sick persons who receive gifts while in the hospital must present gifts to those who remembered them. Motives for the immense quantity, emphasis on quality, and reciprocity in gift giving include face and obligation factors. This is seen in the maintenance of proper relationships between people, especially between inferiors and superiors. Gifts are given in a very formal and elaborate way by inferiors to superiors to express thanks for favors received, to pave the way for favors desired, and to build up a fund of obligations for the future. Likewise, superiors give gifts to inferiors as a means of keeping their loyalty and cooperation.[31]

Japan's major gift-giving times are twice a year: *ochugen* (from the end of June to July 15) and *oseibo* (from the end of November to the end of December), which coincide with companies' bonuses. Companies give gifts to their customers to express appreciation for past business and to attract future business. Companies also reward their employees at those times with large bonuses. Not only businessmen but also ordinary Japanese give gifts during these two periods—to friends, teachers, relatives, and any others to whom they feel indebted in some way or another.

Gifts are viewed as an important aspect of one's duty to others in one's social group. Each Japanese has a well-defined set of relatives and friends with which he or she shares reciprocal gift-giving obligations (*kosai*). Most durable goods such as electronic appliances are purchased during one of the two gift-giving seasons. The giver bestows a gift on the recipient, who, in turn, has a deep sense of obligation and a burden of guilt from having accepted the gift. The receiver reacts by buying something better than the original gift to repay the favor with interest. Giving a gift thus creates an obligation between parties: A reciprocal gift is required if one is given a gift.[32] This can quickly spiral out of control as the reciprocal gift must be more expensive than the gift received.

The wrapping of the gift and the manner of presenting it are just as important as the gift itself. (In fact, in many cases, it is as important or more so than the economic value, the economic value being secondary to its symbolic meaning.) The gift might be soap, but it has a different value to the receiver depending on whether it comes from a prestigious department store or the local supermarket. In the latter case, the receiver is thinking: "If you are not prepared to go to a decent store to get my gift, then you can't think much of me." In Japan, the gift must retain the original department store wrapping paper to be of any value. If one does not go through the effort of selecting the product from a respectable store, one is considered lackadaisical about gift-giving intentions. Nestlé was in tune with the need in Japan for a premium brand of instant coffee for gift-giving purposes; as a result, it holds two-thirds of the Japanese market.

Gifts are beautifully wrapped, but without the ornate bows and other decorations typically used in the West. The color of the wrapping should be consistent with the occasion: red and gold for happy events; black and purple or black for other occasions. Bold colors should be avoided, and rice paper is preferred. Bold logotypes printed on the gifts should be avoided. Certain brands of products are most acceptable and appropriate for business gift giving. The Japanese do not open a gift in front of the giver (so it will not be necessary to hide one's possible disappointment with the present). Favorite gifts include imported liquor, consumables of high quality, and any designer-made products. Anything that cuts (e.g., scissors, letter openers) and handkerchiefs should not be given as gifts, as these items in Japan symbolize the severing of relationships.

This tradition of giving gifts warrants that certain conventions be observed. One should not give old items of little value. Rather, one must attempt to match the recipient's status, the dues given being what he or she deserves. Over- and undergiving can cause embarrassment and be counterproductive. In gift giving, as in everything else in Japan, attention to rank is essential. Gifts must be graded according to rank. If the president receives a gift equal to that given to the vice president, the former will feel insulted and the latter embarrassed. It is also helpful to keep a record of all gifts given because a gift should never be repeated. The gift could be a small thanks for the opportunity to meet the person or to utilize the service, and it could also act as a reminder; gifts are considered a lubricant in human relations. Gifts must be ornate, but not so high in value as to make the receiver feel obligated (although usually the response will be a gift in return). If so obligated, the recipient either returns the gift by mail or delivers to the giver a present of equivalent value immediately; this is considered to cancel out the original gift and release one from any future obligations. Gifts presented after returning from an extended trip (especially when visiting acquaintances in a distant place) are called *omiyage.*

Gift giving can become arduous. On Valentine's Day, most of the chocolate is purchased by women, especially office ladies (OLs), and given to men, particularly unmarried, rising salarymen. Knowing that gifts received must be repaid in Japan, Japanese candymakers launched a second holiday a few days after Valentine's Day called White Day. This is the day men could (and by obligation, must) buy white chocolate (*giri choco,* "duty chocolate") and give it to all those women from whom they had received chocolate on that previous Valentine's Day. Young, single, and popular male managers may receive Valentine's Day chocolates from a dozen or more office ladies, all of whom must be given reciprocal chocolate on White Day that exceeds the value of the chocolate given by them on Valentine's Day.

When Japanese managers are invited to weddings, they incur obligations that are reflected in the gifts they must give: cash, not any other type of gift. The cash must consist of unused bank notes, in denominations of up to 20,000 yen; the higher the manager's rank, the more the manager must contribute, the exact sum expected being understood ahead of time. The gift must be placed in a special envelope. Large contributions cannot be put into envelopes designed for small contributions or vice versa. The cord around the envelope must be red and white or gold and silver; no other combination is acceptable. The gift must be presented to the couple on the actual day of the reception, not before or after. In return, the couple is obligated to give a gift (an article, not money) that must be roughly half the value of the cash received, given on the actual day of the reception, not before nor after. Any violations are viewed as serious gestures of ill will. The consequence of not fulfilling these social rules is the loss of trust and support not only of the party directly affected, but of any observers as well; thus, every favor, no matter how small or insignificant, is remembered by both the giver and the receiver, and they both calculate the appropriate reciprocation.

The would-be renter pays a real estate agent's fee of 50 to 100 percent of one month's rent, makes a deposit of several months' rent, and then gives a gift of one to several months' rent to the landlord (rights money or key money) at the same time as thanks for providing the opportunity to live in this apartment. There are many holidays and occasions on which gifts are given. Department stores and gift manufacturers are always on the lookout for new chances to promote gift giving. For important occasions in Japan, no expense is spared when giving gifts.

Not only gifts, but the gift-giving time is important. Germans start planning their Christmas shopping in October and begin buying at the end of November. St. Nicholas' Day (December 6) is the traditional day when Christmas presents are given. The trend in the UK and France is to squeeze the Christmas period into a shorter giving season, the last week in December. Christmas buying in Hungary has traditionally been on "golden" Sunday, the last Sunday before Christmas Eve. January 7 is Christmas Day for members of the Eastern Orthodox Church. An appropriate gift given at the inappropriate time can be worse than no gift at all.[33]

In general, high-context cultures tend to view gift giving as a requirement; for these cultures, the custom of gift giving is a complex, traditional, meaningful activity that becomes an important communications element and part of the relationship-building process. In contrast, gift giving is an optional, peripheral, and sometimes inappropriate activity in low-context cultures such as those in Germany, the United Kingdom, or the United States.[34]

CONCLUSIONS

The major factors relating to sales promotional tools overseas are legal restrictions and degree of marketing expertise. Many tactics available in the United States are banned from use overseas. Consumers overseas are often unaware of sophisticated promotional tactics that are common in the United States. Point-of-purchase displays work well in environments where self-service behavior is accepted; in many less developed economies where service becomes labor intensive and the shop owner typically provides individual attention to customers, point-of-purchase offerings may not be appropriate. This is not to say they cannot be used nor will be successful in these countries; it is, however, probably worthwhile to do a controlled trial first to see how receptive the consumers may be to the promotional effort and the level of education that must be carried out.

As an example of this approach, one should examine Procter & Gamble's seven-year thrust at the mainland Chinese market. It hired thousands to pass out yellow and orange gift packets of Tide laundry detergent to neighbors. In Fiscal 1995, P&G had shampoo and detergent sales of $450 million (50 percent growth over the prior year) and is the largest consumer products company in China. It has Head & Shoulders, Rejoice (Pert in the United States), and Pantene. The shampoos command a 300 percent premium to local brands but have a 57 percent market share in the major urban markets. P&G succeeded due to thousands of field troops. It also hooked up with washing machine manufacturers to pass out free Ariel and Tide boxes when customers take delivery of their machines.[35]

International usage of sales promotional tactics has also gained notoriety. Terrorist groups have allegedly helped finance their campaigns of violence through a supermarket coupon scam worth $100 million a year. Groups including Abu Nidal and one of the men convicted in the World Trade Center bombing have been linked to illegal coupon redemption rings in New York, Florida, and Missouri. The scam involves buying coupons by the pound, clipping them at special locations, crinkling them to make them appear used and then sending the coupons to clearinghouses for redemption.

Chapter 9

Cross-Cultural Issues in Sales and Sales Management

Personal selling is the largest portion of the promotional mix in business-to-business marketing, exceeding that of trade shows and advertising. Its importance in consumer marketing pales besides the massive dollars spent in mass marketing practices, particularly advertising in the mass media. However, in modern times, with the high growth of direct marketing, personal selling has taken on new life. Even consumer products have a need for personal selling, especially for durable products such as houses, automobiles, furniture, and appliances. In many cases, in both industrial markets and consumer products, personal selling is responsible for the majority, if not all, of an organization's revenues. Products that are higher priced, complex, require demonstrations or hands-on training, or must be customized for each individual customer tend to be sold through the personal sales effort. In many cases, only a qualified and well-trained salesperson can address the questions and concerns of a potential buyer.

The process itself varies greatly across cultural and political borders. Manufacturing Data Systems Inc. (MDSI), a producer of computer software, finds that a sale in the United States requires an average of two calls per sale. In Europe, frequent callbacks are necessary, each time with a higher level of management, expending comparatively more time and cost. In Japan, a sale requires even more time than in Europe. Electrolux finds its direct sales force requires an average of only five demonstrations to make a sale in Malaysia, but 20 in the Philippines. Since bargaining still dominates the exchange process in Saudi Arabia, merchants are heavily dependent upon personal selling to conduct their transactions. In addition, since women are forbidden to participate in most of the workforce, all sales personnel are men; even the cosmetics and lingerie departments of many stores are staffed by males.

CULTURE AND SELLING

Just as the wants and needs of customers around the world differ according to the cultural norms present, so does the process of satisfying those wants and needs: the personal selling process. In personal selling, the unknowing salesperson can quickly stumble by making or ignoring cultural faux pas. Compare this scenario: An American salesperson visits a Saudi official for an introductory meeting for a new product. The Saudi offers the American coffee, which is politely refused. The American sits down and crosses his legs, exposing the sole of his shoe. He passes documents to the Saudi with his left hand, inquires after the Saudi's wife, and assertively pursues the deal. Within the first ten minutes of the business conference, the American had unwittingly offended the Saudi five times.

Arabs like to meet the seller. Most Arab firms have developed a reputation for procrastinating when it comes to correspondence. One must visit regularly and establish a direct personal relationship. For them, there is nothing else besides the relationship. In a ten-year contract between a Canadian firm and an Arab manufacturer, a minimum annual quantity was agreed upon. After the sixth year, the orders stopped coming in and the Canadians cried foul. The contract had apparently been canceled unilaterally by the Arabs because the Canadian contract signer had left the company. The Canadians discovered that the products had never been used and the product was purchased solely out of particular loyalty to the contract signer, not to the company, not because of any felt legal obligation.

In Latin America, social relationships must be developed before doing business; if companies do not do so, they will alienate clients and end up with nonexistent sales. Prospects will want to discuss their company, its needs, and its philosophy with you and learn similarly about your company, its values, and you. Evidence of being *simpatico* (warmth, empathy, and deep understanding) is important. The process of building personal rapport could take months or years and naturally results in a slower sales cycle. Latins complain Americans are too boastful; they become irritated and resistant to American sales pitches. Latins typically find the Americans too direct, too impersonal and pushy, while Latins to the Americans seemed unable or unwilling to stick to the point. To the Latin, the relationship is the important part. It is important that they get to the end, not the path or sequence by which the end is reached. The details of the equipment are less important than the relationship established.

An American company once pursued a contract with a South American customer. The company made a slick, well-thought-out presentation in which it clearly demonstrated its superior product and lower price. Its Swedish competition took a week to get to know the customer. For five days, the Swedes spoke about everything except the product. Though its product was less attractive and higher priced, the Swedish company got the order. The Swedish company knew that business in that country involved more than overwhelming the customer with technical details. The upfront investment in building relationships was more important than the deal.[1]

Likewise, building a personal rapport is important when doing business in Greece. Business entertaining is usually done in the evening at a local tavern and spouses are often included. In Germany, this lengthy approach to selling is called "reflective selling," and emphasizes the establishment of trust and provides the customer with an emotional and logical experience that is a true reflection of the customer's situation, not the salesperson's.[2] Selling is a matter of style. The Japanese may be looking for reliability and commitment; the Chinese wish sincere, hard-working, and even-tempered partners.

In the United States and Northern Europe, nurturing client relationships generally take a back seat to emphasizing product features and competitive pricing. In Latin America and East Asia, the non-economic side of business is the major part of transactions and the client/salesperson relationships are cultivated to establish trust and respect. Often, after-hours socializing is the key to cementing relationships with clients in those countries. Significant business transactions in most developing countries occur face to face; letters, faxes, telexes, or phone calls often go unanswered; if one wants to contact another, it is almost essential it be done in person.[3] The reason is obvious: in countries where the legal system is undeveloped or does not have a tradition of unbiased decisions, the only protection one has is to develop strong relationships with one's associates; the thinking is that "If we do not have a relationship, if he is not obligated to me, how will I know he will do what he says he will?"

In high-context cultures, one tends to go from generalities to specifics, to circle around the stranger, getting to know him or her, and only come down to the specifics of the business later when relationships of trust have been established. This is beneficial, as one does not get trapped in a long-term relationship with a dishonest person because one gets to know him or her early on. High-context cultures take a great deal of time to establish a relationship; low-context cultures will not and some will even avoid personal rapport lest it interfere with clear thinking and sound business judgment. Low-context cultures tend to get straight to the point, to the neutral, objective aspects of the business deal. This is beneficial (to them) as they do not waste time wining and dining people who are not fully committed to the deal. If the other party remains interested, getting to know them facilitates the deal.

Only in the United States and a few other countries is it normal to do business from a distance, between strangers, by mail or phone. Americans tend to be extraordinarily preoccupied with the tangible aspects of a product during the sales presentation instead of the people side. The British believe that Americans talk too much about nothing or talk about things Americans know nothing about. Asians believe Americans are not sufficiently humble and become skeptical when they feel Americans are overconfident. The Swiss say Americans are too absolute in their claims.

The concept of selling in itself is viewed differently from country to country. The Arabs prefer a soft-spoken sell. In Japan, the language used by the seller is much more deferential than that of the buyer—the buyer is always placed in the position of superior status. Moreover, the female speaker is always required to use more polite, differential language. As a result, saleswomen tend to provide a distinctly feminine image that may be beneficial for certain kinds of products but provides a negative image for others.

In many cultures, salespeople are not held in high esteem; in Europe, for example, selling is not considered to be a socially acceptable occupation; in France, salespersons are routinely referred to as "consultants" or "commercial attachés."[4] In Thailand,

Malaysia, and India, this negative perception limits the sales process to persons of similar social strata. In Thailand, family background determines social position. Because money confers only limited status, straight salaries are more respectable and desirable than larger incomes with substantial but variable commission components.[5] Salespeople are frequently recruited from farm families, to whom taking a sales position is a move up the social ladder. Thai society, however, is extremely status conscious and every relationship viewed in terms of superior and inferior; the former farmers are still held in disdain by most potential buyers.

In Japan, the sales function is not a career track or a livelihood as is found in the United States, but to many only a stepping stone, a stone they must undergo in the inevitable job rotation of the average salaryman, a stone they merely tolerate and put in their time, a stone they would rather jump over than submit themselves to. This is the result of the Confucian view of productivity (*shi-noh-koh-sho*): warrior, farmer, craftsman, and merchant. Merchants were ranked at the very bottom because they were considered to be socially unproductive and became the subject of social contempt and humiliation. The merchant caste was a full step below the customer caste. In fact, to the Japanese, as a result of this hierarchy, a merchant's (salesperson's or vendor's) very existence is only justified by the service provided to the customer.

Japanese buyers typically behave like arrogant and spoiled children as they revel in the superior status assigned to them by society. For example, ethical drug salespersons must frequently endure autocratic behavior from doctors;[6] for example, Japanese medical equipment company sales representatives wash the cars of the doctors that they call on. They also even pick up their customers' children from school. A cardiograph company's salespeople will pick up cardiograms from their customers, the doctors, and deliver them to an expert for diagnosis.

It is expected that Japanese sellers should display a suitably respectful attitude toward the buyer in their interactions.[7] The seller must do as much as possible to meet a buyer's wishes. The seller, being in the lower position, uses honorific language, and the buyer, being in higher position, may speak in less-than-polite terms.[8] Sellers or suppliers must accept their subordinate, service-oriented role in the transactions. All employees have direct customer contact; for example, Japan Air Lines (JAL) requires new employees to serve as flight attendants in order to expose them to the front lines; Japanese electronics companies assign new employees to work with customers in department stores as a first assignment in the company.

In Chinese society, an aggressive salesman might frighten customers, who may be humiliated and then lose face. Chinese buyers like to have their shopping in an environment without interference. If a salesman in a store is too eager to help and approaches a customer who has not decided what to buy, the customer will feel uneasy and go away. Chinese tend to chose someone they are familiar with to serve them. Favors done for others are often considered to be social investments for which handsome returns are expected.

In Taiwanese culture, type of work and nature of income are the major factors in determining social position; sales personnel rank low in the hierarchy of occupational prestige. Of even greater importance, the average Taiwanese perceives fixed salary incomes as more desirable and prestigious than commissions, which many regard as the lowest form of income.

An American company invested a large amount of money in recruiting and training 40 young Brazilians in sales techniques for an entire week. On the following Monday, the Brazilians were told they were going door to door selling the product. The Brazilians were appalled; it is beneath the dignity of Brazilian men to ring doorbells and talk to women about a product.

American salespeople are driven by prospecting, seeking new customers; this trait is not as prevalent in European salespeople. American salespeople tend to be order oriented, spending much greater proportionate amounts of time in correcting or following up orders than their European counterparts, that is, in postsales activities. Entertaining clients and overnight travel appears to be American phenomenon not readily seen in Europe.[9]

CULTURAL INFLUENCES ON THE SALES PROCESS

Religious or cultural beliefs often influence the selling process. Salespeople from one tribal or religious group often cannot sell to another such group in their own country. Car salespeople in Japan deliver a car to a consumer on a lucky day; contractors check for an auspicious day before breaking ground; insurance salespeople are careful to pick a good day before asking a customer's signature on a life insurance policy. One American firm arrived in Japan to negotiate a joint venture agreement with a contract already in hand. In the first meeting with their prospective partners, the Americans placed copies of the proposed contract in front of the astonished Japanese. The Japanese perceived the behavior of the Americans in presenting a legal contract at the beginning of the first meeting extremely rude and inept and decided it would not be wise to conduct further business with such a firm.

Infrastructure or regulations often influence the selling process and the sales team composition. Philip Morris had an army of 300 salesmen in Venezuela (due to low wages paid in that country), but only one-third were salesmen; the rest were assistants who helped with deliveries and distribution of the product. These sales assistants were provided with bikes and acted as missionary salespersons. Sunbeam overlapped its own sales force with its Peruvian sales force, but sold two different brands which increased sales and penetration. Pfizer's Swiss representatives vary their sales tasks according to how a doctor prescribes the product; two-thirds of doctors there issue prescriptions, therefore, traditional product detailing is the main assignment; the other one-third of Swiss doctors dispense the product and salespersons do both detailing and selling.

Squibb's sales force in developed countries has special training in anatomy, diseases, and pharmacology to ensure that sales forces have the appropriate technical background.[10] Electrolux sells 85 percent of its vacuum cleaners through retail dealers in industrialized countries; in developing markets, the company found a dearth of suitable outlets, especially in rural areas, so it reverted to its traditional door-to-door sales approach. Russian hospitals and clinics, nearly all state run, buy medicine from drug makers and then distribute it free to patients. Eli Lilly has little trouble convincing doctors of the efficacy of the drugs. The challenge is in coaxing bureaucrats to allocate funds to buy the medicines. Lilly employs 120 salespeople, mainly physicians themselves who have changed careers because of the professions's chronically low wages and tough work conditions in Russia. Most recruits have little selling experience and are drilled on selling practices.[11] Citicorp has captured 40 percent of Thailand's credit card market, relying chiefly on a sales force of 600 part-timers who are paid a fee for each applicant approved.[12] American International Group, Inc., the first foreign insurer in China, has 5,000 door-to-door salespeople in Shanghai alone.

Customs and manners are also important. In Brazil, it is important to dress as your customer dresses, formal or casual. In Switzerland and Germany, it is considered rude to shake hands across desks; instead, executives walk around their desks.[13] The English do not, as a rule, make deals over the phone. A proper Frenchman neither likes instant familiarity nor refers to strangers by their first names. Germans dislike overstatement and ostentatiousness. Visiting salespeople should expect to be invited to long banquets (that could begin in late morning or early evening) when selling to and negotiating with the Chinese; the expected result of these banquets is a drunk guest; otherwise, the guest is believed not to have had a good time.

Language, as in any cross-cultural situation, could provide its share of obstacles. In mainland China, the people say "no problem" frequently; this actually means there is a bit of a problem, but that it is not serious. When they say "there is a little bit of a problem," this implies that a task will not be completed at all unless special action is taken. To those in Taiwan, "no problem" means there really is no problem and "there is a bit of a problem" means just that, a small relatively insignificant problem.[14] This difference can be attributed to the Western influences over the past 40 years in Taiwan.

Title usage varies among countries. Salespersons in Germany should address their customers by title (e.g., "Herr Doktor Schmidt") even if it sounds redundant. In Italy, it is correct to use job titles, but in Switzerland, salespeople should use formal titles. In general, one should not use first names in other countries until invited. Salespeople should not, in general, treat entertainment overseas as out-of-office sales calls. In Latin America and East Asia, business dinners provide an opportunity for clients and salespeople to get to know each other. In these countries, customers prefer to do business with people they consider friends, as relationships are as important as the product. In South America, social conversation dominates the lunch, but a transaction may be discussed over coffee and dessert. Salespeople can discuss general business matters with clients in Northern Europe during lunch.

In Italy, allow plenty of time for appointments, since a customer could very likely spend several hours chatting with a salesperson. In the Middle East, one should not be too distant or aloof, as the Arabs consider the sense of touch a means of communication.

The Japanese selling process is human intensive rather than product intensive.[15] Letters are useful for follow-up communications, but personal relationships are the primary means of conducting business in Japan. Relationships can be established only through extended periods of face-to-face contact. When a personal relationship has not been established, a Japanese buyer will often express skepticism about a seller's claims. A buyer may become unfriendly and aggressively direct. The lengthy process that is typical in Japan for first-time sellers is due to this need to establish a relationship. The Western practice of monitoring calls from faraway centers and scheduling service based on a predetermined schedule for the customer's area is much too impersonal for the Japanese consumers, who prefer a local salesperson to assist them and prefer that he or she be the same one who sold them the product.

Selling in Japan is often a lengthy process with numerous repeat visits. The frequency with which a salesperson meets with the customer correlates closely with the amount of business a salesperson receives. Japanese customers often judge from the frequency of the sales calls they receive whether a company really wants to do business. When a salesperson of one company makes more frequent calls to a potential customer than the competition, he or she will be regarded as more sincere. This also means Japanese companies have to make frequent sales calls to customers for only courtesy reasons.

The Japanese salesperson's role does not stop with the purchase order. For example, a computer salesperson should be present for meetings before installation, at the installation, and even when an engineer adds a piece of hardware or software. When a change in a delivery schedule is inevitable, neither a letter nor a phone call is sufficient—a personal visit is mandated. When a Japanese company asks suppliers to do something, even if it is impossible, they will never say no. They will go through the motions and show they are making a sincere effort to meet the request, no matter how illogical or impractical.[16]

Japanese salespeople usually have poor selling skills. In Japan, the selling profession lacks respect. In the Japanese business culture, the route to the top goes through manufacturing, not marketing and sales as in many an American company. In any company, the sales division is shunned by most self-respecting salarymen. New employees are almost forced to spend time in sales divisions before moving on. Unlike the Chinese, who will spend hours bargaining and enhancing the value of their wares and managing to raise their prices slowly over time, the Japanese want to get the whole thing over with as soon as possible.

SALES MANAGEMENT

Sales management includes the recruiting, training, motivation, compensation, evaluation, budgeting, and supervision of a sales force. Being a management function, it is highly culture bound. In India, sales force management is difficult in a market fragmented by language divisions and the caste system. Swedish Match in India, faced with hundreds of dialects (including more than 50 with over one million speakers each), completely decentralized its recruitment activities to ensure not only that recruits speak the correct dialects for the area, but that they were respected members of their communities and could capitalize on personal contacts. The hiring of locals for sales management positions is more likely in countries with rich ethnic backgrounds.

Large differences in languages (and dialects), social customs, scope of personal influence, and government regulations will sometimes dictate the local hiring practices. Some countries require all sales forces be totally or partly composed of natives. In some countries such as Argentina, severe regulations regarding the firing or discharging of personnel force companies to hire expatriates or be stuck with incompetent or noncooperative nationals who cannot be discharged without a legal struggle. Brazilian law indicates that each salesperson must be assigned an exclusive territory; if a salesperson were to be reassigned, the company is liable to maintain that person's income for twelve months. In other cases, severe regulations regarding the firing of discharging of personnel force companies to hire expatriates or be very stringent with the hiring of natives. Venezuela has one of the more stringent dismissal laws: with more than three months of service in the same firm, a worker gets severance pay amounting to one month pay at the day of severance plus 15 days' pay for every month of service exceeding eight months plus an additional 15 days' pay for each year employed. Furthermore, after an employee is dismissed, the law requires that person be replaced at the same salary within 30 days.

Elsewhere, recruitment can be the major problem. In Hong Kong, Electrolux interviewed 400 applicants to find ten sales recruits; many qualified natives are leaving in fear of the mainland China takeover in 1997. In Saudi Arabia, finding qualified sales representatives is difficult because of a labor shortage and the low prestige of selling.[17] In Central and Southern Africa, MNCs have found the army was a good source of sales recruits because administrative skills, discipline, and steady work habits were stressed in military service. NCR has worked the Japanese market for over 70 years, but has succeeded in recruiting university graduates only in the past 20. In many cultures, particularly Asian, Arab, Latin, and throughout Mediterranean Europe, women are not typically hired for management level sales positions. In Japan, business relationships are typically cemented over drinking and dinner, after business hours. Japanese are typically reluctant to include a woman in their conversations. Although chauvinist and illegal according to American equal opportunity laws, the use of women salespersons in those countries could be ineffective and lead to confusing situations.

Because hiring experienced people is less common in Japan than other countries, managers must invest more in training for their sales representatives. Because most college graduates in Japan join large companies for life, employers' college recruitment practices are incredibly intense, in both time and money. Because employees are more wedded to their companies in Japan, managers reap the rewards of such human capital investments. But because dissatisfied performers tend to stay, and weak performers are not fired,[18] managers must also contend with motivating dissatisfied and unproductive workers.

In the United States, money is the prime motivator, while in Japan and the Middle East, nonmonetary factors (increased responsibilities or greater job security) are more effective motivators. The presence in Europe of high fringe benefits (70 percent of wages in France versus half that in the United States) and often almost confiscatory marginal income tax rates (60 to 90 percent) means sales commissions have much less effectiveness there. In Brazil, sales force compensation has been complicated by repeated episodes of hyperinflation.

Straight salary and bonuses comprise the usual Japanese compensation package. The motivation for getting the order is that it is the honorable thing for the employees to do; making the sale is what a salesperson owes to the company. Recognizing, rewarding, or praising employees is almost unheard of in most Japanese companies; the employees are supposed to do well. In Japan, satisfaction is often not communicated through praise, since praise carries with it the implied message that one did not really expect such good work in the first place; to praise an employee, therefore, may be considered an impolite communication. Supervision is looser in Japan than in the United States.

Motivation and evaluation differ cross-culturally as well. Written job descriptions, a key feature in American sales management, are scarcely used in Japan. Salespersons are oriented through on-the-job practice rather than job descriptions. In Japan, individual recognition of sales reps is still at odds with the team approach to business. A Japanese sales force needs direct administrative guidance in the form of morning meets to bestow a group identity. In Japan, a person who looks a subordinate in the eye is felt to be judgmental and punitive while someone who looks his superior in the eye is assumed to be hostile.

Management practices differ between cultures as well. Matsushita provides two distinct kinds of sales training: one is basic skills training and the second and more fundamental one is training in the Matsushita values. These values are continually being absorbed by the new hire. U.S. managers tend to be in closer contact with their salespeople and place greater importance on spending time in the field with salespeople, observing and discussing performance, paying attention to travel and expense accounts, evaluating sales results, and using incentive compensation than their Australian counterparts. Australians, in contrast, assign greater importance to watching credit terms and evaluating profit contribution than their American counterparts.[19]

SALES CONCLUSIONS

Today's global economy requires global sales managers, ones with an international or global perspective. Global megatrends occurring include:[20]

- globalization of markets;
- microsegmentation of markets;
- rising personal selling costs and the shift to direct marketing alternatives;
- advances in telecommunications and computer technology;
- more expert and professional buyers;
- rising customer expectations;
- influx of women and minorities into sales; and
- development of androgynous sales management.   = hermaphrodite?

To succeed internationally in sales and sales management, one should:

1. Become culturally sensitive and seek out cultural differences and the implications they may have for the sales process. A contract between Boeing and a Japanese supplier called for the delivery of fuselage panels to have a "mirror finish." Labor costs were higher than expected because the supplier polished and polished the panels to achieve what it believed to be the desired finish, a literal interpretation. All Boeing wanted was a shiny surface.
2. Research the business protocol for countries in which one plans to do business. Be respectful of local business protocol. Know when to talk business and when not to.

3. Expect a slower selling cycle.
4. One should walk a fine line between being ethnocentric (using the same sales management policy everywhere) and being totally polycentric (adopting a total "host-country" orientation in each country). The polycentric orientation, if carried to extremes, can cause the company to miss opportunities for capitalizing on economies of scale and those that can come from some degree of worldwide standardization of policies, practices, and procedures.[21]

DIRECT MARKETING

In January 1996, Dell Computer opened an Asian hub—a PC assembly plant and customer service center—in Penang, Malaysia. Concern exists about whether or not Dell's model of direct sales of personal computers that bypasses traditional retailers and distributors will work in Asia, where even corporate buyers are used to browsing showrooms for PCs and haggling in their local tongue. Dell sells direct to its customers in Australia, Japan, Hong Kong, Malaysia, New Zealand, and Singapore. Similarly, Dell is selling computers in Japan and Europe by mail and telemarketing although it was told that in every country, mail orders would not work. Dell's low price was supposedly a major hurdle; European buyers have a long-established prejudice: high price equals good quality, low price means shoddy quality. Dell sold over 35,000 PCs in Japan while its sales in Europe are ten times higher.[22]

The world's second largest direct marketing market is the UK, where 90 percent of the $6 billion in annual sales are generated by just five companies. These companies, which started after World War I to sell to the working class on credit, still cater to lower income households. British mail order has long been seen as a peculiar business, hobbled by an archaic agent system designed to provide choice, convenience, and credit to the low class. Direct mail users in Britain enjoy their shopping more than anyone else, even though they are also the busiest people. They also hunt for bargains more enthusiastically and are more likely to try new brands.

Interestingly, Hispanics are high users of direct marketing because many wish to avoid the threatening experience of the retail scene. They tend to prefer direct response television that is produced in Spanish. Many do not mind receiving calls at home but only one in five indicated the calls were in Spanish.

Major factors for success for direct marketing overseas include the standard of living, reliable postal delivery, and a stable currency. Expansion of global direct marketing has been relatively slow because it requires sophisticated national infrastructures and a social acceptance of this type of purchasing. As an example of the former, credit cards, being for the most part new, are not highly penetrated outside of the United States, thus providing another infrastructure barrier. In Northern European countries, 70 to 90 percent of letters are delivered the next day; in Italy, this is only 10 percent; in Spain, it is 40 percent. In Mexico, a major problem mailers are faced with is the lack of correct zip codes, since the majority of consumers themselves simply do not know their own code. In every European Union nation except Sweden and the Netherlands, the postal service is controlled by government monopolies. Most are fiercely protectionist and strongly resistant to change.

Threats to direct marketing include a value-added tax system that is still not uniform across Europe and data protection, since personal information collected on computer databases is the raw material for mailers, lists whose demographic information is invaluable to marketers. In the United States, sales of such lists are virtually unrestrained. Banning the sales of lists has been discussed from time to time in the European Union. Companies could use the detailed information they have already gathered to sell to their existing customers but could not go prospecting for new ones.

Direct Mail

A multiple of postal and legal restrictions continue to inhibit the growth of direct mail. In Germany, companies are not allowed to offer prospects free gifts. In most European countries, if a letter is addressed to a certain name, it is against the law for anyone else to receive it. In some countries, a company name is used at the top of the address, followed by the job title and finally, the name and postal details. In others, the name or title comes first. In Britain, the address is always placed at the bottom left of an envelope; elsewhere in Europe, it is placed on the right. Not correctly addressing a letter will result in its return. In the United States, one's mailbox is technically owned by the U.S. government and exists solely for the use of the U.S. Postal System. Elsewhere around the world, the box or slot is considered to be the property of the resident and is fair game for privately delivered solicitations. And all this is beside the fact that postage rates are much higher than in the United States.

Advertising sales letters are unlike written business communications in that the burden of interpretability (the meaning behind words) lies in the originators of the text, not the recipients. Where, in ordinary business correspondence, pragmatic understanding must be interpreted in light of the writer's language and cultural background and the location of business operation, advertising sales letters must be written in light of the reader's language and cultural background and location.[23]

Another major problem for direct mail internationally is the availability of customer lists. France and Germany have a limited range of customer lists available while markets such as those in Italy and Spain have considerable structural problems that inhibit list sales. In Japan, magazines are sold via newsstand, not subscription, so few if any subscriber lists are available. Procuring lists from Japan is difficult because the nature of Japanese culture is not to share information openly; Japanese companies are hesitant to sell Japanese lists to anyone, even to other Japanese companies. Any lists that are available are typically in Japanese characters rather than English. Lists, however, can cost three to four times those of the United States (approximately $250 per thousand in Japan compared to $90 per thousand in the United States). In addition, Japanese credit card companies charge "usury" fees as high as 12 percent of revenues for use of their lists.[24] One must also translate to Japanese as it is disrespectful to send mailings in English. It can be profitable; of the estimated $20 billion the Japanese spent via mail order in 1994, nearly $2 billion went to U.S. companies, up 30 percent from 1993.[25] Pan-Asian lists from American business publications are excellent sources since their Asian buyers must be English speaking to read the publications. An offer to an international list will tend to pull more than an equivalent U.S. list because it has not been exhausted by repeated offers and will tend to have higher response rates.

Successful campaigns can be achieved by careful attention to details. *National Geographic* magazine mails out one million marketing items per year to 167 European countries. It has 750,000 names on the database: 300,000 in the UK and 450,000 elsewhere. Marketing is conducted from the UK. Marketing communications have to be consistent across borders. Cosmetic changes are made from country to country.[26] In Novell's campaign, the consistency of message and marketing materials was essential. An integrated European campaign was launched every three to six months. The flyer was the same except for language.[27]

Many places in Europe are nearly ten years behind the United States in direct marketing volume and sophistication. Factors inhibiting growth in Europe include its cultural heritage, the multilingual nature of the continent, limited availability of lists, poor quality of those lists that do exist, higher postal costs, stricter privacy laws and restrictions, low credit card penetration, fragmented markets, few address and phone number standards, and poor delivery systems.[28]

How long direct mail has been used in a country heavily affects how well it is accepted in that nation. It has a much longer tradition in countries such as Sweden and Germany, while in the UK, direct mail has been in existence for only two decades. In the UK, the feeling is that companies use direct mail because it is cheaper than space advertising. Most British are skeptical about direct mail they receive.[29] Spanish consumers are also apprehensive about the quality and delivery of mail-order goods[30] (although the mail-order market has had remarkable growth in the past decade in Spain). Teleshopping and Ibertext are popular forms of direct marketing in Spain.

Direct mail is not as popular in Japan. Japanese marketers estimate that the use of direct marketing is between 15 and 20 years behind that of the United States. One reason for this discrepancy is that the Japanese feel printed material is too impersonal and hence, not sincere. If printed material is going to be used, Japanese prefer communications written out in longhand by someone who has fine penmanship. Japanese will often not open direct mail if their names and addresses are not attractively handwritten or beautifully printed.[31] The Japanese favor face-to-face communications, so response rates for direct mailings are half those found in the

United States. Direct mail marketing accounts for less than 1 percent of all Japanese retail sales compared with 17 or 18 percent in the United States (although growth has been 10 to 15 percent annually for direct mail sales versus 3 to 4 percent for retailing).[32]

Sophisticated direct mail techniques are less accepted and used less often. Few database companies exist and fewer still offer quality lists. However, over 4,000 direct mail marketing companies now exist in Japan and the field is expected to grow as more Japanese consumers change their lifestyles and become aware of the convenience of direct mail. The mail order business has expanded rapidly in Japan, with annual growth rates in the 1990s of over 17 percent. The average Japanese consumer receives 166 pieces of sales promotional direct mail a year versus nearly four times as many for Americans. The Japanese spend more, return less, and buy more often than Americans. According to a survey by the Japanese Direct Marketing Association, the products most successfully marketed by mail in Japan are fashion accessories (shoes and handbags); jewelry and precious metals; watches, glasses, cameras, and optical instruments; ladies' wear; and furniture and interior goods. The increase in catalog sales reflects status seeking as well as cost consciousness. L.L. Bean's international sales increased 73 percent in 1993 to over $100 million. The company has even opened two retail stores in Tokyo to help popularize its products. Catalogs and order forms in Japanese, with explanation of how to order and deal with overseas delivery, ease the difficulties of Japanese consumers who are not well versed in direct mail ordering.

Several major challenges are inhibiting the growth curve of direct mail in Japan. These include extremely high postal rates (80 yen to mail a domestic first-class letter, almost four times those found in the United States; airmail from the United States or Hong Kong to Japan is only 50 yen; a Japanese marketer could send direct-mail pieces to Japanese households from the United States cheaper than he or she could from Japan, except the Japanese government has made it illegal for Japanese companies to mail such materials into Japan from other countries), restrictive postal regulations (Japan has compartmentalized the distinctions between personalized mail and advertising; the term "business executive" or "head of household" as an addressee means the post office will treat the letter as personal mail and charge the higher postage rate), and the fact that list management is still in its infancy compared to the West (only 20 percent of all lists are computerized, and the remainder are on three-by-five cards; many are not language standardized).

Many Japanese companies are reluctant to share lists, especially with potential competitors. When lists are available and can be rented, direct mail vendors will tend to pay anywhere from $.22 to $.75 per name, three to five times as much as in the United States. Lists are often "dirty"; that is, they include a high number of incorrect, duplicate, or out-of-date addresses. Most national lists are either compiled from paid subscriber publications or based on specific types of mail-order purchasers; many, though, are compiled from government and trade association directories, which means that people on the lists are not proven responders to direct mail offers and the addresses are often not up to date. Japan does not have a standard industrial classification (SIC) system such as that of the United States or Europe, so refined segmentation by industry is difficult to find among national lists.

Procuring lists from Japanese owners is difficult, since the Japanese tend to not share information openly with strangers. Many publications are hesitant to rent their subscriber lists. Japanese consumers typically desire to meticulously inspect a product before deciding to buy it and demand a higher level of service. Nevertheless, because the Japanese receive relatively few direct mail pieces, direct mail is a unique medium. Added to the increased penetration of credit cards, this is a viable promotional tool in Japan. Shop America joined forces with 7-Eleven Japan to distribute catalogs and place orders in the convenience stores; Shop America offered high-quality brand name goods at 30 to 50 percent less than found in retail stores.

Telemarketing has become the largest direct marketing medium in the United States (2.6 percent of GDP), while considerably underutilized elsewhere in the world (1 percent of GDP in UK and Canada). Factors to be considered when assessing how a country's telecommunications network affects telemarketing include how much of the market is reachable by telephone, the availability of bulk discounted outbound and inbound long-distance services, and the rate of improvement over time. Cultural factors that influence the diffusion of telemarketing include approved methods of social interaction within a country, limited use of credit cards internationally (only 20 percent of telephone orders in France can be charged because most French do not have credit cards), and population distribution.[33]

out of date

Telemarketing is a relatively new phenomenon in Japan. The 800-number concept (dialed 0120 in Japan) was only introduced in 1986 and is expensive, with merchants charged at the same rate as for commercial calls. The toll-free service (for consumers), when first implemented was rather expensive; even with rate reductions implemented later, it is not a bargain. Telemarketing has traditionally not been well accepted in Japan, since the Japanese culture promotes privacy within the confines of one's home and therefore, Japanese tend to resent strangers calling their homes at any time.[34] It is more successful in business-to-business marketing than in consumer marketing.

Unlike Americans, many foreign nationals use telephones only for very limited and specific reasons; telephones are the last instead of first resort. In some countries, telemarketing cold calls are forbidden. Other countries have restrictive privacy and consumer credit laws. Some national telecommunication networks are government monopolies. Not unexpectedly, phone rates often are considerably higher outside the United States. Lack of a standard 800-number system also inhibits growth of international telemarketing: in Spain, it is 900; in UK, 0800; in Norway, 050; in Sweden, 020; and is 0600 in Holland. In some countries, outbound telemarketing is illegal; in Germany, outbound calls can only be made to a company's customers or to noncustomers who have requested contact. In France, telemarketing to consumers is limited by legal restrictions on list maintenance.

In the early 1980s, the French PTT (Postal, Telegraph & Telephone) created the Minitel to replace the costly publication of annual telephone directories. Millions of computers and modems were placed in private homes and businesses at no cost to the subscriber. Subscribers pay the equivalent of $.10 per minute to access the directory. Outside companies place products and service on the information for access by the subscribers. Approximately 50 percent of Minitel households use their systems for interactive transactions and approximately 15 percent of all mail-order (catalog) orders come from the Minitel system.

Door-to-door selling is popular in Japan. As many as half of the cars sold in Japan are sold by door-to-door salesmen. Toyota Motor Corporation alone has more than 100,000 door-to-door salespeople (half as many as the entire sales force in the United States for all kinds of cars).[35] Many Japanese car buyers never set foot in a dealership. Pitches are made and contracts are signed in people's living rooms. A typical Toyota salesperson has 3,000 doors in his or her turf. The salesperson's book contains notes and details on over 370 customers to whom he or she has sold cars; many are repeat buyers. Salespeople time their pitches to just before a customer's car turns three years old or every two years thereafter. (That's when the owner faces the government inspection system known as the *shaken*, which often can cost a Japanese owner thousands of dollars in repairs before the car can be certified.) These extensive face-to-face meetings establish trust long before business discussions begin. These relationships do not end with a sale; salespeople maintain constant contact with their customers. There are calls after a purchase to inquire how a car is running, handwritten greeting cards, and special invitations for low-cost oil changes, dealer events, and even driving schools in larger cities to help people obtain licenses. Most new customers are introduced by a previous buyer. Buying a new car is like joining a fraternity: once in the family, many never consider leaving. It is not unusual for a salesperson to follow a lead for a year or even longer, paying a visit to a prospective buyer's home every month before a sale is finally made. When the deal is sealed, the salesperson may invite the car buyer out to dinner and fit the car with an additional accessory as a "present." The service department does its part in keeping the customer satisfied by bringing the car into the shop for the semiannual checkups mandated by the Japanese Vehicle Code. The service department calls a customer when the maintenance is due and then sends a man around to pick up the vehicle and drive it to the shop. The vehicle is always returned washed and its interior vacuumed.

Network marketing, especially the home party approach, which involves gathering friends and relatives, is popular in Japan. Japan is the largest and most competitive market in the world for direct sellers, representing more than half of the global volume with total sales of $40 billion in 1996. Amway has had remarkable success in direct marketing in the Japanese market. It has set up its own network of warehouses and a direct sales force. Amway also set up its own distribution system, which uses independent distributors. Amway distributes over 200 consumer products, ranging from home care products to housewares to nutrition products.

However, since the Japanese rarely invite strangers to their houses, this eliminates the familiar sales plan for home distributors as is typical for Amway. So Amway's alternative successful approach was to hold sales parties in local coffee shops instead. One advantage Amway has is that the Japanese rely strongly on the recommendations and experiences of friends and relatives; word of mouth and opinion leaders aid Amway in both selling and recruiting, thus playing to its strengths. Amway relies heavily on personal relationships with friends, neighbors, and relatives; this works only when the product is of good quality and earns quick acceptance. Only good products sell because distributors will not compromise personal relationships just to sell products.

The ability to work for themselves has attracted would-be entrepreneurs and refugees from Japanese big businesses. The attraction is the ability to earn according to how you perform, not according to one's age or seniority. In contrast to the United States, where many Amway distributors are retired, the majority of Japanese distributors (2.5 million in 1994) are in their twenties and thirties. In Japan, where one's network of human contacts (*jinmyaku*) is everything, network marketing such as that used by Amway thrives. Amway's culture encourages group meetings and pep rallies, which only mesh more so with the Japanese culture. As a result of such effort and devotion, Amway sales in Japan have exceeded $1.5 billion (with double digit increases for over a decade), more than one-quarter of the company's worldwide sales are derived from Japan, nearly equaling that received in the United States (with net income approaching $200 million). Amway's direct distribution system bypasses the complex and multilayered Japanese system, another advantage well suited to success in Japan. Tupperware has also had great success in Japan in selling its products in the traditional Tupperware way. Amway has had great success in selling its concept to new markets; for instance, in the Czech republic, Amway signed up 25,000 Czechs as distributors and sold 40,000 starter kits at $83 each in its first two weeks of business in that country.[36]

The experts said that Avon would not succeed in its door-to-door sales in Mexico because the Mexican middle-class wife would be out of the home, either shopping or playing bridge. The wall around the house would keep a saleswoman from reaching the front door. When she rang the doorbell, the maid would not let her in. Avon mounted a massive advertising campaign to educate the Mexicans as to what they could expect from the visits before sending its salespeople out. Avon recruited educated, middle-class women as representatives and trained them well. They were encouraged to visit their friends. Since entering Mexico in 1990, Avon has built is sales force to 170,000 with sales of $370 million.[37]

Avon is also extremely successful in Thailand, thanks to the inherent cultural bias of "obligation to one's friends and the great difficulty of saying no when approached by someone directly." In many parts of Asia, direct selling is the ideal way since labor is plentiful and inexpensive, the cultural acceptance is there, and the marketing infrastructure is very weak. In the Far East and Southeast Asia, Avon and other direct selling representatives rely mainly on extended family kinship patterns and go-betweens in order to gain contacts. However, Avon toned down its sales presentations in Britain because British Avon representatives disliked pressuring friends to buy. Avon's Chinese ladies do not press doorbells, as the door-to-door cold-calling technique used in the United States arouses suspicion in China. Sales are made to friends, relatives, neighbors, and co-workers. Avon ladies are invited in to the communist work units (*danwei*) to give informal seminars on skin care, make-up, and grooming skills.[38] American women are big buyers of make-up; Chinese women are drawn more toward skin care products.

Acceptance of direct or network marketing varies cross-culturally. Northern Europeans are not enthusiastic about direct marketing. Laws restrict market entry and access to homes. The ideological climate is hostile since the countries tend to be more socialistic and the free enterprise spirit is not as prevalent. By way of contrast, Southern Europe, Italy, and Spain are good arenas for network marketing. Fewer worker protections and social welfare benefits exist in these countries. These areas have growing informal sectors. The family is more important and the extended family provides a fertile beginning for distributors. Mary Kay has also prospered in Russia, averaging $350 per month in a country with average incomes one-third as much. Mary Kay's Russia sales have relied on word-of-mouth advertising to develop business.

The Pacific Rim is an entirely different story. In 1985, Japan's one million distributors sold $11 billion worth of products. By 1995, direct selling in Japan had reached $30 billion. Taiwan had $1.7 billion and Korea had $1.3 billion. Malaysia and mainland China are rapidly growing markets. Amway has shifted its international focus from Europe to the Pacific Basin. Why has network marketing been so successful? Asian societies tend to be structured societies. Asians recognize status gradations in their everyday life and have multiple social institutions, from the family to the firm, built on the notion of status hierarchy. Therefore, network marketing fits Asian preconceptions about the proper ordering of social relations. Entrepreneurial spirit is strong in the area. Relationship selling is how business is done in the Far East. Extended family networks make recruiting and selling easy. In China, being an employee is considered low status; everyone wants to be his or her own boss.[39]

The concept of door-to-door selling is not equally accepted in all countries. In some cultures, making a profit from selling to a friend, colleague, or neighbors may not be socially acceptable. The ability to find suitable salespeople on a part-time basis may also be limited because of bans, legal or cultural, on women and students working part-time.

For direct mail, accurate translation and knowledge of mail patterns are necessary. This is also true for telemarketing. For either to succeed, efficient infrastructure must be available in the target market. In telemarketing and door-to-door efforts, if locals are not used, familiarity with not only the language, but the correct dialect and accepted telephone courtesy for the target market is mandatory.

Chapter 10

A Cross-Cultural View
of Channels of Distribution

A channel of distribution is the path the goods take from the manufacturer to the ultimate user. A channel provides the services needed to make a product available when it is demanded and in the quantities demanded by the customer. For business-to-business goods, the path (or channel length) is short, usually directly between manufacturer and the customer via the direct sales force of the manufacturer, or often with an industrial distributor or manufacturers' representative (agent) acting as intermediary between two endpoints. For consumer goods, channels are usually longer and typically have one or two levels of wholesalers before reaching the retailer and the final consumers.

Intermediaries perform functions that the manufacturers cannot or will not do. Their presence usually adds efficiency and effectiveness to the marketing process. These functions include: shipping, advertising and promotion, financing, buying, selling, bulk breaking, negotiation, stocking (inventory), materials handling, standardization and grading, market research, documentation, risk taking, and final assembly, if necessary. In addition, international channel members may provide the export activities such as customs and tariff documentation, insurance, and shipping. International channels of distribution must not only consider the problem of marketing within a country but between countries.

International channel alternatives are many. Distributors, agents, commission houses, import merchants, brokers, jobbers, trading companies, cooperative exporters, state trading companies, vertical marketing systems such as franchises and cooperatives, and *norazi* (black marketers such as the mafia) are among the potential intermediaries. It is not our purpose in detailing and defining each and every one or discussing advantages and disadvantages of one intermediary over another. We are interested in these only in how some intermediaries may be preferred and some ignored due to cultural reasons within a country or between countries.

In 1993, the top 100 retailers in the world represented over $1 trillion in sales. The average top 100 company operated nearly 2,000 outlets. Supermarkets, diversified companies, and department stores predominate.[1] These numbers do not include revenues from all other channel members. These numbers indicate very clearly the importance of channels of distribution in the international marketing mix.

CULTURE IN THE CHANNEL

One of the main functions of culture is division of labor among various actors within a society. Since the global environment is characterized by diverse and deep-rooted cultural norms and values, the nature of this division of labor across cultures should be considerably different. Since channels of distribution are primarily designed to facilitate division of labor, channel relationships should therefore reflect the underlying cultural values of systems.[2] An example of this culturally determined difference in distribution channels can be seen in a survey of dealers in India and the United States. Compared to the American environment, the Indian environment was characterized by greater unidirectional communication from suppliers to dealers, lower communication frequency, greater use of formal communication modes, and greater supplier use of direct influence strategies.[3]

Distribution in underdeveloped countries is characterized by small intermediaries. Distribution is slow and inefficient in underdeveloped countries because the population is widely scattered, inventories are low, costs of capital are high, middlemen are few, and margins are high. Developing countries are typically sellers' markets where the balance of power within the channel tilts toward the supplier (manufacturer). Coupled with the fact that the typical dealer (retailer) in developing countries such as India is small and is attributed a relatively lower social status, this leads to asymmetrical power relationships and communication flows that are mostly unidirectional from suppliers to dealers. In such economies, the suppliers are typically provided with a superior position as the providers in an undersupplied economy.

The attitude toward the middlemen in underdeveloped countries is generally negative. This feeling exists because the people tend to emphasize production and consider the intermediary unproductive. The result is often that this function is done on the side or secretly, which makes distribution overly difficult. In addition, since intermediaries in such undeveloped markets are typically not considered productive by the locals, few locals act as intermediaries; the vacuum is usually filled by foreigners. Middleman minorities (e.g., Jews, Chinese, Lebanese, Indians, Ibos of Nigeria) perform these locally neglected intermediary functions, such as lending money and keeping retail shops, that increase the efficiency and hence, the wealth of their new countries. The belief that middlemen are useless parasites is overturned when governments have expelled some groups en masse[4]—only after prices and interest rates have risen in the wake of such actions, and in some cases, the economy in general has collapsed, it then becomes clear just what and how much middlemen contribute to a nation's economic well-being.

In Asia and Africa, these foreign middleman typically were Indian or Chinese. For former colonial countries, individual mother countries controlled the intermediaries. Many links still exist today to companies of the former colonial power. The end result is that for undeveloped countries, intermediaries are often perceived to be gougers and cheaters rather than mechanisms for an efficient economy.

This view of the middleman as parasitic in nature can be ascribed as a Marxist view of distribution channels which views distribution as a social waste because distribution does not add value to products. It is further perceived that wholesalers and retailers create anarchy by constantly fighting for profits; therefore, to create order and reduce anarchy, the State should centralize the apparatus for distribution. Soviet cooperatives supplied and operated outlets primarily in the rural areas while the State did likewise in the urban areas. Retailers were given geographical monopolies and were generally specialized according to categories.[5]

Retailers in underdeveloped countries are small and number in the thousands; many carry few lines of goods, serving few customers.

The level of services that retailers provide varies according to the retailer's size. Large retailers generally carry inventory, render financial help, display and promote merchandise, and furnish market information. On the other hand, smaller retailers often depend entirely on a manufacturer or wholesaler. They carry limited number and lines of product and expect vendors to provide credit. Promotion and display is handled by wholesalers. The typical retail establishment in underdeveloped countries is a small, family-owned business that specializes in a narrow line of products. In these cultures, the weekly market continues to be an important source of goods. As economies develop, retailers tend to increase in size, widen their assortments, offer less personal service, and segment their markets.

As economies develop, channels shorten and intermediaries become more skilled and larger. Each channel member tends to be able to cover a larger geographical area since with a well-developed infrastructure, the physical movement of goods is facilitated and communications infrastructure exists. With a well-developed capital market, channel members are able to secure more financial resources.

Nonetheless, inefficient channels are not necessarily restricted to developing or underdeveloped economies. Distribution in Japan is typically complex, multilayered, inefficient, and highly unique. The field of distributive trades may still be considered as a "dark continent in the economy in Japan."[6] While the United States needs two people to build a car and one to sell it, Japan requires one person to build the car and two to sell it. The average retail price of a car in the United States is 1.7 times the factory invoice price; in Japan, it is an incredible three times the factory price. It costs two to three times as much to sell a car in Japan as it does in Europe or the United States. An extremely efficient manufacturing industry shields the gross inefficiency of the distribution system and the agricultural and service sectors. In reality, modern Japan is an industrial power only in mass-produced products such as automobiles and consumer electronics.

Japan has more wholesalers and retailers per capita than any other advanced industrial nation.[7] The per capita number of wholesalers and retailers are twice that found in the United States. Half of the wholesalers employ fewer than five persons; only 5 percent have 30 or more employees. The ratio of wholesale to retail sales in

Japan is four to one, three times higher than that found in the United States. Japanese wholesalers sell their goods to other wholesalers twice as frequently as do their Western counterparts. Japan has over 30 times the number of food wholesalers as does the United States.[8] A product ends up in a consumer's hands only after it has passed through a distribution chain consisting of at least two (and sometimes as many as five) layers of wholesalers before landing on a retailer's shelf. Prices escalate rapidly as each intermediary takes its own cut. Apples from the United States move through the hands of more than a dozen middlemen in less than a day; starting at $.25 at the dock, each apple eventually costs Japanese consumers nearly $4.

Japan has one million bars and restaurants, giving it three times the per capita number of those in the United States. Retail firms are typically small (three employees on average, with sales less than half of the U. S. average). Most are independent operations that need frequent deliveries. Campbell Japan Inc.'s typical delivery of soup to a retailer in Japan is six cans; Campbell's average shipment to wholesalers in the United States is three to twenty-five cases, each case containing twenty-four cans. So it is not surprising that soup in Tokyo costs four to five times that found in New York. Many food superstores have twice the number of salespeople as found in typical American stores, yet the American stores have five to ten times the sales of the typical Japanese store.[9]

The importance of distribution even in a closed society can be seen in the example of Korea. Kodak Film has become Korea's most popular brand of color film through its link with the Doosan Group, while Coca-Cola, not being allowed to participate in the distribution business, assisted its bottlers in marketing, promoting, and selling its products by training its sales agents, and even providing marketing kits for the retail outlets.[10]

CULTURAL INFLUENCES ON DISTRIBUTION CHANNELS

Intermediaries differ considerably on a global basis. Hong Kong supermarkets, compared to those in the United States, carry a higher proportion of fresh goods, are smaller, sell smaller quantities per customer, and are located more closely to each other. The Japanese emphasize the freshness and quality of produce; Lawson, a leading convenience store, has food delivered three times daily—midnight, before noon, and in the early evening. Shoppers visit stores frequently for small quantities rather than buying in bulk.[11] Germany and the UK have 160 inhabitants per retailer, compared to Greece and Italy with 64 to 67 inhabitants per retailer. The number of retail establishments continues to decline, more so in Northern Europe. Northern Europe has a greater concentration of large retail establishments than found in Southern Europe.

Italian distribution is characterized by a very fragmented retail and wholesale structure. In the Netherlands, buyers' cooperatives deal directly with manufacturers. In Germany, mail-order sales are important; it is not so in Portugal. In Norway, regional distributors predominate. Consumer cooperatives have traditionally been popular in Europe; they control almost one quarter of food sales in Switzerland and claim one-third of Swiss households as members. Over 80 percent of Kenya's retail and wholesale businesses are controlled by Asians. Chinese dominate in the Philippines, Indonesia, and Malaysia. Finland has fewer stores per capita because general line retailers predominate. In Finland, four wholesaling houses handle the major portions of all trade; one such wholesaler, Kesko, controls over 20 percent of the market.

Channels must differ by country and culture since where consumers buy certain goods also differs country by country. In Germany, contact lens solution is only found in stores that sell eyeglasses, while in France, it is found in most drugstores as well; magazines can be found in retail stores in the United States while news agents are the exclusive channel for magazines in the UK. Baby foods are predominantly distributed through pharmacies in Italy, while Germans can buy them in grocery stores.

Sometimes what works in the United States does not work elsewhere in the world; the converse is also true. Although the number of Benetton stores worldwide reached 7,000 in the early 1990s, the number of U.S. stores dropped below 400, half of the total number of U.S. stores five years previously. The reason: Benetton's controversial ads (AIDS, rainbow condoms, nuns kissing priests) may have been acceptable in liberal Europe, but backfired in more conservative American locales.[12] Hypermarkets, a French idea successful since the late 1960s, are three times the size of typical discount stores; selling everything from groceries to durables, they proved to be a major flop in the United States. Wal-Mart (Hypermart USA), Super-Value, and Kmart (American Fare) all opened outlets which were the size of several football fields and then just as quickly closed them down. The stores were simply too big: aisle after aisle had shelves that rose several stories high. To have been successful, a store had to draw four times as many shoppers as would have a normal discount store at double the average transaction.[13]

Wal-Mart Value Club shoppers in Hong Kong seem to be voting for better locations, smaller product sizes, and products more familiar to Chinese households by spending fewer dollars and visiting the stores less often than forecasted. One reason is that Hong Kong customers seem to place a premium on convenience, quality service, and store values. This, along with Hong Kong's small living quarters, limited number of parking spaces, relatively few automobiles, and traffic congestion, implies that the fundamental nature of warehouse clubs may be incompatible with Hong Kong.[14] Value Club outlets are located away from the public transportation backbone, thus requiring extra time in taxis or buses; the lower prices at the store may be offset by higher transportation costs. The traditional practice of Chinese wives is to shop every day and the most convenient places for them to shop are stores on the way home from work or near their apartment complexes. Lack of familiarity of products also hurts Value Club. Lack of space in living quarters means gallon jugs are not preferred, smaller containers must be available to handle and store.

A fragmented wholesaling system in Mexico means higher transactions cost and inefficiency. Warehouse clubs which reject credit cards in the United States have found that they cannot maintain that policy in Mexico because so many Mexicans use credit cards to manage their cash flow on basic purchases. With the advent of NAFTA, Mexico appeared to be the shining star for retailers. At one time, Wal-Mart planned to open (with CITRA) five warehouse clubs called Club Aurrera. Price Co. was teaming up with retailer Commercial Mexicana to launch two new warehouse clubs outside of Mexico City. Sears, in Mexico since 1945, planned to spend $150 million opening new stores and malls in Mexico as well as renovating its old stores. McDonald's planned to spend $500 million to open 250 new restaurants by the year 2000. The peso devaluation in December 1994 sprinkled a huge dose of reality on these plans and many retailers have scaled back or put on hold their plans until the Mexican economic situation clears up.

Wal-Mart attempted to enter Mexico in a large fashion only to find its American ways do not always work there. Mexicans tend to shop as families as part of a weekend's entertainment, necessitating wider aisles in stores. Retailers must place their stores close to residential areas since car ownership is not as high in Mexico as it is in the United States. In a grocery's food section, Mexicans prefer produce and meat displayed as they are in a local market. Mexican consumers who see prepackaged food do not think it is fresh.[15] Wal-Mart is competing for the 8 of Mexico's 82 million people who are middle class or above. The Wal-Mart in Monterey has prices 12 to 20 percent more than its Laredo store 150 miles to the north: transportation costs and duties are to blame. Its Mexico City stores are accused of gouging the customer.

Most Mexicans buy their eggs, produce, and packaged foods in different stores, visiting three or more shops in their daily or twice-daily trips to the store. They most often visit self-service supermarkets for highly packaged and processed products. For fresh items, shoppers tend to frequent corner stores and open markets. Speciality stores are for bread, red meat, and chicken. The most important factors for Mexican shoppers when selecting a food store are good quality, low prices, personal safety, a clean shop, customer service, and good variety.[16] Fewer than one in seven had changed the food store where they shop the most. Mexicans reported high levels of satisfaction and rated the stores excellent. The Mexican *mercado*, the traditional marketplace, is making a comeback and breaking even with supermarkets and hypermarkets. The Nave Mayor mercado in Mexico City has 100 acres of vegetables, all under one single roof. Mexican homemakers prefer the mercado, to go to a favorite merchant whom they know (not an impersonal supermarket), even though the merchant may not have the best produce, because he or she is their friend.

Wal-Mart entered Brazil and has also taken a humbling performance. It started operations in 1995 boldly predicting a retailing revolution. Wal-Mart was very arrogant to think that just by cutting prices, it was going to immediately eliminate retailers who have serviced Brazil for many decades. Typical Brazilian shoppers have long-established relationships with their Brazilian retailers that Wal-Mart cannot match.[17]

The Japanese distribution system stems from the early seventeenth century, when cottage industries and a burgeoning urban population spawned a merchant class. During Japan's feudal period, the country consisted of many small, largely self-contained provinces, each of which developed its own distribution system. Manufacturers who wished to penetrate these regions successfully needed to develop relationships with wholesalers in each area; 500 such regions existed in Japan at that time.[18] As it is difficult for many manufacturers to sell in volume directly to the retailer or the end user, a large network of wholesalers is usually required. This system endures because most Japanese companies typically operate with little equity capital and much debt. Manufacturers supply goods to wholesalers in return for promissory notes with terms ranging up to six months or more. Strong personal relationships between channel members are the norm. Channel members routinely pool and share information. This behavior has its roots in traditional village life where planting, irrigating, and harvesting rice are activities that have to be shared to succeed.

The Japanese distribution system exists to serve social as well as economic purposes, and the social or societal goal sometimes overshadows economic logic. Channel members are not altogether different from family members, with all levels and members tightly interlocked by tradition as much as by emotion. It is a traumatic and sometimes tragic decision if channel members have to be dropped; such members may be unable to bear the social consequence of losing face and pride. Because of these implications, small or inefficient channel members are often retained and tolerated.

With no social welfare system comparable to Social Security or unemployment compensation found in the United States, the Japanese distribution system acts as an employment buffer by maintaining employment and income flows, acting as a social welfare security net. Most Japanese retire at age 55 with a lump sum pension (of up to three years' salary), but live to well past 70. Those who cannot find a part-time job with one of their former employer's subsidiaries or suppliers and who do not have sufficient funds to live out their lives—that is to say most retirees—often invest their severance pay in small retailers or wholesalers to provide steady income during their retirement. It is a flexible, make-work device, acting as a buffer to absorb excess workers, especially those of retirement age and those who cannot find other work during economic downturns.

Proctor & Gamble worked within this traditional system. In Japan, P&G's marketing task was to convince Japanese mothers (and their influential mothers-in-law) that they are not lazy or uncaring if they use disposable diapers. P&G entered the Japanese market for disposable diapers by giving away millions of samples to consumers. This not only provided consumers with a free taste of the product but also established *amae* (obligatory) relationships throughout the distribution channel. Wholesalers and retailers had to return the favor, which they did by setting up special displays showcasing the P&G product in supermarkets, department stores, and family shops.

By way of contrast, Mattel bucked the system. After Mattel decided to sell its toys in Japan as it sells them in the rest of the world, it decided to sell the same ones rather than specially designed versions. Mattel bypassed the wholesalers and linked up with 1,400 mass-merchandise superstores, Western-style shopping malls.[19] (Note: many Japanese girls thought Barbies belonged on display, like traditional Japanese decorative dolls; as a result, they purchased fewer accessories for their dolls.)

Matsushita, part of the system, sells through 56,000 retail outlets, half of which sell only Matsushita products and are, therefore, solely dependent on Matsushita. If Matsushita products fall behind those of Sony, the associated retailers suffer. This exclusivity puts much pressure on manufacturers to innovate and to match competitors' innovations. It also provides the manufacturers with a built-in base of customers and a firm starting point for any products it manufacturers. Manufacturers are increasingly at war with independent discount retailers who disrupt the manufacturers' price structure and other channels. Matsushita is restructuring its rebate system, which used to reward stores based on the percentage of Matsushita brand products in its inventories. The company will now base its rebate on the stores' actual sales of Matsushita goods. The National stores, named after Matsushita's brand of household electronics sold in Japan, have played an important role in making Matsushita Japan's largest consumer electronics company. These stores account for as much as 60 percent of Matsushita sales in Japan.

Global opportunities for retailers are a dicey proposition. The critical question for a would-be international retailer is: "What advantages do we have relative to local competition?"[20] The objective answer oftentimes is no. In such cases, there is no reason to expect profitable operations to develop from such ventures. However, retailers can offer selection and setting. JC Penney is expanding internationally after its research indicated that many foreign retailers often lack marketing sophistication in their displaying of products, optimizing customer traffic, and grouping products—areas in which JC Penney has comparative strengths.[21]

FRANCHISING

Franchising is growing in popularity in every corner of the globe; much of its success is attributed to the 94 percent success rate it has achieved in the United States. However, a mere 10 percent of U.S. franchisers have entered markets outside of North America. In 1990, 350 franchising companies operated more than 31,000 outlets outside of the United States. However, the International Franchise Association estimates that before the end of the decade, more than half of U.S. franchise systems will be foreign bound. International franchising requires only about one-tenth as much capital as does traditional expansion. Franchisers often prefer English-speaking countries, but Japan and Mexico are also high on many lists.

McDonald's put its first European fast-food outlet in a suburb of Amsterdam, thinking it would be just like a suburb in Chicago (KFC Japan did likewise with its first outlets in Tokyo); in both cases, the companies found that most Europeans and Japanese live in central cities and are less mobile than the average American. Central city locations were more efficient, productive, and profitable. When McDonald's chose a French partner, it did so after extensive review and reference checking. However, initial inspections of the French restaurant alarmed the American staff. Hygiene habits were observed that were considered unacceptable in its U.S.

outlets; the French are less concerned about cleanliness than are American attitudes at home. These habits were not viewed negatively by the French partner or by most of the French customers. The major problem was that many of the outlets' customers were American tourists expecting American standards.[22] Other franchises have adapted well to foreign cultures. Big Boy serves no pork in Saudi Arabia (turkey is used for its Slim Jim sandwiches), male waiters are substituted for waitresses, and separate seating areas are provided for men, for families, and for women and children.

Both KFC's Japanese partner (Mitsubishi) and McDonald's Japanese partner were the most critical element in their success in Japan. Chinese and Japanese insist upon social relationship. They favor nonadversarial, nonlegalistic mediation and compromise. The strategic alliance is more interested in long-range goals. An emphasis on reciprocity in social and business relationships exists. Franchising seems to fit well with the existing structure of most Asian businesses; it is an ideal form of family-run business. Long-standing Asian traditions such as master-apprentice are compatible with the franchisor-franchisee relationship.[23] Other Asian qualities such as work ethic, loyalty to the organization, and attraction to Western products suggest the success of the franchise concept in Asia. Mister Donut found success in Japan when it decided to target its marketing at singles looking for a wholesome alternative to the usual bar scene.

The Chinese market is ready for fast food and hotel franchises. Franchises in China should remember that the country has ten provinces, each of which requires a separate deal, including differences in joint venture partners and restrictions.[24] Inconsistent government policies, fluctuation in currency exchange, inadequate intellectual property rights protection, high inflation rates, high operating costs, and a complicated taxation system provide major obstacles for operating in China.[25]

CULTURAL RATIONALE
FOR REGULATORY RESTRICTIONS

Although regulations and nontariff barriers are not culture bound per se, culture and the norms within a culture certainly affect the regulations and legal standards within a country. If the regulations were not acceptable to the country's dominant culture, they would not stay on the books for long. Therefore, by gazing at the regulatory restrictions that affect international channels of distribution, we are also examining culture. Europe and Japan, even though industrialized and developed, offer a variety of interesting and restrictive practices within the distribution network. Sweden, for example, has its town planners decide on the locations of retail outlets, so that thinly populated areas, as well as elderly and handicapped customers, will be served. Many European countries protected owners of small shops by regulating the placement and types of new stores that could enter the market.

In Germany, local authorities can and do bar new stores if they believe existing ones will suffer; at best, it takes about five years for a business to get authorization. If a community opposes a store, there is no chance for approval. Mr. Max has spent three years persuading more than 20 farmers to sell their land and petition the government to rezone it for commercial use. If successful, next comes at least 18 months of haggling with local merchants who legally can demand concessions when new stores open nearby. Mr. Max expects to open its store in 1997, but will almost certainly will shrink the store's planned size at least 20 percent and pay inflated membership fees to a local trade association.[26]

Germany has traditionally limited store hours and competition. Stores were allowed to be open only 68½ hours a week and had to close at 6:30 p.m. on weekdays and at 2 p.m. on Saturdays; Sunday shopping was forbidden. In July 1996, a new law was passed (which took effect on November 1, 1996) that lets stores stay open until 8 p.m. on weekdays and 4 p.m. on Saturday. Bakeries can sell fresh bread on Sunday mornings, though other stores must remain closed. The old law banning commercial baking on Sunday dated from 1915, when bread sales were limited because of grain shortages during World War I. To cope with the old law, many Germans flocked to gas stations and train stations, which exploited a loophole in Germany's dense web of trade rules to sell food and alcohol outside normal store hours—at premium prices. Still, German stores can hold full-scale sales only twice a year, usually in January and late July; even then, they cannot discount food. German clerks earn the equivalent of $16 per hour, get six weeks of vacation, and are unionized. Heavy severance pay is required if a store is closed.

In Italy, small mom-and-pop stores still dominate the retail grocery industry with an average of approximately 30 families supporting the typical grocery outlet. Italians' strong, traditional sense of community and neighborhood, coupled with laws that strongly protected small stores and made supermarket expansion a difficult and time-consuming process, explain this phenomenon. Italy's stores typically take a two-hour lunch break and close down operations during lunch. In Italy, retail operations are chaotic. Rules not only vary according to store type and season, but also from city to city. Some food stores can only sell cooked food on Thursday afternoons. Some apparel stores are closed on Monday mornings while others close on Saturday afternoon.[27] In France, medicines must be sold through pharmacies; the Lang Law limits book discounting to only 5 percent.

British store owners are finally able to open their doors on Sundays. However, the new law also indicates large fines if large stores stay open for more than six continuous hours between 10 a.m. and 6 p.m. Before, it was legal to buy a newspaper on Sunday but not a book. It was also legal to shop for fresh vegetables and fruits but not the same foods in cans or bottles. Oftentimes, shops close for one afternoon a week.[28] The British, like many other Europeans, like the modern convenience of larger supermarkets, but miss the social relationships they have established over decades with their local shopowners, social practices the impersonal supermarkets are not prepared to handle. Some even have scheduled buying practices to formalize the daily shopping social.

In Japan, resistance to large competitors by small mom-and-pop stores, called "papas-mamas," can be extreme. A construction worker building a chain store in Tokyo was beaten by irate small shopowners. Gangs of other small shopowners repeatedly stormed the store screaming at employees and intimidating customers. Many cities enforced the former Large-Scale Retail Store (LRS) guidelines, which required a national retailer to get approval from all existing shopkeepers within a third of a mile before opening a store; councils of consumers, academics, and representatives of small and medium-sized stores and local department stores operate under the aegis of the local chambers of commerce to evaluate all plans for new stores. The national law decreed that no retailer could open a store larger than 1,500 square meters without having such approvals. Seventy-one licenses were needed before such a store could begin operations. As a result, Japan only had one shopping center per 100,000 residents, one-tenth of the per capita rate in the United States. MITI, which administered the LRS law, took from eight to ten years to approve a store; consequently, only about 30 large stores opened each year in Japan at half the size requested. In order to circumvent the law, stores were opened with slightly less than 1,500 square meters of selling space; chains would form groups of companies that would purchase a building and open "different" stores on each floor, with each floor being slightly under the space limit.

Mr. Max can stay open until 8 p.m. in Japan, but is required to close for 24 days of holiday a year. It cannot give discount coupons (for fear of violating laws designed to protect consumers from confusion) and cannot discount copyrighted products such as CDs, books, or magazines. Mr. Max pays its predominately part-time employees lower hourly rates in Japan, while its full-time employees start at the same salary as a store manager.[29] Small enterprises do not have to keep accounts of their transactions. Japanese tax regulations favor small enterprises. Government facilitates the continuation of family stores because residential taxes are lower if one operates a business at home. The government also encourages small enterprises to continue business: Legacy duties are considerably lower for such continuation.

Renting practices also favor the continuation of operating a smaller store. Renting a site in Japan involves the payment of large sums of key money (up-front payments of as much as a month's rent or more to a landlord in appreciation of his/her renting the property to the tenant; this is in addition to any deposits required). The key money is an assurance of a long-lasting and close relationship between landlord and tenant. Rents increase only by a small amount as long as the same tenant is renting the place, a practice that thus favors already established retailers, inhibits new retailers, obstructs the intentions of retailers to enlarge their stores, and almost forbids established retailers from moving. Government subsidizes and facilitates the modernization of stores of small- and medium-sized retailers and shopping street associations, the *shotengai.*

International retailing groups are marching into China, unwilling to be left out of the huge market. Problems include securing favorable locations at reasonable prices. Rents in Shanghai are equivalent to those found in Hong Kong, although both cities have incomparable income levels. Every outlet has to pay tax on sales revenue through the local taxation bureau. Joint ventures must be set up with each company that owns a location; Jeans West has 16 locations and 16 joint ventures.[30]

Developing countries often discriminate against franchising because it is viewed as a marketing system rather than as an economic contribution to the country. Many Asian countries view franchise agreements (particularly trademarks licensing) as instruments of exploitation. It is argued that trademarks cause prices to rise without a corresponding increase in the quality of the product and/or service. These countries fear that persuasive advertising will lead to resource misallocation and ultimately to an adverse balance of payments.

An often overlooked but critical factor is termination rights of the intermediary in another country. In the United States, termination for nonperformance is a relatively simple and accepted practice. In other cultures, termination can be a costly and lengthy process. In Honduras, the termination of an agent can cost a company up to five times its annual gross profits, plus the value of the agent's investment, plus additional payments. In Belgium, termination compensation includes the value of goodwill plus expenses for discharged employees; the minimum termination notice is three months.

CONCLUSIONS

The four main variables which affect the international marketer's choice of distribution channel are (1) availability of intermediaries, (2) the cost of their services, (3) the functions and effectiveness in which they are preformed, and (4) the extent of control the manufacturer can exert.

The increasingly developing world economy means that channels and intermediaries must in turn modernize and mature. The number of stores (are) shrinking and the size of the survivors is increasing. Japanese toy manufacturers have traditionally sold through the convoluted, multitiered distribution system of Japan and initially refused to sell to Toys "R" Us. Toys "R" Us retained its marketing strategy of signing low-cost direct supply contracts with manufacturers who also provided promotional funds. Toys "R" Us, by buying direct from manufacturers, eliminated the multiple layers of wholesalers which was so prevalent in Japan. Toys "R" Us has been in Japan only since 1992. By 1994, it had opened 16 superstores; by the end of 1996, the number of stores opened had increased to 35. Whereas a typical American outlet has $10 million in sales a year, Japanese stores average $15 to $20 million each. With almost 4 percent of the Japanese market, it is projected to increase its share to 10 percent by 1996.[31]

Despite earlier Japanese prophecies of failure, its stores have been so popular that nearby department stores are feeling threatened and are upset. Some of the local stores in Osaka and Tokyo have responded by discounting toy prices by as much as 30 percent. The Toys "R" Us store in Niigata has 5,020 square meters of sales space—almost half the combined size of the city's 63 other toy stores. In 1988, these stores had combined annual sales of $31 million; Toys "R" Us surpassed that amount by itself during the first year of operation. The typical Japanese toy store tends to stock between 1,000 and 2,000 different items, compared to between 8,000 and 15,000 stocked by Toys "R" Us. Initially, few Japanese toy companies were willing to risk offending wholesalers by supplying merchandise directly to Toys "R" Us. It has now become too successful to ignore. At first, faced with opposition from local retailers, landlords were reluctant to lease locations. But as it became apparent that the stores were drawing large crowds, tunes changed and landlords now seek it out. Toys "R" Us is a harbinger of the future for the Japanese distribution system.

Japanese retailers also are undergoing radical changes that reflect changes occurring in many developing countries. The retail trade has been shrinking. Although the number of stores is declining in most sectors, this overall trend is almost offset by growth in the number of large, general merchandise stores and marked growth in certain sectors, notably women's and children's clothing stores, motor vehicle dealers, and secondhand stores. There were 1.6 million retail outlets in 1994, down from 1.72 million in 1990, and MITI forecasts the number will shrink by over 20 percent to 1.2 million by the end of the century. The Distribution Policy Institute in Tokyo estimates that 400,000 retail outlets will disappear by the year 2000, with the majority coming from the independent retail sector. By some estimates, two-thirds of all retail stores in Japan could be eliminated without lowering output, yielding great increases in productivity. It is estimated that the effect of national supermarkets and discount stores will result in retail prices dropping 2 percent annually until 2000. In wholesaling, as few as one-tenth of the number of existing Japanese companies could handle the current wholesale distribution volume in Japan without any loss of output.

Channels chosen must take into account the country and culture so as to maintain acceptability and credibility within the target market.[32] Traditional affluent European markets are too saturated for U.S. retailers to have much chance of success. There is little room for firms that are insensitive to local cultures, that lack a differential advantage, or enter the market without a sound strategy. Mass retailing concepts are much less likely to succeed. Marketing and retailing know-how of leading U.S. retailers provide a sustainable competitive advantage because consumer research, global sourcing, and automated distribution are difficult and expensive to imitate in Europe. These practices are still in their infancy in Europe, and information technology is unmatched by European retailers. U.S. retailers are particularly strong in customer service, and this expertise can be a distinct advantage in Europe, where tradition of consumer orientation lags significantly behind that of the United States.[33]

Global companies must trust intermediaries for operating expertise in local markets. Global intermediaries offer these advantages:

- Cost savings from global intermediaries can be substantial.
- Familiarity with the native language.
- Assist with culture-related idiosyncrasies of operating in a given environment.
- Assist in import/export documentation, custom clearances, and international banking requirements.
- Offer more consistency and continuity of call coverage.

Chapter 11

Pricing

Pricing is affected by factors such as cost differentials, demand conditions, and national laws. Pricing can be set by any number of techniques including cost (computing all relevant costs and than adding a desired profit markup to arrive at the final price), market (set the price at the market level or at par with competitors), demand-based (penetration or skimming techniques), or profit (setting the price to allow a predetermined level of profit). Each technique has its advantages and disadvantages. Each culture has its own preference on pricing strategies and of which techniques to use. The final determinant of price may be irrelevant to costs; image and quality may become the primary determinants (as in many cultures, price and perceived quality are directly related). For instance, a BMW may have a comparable cost as an Oldsmobile, but to price it likewise would cause BMW to lose much of its image quality.

Two major pricing tasks face the international marketer: pricing for export and pricing for the foreign market. Export pricing involves a marketer in a firm's home market, setting the price that will be paid by an intermediary in the foreign market, cross-border pricing. Foreign market pricing involves setting the price that will be paid by local buyers within the foreign market. The pricing role is determined by the emphasis placed on price competition in the total marketing mix. Traditionally, U.S. companies have relied more on nonprice competition than on pricing. U.S. companies generally avoid price competition in the European Union and often went after competitive leverage through promotional and product differentiation. During the 1980s and 1990s, price competition has been stressed more than before.

Price is also related to value; the price that a customer may be willing to pay depends on its perceived and actual values received. These customer values are often related to cultural mores. The price set for a particular country must be appropriate to the value delivered in that market if a company wishes to avoid over- or underpricing its product. The value of goods imported from a Western company is often perceived to be much higher than those made in a developing country. Indians and Russians perceive imported products as being superior to those manufactured locally and thus, many Western brands sell at an inflated price in those two countries. This price-quality value relationship can be seen in the country-of-origin effect, whereas premiums are paid for goods produced in some countries, but not for those manufactured elsewhere. An American product in Europe may be perceived as equivalent to local products and thus must be priced similarly; in developing countries, it could be per-ceived as a premium product with higher quality and could therefore demand a higher price. In addition, the level of consumer education and sophistication makes a significant difference in price setting. Shoppers in markets that are not familiar with or do not have dis-count stores may not have formed the habit of waiting for sales when making large purchases. Consumers may not have developed the habit or ability of obtaining information about competing brands to assist them in evaluating and choosing one brand over another.

A preference for many multinationals is the concept of standard-ization. In setting a worldwide standard price, a firm establishes a uniform price for its products all around the world. Although ele-gant in theory, the concept breaks down in practice. Marketers generally agree that price is probably the marketing mix element which is most difficult to standardize because of country-to-country differences.[1] The single uniform price may be too high for consum-ers in less developed countries. Masterfoods introduced several different brands of dog food in Russia, a country with little previous familiarity with packaged pet foods. Seeing a market potential among consumers who often pamper their pets by preparing a meal for them, Masterfoods priced its dog food at a premium; at the set price it exceeds the Russian average monthly salary.

The multinational company has a dilemma in the use of standard-ized pricing: if it prices too low, it cannot earn a profit in the industrialized, higher cost portion of the world; if it is priced too high, it prices itself out of the market for the developing and undeveloped markets. As a result, standardized price is seldom used. Marketers realize that demand elasticities differ between markets and thus, different prices can be charged for different markets. (Note: such behavior can lead to parallel imports between two differently priced markets or even to claims of dumping.) Corporate objectives could also vary between countries and cultures: entry into one country could be a long-term endeavor and hence, penetration, or at the very least, market prices would be charged. If entry into a foreign country is perceived to be short ranged and taking advantage of a momentary vacuum, premium prices through skimming could be charged.

Even after the benefits of economic union in Europe after the 1992 mandate, prices in Europe still vary significantly. Enormous price differentials exist between European countries. As a result of devaluations, some car models cost 30 to 40 percent more in Germany than in Italy. Some car dealers in Europe—especially in Germany—specialize in "Eurocars," their name for gray market imports from other European countries. A car buyer can order a car from a catalog for delivery in about three weeks; a buyer's average savings are approximately 12 to 20 percent of the German authorized dealer prices.

For identical consumer products, prices can typically deviate 30 to 150 percent. The biggest price differences found by Nielsen in the 45 products that it frequently surveys amount to 100 percent between the cheapest and dearest countries. In two cases, Kellogg's cornflakes and Palmolive hand wash liquid, the differences were much higher.[2] These variations consider differing value-added tax rates, sales volumes, inflation, and exchange rates. These differentials are rooted in consumer behavior, distribution systems, market positions, and tax systems.

Cross-border shopping and parallel import (grey markets—products sold through unauthorized channels) flows result from such price differentials. Japanese can buy cameras from catalog retailers and have them shipped to Japan for a price below that charged at a corner store. Kodak prices its film higher in Japan than in other parts of Asia; arbitrage merchants buy Kodak film in Korea and resell it in Japan for less than the authorized Japanese Kodak distributors sell it for. Coca-Cola imported from the United States sells for 27 percent less than Coke's own Japanese product.[3] A Japanese subsidiary of a prestigious high-priced liquor company complained to its corporate headquarters about the substantial quantities of the product that had entered Japan through the gray market, which were cannibalizing products sold through authorized dealers and threatening the high-prestige image of the product in Japan.[4]

Prices are sometimes affected by factors outside a company's control. Price escalation is a common phenomenon that is caused by the extra costs involved in functions involved in export-related activities that are not found domestically (e.g., insurance, tariffs and customs duties, overseas shipping, political risk insurance, and extra distribution channels). These factors can double or triple the domestic price of an item. This often requires changes in the promotional strategy from a regular to a premium product. Currency fluctuations can also have similar effects.

A joint U.S.-Japanese price study of 112 products sold in Japan released in May 1991 found that prices of comparable products were on average 37 percent more expensive in Japan than in the United States; of the 40 products in the survey made in Japan, 12 were more expensive in Japan, including a bottle of sake that was 44 percent more expensive than in the United States. Nineteen of 20 products surveyed were also more expensive in Japan than in Europe. Prices of most consumer products are two to three times the prices found in the United States.[5] As a result, Japanese consumers pay unfairly high prices, and imported goods face major obstacles in Japan. An imported car is inspected thoroughly. For example, automobile identification numbers are repeatedly scrutinized; even a minute variation in the length of the downstroke of a single letter has held up the release of a car for weeks. After taxes, an imported car costs nearly double the price of the car in the domestic market; a comparable Japanese car costs less in the United States than in Japan. Producer subsidies and import barriers, as well as export incentives, can come to 75 percent of farmers' incomes in Japan compared to 9 percent for cattle ranchers in the United States, the result being that steak costs over $50 per pound in Japan. Tokyo stores did such a strong business in Washington apples after they were introduced, some stores doubled the prices of the apples (from 50 yen to 100 yen each—$1 apples). Apples in Japan are not thought of as casual snack food, but are often given as gifts and are highly prized; thus, the high price is a connotation of apples' value as gifts, not their value as a food product.

The impact of cost consciousness on Japanese consumers during the 1990s can be seen in the use of "callback" numbers. A callback subscriber places a call to the United States using a specially assigned user number, but hangs up before the ring is answered. Sophisticated switching equipment in the United States recognizes the encoded number and returns the call. The subscriber answers, receives an American dial tone, and then dials a number to anywhere in the world. Its widespread success is due to American phone rates being anywhere from 25 to 60 percent lower than Japanese rates.[6] It is often cheaper for consumers in Japan, even with duty and international shipping charges, to buy U.S. products from the United States and ship them to Japan rather than buying the same products at a store next door.

Reflecting an inherent desire to provide customers with good value, a high price-quality ratio exists in Japan. Japan is not a price-sensitive market; competitive price ranked seventh among ten factors impacting success in Japan. Since most Japanese consumers are pressured by high housing prices and increased costs of living, they are not so different from Americans and Europeans. They all want maximum value for purchased items. In fact, in one survey, 70 percent of respondents stated that they wanted reasonable prices more than high-priced quality goods.[7]

CROSS-CULTURAL ASPECTS OF PRICING

Incomes, cultural habits, and consumer preferences differ from country to country. All three influence desire for a product and hence elasticity necessarily differs between any two countries or cultures. Thus, for the same product in two different countries or cultures, two different prices may be demanded and received.

The cultural background of parent company executives often influences a pricing strategy. Canadian and Scandinavian firms prefer market systems; U.S., English, French, and Japanese firms use predominantly cost-oriented ones; and Italian, German, and Dutch firms tend to use combination systems. Tax avoidance preference can explain the French preferences while the complex tax and collection procedures in Italy make it preferable to maximize income in Italy. The Germans' apparent lack of interest and concern with transfer pricing can be explained in terms of their emphasis on fixed assets and long-run stability of the firm.[8]

British exporters favor supply and demand approach because they are looking for the soundness of the market. German exporters prefer the product market strategy because they want to match price and quality attributes for their customers. Japanese exporters price according to the transaction with the goal to increase market share. Americans, British, and Canadians tend to be reactive price setters, pricing their wares competitively. Germans, Swedes, Dutch, and Italians are neutral setters of prices and are not as concerned with matching competitors' prices. The Chinese and Southeast Asians are proactive setters of prices, with their prices based on the overall marketing strategy.

Pricing strategy can be skewed by government competition. When Renault was owned by the French government, its primary goal was to maintain employment rather than to maximize profits. For this reason, Renault was often willing to accept lower prices than its competitors. As a result, the entire auto industry in France, in order to compete with a nonprofit-based entity (as Renault was), was forced to keep its prices at unprofitable levels. By way of contrast, German auto companies were profit-led and provided more opportunities for competitors to have profitable price levels.

Profit tends to be disregarded in Japan. Historically, Japanese merchants were bitterly criticized and often ostracized because they sought profits. One classic Japanese proverb is "A folding screen and a merchant cannot stand up unless they are crooked." To a Japanese, normal profit means that the cost of capital (essentially, debt) is covered. Therefore, a normal profit is obtained when the interest on the borrowed capital is paid on schedule. *Kami yori usui kosen* (a margin thinner than paper) is a common saying in Japanese business. In some cases, Japanese agents' total disregard for manufacturers' list prices when selling products reflects the Japanese philosophy that "some business is better than none at all."

Japanese sellers view prices as a highly flexible marketing instrument. In the West, factors that determine pricing are primarily related to the product. In Japan, pricing is a strong tool used by producers to gain influence and control over their distribution channels. Fujitsu won a contract to design a computer for the city of Hiroshima by bidding 1 yen; in the past, both Fujitsu and NEC had submitted bids of 1 yen to design a library computer system; they drew straws and Fujitsu won. Fujitsu intended to give away the design job that would lead to the equipment order.

Prices may be cut at any level in the Japanese marketing channel by firms that must have sufficient immediate income to meet their unavoidable costs. Small wholesalers and retailers have no competitive devices except for price competition and relationships, but vigorous price competition at the retail level is not at all common in Japan. Instead, price coordination is widespread due to the oligopolistic structure of Japanese industry. In most branches of industry, many companies or industrial groups (*keiretsu*) exist, each of which has strong connections in the financial sector, the Diet (the Japanese national legislature), and the bureaucracy. Any attempts by one company to engage in heavy price competition could cause such a powerful negative reaction from the others that they would probably produce more harm than benefit.

Cost-plus pricing is not the recognized price-setting formula as found in the West. Management must first set the price and then see how costs can be brought into line. This is similar to Texas Instruments' famous learning curves approach. The selling price is dictated by competition with other companies in the same industry. Companies must then reconcile costs with selling price. The main weapon of a sales department is low price. This strategy involves aggressively setting low prices to win market domination and then rapidly improving production to bring costs in line with prices. Japanese marketers spend as much time discussing the right price for an article as they do discussing the product or its promotion. The price has to be what the consumer expects to pay. Once a price is established for a product in Japan, considerable difficulty exists in raising it. This makes initial price setting more important than in the West because prices must not change; one has to pick a price that one expects to be bound to for many years.

In the United States, new fashion items are given high prices because high prices have traditionally been associated with high quality and premium items. In countries where change is less desirable, a premium price does not necessarily denote premium items. Levi's 501s were priced higher in Spain than elsewhere in the European Union during the early 1990s because they were regarded as a fashion item and priced as such. Although soup was priced at a premium in France because most French housewives considered soup to be a minor appetizer, they were unwilling to spend the required amount for the product and the soup did not sell well. Thus, products are not prized the same in all countries, so what some may be willing to pay highly for, others may not.

Kmart found when entering the Czech republic that customers were unaccustomed to and leery of price reductions, especially the company's blue light specials. This resulted from that country's history of communist control, during which time unsold merchandise would be stored and then brought back in about five years.[9] German stores discount prices through sales for only a few days per year and they all do so at the same time.

In Japan, perceived value is a major determinant of product success; qualitative images are far more important than product value; high prices portray high quality. BMW and Mercedes have dominated the foreign import market using the image of high cost equalling high quality. Mercedes advertises in *Nibon Keizai Shimbun*, an upscale business journal that is Japan's equivalent of *The Wall Street Journal*. BMW spends close to $5 million per year on sixty-second prime-time television spots that are run weekly in Japan.

Johnnie Walker Black and Red and Chivas whiskies have long cultivated high-status images in Japan. They are very expensive in bars or clubs and are highly prized as gifts. Hoping to take market share away from Chivas, Johnnie Walker dropped the price of its Black label brand. Instead of increasing sales, the opposite happened: sales dropped drastically. Japanese consumers saw the price reduction as somehow related to quality problems with the beverage, and, as a result, the whiskey suffered a drop in status. While the Black label brand fell out of favor and is still today on the cheaper end of the drink menus, the Red label has maintained its high-end status position.[10]

P&G introduced Cheer into Japan by discounting its price, a common practice in the United States. This only lowered the soap's reputation in Japan. P&G also discovered that once it discounted its product in Japan, it is extremely hard to raise the price again. Wholesalers were alienated because they made less money due to lower margins. Small retailers have limited shelf space and do not like to carry discounted products because of the lower per unit profit earned.

In negotiating, especially about price, Americans expect give and take and begin their negotiations at a far lower price (or higher if selling) than they expect to get. When hesitation is encountered, most Americans tend to assume that the price is unacceptable and improve the offer even before it is rejected. This can easily lead to situations where Americans continually change the price even after the other side has found an earlier price acceptable. Hesitation and discussion between members of the other side were not necessarily a result of unhappiness over the price quoted but that time was needed for a check with other colleagues.

Japanese Pricing Strategy

An aggressive penetration pricing strategy in Japan is directed toward gaining and holding market share, particularly abroad. When operating overseas, the Japanese concentrate on pursuing market share rather than profits. Most local companies cannot do this because it is not economically feasible. But as long as the Japanese companies have adequate financial backing (as many do), they have a high probability of success. Japanese exporters absorb significant costs, which impact profits in their home currency, to maintain and perhaps expand market share in their export markets. Import prices start low and generally remain low. Marketing arrangements such as price collusions, limits on competition, and advertising discounts are legal and extensively used in Japan.[11]

Market penetration traditionally has been a much more important pricing objective than quick profit taking with a skimming approach. Entry into a market is viewed as a long-term investment. Individual markets are seen not as profit centers, but as pieces in one large, global puzzle. If a firm can generate sufficient funds at home and in some selected country markets where its market share positions are strong, it can survive the lower returns from a low-price penetration strategy in newer markets over a relatively long period of time.

The Japanese system of sales price determination is known as *tatenesei*. A manufacturer fixes the retail price of each product, tells a wholesaler the price at which each product is to be distributed to retailers, and demands that retail stores throughout Japan strictly observe the retail price set by the manufacturer. The standard price is so commonplace that Japanese ads will often include the standard price for the item in commercials on national media. The standard used is retail price equals 100, wholesale price equals 70, and manufacturer's price equals 60. This general formula has become established as the method for determining prices.[12] This system infringes on the fair trade provision of the Antimonopoly Law. Nonetheless, it is tolerated. The system attracts public attention only when retailers dispute a manufacturer's right to bind them to a set price.

Both wholesalers and retailers accept the system because it has advantages for them. If wholesalers abide by the price set by the manufacturers, they are assured of receiving rebates in addition to the regular margin. If a retailer goes along with the price fixed by a manufacturer, he or she is free from the competitive risk and assured of having the manufacturer take back unsold stock at the price the retailer paid for it. The distribution industry accepts the system as the price for getting the manufacturing industry to take over risks. Price coordination and resale price maintenance have advantages for both the manufacturers and the retailers. When prices are uniform, consumers do not have much incentive to prefer large outlets (which can cut prices as a result of economies of scale) over small, more expensive shops. Retail price maintenance thus serves to protect small retailers. Consequently, price coordination and real price maintenance are strongly supported by small retailers, who are a politically visible and numerically large segment of the population. One example of this can be seen during the summer. Electric fans which are identical in color, shape, quality, and price are on the market, but produced by several different companies. Numerous outlets will offer identical models of products at discount prices, but the discount prices are the same for all the discount outlets.[13]

Haggling

Consumers are also willing to bargain in a variety of cultures; bargaining occurs in about 60 percent of the stores in India and Kenya, but less than 5 percent in China and South Africa. This often leads to a condition called haggling, to bargain, to dicker, or to argue in an attempt to come to terms. As a highly structured behavioral system, haggling is marked with verbal threats, counterthreats, disclaimers of interest, and sign language. Its structural format is composed of several steps. These steps include a first offer by the merchant, followed by an initial rejection by the potential buyer—made after objecting that the offer is ridiculous—followed closely by a counteroffer from the merchant, another counteroffer by the buyer—after an exchange of indignant words—another counter by the seller, a feign of interest in different items, a move to leave by the buyer, then finally, a completed transaction.[14]

In the modern world, haggling is most often found in the Middle East, Africa, and to a lesser extent, in the developing countries of Pacific Asia and Latin America, including the Caribbean. Haggling is not generally considered to be a legitimate part of typically American business dealings. This tends to be gender-specific; as a sex, women predominantly wish to avoid haggling; this distaste is not as prevalent among men. In many developing countries, where a majority of consumers cannot read and write, goods often do not have price tags, and advertised prices may not have much meaning to the average consumer in these markets. In these markets, haggling traditions provide strong influence over the manner in which many goods are marketed. In some cases, variations in quality and the absence of standard systems for the establishment of weights and measures make it difficult to implement a "one price" system. The initial price offered by the consumer betrays the level of experience with similar goods. Some consumers may get more out of haggling than others because of differing experience levels, social or economic status, and the ability to speak the language used to make the sale.

Haggling offers some advantages to both the buyers and the sellers. From the buyer's perspective, haggling affords the opportunity to get a lower price by refusing the seller's initial offer. This also allows the seller to size up the customer and change his tactics in order to entice an unenthusiastic customer. The seller's main problem is keeping other customers from noticing any price discrimination. If another buyer picks up on the results of a prior sale, it may severely compromise the bargaining position of the seller. Haggling also gives the customer a feeling of some control over the price to be paid. For the seller, a commitment to a higher price is to his advantage in an individual transaction, but he may risk losing customers if he shows no price flexibility.

Since haggling is in most cases a social engagement between equals, it is most likely to be found in cultures that have a relatively low level of status consciousness within the society. As a time-consuming activity, it is less likely to occur in highly time-conscious societies. In societies that discourage most forms of argument or confrontation, such as Japan, China, and most other Far Eastern cultures, haggling is not commonly encountered. Haggling takes place as a one-on-one activity. Any bargaining that involves large groups of people or takes place between firms will gravitate toward negotiation and away from haggling. Similarly, owners of small shops are more likely to haggle than proprietors of larger stores. Another distinguishing characteristic is context: Generally, one would be more likely to find haggling in high-context societies than in low-context societies.

Another salient characteristic of haggling is that there is a price range that is acceptable to both the buyer and the seller. A buyer with skill can narrow this price range and maximize his standing within the negotiating range. Of course, the seller is going to try to keep the price range at a higher level in order to retain as much profit as possible. For both parties to emerge as successful, each must be knowledgeable as to the general worth of the product or service under consideration. If one party is not well informed as to the value of the product or is innocent of the process of haggling, he may not only strike a poor bargain, but he may also lose status among his peers. As a result of this, Westerners tend to feel that they have been cheated when they conclude a deal while they are still not satisfied with the results. This tends to contribute to an unsavory reputation for bazaar merchants and others who haggle as unscrupulous merchants. In their own defense, they reason that all would-be hagglers should know the rules of the game beforehand.

The key to haggling in any country in which it is performed is establishing a personal relationship. In Middle Eastern countries, the act of haggling is a practice of the "common man"; therefore, men of honor and prestige do not haggle. Practically speaking, persons of high social rank may conclude a deal after an agent has haggled to a point of near conclusion, but almost never engage in the actual haggling process. In the classic *suq* (market) model of haggling, there is a preliminary period of discussion involving items of some general interest that go well beyond the scope of the initially intended transaction.[15] The purpose of this seeming waste of time is to establish a personal connection between the bargainers. Once accomplished, the actual bargaining can begin. Possible loss of face is at stake for both participants, so in order to get over this hurdle, a very strict collection of rules that form the basis of a tacit bargaining etiquette is followed. Both parties will begin the process far outside of the expected price range so as not to give away any advantage that the opponent might attain from being able to estimate the final position. Both parties have a reasonably well established idea as to how much they would be willing to compromise before the actual conversation begins.

Since haggling is also a process of price determination, the customer has the right to handle and examine the product closely before making an offer. Only when the customer is satisfied and has made up his mind is his bid for the item binding. Consultation with others is often a part of the process. Written contracts are quite uncommon. Haggling, in many cases, is an endurance test for both the seller and the buyer.[16] Haggling over prices is considered a pleasure of doing business in Middle Eastern bazaars. Tips for effective haggling at such bazaars include dressing down, shopping around, being knowledgeable concerning the merchandise one is haggling over, negotiating only with the proprietor, being patient, and offering to pay cash.[17] By doing so, a buyer will secure the best deal as well as impress a proprietor with the respect and appreciation shown for the proper way of doing business in the proprietor's homeland. Haggling is generally seen as an unacceptable route to final transactions in most countries with highly developed economies; the more economically developed and industrialized a country or society becomes, the further from its primitive roots it evolves and the more structured the market the country or society tends to evolve toward.

ENVIRONMENTAL PRICING CONSIDERATIONS

International marketers must recognize differences in the country environment governing prices in each national market—differences in the legal and regulatory environment, the volatility of foreign exchange rates, market structure, and competitive environment. Many European PTTs (governmental Post, Telegraph and Telephone ministries) are public monopolies, which allow them to charge high rates with little risk of competition. For example, monthly telephone costs in Spain and Italy (with government monopolies) are twice the cost as found in the UK (with competition).[18] Eighty-five percent of German retailers are cooperatively organized versus only 10 percent for Italian retailers. Germany has over three times the number of persons per food store compared to Italy. Germany has multitudes of self-service food stores compared to Italy. It is no surprise that Italian food prices are the highest of any country in the European Union. Campbell Soup company found its distribution costs in the UK to be 30 percent higher than in the United States; extra costs were incurred because soup was purchased in small quantities—24-can cases of assorted soups which required hand sorting by the wholesalers.

In 1991, Thailand opened its cigarette market to imports, but only after imposing high import duties, a cumbersome customs clearance procedure, and a stiff ban on cigarette advertising. The result was unit sales: large quantities of imported cigarettes are sold one at a time by enterprising young street vendors.[19]

Rampant inflation and/or governmental cost controls provide additional challenges for the international marketer. In Brazil, during the early 1990s, inflation was above 1,000 percent annually. During the 1980s, Brazil had 8 monetary stabilization plans, 4 currencies, 11 inflation indexes, 5 wage and price freezes, 14 wage policies, 18 changes in foreign exchange rules, 54 changes in price control guidelines, and 19 decrees on fiscal authority.[20] Some of Brazil's policies encouraged inflation: salaried employees whose pay is indexed, debtors whose debt shrinks in value, and firms whose cost increases are easily passed on. To operate in such conditions, firms issued new prices on a periodic basis (often raising their prices 7 percent on the first of each month, sometimes on a weekly basis at the worst times of the inflation). In countries with hyperinflation, prices are changed daily if not hourly, which practically eliminated accounts receivable (two weeks to a month at most, if not stopping free credit entirely), extended accounts payable whenever possible, and cut back on credit card grace periods (from one month to less than one week). Under such conditions, credit becomes meaningless (P&G did likewise in Peru). Heinz introduced a new fruit drink in Brazil and sold the product to retailers under consignment; faced with a rate of inflation of hundreds of percent per week, profits vanished. Even then, it was not enough. The purpose of Government price controls is generally to limit price increases. This obviously limits a firm's pricing flexibility. In January 1991, then President Collar again froze wages and prices but raised utility rates and fuel prices, thus raising costs but limiting firms' abilities to raise revenues.[21] As a result, many foreign producers withdrew their products from the market or left the market. Oftentimes, price controls are limited to specific product groups; for instance, pharmaceuticals are the products most frequently subject to price controls. Proctor & Gamble encountered strict price controls in Venezuela in the late 1980s. Despite repeated requests for price increases in lieu of increases in their costs of raw materials, permission was stalled for months. When permission was granted, only 50 percent of the price increase requested was granted. By 1988, detergent prices were less in Venezuela than in the United States, with profits having disappeared.[22]

CONCLUSIONS

Effective pricing is a major element in the successful international business operation. While domestic pricing is difficult, a number of factors make pricing in the international marketplace even more difficult: (1) variable distribution and marketing costs, (2) fluctuating exchange rates, (3) differing perceptions of the product (the value of the product may vary according to the marketplace), and (4) local competition.[23]

Traditionally, foreign products in Japan have been marketed as luxuries and customers have been willing to pay high prices to get them. Retailer J. Crew charged Tokyo customers $130 for wool sweaters that it sold for $48 in the United States; Polartec caps were sold for $39, retailing for $14 in the United States. However, the recession in Japan has turned many Japanese consumers into bargain hunters; those same J. Crew sweaters now sell for $72. Eddie Bauer and The Gap are practicing what they call "fair pricing," meaning that their prices are only about 1½ times those in the United States ($45 for jeans in Japan that sell for $30 in the United States). The price difference is mainly the result of high labor costs (twice those in the United States) and rents (as much as four times or more that found in the United States), although import duties and local advertising costs are also factors. In the past, prices as much as twice or more than those found in the United States have been the norm in Japan due to regulation, cartels, and legal sanctions against discounting (which are beginning to go away). As the average Japanese become more cosmopolitan and international, they have begun to recognize the extent of higher prices in Japan; for instance, Clinique facial soap costs $40 in Japan; the same soap is available in the United States to Japanese businessmen or tourists for $10. This differential has created a market for parallel importers (grey marketers) who import products directly from the manufacturers.[24]

Chrysler agonized over how to position its Neon in the Japanese automobile market when they introduced the model in 1996. Originally, the company intended to compete solely on price, focusing efforts on a low-end, stripped-down, $12,000 model. But Chrysler decided that low price alone wouldn't sell in Japan. Instead, Chrysler decided to push a midrange Neon at $15,000, the same price category as the most popular Toyota Corolla. But Neon buyers will get a bonus—a more powerful, 1.96-liter engine versus Corolla's 1.5-liter engine.[25]

Companies that tend to conduct all other marketing activities in an uniform manner and thus tend to standardize their pricing practices typically do not depend on international business as much as those companies that do adopt. Standardized companies typically do business only within the industrialized world, function mainly in markets that are similar to American markets, or in familiar domestic markets. Companies that are multilocal tend to have substantial international growth, are more demand driven, and are more in tune with market conditions in different international markets. These companies are more inclined to do business in Third World countries, the Middle East, and in Eastern Europe. Those who use prestige pricing have brand names and products; these companies charge what the market can bear.[26]

Local customs influence customers' expectations of the way in which they are charged for a service. While customers in the domestic market might expect to pay for bundles of services, in an overseas market, consumers might expect to pay a separate price for each component of the bundle. While it is common in the United States for customers to pay a tip to a person providing them a service, other cultures expect to pay an all-inclusive price without the need to subsequently add a tip.

A global company needs to pay attention to the possibility of parallel imports because they can cause irreparable damage to a company's image and profits. When a company goes global, it has to price its products in different countries and develop a standardized pricing policy. However, it is realistically not practical to set the same price in every country because of the differences in power purchase parity. Parallel imports develop when importers buy products from distributors in one country and sell them in another to distributors who are not part of the manufacturer's regular distribution system. For example, if a company sells its products to Indonesian distributors for $2.00 apiece and to the German distributors for $4.00 apiece, assuming ceteris paribus, the Indonesian distributors could sell the product directly to the German distributors at a cheaper price. The possibility of a parallel market occurs whenever price differences are greater than the cost of transportation between two markets. Countries or regions with free ports are very famous for parallel imports. For example, the Canary Islands are famous for having shops that live exclusively out of the parallel import inefficiency. Parallel imports cause serious concerns because companies lose revenue when competitors sell their product at a lower price. The biggest problem involves warranties; authorized dealers may decline to accept or repair the product if it breaks down because no profit was realized from the sale. The problem is exacerbated because the consumer does not understand this line of reasoning, which causes the product/company's image to deteriorate.

Pricing can be a bottleneck to the entire marketing process. McDonald's Corporation set its prices at its restaurant in Beijing low compared to its prices in other countries, but a meal still cost a sizable portion of a Chinese family's weekly income. As a result, the Chinese families that frequented the restaurant spent hours at the restaurant, converting what was designed to be a fast-food experience into a long dinner affair. McDonald's failed to recognize the Chinese need to savor and prolong what was, to them, an expensive meal. Consequently, McDonald's seriously underestimated the seating capacity required for profitable volumes.[27]

PART III:
POSTMARKETING

Chapter 12

Cross-Cultural Aspects
of Services Marketing

Three definitions of service(s) exist: (1) service as segments of
the economy such as entertainment, utilities, banks, or gardening;
(2) service as in repair and maintenance and other after-sale support
activities; and (3) customer service as in service quality. The cross-
cultural implications of each meaning of service will be reviewed in
the next three chapters.

ATTRIBUTES OF SERVICES

Services are activities, benefits, or satisfactions offered for sale
when there is no exchange of tangible goods. Services in general
possess four predominant characteristics: *intangibility, perishability, inseparability* (simultaneous production and consumption), and
heterogeneity (lack of standardization). The differentiation of offerings is difficult for most marketers to achieve, but it is an especially
difficult task for service marketers. It is hard to differentiate an
accounting audit, a title search, and an eye examination. Unlike the
case of a consumer product such as breakfast cereal, one cannot
accomplish differentiation through simply sprinkling on a new coat-
ing or stamping out a new shape. The amount of variation in the
way a service can be provided may be quite limited, particularly if
professional standards restrict methods of provision. Additionally,
even if a service is provided that substantially differs from competing services, it may be difficult to get clients to perceive and recognize the real differences.

Customers often infer quality via brand name and reputation of
the service provider. Producers with strong reputations are asso-

ciated with high quality and are often able to charge higher prices for their services. The Big Six international accounting firm brand name is associated with premium audit fees. The Big Six name is perceived as a high quality producer of audits. Companies are willing to pay higher fees for the Big Six brand name service even though the nature and scope of the audit is identical to those of other accounting firms. This is very important in audit services, since the conduct of an audit is unobservable to investors and the outcome of the process follows a standard format. The credibility of an audit appears to be based upon the auditor and its reputation. International accounting firms spend considerable sums to protect and enhance their reputation and brand name, and are consequently awarded with higher fee income.[1]

If a service is *intangible*, it cannot be observed, touched, felt, or tried out before it is purchased. Intangibility makes a service significantly different from a product. Although a service may have tangible trappings, no amount of money can buy physical ownership of such intangibles as movies, consulting, or dry cleaning. When a company purchases engineering services or consulting services, the result, the intellectual outcome, is not a physical entity. This dimension of intangibility makes it difficult to evaluate quality prior to purchase and even quality subsequent to purchase. The benefit of a service cannot be experienced until the service is provided. This intangible feature represents a considerable amount of uncertainty and risk for many customers.

One of the challenges of a service business is to provide a physical component to the service by stating the benefits in a perceivable manner; the promotional focus may emphasize office decor and dress rather than the service benefit. Other physical components could include logos, trademarks, brandmarks, membership cards, and characters or mascots. Tangible cues can also emphasize the benefits of the service by simply describing the features; for example, a dentist can talk to a patient about the better smile he/she will have once his/her teeth are straightened, rather than the technical steps in straightening his/her teeth. Interiors should be designed to be pleasing to target markets and to project an image consistent with the positioning strategy. A storefront law firm that wants to target lower- and lower-middle-class clients would want to decorate its offices with inexpensive paneling, inexpensive furniture, and potted plants. On the other hand, a dentist seeking upper-class patients would have plush carpeting, leather chairs, contemporary art, exotic plants, a stock market ticker tape, and perhaps even stained glass windows— in other words, an atmosphere conducive to its desired clientele.[2]

Perishability means that services cannot be inventoried or sampled in advance. This results in difficulties in matching demand with capacity. Fluctuating or seasonal demand poses excess capacity or shortage problems. During the off-season or a recession, the available capacity may be underutilized, requiring a reduction in capacity (e.g., a ski resort in summer); during a peak season (e.g., early April for tax accountants) or certain promotional periods, the capacity may be inadequate and may necessitate expansion. If capacity is not expanded to match growth in demand, revenues may be lost or quality of services may deteriorate, resulting in customer dissatisfaction. In contrast, if capacity is not reduced or adjusted when there is a decline in demand, profits are adversely affected. The tendency is to maintain the capacity and to expand demand during off-peak times and use differential pricing to control demand during peak periods. The solution here is to better train service providers to better understand and empathize with customers' peak needs and to provide for a careful assessment of customer needs through research.

A doctor's appointment missed will never make up to the doctor the opportunity cost of that time which could have been spent profitability with a client. This is not a problem when demand is steady but becomes a severe problem with fluctuating demand. Service firms can influence demand levels in many different ways: differential pricing to shift demand from peak to off-peak periods; off-peak demand can be cultivated; complimentary services can be developed during peak time so that customers do not have to spend as much time waiting; or other services may be offered during off-peak times (for example, a ski resort becomes a summer dude ranch to enable year-round operation). Reservation systems can also be installed to help manage the demand level. The supply level can also be influenced in several ways: part-time employees can be hired to serve peak demand; peak-time efficiency routines can be introduced whereupon employees perform only essential tasks during peak periods; increased consumer participation in the tasks can be encouraged; shared services between multiple providers can be fostered; or facilities can be developed which make potential expansion possible. Risk is involved in any of these alternatives. All of these strategies present signals to the consumers of the provider's willingness to work with and understand customer needs.

Simultaneous production and consumption, also called *inseparability*, means that a professional who provides a service also markets it. This makes economies of scale difficult to achieve. The service requires the presence of the service provider. Several possible solutions are for a provider to work with larger groups, take less time with each client, or train more providers; for example, lawyers can have paralegals work on the lesser legal problems encountered. This particular feature becomes critical. The nature of the encounter between provider and client to a large extent determines the continuing business relationship.

Instead of fine tuning a machine to maintain quality, people-intensive service organizations must emphasize finding good people and exhorting them to work conscientiously. Many service organizations have to contend with the additional problem that the quality of their service often depends on the behavior of their clients (inseparability). A consultant's or doctor's services will usually be more helpful to those persons who follow the professional advice they have received. Uncooperative clients can, unfortunately, produce poor results and a poor track record for a professional to try to build upon.

The lack of standardization, or *heterogeneity*, means the quality of service varies with an individual provider. The quality of service may vary significantly from one provider to another or from one time period to another, even within the same selling organization. Service buyers are aware of this high variability and frequently talk to others before selecting a service provider. This heterogeneity, along with the intangibility feature, often force customers to dwell on dissatisfaction rather than satisfaction from the consumption of a service. A customer's preoccupation with dissatisfaction could prevent the consumer from trying out a service initially or it could force the consumer to look for another provider in the event that dissatisfaction emerges from the service.

Customer satisfaction and loyalty are often quite difficult to achieve and maintain. This variability in quality is particularly evident in multisite locations and multiproviders of the same service within the same office. This results in difficulty in setting prices because it is almost impossible to draw price/service comparisons accurately. Therefore, any reduction in price to lure customers away from the competition is questionable in practice and outcome. The best solution is for the provider to standardize service procedures whenever possible and do a careful cost analysis to set prices. Quality control can be exhibited in careful personnel selection and training as well as by constant monitoring of customer satisfaction through suggestion and complaint systems and surveys. (See the discussion on SERVQUAL in Chapter 14.)

Differences in the perception given and the importance of each of these attributes occur between cultures. Because services generally involve close social interaction between the service provider and the customer, cultural variables naturally affect user satisfaction and the nature of the interaction with the customer. Intangibility makes selling services overseas more difficult because the buyer must often take the quality of the seller on faith. A corporate brand name and a sound reputation helps. Intangibility also limits the ability of the firm to wade into a market; oftentimes, it becomes a choice of dive in, sink, or swim. The direct interaction between customers and providers inherent in services often means cultural differences must be accounted for in seeking buyer satisfaction. Establishing a local physical presence and hiring local personnel are often the only workable alternatives.

IMPORTANCE OF SERVICES INTERNATIONALLY

Services continue to increase in importance within national economies. Services make up 20 to 30 percent of world trade and have a growth rate estimated to be up to 20 percent annually. Thus, opportunities for growth at world market level are considerable. Yet, barriers to services exist and can be immense; most of the nontariff barriers are aimed at services. Services have particular product dimensions that make global service marketing management different from that of physical goods.[3]

The growth in services internationally can be attributed to two principal factors: changing lifestyles affected by affluence, leisure time, and women in paid employment; and the changing world affected by the increased complexity of life, ecological concerns, and the variety and complexity of products available on the market. World trade in services is gaining increasing importance as seen from its inclusion as one of the three major topics in the now-completed Uruguay (eighth) round of GATT talks; these talks failed to resolve many issues, thus the WTO will become involved in their resolution. The growth of services has also been driven by the need of many service providers to follow their clients overseas. American banks were encouraged to become global to meet the needs of their American multinationals who had established foreign operations. Travel agents followed American-based airlines overseas. Japanese personal and business services firms followed the Japanese auto parts companies that followed the Japanese auto transplants to the United States.

With over three-quarters of its GDP in services, the United States has a vested interest in that segment of the economy. In fact, every industrialized country has over 70 percent of its GDP in services. What becomes paramount to the United States and other developed countries is that, for the most part, comparative advantages are to be found predominantly in service industries: for the United States it is entertainment, publishing, finance, insurance, tourism, high tech, and construction services. International trade in services exceeds $1 trillion worldwide annually; the United States is the world's leading service exporter with over $200 billion, almost 30 percent of total U.S. exports. The importance of services in the United States can also be seen in the fact that services provide a trade surplus exceeding $60 billion.

By way of contrast, Japan suffers a chronic deficit in its service trade; its share in world service trade is low. Growing international activities by Japanese firms have heightened the deficit. Payments exceed receipts by a wide margin in technological trade. Finally, the travel and tourism deficit is significant as more and more Japanese take holidays abroad. Japanese consumer demand for services has exploded as leisure time has increased; greater female employment (working wives) has increased demand for food services; the aging of the population has increased demand for medical services; and the demand for higher education has skyrocketed. On the positive side, Japan is the largest exporter of capital in the world. Tokyo is a leading financial center. The Tokyo Stock Exchange is one of largest in the world. Seven of the largest commercial banks and four of the largest securities companies in the world are Japanese. Countering this is the fact that Japanese manufacturers still get more of their financing, distribution, travel, and advertising services from in-house sources than is common elsewhere. Manufacturers provide the bulk of the nation's vocational training.

Japan's production sector has been characterized by low-cost, lean employment, and high efficiency. The retail/service sector, on the other hand, traditionally has been overstaffed, with high prices and gross inefficiencies. Whereas the productivity gap between the more efficient manufacturing and the less efficient service industry is about 15 to 1 in the United States, it is around 80 to 1 in Japan.[4] The Japan Productivity Center indicated that to reach overall U.S. productivity levels, Japanese companies would have to eliminate 39 percent of their employees. Nearly 20 percent of white-collar workers are excess; as many as five to six million are redundant workers.

Without the challenge of international competitors, the majority of Japan's domestic companies (80 percent of the economy) have become complacent; this is especially true in their service, construction, and food production sectors. Japanese department stores, specialty retail shops, and banks provide service personnel who in the West either have been replaced by customer actions themselves (e.g., elevator operators) or simply would be absent (e.g., greeters and receptionists). Even if the automated equipment has been installed, human workers may be standing by performing redundant functions. At the gate checking for domestic flights at Haneda Airport, boarding passes are inserted into a machine that retains the airline's portion and returns the passenger's ticket stub. This transaction is handled by two workers: the first takes and inserts the pass; the second hands back the stub.[5]

POTENTIAL HURDLES
IN INTERNATIONALIZING SERVICES

Several other potential problems of the service industry are found when the subject of internationalization is discussed. Services tend to be labor intensive and internationally, barriers to labor mobility across countries exist; as such, services tend to export capital, technology, and information that can be combined with local labor to recreate the imported service locally. A second potential barrier is the mobility of the service product offered. Mobility is prized in international trade; this is especially true for financial instruments and skills. Some services are more mobile than others. Retail establishments, due to their need for physical plants, are not as mobile as are insurance industries, for example.

The third potential hurdle is infrastructure. All service operations have some physical aspects; for example, a bank building and vault, a movie theater, and aircraft for airlines. In order for a service entity to be successful, the required physical infrastructure must be present. As much as an airline could wish to serve northern Nigeria, if no acceptable airports exist, service cannot be performed. Credit cards may be a lucrative market in Pakistan; however, phone lines from retail outlets to computers must be available to check on credit and to make the necessary transactions. The lack of availability of the phones, the modems and terminals at the retail outlets, or the computers themselves would cause the entire concept of credit cards to be inoperable.

The fourth potential problem is the theme of this entire book: cultural transferability. Some markets may be more culturally indifferent to particular services or prefer particular services than others. Consumer services in particular travel poorly. Those involving entertainment and communication must be adapted to language barriers. Food and lodging industries may be affected similarly. For example, non-meat-eating India was a market dismissed by McDonald's until the company decided to offer lamb burgers and soyburgers instead. Burger King in Venezuela must have sweeter milkshakes and ketchup to satisfy local tastes. In addition, advertising prepared for viewing in one part of the world may not be suitable in another.

American rap music does not transfer easily; the lyrics conjure up the things Europeans and Asians fear most about the United States—crime and violence. French teens are opting for "*rai*" music and Italians, "*ragamuffin*"; both are tamed European equivalents of rap. In 1985, U.S. and British artists accounted for 65 percent of music sales in Europe; in 1995, it was just 45 percent. One estimate indicates 80 percent of the music sold in Latin America is by Latins, while 60 percent of that sold in Asia is by Asians. Over 3,000 students from Beijing colleges reveled in a live concert which included two of China's hottest rock stars—He Young and Dou Wei—blaring out Chinese versions of rock, grunge, and heavy metal. No tickets were sold; however, word of mouth brought the crowds; once there, attendees bought tapes and CDs by the hundreds.[6]

CROSS-CULTURAL INFLUENCES ON SERVICES MARKETING

Credit Cards and the Finance Industry

Germany poses a cultural-bound problem in the use of credit cards. Historically, Germans have shunned debt and have used their cards as electronic checkbooks instead of revolving credit; the German word for debt (*schulden*) also means guilt. German privacy laws also make it difficult to get an individual's credit history for commercial purposes. Citicorp, in an attempt to increase the perception of credit cards, coined a German phrase for their credit cards: *Ruckzal-Wahl*—"credit that empowers." The desirable high-end market is seemingly saturated. Even if the market takes off, the business might never be as profitable as elsewhere.

In Germany, cash has long been king. Although Germany is Europe's largest country, it has only 3 million Visa cardholders, compared with 30 million in Britain (45 percent of British population owns at least one credit card). Eurocard (tied to MasterCard) has 6.7 million members in Germany. American Express has only 1.2 million members and has been stuck at that level for the last three years. Germans make only 1 percent of their purchases with cards, compared to 18 percent in the United States. Germans might be so satisfied with their current payment systems that they have little interest in new ones. Germans prefer to pay their bills with debit cards, bank transfers (17 percent compared to 5 percent in the United States), and most of all, cash (80 percent versus 42 percent).

German customers tend to pay their credit card bills immediately rather than using the borrowing privileges; banks, therefore, must make their money almost exclusively on fees charged to merchants instead of on interest. Competition is keeping down the fees, which range in Germany from 2.4 percent to 4.5 percent of the purchase amount. German law prohibits companies from offering bonus programs; American Express' Membership Miles program, which gives customers frequent flyer miles with each card purchase, is in jeopardy of violating that law.[7]

Smart Cards—credit-card-sized pieces of plastic with embedded microprocessors—got their start in France in the early 1980s. Putting a tiny computer that can hold vast amounts of information onto a wallet-sized card creates a card smart enough to contain its own verification codes and passwords. Smart cards are used by almost all banks and pay phones in France, and are quickly being adopted by banks in Austria and Germany. The U.S. military is testing the cards as electronic dog tags. Visa promoted smart cards as a substitute for cash at the 1996 Summer Olympics in Atlanta. Banks in Belgium, Denmark, Portugal, and Finland have programs in place for electronic cash. Global card sales have increased from 260 million in 1992 to 720 million units in 1996 and are predicted to reach 2 billion units by 1999. Revenues are expected to rise to $1.5 billion in 1998 from $400 million in 1996. The use of such cards is inhibited by local restrictions. In Germany, where the health care system has already issued more than 60 million smart cards, privacy laws prevent basic medical information such as a penicillin allergy from being recorded on them; most German cards store only a patient's name and address. However, on a voluntary basis, personal medical data is beginning to be included.[8]

Visa International announced in June 1996 the first true credit card in China, in cooperation with Industrial & Commercial Bank of China. Previously, credit cards with preset limits, interest charges, and revolving credit have been virtually unknown in China. Banks have instead issued debit cards, which require a deposit from which purchase amounts are deducted monthly. Visa's Chinese credit card is much like the Western version. The annual percentage rate is 2 percent interest every month on the unpaid balance with a grace period of 61 days. The government has set a

$12,000 limit on each transaction made on any credit or debit card in China. Visa's card must be paid in dollars because China's yuan is not fully convertible. Hence, only people who can use foreign currency in China are eligible.[9] Spending per card is higher in China than in almost any other country because almost all of the cards issued are solely for business use.[10] In contrast, card usage by Taiwanese is so widely accepted that one of the country's top vocalists hit the top of the charts with the song, "Do you love me or your Visa card more?"

Citicorp is creative in its credit card endeavors because many places it targets do not have centralized credit reporting bureaus; Citicorp solicits owners of TV satellite dishes in Indonesia. In Singapore, by law, only well-to-do people, 200,000 of the 3 million residents, can legally be offered a card. Ten other issuers, including American Express, have put 700,000 cards into hands of these elite residents. Citicorp chose to go after the upper-income segment with a premium card ($75 for gold), fatter credit lines, around-the-clock customer service worldwide, and a heavy promotional blitz: it has issued over 50,000 cards and has targeted a 10 percent share of the Singapore market.[11] In Thailand, Citicorp has captured 40 percent of the credit card market, relying chiefly on a sales force of 600 part-timers who are paid a fee for each applicant approved.[12] Citibank played to Koreans' status consciousness by introducing a product called VIP banking: a special service for customers who could open an account with a large minimum (over $100,000). Customers can use an office in the bank for their private meetings any time they want and are served tea and cake whenever they are there. Also, if customers do not want to go to the bank, a bank employee picks up the money for deposit or delivers it for withdrawal.[13]

Citibank is pursuing its goal of becoming a global consumer bank. One strategy is to have ATMs located throughout the world. Citibank focuses on the top 30 percent income bracket of the population, to whom the bank markets itself as a status symbol and a leader in service in a competitive banking environment. Its target is to reach 10 million affluent Asian households by the end of the decade. It emphasizes local banking: in Taiwan, the idea of a mortgage was revolutionary until the mid-1980s and the government was reluctant to let Citibank offer mortgages. Home purchases in Taiwan were financed in the Chinese tradition, borrowing from family or tapping lifetime savings.[14]

ATMs are also becoming a hot item in South Africa due to a lack of consumer knowledge for the recently freed poor black population. The typical savings method for such consumers was to hide money in jars in their houses. Many are used to being robbed. With the use of banks and ATMs, they can save and feel secure. Prior to the ending of apartheid, 80 percent of the population was estimated to be too poor or illiterate to be of value to banks in old South Africa. ATMs provide a challenge to such consumers. They must learn not just how to use them but how to use savings accounts and checking accounts. The entire concept of being a consumer must be learned.[15]

Japan's banks (JCB-Japan Credit Bank which has the top-selling credit card in Japan) have an international credit card dilemma: being domestic, they could control the local (Japanese) credit and debit card industry; however, having little international presence or brand name awareness, few if any establishments overseas accepted their cards. Most spending on credit is done when traveling abroad, to avoid carrying cash. Japanese travelers, therefore, adopted American cards such as Visa, MasterCard, and American Express, which were accepted worldwide. Most Japanese have a credit card but card purchases amount to less than 1 percent of all consumer transactions in Japan.

Japanese banks, although the world's largest, are rich in assets, but poor in capital and innovation. They tend to have had little experience with aggressive competition, having been fully protected until 1992. In home markets, many of the larger Japanese banks were able to enter investment banking and insurance, businesses denied to their American and European rivals. National banking is allowed.[16] European and Japanese banks also have extensive stakes in industrial companies. Nevertheless, American banks have the technological and innovative edge that allows them to design and distribute new financial offerings.

Definite cultural preferences and distinctions can be seen in the credit versus debit card phenomenon. In Japan, debit cards dominate. One reason is the Japanese Confucian tradition of saving before consuming, the fear of debt, and the fear of obligations that debt would impose. In the United States, credit cards dominate. No such fears of obligation or debt occur in the United States. Rather, it is a buy-now, pay-later society, perfectly suited for credit cards.

Air Transportation

Federal Express decided to build a European hub in Brussels in 1985; imitating its hub system, it planned to run nightly flights from several countries and return the planes early in the morning. It hoped that knowledge of running such a system in the United States would work to its advantage. However, in Europe, customs officials must clear each system upon arrival, thus considerably slowing the process. Overseas regulators were in no hurry to let Federal Express develop an efficient hub and spoke system, often preferring to nurture their own companies.[17] After this effort failed, Federal Express restructured by stopping deliveries between cities in Europe but still handling intercontinental deliveries by setting up European partners. The problem in that approach is that volume from Europe to the United States is less than half that shipped in the other direction, and the imbalance is costly. The hub approach in the United States worked since the volume was present that could accept the high-cost solution that necessitated high capacity utilization that has never been approached in Europe.[18] Another drawback was that it started late in Europe after companies such as DHL and TNT were already providing such service. Instead of being the leader and pioneer, Federal Express was a follower.

DHL, by way of contrast, traditionally used couriers who flew with the plane treating their shipments as personal baggage. UPS took a slower track. Starting in 1976, it took UPS 12 years to build its German operation to 6,000 employees. Instead of starting from scratch, it acquired several local courier companies. It grew slowly and learned how to operate in Europe. In 1992, UPS bought Star Air Parcel Service in Vienna as a gateway to Eastern Europe. The company supports its service with a pan-European media program.

American Airlines' Latin American division has captured 64 percent of the region's passenger traffic flown by U.S. carriers and produces about 25 percent of the airline's total operating profit. Over 80 percent of the airline's traffic comes from Latin American residents. To address local sensitivities, each of its top managers in Latin America is a native of the country managed. Free flights are given to universities, hospitals, and other local institutions to increase local goodwill. In response to American Airline's success and to compete with American Airlines and other U.S. air carriers, Latin American airlines, such as Varig, Chile, and Aerolineas Argentinas have upgraded their fleets and provide premium services for their more valued customers. Being on time and quality of service seem to be key to American Airline's success in Latin America.[19] To differentiate itself from the multitude of European airlines, British Airways has developed seven brands under the umbrella of its corporate name—Concorde, First Class, Club World, Club Europe, World Traveller, Euro-Traveller, and Super Shuttle.[20] Many countries have national airlines that are government owned and as such tend to be inefficient, providing marginal service, and having poor on-time records. Privatization or acquisition is a last resort due to the national prestige associated with owning an airline.

Entertainment

The Japanese, having purchased many American entertainment companies, call the industry *omizu shobai*, or "the water business," meaning that it is tricky to get a hold upon. The American movie industry is the only truly international entertainment industry. It appears that Americans have the know-how to entertain people. The most popular film of the 1980s in Israel and Sweden was *Pretty Woman*. Many traditional European theaters even lack soft-drink machines, to say nothing of the U.S.-type full-service highly profitable concession stands. In Italy, 40 percent of the theaters do not have air conditioning, making the summer months a bust. Overseas promotion, therefore, becomes extremely different and difficult. In Germany, where the limited supply of television advertising is booked far in advance, Columbia Pictures had to resort to a direct mailing to German households inviting them to sneak previews of its films. In France, television advertising of films is simply banned for fear of American cultural imperialism. In Japan, growth is constrained by high ticket prices and a shortage of movie houses (one-tenth the number of screens for a population half that of the

United States, 500 of which are effectively reserved for Japanese movies).[21]

Entertainment is a culturally sensitive industry. Fear of foreign influence polluting the local culture and protectionist policies on local entertainment companies have fostered considerable levels of restrictive legal barriers. (GATT did not help matters, as this was one facet that was not decided upon prior to the final agreement.) Indonesian television stations generally shun foreign movies. Singapore does not allow private citizens to own satellite dishes. In Manila, movie theaters are expected to devote at least one-fourth of their screen time to Philippine productions. Australia has a 50 percent rule: at least that amount of Australian content must be broadcast on its commercial television stations. Korea forbids the playing of Japanese movies. A Canadian rule forbids cable outlets from carrying a foreign speciality service if the Canadian version is available. Canadian advertisers can face tax penalties for using American magazines to reach their Canadian customers.[22] In England, only 14 percent of daily airtime can go to imports. In Muslim countries, every item must meet a test of religious acceptability. The mainland Chinese are so afraid of radical thoughts such as freedom being emitted from the airwaves that they have launched a program to review and censor all incoming signals to the entire country. Communist European countries routinely prohibited programs with religious content entirely.

Brazil had some of the most widescale restrictions in the world on foreign motion pictures during the 1980s. These included:

- Companies had to show Brazilian short-subject films along with any foreign feature films that were showing at a theater.
- 3.4 percent of gross box office profit was specifically allocated toward Brazilian film development.
- Brazilian censors reviewed, cut, or forbade some films before they were released.
- Brazilian feature films had to be exhibited at least 140 days per year at each theater.
- All color feature films had to be printed in Brazilian labs.

Entertainment preferences also vary culturally. The British are more tolerant of nudity in television programming than Americans;

Americans are more tolerant of violence than the British.[23] The Japanese allow levels of human sexuality unheard of in the United States; frontal nudity is acceptable in prime time television as long as pubic hair is not shown. Despite Mexico's being an extremely conservative country insofar as sexual matters are concerned, Mexican television series tend to be risqué and provocative.

The video rental industry also varies considerably worldwide. In the Czech Republic, a customer reviews a list of store offerings and gives an attendant behind a desk his or her selection; in Britain, corner news stores are the most common video outlets. In Germany, most video shops are legally required to cover their windows, lest the pornographic movies inside offend pedestrians. By German law, no one under 18 is allowed to enter a video shop. In Italy, open-air markets are the best places to find cheap, pirated videos. Violent films are the most popular in Brazil, while in Japan, locally produced offerings of soft pornography are market leaders. In Britain, the top 50 rental videos typically are all American-produced films. The French tend to purchase rather than rent videos. Germans go for porno and action films. Mexicans tend to buy Hollywood films with Spanish subtitles. Canadians are also Americanized in their video habits, but have a special fondness for hockey videos.[24]

Saklambac, Turkey's number one show with 15 million prime-time viewers, is a remake of *The Dating Game*. *The Price is Right* is the rage in Spain. The French love *Jeopardy* so much, it is number one in its time slot. *Wheel of Fortune* is cloned in 15 countries, including Poland. The secret to these successes is in keeping the format as much as possible to that of the original U.S. version. Cultural variations are necessary (e.g., local actors, local languages, and local trivia). In Germany, farm animals are often used as booby prizes on *Let's Make a Deal*. This policy was stopped in Greece, where contestants actually wanted to take the animals home to stew.[25]

Thomson Consumer Electronic's DSS (Digital Satellite System) was launched in Mexico in mid-1996 and expanded to Brazil and Venezuela later that year. First-year sales were over 500,000 units. Fewer than 10 percent of households in Latin America get more than a few channels. Cable television does not exist in many urban areas. Since the satellite is different from that serving the U.S.

market, DSS dishes for Latin America must be 24 rather than 18 inches in diameter. On-screen programming can display any of three languages: Spanish, Portugese, or English. Multiple voltage requirements were also necessary, as household voltages vary from 80 to 240 volts in Latin America.

Tourism

Tourism is the largest business in the world. It generates more than $3.4 trillion in sales, accounts for 10.1 percent of worldwide GDP, employs more than 204 million people (one in nine working people in the world), and contributes more than $654 million in tax revenues.[26] Tourism is not uniform across the globe; while 40 percent of Europeans have visited other countries, only 7 percent of the Japanese have traveled abroad. The United States leads in market share of tourist expenditures, followed by France and Germany; Europe is the most visited continent and receives nearly 60 percent of all international tourist visits (compared to just 3 percent for Africa).[27] While most tourists visit industrialized countries, they are increasingly visiting Third World countries. The inevitable cross-cultural contacts of tourists in a foreign land provide many opportunities for negative encounters and dangers. Commercialization of a culture is an effect or consequence of tourism, but changes in culture have occurred prior to the advent of increased tourism and continue to take place in response to other forces of modernization.

An interesting cross-cultural tourism example was that of promoting India to the U.S. tourist market. The cultural differences between India and the United States provides an explanation for the campaign conducted and the poor response received. India and the United States differ considerably in two Hofstede dimensions: individualism and power. American individualism requires that all promotional appeals be directed toward an American traveler; the message must be addressed to and made relevant to the individual as well as reflect friendliness and informality. The prospective American traveler needs to be assured of adequate free time to relax or explore, ample opportunities for shopping, and the flexibility to select activities that suit the individual. The fun aspect of vacation travel should be emphasized.[28] The original Indian approach which stressed typical Indian values failed; the revised approach which appealed to American values was considerably more successful.

Lufthansa stresses the primary benefit of punctuality which appeals universally to businesspeople. A Bahamian tourism advertising campaign emphasized the Bahamas' clean water, beaches, and air, but in Germany, specifically focused on sports activities available in the islands, while emphasizing humor in its UK version.[29] Resort owners catering to Japanese tourists find they must import sake to quench Japanese thirst. A Japanese tour is not for the faint of heart. Japanese take few long vacations and their vacation packages are crammed with activities, encompassing a long day (from an early rise to a late night, the agenda is fixed). The Four Seasons Hotel chain provides special pillows, kimonos, slippers, and teas for Japanese guests. The Japanese are not adventurous and do not necessarily want exotic surroundings, but a replica of home. As such, special furnishings and food products must be imported to satisfy their needs.

Golf architects have been pulled toward Japan in their desire to build championship golf courses. Golf courses are different in Japan than those in the United States, since Japanese golf courses are meant for golfers with high handicaps. (Japanese golfers take up the game late and have little time to practice or improve their game.) Due to limited amounts of flat land, Japanese golf courses are usually built into hillsides, taking the terrain as it is. Clubhouses must be huge because most Japanese live in cramped quarters and want opulence during their leisure time. Japanese golf courses typically have wide-open fairways. In addition, all Japanese golf courses must have large reservoirs to hold water in case of torrential rainfall and typhoons, which are common in Japan.

Tourism can affect national economies. Cuba expects tourism to become its number one industry in the late 1990s.[30] The Nicaraguan Ministry of Tourism projects the number of tourists visiting Nicaragua annually will increase from 200,000 tourists in 1993 to 500,000 by the year 2000. The income generated during this span will increase from $29.6 million to $250 million. In Votualailai, Fiji, the majority of village adults, both male and female, are employed by the nearby Naviti Resort, and all, while mostly employed in service and unskilled jobs, are earning far greater incomes than people in Navutelevu, a nearby village not impacted by tourism.[31] In this case, tourism has an effect on income distribution of those regions which offer such destinations.

Tourism may also deprive indigenous people access to the resource areas they traditionally have used for hunting, fishing, and foraging, potentially driving them further into vulnerable ecosystems or into resource-degrading employment. Tourism is also an unstable source of income, subject to widely fluctuating demand scenarios; local economies that rely heavily on tourist dollars can be severely disrupted by a sudden decline in tourist arrivals. In Cuzco, Peru, in response to extreme terrorist activities, tourism dropped more than 80 percent, causing 43 of the area's 128 officially registered hotels to close and most hotels to operate under 30 percent occupancy rates during 1992.[32] Specific terrorist groups in Kenya, Papua New Guinea, Egypt, and Peru have harassed or killed tourists in an effort to destabilize government regimes in those countries, which are highly dependent on tourism revenues. Japanese tourism in the Philippines dropped significantly after only one incident in which a Japanese businessman was murdered.

SUCCESS FACTORS

The marketing of services is significantly different from the way goods are marketed. These differences are tremendously magnified when dealing with the cross-cultural elements present in international marketing. Restrictions on what one can do domestically may not apply to one's competition abroad. For example, Britain's postal service is also responsible for providing a much more extensive range of services than that allowed by its peer in the United States, including a large banking operation, the National Girobank, and the nation's telecommunications services (prior to its privatization). In Britain, postal outlets serve as outlets for government services and provide more than 100 different kinds of transactions, such as sales of licenses, payments, and government securities. High postal rates and a small densely populated country have allowed its postal service to make profits each year.

Customer involvement with services becomes more critical and also more complex (due to cultural factors) when dealing internationally. The following is a noninclusive list of success factors when involved in cross-cultural service marketing efforts.

Provide a flexible offering. Software makers are developing ways to make their programs more polyglot. Most personal computer software is written in American English for U.S. computer keyboards. Translating and adapting software can be immense task. Lotus keeps nearly 300 employees working on translation overheads. The solution entails two items: designing every new program from the beginning to accept any generic language and specifying afterward which language the program is going to use. The second part is specifying a standard code for every alphabet that a computer could instantly retrieve and use.[33]

Adapt to local markets. Modifications made by service providers include Wendy's adding shrimp cake sandwiches to its menu in Japan, Shakey's adding charizo in Mexico, and squid and cuttlefish in Japan, Arby's deleting ham sandwiches in Arab countries, KFC serving chips instead of fries in Britain, and rice and smoked chicken in Japan, and Dairy Queen changing its name in England to Huckleberry's to avoid insulting Queen Elizabeth. American International Group, Inc., the first foreign insurer in China, has 5,000 door-to-door salespeople in Shanghai alone.[34]

Offer support services. Charles Schwab operates a telephone center in San Francisco that offers services in seven Chinese dialects and a center in Florida that offers services in Spanish and Portugese.[35]

Understand the necessary physical infrastructure and its availability and restrictions before entering a market. Credit cards need computer systems, phone lines, and means to check validity of the cards before mass penetration can be accomplished. If the infrastructure is lacking, introduction and penetration of a market will be difficult and negligible, if not impossible.

Make a commitment to foreign clients. Before a new KFC is opened in Japan, a Shinto priest is asked to bless the new store and nearby tradespeople are invited to the opening ceremony.

Chapter 13

Cross-Cultural Implications of the Aftermarket

The second definition of service is that of after-sales service. The after-sales or postsales service (also called the aftermarket) includes customer service (e.g., repair and maintenance), training, warranties, manuals and instructions, installation, consultation services, delivery, and availability of spare parts. Repair and maintenance servicing constitutes an offer to maintain the original product through overhauling, replacement of parts, adjustments, and the satisfaction of outstanding warranty items. Most industrial products and many consumer durables require servicing on a regular basis. Service often must be provided to comply with a warranty policy; a manufacturer must make arrangements for service training, appropriate service facilities, and spare parts to accommodate and fulfill the terms of the specific warranty.

Postsales services are a critical part of the total product package for consumer durables and industrial products. If the product breaks down and the repair arrangements are not up to standard, the image of the product and company will suffer. Service can also be a promotional tool: when a product requires after-sale service, the service could provide the edge over a competitor which does not provide after-sales service or provides an inadequate level of service. A company which provides more effective after-sales service has an immense, often insurmountable, edge over a competitor. Customer service, therefore, is integral to any marketing effort, international or otherwise.

Service is crucial to the industrial buyer, since any breakdown of equipment or product is apt to cause substantial economic loss. Service internationally provides complex problems including the dilemma of establishing a base with its own trained service personnel or selecting an independent service company or local distributor to perform the service. Adequate training must be provided to an agent, in any case. An adequate inventory for spare parts is mandatory. Sufficient inventory must be in place within reach of a company's markets. Fujitsu combined forces with TRW for its sales operations in the United States; TRW provided the extensive service organization Fujitsu needed[1] to compete effectively in the United States. In the United States, customers usually have a multitude of service options and easily available service parts from many different outlets. Customers in developing countries, however, may only have a few of the many options available in the United States.

Customer service is an important competitive weapon in international markets because of its ability to acquire and retain overseas customers and enhance overall company revenues. Customer service is especially critical when foreign vendors are perceived as offering similar products at comparable prices or purchasers have doubts about foreign suppliers' willingness to provide adequate postsales support. The customer service programs of international marketers can increase sales, reduce costs, improve bottom lines, build market share, and obtain a sustainable competitive advantage. These benefits are frequently achieved through such customer service elements as emergency shipments, on-time delivery, order status reporting, and frequent inventory replenishment, which are integral parts of companies' logistical operations; they are powerful weapons in acquiring and retaining overseas customers such as manufacturers and distributors.[2]

As the suppliers' products and prices become more similar, more emphasis gets put on customer service as a differentiation tool by the sellers and more emphasis is placed on sellers' customer service capabilities by the purchasers. Foreign firms are often fearful that if they purchase from a foreign vendor, there will be lack of adequate follow-up; suppliers which are viewed as faithfully performing these after-sale activities will have a decided competitive advantage. In one study of customer service, after-sale service and product availability were the two most crucial components of customer service for companies operating internationally.[3] Cybex has focused on service and has provided a strong international sales and service staff for its fitness systems; as a result, it has prospered internationally. Kulicke & Soffa Industries, a semiconductor equipment manufacturer, recovered global share in its industry after it improved its response to customers' after-sales needs.[4] As rising real wages give Poles an incentive to replace obsolete home appliances, Whirlpool has discovered that after-sales service is increasingly the decisive factor in consumer choice of appliances in Poland.[5]

In some cultures, the concept of routine maintenance or preventive maintenance is not part of local norms. To many businesspeople in those cultures, the marketing process terminates with the sale; once the transaction is completed, generally, no services are provided after a sale and there is no concern for customer satisfaction; it is extremely difficult for a customer to return a product. As a result, products may have to be adjusted to require less-frequent maintenance, and special attention must be given to features that may be taken for granted in the United States.[6] A simple term in one country may be incomprehensible in another. Customer satisfaction policies such as a 30-day money-back guarantees and multiyear warranties are virtually unknowns to domestic Korean companies. ? see p 248 In some cases, products abroad may not even be used for their intended purpose and may thus require modifications not only in product configuration but in service frequency. For instance, snow plows exported from the United States are used to remove sand from driveways in Saudi Arabia.[7]

The Japanese have long understood the international importance of customer service. Nissan's new multimillion pan-European advertising campaign emphasizes the company's after-sales activities to consumers.[8] The success of its entry strategies, notably in the United States, linked price, quality, and service. Japanese manufacturers built immediate repair and maintenance services into the package they offered their U.S. customers.[9] Japanese distributors prefer small orders, short lead time, and order reliability; as a result, these factors often outweigh price competitiveness, especially when evaluating foreign suppliers.[10]

The Japanese consider early problems to be a sign of poor long-term reliability. For all major purchases, the Japanese expect prompt service and a wide choice of items. Their major concerns with imported goods are safety and after-sales support. Unless a proper guarantee or warranty is offered with their products, foreign manufacturers usually experience difficult times.[11] Japanese Web pages on the Internet should state their return policies since the Japanese are often leery of overseas companies and a return policy seems to ease their worries.[12] Therefore, foreign businesses in Japan must carry a large and complete inventory of parts and provide trained service personnel.

This is especially important in the Japanese automotive segment, since many Japanese fear that buying a foreign car means they will not be able to get necessary parts or good service. BMW built a warehouse near Tokyo to guarantee delivery of spare parts within 24 hours, a move that helped it capture 25 percent of the imported car market in Japan. BMW also found that its customers in Japan expected only the finest quality. No mistakes were acceptable; cars often had to be completely repaired prior to customer shipment. Whenever a service call was made, the car was picked up at the customer's home and returned when repairs were completed.[13] In BMW's case, outstanding after-service support did indeed provide a marketing advantage by distinguishing the company from its competitors. In this chapter, we discuss the cross-cultural aspects of the second definition of service: those of after-sales service.

IMPORTANCE OF THE AFTERMARKET

An essential part of marketing strength is the service support component. When customers buy a product, they expect certain levels of postsales support to go along with it. Defining those expectations is critical to marketing success and will be even more important when markets mature. Support is a poorly understood part of the marketing mix in most companies.

Why is service so critical? It is critical because companies will find technological differentiation increasingly difficult to maintain in the years ahead because of the increasingly high costs of doing so. In business-to-business marketing, customer service offers firms the opportunity to differentiate themselves from competitors and thereby establish a competitive edge.

Service support is emerging as a major source of profits and competitive maneuvering. For example, in 1991, U.S. businesses spent nearly $20 billion on computer service and support predicting double-digit increases for the rest of the decade. Profit margins for aftermarket services are typically about 15 to 25 percent before taxes, whereas those for products are only 7 to 11 percent. Return on investment in the service sector is in the vicinity of 70 to 80 percent, even allowing recovery in some cases in less than a year. Often, up to 25 to 40 percent of corporate revenues and from 20 to 50 percent of corporate profits can be generated from the aftermarket service components of a business.[14]

Several reasons exist for this evolving strategic emphasis. First, service is perceived as a high-profit, high-growth opportunity. With profit margins for equipment sales under pressure from foreign and domestic competition, many U.S. firms are targeting after-sales service as a key area for investment, a sharp contrast to its historical low-level image meriting little attention from top management. Managers are also beginning to realize that customers will buy more often and in greater quantity from a company they feel will support them and give maximum postsale satisfaction. Therefore, after-sale service becomes an important aspect of a company's marketing mix to build loyalty and repeat business. The aftermarket is a crucial ingredient for success in international marketing.

Companies are also realizing that technological and feature advantages are short lived. The rapid diffusion of technological change makes it increasingly difficult to maintain a competitive advantage based on product features or design. As a result, both customers and manufacturers are focusing on service as the key differentiator. Moreover, a firm's ability to provide service support has increased significantly. A number of technological advances allow companies to provide radically greater service support today as compared to 20 years ago. This capacity creates opportunities for new entrants and threatens existing players. Last but not least, customer expectations are increasing and buyers today are demanding even higher levels of service support.

Customer expectations will create opportunities for innovative products that meet changing service support needs and will increase competitive pressures to continually improve product reliability and serviceability. They will make "conventional" service contracts an endangered species. They will force manufacturers to "unbundle" the prices of products and support services. They will also create a major profit squeeze in key segments of the "information age" industries—telecommunications, computers, and office automation.[15]

Design-related strategies are of three generic types: those focusing on increasing product reliability, those changing the product design to make it more modular in construction, and those building in redundancy. Strategies which relate to support systems concentrate on changing the way service is provided in order to reduce the costs incurred by customers when equipment fails. Strategies that reduce customer risks include warranties and service contracts. Warranties are used to minimize customers' out-of-pocket costs immediately following the purchase and to ease customer fears about product reliability.

Traditionally, service support has been marketing's stepchild. It was something companies had to do to keep customers from revolting, or it was a profitable cash cow that they could milk forever. The traditional approach to service support has some or all of these shortcomings:[16]

- An explicit service support strategy is lacking.
- Responsibility for service support is diffused.
- Support needs are considered late in the product development cycle, after design is frozen and marketing strategy decisions have been made.
- Management focuses on individual support attributes ... internal, functional measures—engineering reliability, parts-fill rate, or warranty costs—rather than on customer-oriented measures such as downtime per failure.

Why has service support been so neglected, so often, so thoroughly, by so many companies? Because, in periods of market decline, customer service has often been an area for budget cuts, especially in firms that view it basically in terms of cost and not in terms of market projection or profits.

The International Importance of the Aftermarket

When exporting a product that requires after-sales service, four basic options are available to a firm:[17]

- Disregard service issues altogether.
- Contract with locals to service the product.
- Train distributors (if utilized) to provide repair and maintenance.
- Establish service personnel in the country or be prepared to provide these services long-distance from American-based service centers.

One of the most important considerations for any firm is how to service products shipped overseas, followed by the need to maintain long-distance customer relationships. Before foreign customers buy nonnative equipment, they want to be sure they will be able to get service to operate, maintain, and repair it. To maintain a long-term relationship with representatives, an exporter must take into account the provision of service to overseas customers. Exporting ventures that overlook this issue are inadvisable since such action may permanently damage the foreign reputation of a firm and its product, which creates a prohibitive barrier to international expansion at a later time. Overall, the delivery of service can make or break a sale. In order to remain internationally competitive, an exporter must provide the best service possible. The support delivered for a product determines how enthusiastic customers are about placing another order. In addition, a premium price can be commanded for a product based on servicing capabilities.

Providing adequate service is a problem in international marketing. The customers' need for service is a function of their use of a product and maintenance conditions; these may vary from market to market. On the other hand, a manufacturer's ability to supply service is a function of a firm's international involvement. Most companies selling internationally do not have subsidiaries in all their foreign markets. They must rely on their distributors to provide service where they have no facilities of their own. Finding good distributors that can also service the product is critical. The distributors' service programs must often be supplemented by the efforts of the producers.

One of the service difficulties in multinational marketing is the parts problem, which involves either expensive parts inventories in each market or shipping and importation delays in receiving the part from some central storage. No one has found an easy answer, but General Electric tried a novel approach. With each group of appliances sent to a distributor, GE sent along a spare parts kit, compiled on the basis of a statistical analysis of failure rates of various parts in various countries. It was expected to contain at least enough parts to cover the warranty period. This was sent out prepaid, supplanting the cumbersome system of giving distributors credit for each part replaced on the warranty. For GE, the advantages were savings in freight and customs costs (because of bulk rates), elimination of wasteful accounting, and most important, elimination of shipping delays.[18]

CROSS-CULTURAL DIFFERENCES IN AFTERMARKET FUNCTIONS

Warranties

A warranty is a guarantee from a manufacturer that its product will perform as stipulated. A warranty serves as a competitive tool and provides differentiation in the marketplace. It also enhances customers' confidence in the product. Warranties can be used aggressively to promote sales. If an international company has a stronger quality control program and a more reliable product than national competitors, it may gain a promotional edge through using a more liberal warranty policy. A warranty could be the difference between winning and losing a contract.

Warranties and service policies must be considered as an integral aspect of a company's international marketing strategy. Companies doing business abroad frequently find themselves at a disadvantage with the local competitors. With a supplier's plants often thousands of miles away, foreign buyers are naturally leery and expect extra assurance that a supplier will back the product. Thus, a comprehensive warranty and service policy becomes as vital a part of the marketing mix as the product or price. A warranty may only hold if a product is regularly serviced; thus, service contracts are regularly sold with many items. (Xerox's Total Satisfaction Guarantee program requires that its machines be covered by the manufacturer's maintenance program, which is usually purchased upfront.)[19]

Warranty differences may result due to environmental differences. A warranty may have to be made much more restrictive if wear and tear on the product is likely to be excessive. For example, in the dusty conditions and hot climate of Saudi Arabia, equipment such as air conditioners would wear out in a shorter period than in Finland or Sweden. A company, therefore, may offer a more liberal warranty in Switzerland than in Saudi Arabia.

Differences between legal systems affect the nature of warranties that can be offered. Competitive practices and the level of technology also influence a firm's ability to offer certain kinds of warranties and service. In the United States, most computer manufacturers provide 60- or 90-day warranties on their products; the norm for Europe or Japan is 12 months. In developing countries, where technical sophistication is below developed countries' standards, maintenance may not be adequate, causing more frequent equipment breakdowns. Until recently, many office electronics customers in Russia did not demand warranty service—because they believed that vendors could not live up to any promises made. The proportion of customers in Moscow expecting after-sales service has risen from barely 5 percent in 1994 to nearly 40 percent in 1996.[20]

Warranties have a unique meaning for the Chinese. Customarily, in China, a reputable firm is expected to stand behind its product indefinitely. The Chinese have the tendency to attribute failure of products or services to fate rather than to the company from which the product was purchased or even the manufacturer. Therefore, Chinese consumers would generally have low expectations toward products they purchase or consume; when the performance does not meet with their expectations, they would feel less dissatisfied because they think they should conform to the *Yuarn* (predestination); therefore, Western measures of dissatisfaction would tend to be irrelevant in this setting.[21]

The Japanese feel that if it is a quality product, it won't need to be repaired. If it does need service, it should be forthcoming as a matter of course. In general, the Japanese expect free after-sale service and longer warranty periods. No strings are attached when providing services for the products and typically no additional charge for any warranties exists.[22] In Japan, a product is supposed to work even after the initial warranty period expires and any minor problems are to be taken care of without additional payment. Typically, the Japanese see no need for service contracts. A reluctance exists in Japan to charge for service!

If there is a problem at a customer site, it must be fixed with no regard to cost. The Japanese customer, being a long-term partner, will tend to work to find an amenable settlement for services rendered, often without any written communication. Otherwise, charges usually must be either bundled with the parts or as upgrade packages.[23] The level of customer support in Japan does tend to require more engineering per piece of equipment of more after-sale support on products—it often seems as if service people must always be on call! The extra effort required to do business in Japan can be worth the cost in the long term and actually sustains the business being conducted. Knowing that building customer loyalty is a prerequisite to effective selling in Japan, salespeople put forth tremendous effort to achieve this end.

Koreans have traditionally paralleled the Japanese and Chinese programs. However, Samsung Electronics in 1994 launched three new after-sales service programs which cost $125 million annually. Samsung extended the warranty period for most of its consumer electronic products from one year to two years and agreed to replace any product that had to be repaired within six months of its purchase if a customer was not fully satisfied. Previously, Samsung only allowed replacements of defective products during the first month following the sales date.[24]

Warranties can be standardized if:

- the product is totally standardized, warranty variations make little sense;
- the product is taken regularly across country borders; or
- if legal standardization exists (such as in European union).

Problems do arise, however, when a manufacturing source or operating conditions vary between countries (e.g., differences in climate adaptations between cars for Spain and Sweden). IBM began in 1994 to offer its multinational customers standardized IBM pricing and warranty services by region, rather than by country.[25]

Training

In the 1950s, some European automakers entered the U.S. market without sufficient consideration of the importance of training. After the initial sales, customers were shocked and angered to find they had to wait weeks or months for parts and to find trained mechanics for their newly purchased cars. Volkswagen, having learned lessons from these prior entrants, entered the market later; Volkswagen invested heavily in parts depots and training and became successful as a result.[26]

Adequate training has become an essential element in marketing. Unlike many Americans who grew up owning automobiles and working with tools, mechanics and operators in many foreign companies rarely have had such experience before training; for many, it is on-the-job training. Improperly done, poor or no training can lead to disastrous results. A bulldozer operator learns that if he or she pulls a lever and steps on a pedal, the machine will push whatever is in front of it. When a bulldozer meets an immovable object, the operator will continue to push until the engine fails or a part breaks. In another example, despite careful instructions concerning cleanliness which the ball bearing manufacturers have included in the package, in developing countries, it is not unusual to find a mechanic removing the protective oiled paper to leave the bearing exposed to dust and grime before using it (the mechanic probably being a low-paid, uneducated, and illiterate worker). Thorough training programs by such companies as Caterpillar and Allis-Chalmers are meant to overcome such difficulties. Simple instructions with plenty of pictures get the message across to those with low levels of literacy. Having been burned many times in situations such as those described here, these companies know that whatever can go wrong will; therefore, these companies intend to assume nothing and are as complete as possible in their training courses and manuals.

The preferred Japanese training method is that of learning by doing. Training is accomplished by working together in a group. The group will train together, will be evaluated together, and will be tested together. The group discovers the source of a problem and fixes it as a team. Groups are small, designed for functional harmony. They usually will continue their training informally after hours. The emphasis is on doing, sharing experiences, having intra-group discussion, and role-playing; the orientation is highly visual (including slides, videotapes, samples, and actual hands-on demonstrations). Prereading is not highly valued unless special time is allowed for group discussion of the material. Prior to the formal training session, the Japanese may oftentimes conduct a group orientation in order to build group harmony, giving everyone a chance to get acquainted and build team spirit. A sharing of experience and learning is desired. Each person in the group must contribute to the learning environment and become part of the team. Tests of practical skills are more valuable than written tests on the same material.[27] The two-week training of KFC workers in Japan would be uneconomical in the context of U.S. workers with its high level of labor turnover, but is appropriate in Japan given the higher levels of job loyalty and the greater demands of customer service placed upon the Japanese worker in terms of politeness, courtesy, and information demands. Instructions are given, for example, on how to greet people, what tone of voice to use, and how to handle complaints or difficult inquiries. (One trainer at KFC claims she knows how to say "thank you" to the customer in over one hundred different ways.)

Most Japanese stores provide a minimum of two weeks of full-time training, the aim being to integrate the staff into a productive and loyal team. The second week is spent on in-store training. Afterward, the staff is inspected daily on the floor in a military fashion to check that its appearance is up to the typical high Japanese standard. Substantial role-playing, customer interactions, and videotaping are used in the training process of even the lowest level employees.[28] American companies such as KFC, McDonald's, and Pizza Hut have mastered this and have had great success in appealing to Japanese consumers and affecting cultural change in dining habits. The training of customer contact people is very detailed in Japan.

Many of the training methods developed in the West may not be appropriate for other cultural settings. For example, role-playing is a commonly used and effective training method in the West; it may not be as effective in a culture which is characterized by a high degree of risk avoidance. When role-playing is used in such cultures (the Chinese, for example), the participants usually do not actively participate since they have a difficult time in play acting another role.[29] Similarly, techniques used in sensitivity training may require substantial modification to be used successfully in an Asian culture.

Microsoft understands the importance of training in a successful overseas operation. Microsoft is spending $2 million annually, training thousands of technicians and programmers at centers and universities throughout China. One of its principal purposes in doing so is to alleviate the dearth of Windows applications present in China. It must also train thousands of technicians at Chinese banks, state-owned industries, and other government bureaucracies to work on Windows. Microsoft has set up training institutes at the Chinese Academy of Social Sciences—three universities and more than 70 centers employing 32 full-time Chinese instructors, who trained in the United States. The payback is thousands of offices running ten thousands of PCs, most of them running Windows 95 and Windows NT and connected with Microsoft servers. The Chinese government wanted an operating system especially designed for mainland China's character fonts. Microsoft fully expects to establish Windows as the national platform.[30]

The Chinese, like most East Asians, expect and demand structure. Therefore, Chinese training programs should be highly structured. Trainers should clearly outline the goals of the course to participants. Participants should receive checklists of what they are supposed to learn so they can measure their own progress. Giving clear, immediate, and frequent feedback to participants is essential. Chinese managers are thirsty for new ideas, new tools, and new information, so any course should be challenging. Interactive training is a foreign concept to most Chinese, who are accustomed to rote and lecture methods.[31]

While training is an important element in any service organization, training becomes critical, complex, and the greatest need for an organization in any culture where service is perceived to be synonymous with servitude or unskilled labor. Where this is the case, understanding the concept of marketing and service is difficult and behavioral changes will be a necessary element in the training program, a cultural transition to move the organization and its employees from a traditional unit to a service-oriented unit.[32] For example, in Eastern Europe, employees were literally trained to have very low levels of self-esteem; management wanted to discourage any behavior on the part of the employees which could lead to a potential rebellion against the system. Obviously, this mentality is completely contrary to what one would want to install in any profit-oriented firm. Furthermore, managers have historically worked for the state and employees learned not to like or trust managers. As a result, teaching employees to believe in themselves, to take pride in their work, and to trust their management becomes a major cultural change[33] and must first be performed before any subsequent training can be effective.

Manuals

Any American who has assembled a foreign-made bicycle at 2 a.m. on Christmas morning will empathize with the need for properly constructed and translated manuals. Many manuals are horrible because they are often translated improperly. Literacy rates and educational levels may require changes in instruction manuals and training procedures. Brazilians have overcome this by including videotapes with detailed repair instructions as part of the standard instruction package. They also minimize spare parts problems by using the standardized off-the-shelf parts available throughout the world. While translating is almost mandatory, many of the idioms in manuals need to be clarified as well as translated. Most companies want manuals that are quick and cheap. Usually, they have an engineer—one who hates to write—write the instructions. These engineers do not write for consumers but for other engineers. To make matters worse, instructions written by engineers are often translated by people who are not totally familiar with the language. What results is totally incomprehensible material.

The Japanese Philosophy of the Aftermarket

Customer service, along with product quality and after-sales service, are the triple pillars of marketing and selling in Japan. Japanese business is strongly oriented toward providing service to its customers and is concerned about meeting their needs. Great attention is paid to research on what customers want. One of the frequent complaints about foreign business is that certain firms do not take the trouble to find out what their Japanese customers want. They ship clothing that doesn't fit the Japanese physique and appliances that are too large for Japanese living space and not adapted to lower voltage and frequencies. On the other hand, Japanese manufacturers tend to be well attuned to their own customers' special needs. Japanese machine tool producers found that their American customers used (punished) the machines more than their Japanese customers. Because of their higher labor costs, American firms used the machines more intensively and could not afford downtime for maintenance. The Japanese producers had to modify both their product and their service program when selling in the American market.

The Japanese have developed exacting standards for product quality, durability, and reliability. Consumers also tend to place emphasis on the appearance of products and packaging. Form is as important as function. Many customer complaints center around scratches and other exterior damage to daily necessities and household goods. Retailers must then take extra care in handling merchandise to prevent damage. Standards for product performance are also strict. Consumers demand reliability and good after-sales service and will change brands if they find an item functions poorly. In this instance, a Japanese consumer expects an immediate response from the manufacturer. Japanese customers feel it is their right to be treated as the central figure in any transaction, to receive careful, respectful service. A major concern with Japanese purchase of any imported products is the length of time it takes to have them repaired.

An example of Japanese concern for the aftermarket can be seen in their thoroughness in doing business in the Middle East. As the Mideastern automobile market expanded, so, too, did demand for spare parts, gas station equipment, tires, repair shop tools, and mechanical services. Japanese motor vehicle manufacturers were quick to see the potential of this market and trained auto mechanics all over the region in the art of auto repair. In one such venture,

Toyota, Nissan, and Honda helped Libya set up service shops in 44 towns and cities. Toyota sent three experts to Libya to give technical advice on building a repair shop in Tripoli, and Libyans went to Japan for training in motor servicing techniques. Honda also sent auto experts to Libya, while Nissan trained mechanics at its service centers in Athens as well as in Japan.[34] The automakers counted on the service market not only to provide a lucrative sidelight to the main business of selling cars, but also to boost Mideast demand for Japanese vehicles. The region is now Japan's second largest market for automobile sales, but still way behind the number one market— the United States. If Mideast mechanics are trained to service Japanese cars, the reasoning goes, people in the market for a new car are more likely to choose a brand they know they can have repaired locally. By way of contrast, neglect of the aftermarket requirements of the automotive industry cost GM dearly in Thailand: Its Opel brand sold nearly 7,000 models its first year in 1994; by 1996, sales were merely 783 cars, primarily due to lack of service centers and troubles getting parts and service from GM/Opel.[35]

The Japanese cultural traditions of expecting and receiving a high degree of quality service and aftermarket support appears to have become common practice in their international business activities. For Japanese businesses, service is now an integral component of their marketing mix. For the Japanese, "value-added" is not just in terms of a product itself, but in the service that accompanies it.

SUMMARY

In the United States, no one has to be sold anymore on the values of customer service. Whether their customers come from the consumer or industrial sector, just about every distribution department worth its salt now knows how a vigorous customer service effort can pay off directly in enlarged market share and higher profits. Usually, the foreign customers of these same U.S. firms have had their service problems handled by third parties. The belief has been that these services should be left up to the importer in the host country. The result, unfortunately, has been that foreign customers have not received effective service from their U.S. suppliers. In essence, companies are going to have to rethink their traditional beliefs about customer service just to maintain their present market positions.

In general, most U.S. companies do not get much respect in the international marketplace. In the past, U.S. companies have often been regarded by their overseas customers as too slow, too narrow, and too half-hearted in their approach;[36] unfortunately, these complaints are largely legitimate. One ingredient to success is flexibility, being able to adjust the system to needs as they arise. A willingness to listen and learn is so important to international customer service; nothing can be assumed to be standardized when dealing with foreign customers. In one survey conducted, the U.S. companies had acceptable speed of delivery and integration with production but had negative, unacceptable ratings for support punctuality and satisfactory delivery. An international marketer of technical products needs service capability to accredit his or her firm with foreign buyers. The marketer will hesitate to purchase a product, however good, unless he or she is assured of service backup. A firm with a strong service program can gain a competitive edge.

American businesses typically divorce the warranty from the product, making it just another saleable item; this only reinforces the impression that U.S. companies have no confidence in their own products. In an evaluation of many of the Fortune 500 companies, it was found that only 13 of the top 50 have international distribution or international customer service departments.[37] The aggressive sales function in the corporate marketing effort is nurtured and rewarded while the service and support (utility) function goes unappreciated. This is changing, but slowly. Many companies are beginning to see the light and the potential rewards in the aftermarket and in establishing and maintaining long-term relationships, that is, those which extend past the next quarterly report. However, these firms are still all too few in number.

American firms must learn to understand, appreciate, and deliver the same exact standards of service and aftermarket attention as their Japanese competitors if they are to become (or remain) major players in the world markets. Customers expect service quality as part of every purchase, but only a minority of American companies really deliver it. Advertisements, slogans, and lip service will not do—managers in most U.S. companies have not yet accepted the full responsibility for satisfying customers. The secret of Japanese success is quite simply a commitment to customers for life. Customer-driven strategy requires quality and service excellence at every level; customers are brought into every department of a company, their voices heard, and feedback acted upon.

The sales function in Japan is intimately mixed with the service function. Free service is usually expected on products. For example, with orders for heavy machinery, a supplier is responsible for installation, operator training, maintenance, and service long after the warranty on the equipment expires. Indeed, many suppliers have automatic checkup inspections for their machinery. This may continue for up to 20 years after purchase. This ongoing inspection serves to cement the relationship as well as to ensure proper performance. Having one person coordinating both sales and service forces the employees to look on service as a sales function.[38] Frequently, repeat orders/business are sold not by the salesman, but by the serviceman.

International customer service is not a new management discipline, but it is still an area on which companies must constantly refocus their attention if they are to compete internationally. American industry currently has a poor image in the minds of foreign customers with regard to its degree of concern for customer service. This is a costly image problem. As many foreign customers have said or thought: "Americans are more concerned about their home markets than about foreign customers. Why should I buy goods from an American company when I know the service will be bad, when I can get a better product and better service from a supplier in another country?" American companies realize the importance of customer service in marketing to international customers, yet customer service for international markets is not considered to be appreciably more important than it is for domestic ones.[39] Some American firms, though, have just not learned their lessons, but are teaching the class. Leading U.S. distributors, such as Avnet, Inc., offer a range of sophisticated services that have become key competitive weapons overseas as well as major profit generators. Part replenishment programs and logistics management it offers to its customers are far superior to those available from European and Asian distributors.[40]

International standardization has begun. The European Union nations have legal provisions on the guarantees offered by sellers in the event of a defect in their products: in the case of a defect, the buyer has the right to reject the contract or to obtain a price reduction. The purchaser has the right to sue for damages where there has been negligence or deliberate deception on the part of the seller. No standards exist on legal guarantees, though.[41] Liberalization and standardization in Europe's telecommunications industry has made it feasible for midsize firms to organize centralized after-sales and support centers that allow seamless routing of toll-free calls across the European Union.[42] Although the cost of setting up such after-sales support systems is high, the long-term benefits, including creating loyal customers and collecting marketing intelligence, far outweigh the expense. Volvo trucks used the following methods to create a pan-European before- and after-sales network:[43]

- Marketing information systems standardized format across Europe
- Common standards were developed in conjunction with dealers and importers
- A manager in each dealership was appointed to work on common standards
- Three-day training seminars for importers and Volvo headquarters staff

The aftermarket function is beginning to take preeminence even in promotions. Daewoo kicked off the launch of its luxury car, not stressing the product, but totally emphasizing the service and after-sales care available for the car.[44] This is also true in high-tech companies which are discovering that they need to differentiate themselves from rivals to appeal to their customers. Technology alone is insufficient; after-sales support is the differentiator. Yet, the steady rise of customer expectations means that suppliers must continue to not only provide but to continually improve their services. This is being done by setting up around-the-clock support lines, better-educated staff, creating overseas customer support centers, and establishing crossborder telecommunications links.[45] Hewlett

Packard created its Worldwide Customer Support Operations (WCSO) to centralize its aftermarket services. Employing 16,000 people, HP offers seamless service at any hour of the day from anywhere in the world through a global chain of response centers, including major centers in the UK, Atlanta, California, and Australia. Problems which cannot be resolved in a smaller center may be transferred to a major center, one of which is always in full operation. It now not only delivers support services but also global account management.

Chapter 14

Cross-Cultural Dimensions
of Service Quality

The third of the three service definitions is customer service, that is, service quality, how a service is performed, and how a customer perceives a performed service as compared to expectations. Quality has traditionally been defined in one of three ways:

1. Quality is conforming to specifications.

The quality of an item depends on how well it measures up against a set of specifications; quality is achieved when a product is produced the way it is supposed to be.[1] According to this definition, a Mercedes may be of lower quality than a Chevrolet if the Chevrolet conforms better to the design and performance standards set for it. The Japanese see low quality as the result of inefficiency: a "good" product is both error-free and made as cheaply (efficiently) as possible. This managerial definition is inadequate because it misses the difference in perception between two similar products. *? which ?*

2. Quality lies in the eyes of the beholder.

Different users have different needs, and to the extent that a product is designed and manufactured to meet those needs, quality is dependent on how well it fulfills them. Individual consumers are assumed to have different wants or needs, and the goods that best satisfy their preferences are the ones they regard as having the highest quality. This is an idiosyncratic and personal view of quality, one that is highly subjective. For business travelers, the highest quality airline is usually the one with the best record of on-time arrivals and departures; for vacationers, it may be the airline with the finest food, the quickest in-flight service, the cheapest fares, or the most interesting movies. In the marketing literature, subjectively viewing quality has led to the notion of "ideal points": precise combinations of product attributes that provide the greatest satisfaction to a specified consumer. This concept, however, faces two problems. The first is practical: how to aggregate widely varying individual preferences so that they lead to more meaningful definitions of quality at the market level. The second is more fundamental: how to distinguish those product attributes that connote quality from those that simply maximize consumer satisfaction. This definition is incomplete because quality is extremely subjective: quality is simply what a user says it is, be it rational or not.

3. Quality is innate excellence.

This definition reflects the belief that although styles and tastes change, there is something enduring about works of high quality. They provide a standard against which other products are judged. According to this view, excellence is both absolute and universally recognizable; whatever it consists of—and the writers in this camp are distressingly vague on that point—people all know it when they see it. Michelangelo may not be everyone's favorite artist, but it is hard to deny the quality of his work. While recognizing the universal aspects of quality, this definition lacks specifics.[2]

In essence, quality is a word used by an individual to describe whether his or her perception of a product or service has reached a satisfactory level of excellence. If customers believe a product or service will provide certain benefits at a satisfactory level time and again, they may deem the product a quality product. Quality can and should be used as a market differentiator. Adding service to the core product may differentiate the product over competitors' products, provided the consumers are able to recognize (and appreciate) such differences and have actually experienced the product of competitors. If a customer does not have the experience of comparisons between competitors, this usually results in brand indifference. This was the case in Eastern Europe during the communist era. Consumers did not have a choice in the products they could buy, so they waited in long lines to just buy whatever was available. As a result, consumers did not gain consumer experience in comparing brands. Consumer satisfaction was not a concept that existed during that era.

DIFFERENCES BETWEEN GOODS
AND SERVICE QUALITY

A product may be defined as a good or a service, but more often, it has both intangible and physical elements (the "service goods continuum"). This dualism affects quality perception. For service-related companies (and the service-related component of goods), quality is a particularly elusive concept. In labor-intensive services, quality occurs during service delivery, usually in an interaction between a client and a contact person from the service firm. The service firm may also have less managerial control over quality in services where consumer participation is intense (e.g., haircuts, doctor visits), because the client in these instances affects the process. In these situations, the consumer's input (description of how the haircut should look, description of symptoms) becomes critical to the quality of service performance. When purchasing goods, a consumer employs many tangible cues to judge quality: style, hardness, color, label, feel, package, fit. When purchasing services, fewer tangible cues exist. In the absence of tangible evidence on which to evaluate quality, consumers must depend on other cues such as a service provider's physical facilities, equipment, and personnel.[3] In judging product quality, customers often use intrinsic cues such as price, advertising, or brand name. Due to service intangibility, a firm may find it more difficult to understand how consumers perceive services and service quality.[4]

In general, these differences between service quality and goods quality are true:

- Service quality is more difficult for consumers to evaluate than goods quality.
- Service quality perceptions result from a comparison of consumer expectations with actual service performance.
- Quality evaluations are not made solely on the outcome of a service; they also involve evaluations of the process of service delivery.
- Service quality is a measure of how well the service level delivered matches customer expectations. Delivering quality service means conforming to customer expectations on a consistent basis.

SERVQUAL AND CULTURE

The introduction of the Service Quality model (SERVQUAL)[5,6] revolutionized the discipline of services marketing. The service gap concept discussed the existence of service gaps on the service provider's side that can impede delivery of services that customers perceive to be of high quality. The model proposed five gaps that are major hurdles in attempting to deliver proper service.

The SERVQUAL model resulted in five dimensions which describe the customer experience: (1) reliability is providing what is promised, dependably and accurately; (2) assurance is the knowledge and courtesy of employees and their ability to convey trust and confidence; (3) tangibles are the physical facilities and equipment and the appearance of personnel; (4) empathy is the degree of caring and individual attention provided to customers; and (5) responsiveness is the willingness to help customers and provide prompt service. According to survey results, reliability is the most powerful dimension, responsiveness is second, followed by assurance, empathy, and tangibles. Most organizations are best at tangibles, which is the least important, and perform lowest on reliability. The SERVQUAL model has been predominantly tested and domestically enhanced within the United States.

Internationally, the results of studies using the SERVQUAL model on non-American respondents have more than occasionally disputed those found in the United States. A SERVQUAL study of the Dutch car service industry found that the American five dimensions did not emerge; instead three dimensions were discovered: customer kindness, tangibles, and faith,[7] with only customer kindness contributing directly to the measured service quality. A study of SERVQUAL in the banking services in Hong Kong appears to indicate that SERVQUAL can be a consistent and reliable scale to measure service quality; however, the five American dimensions of SERVQUAL could not be confirmed.[8] A SERVQUAL survey of Singapore's five major banks measured gaps between customers' expectations and the perceived performance of the service; the widest gap between perceived performance and expectations was in the dimension of empathy while the dimension of tangibles showed the smallest gap. Banks' customers' expectations were highest for reliability;[9] thus, the results were similar to those found in SERVQUAL-United States, but significant differences were noted as well. A study of retail banking in the United Kingdom used SERVQUAL to describe both customer and staff perceptions of those factors which determine service quality. The study determined SERVQUAL model was of limited value and proposed an alternative basis for modeling service quality based upon the three dimensions of process/outcome, subjective/objective, and soft/hard.[10] A SERVQUAL study of Turkish hotels showed that users expect to get friendly, courteous, clean, expert service but without special, personalized attention. The survey confirmed several of the SERVQUAL attributes (particularly reliability), but also introduced other dimensions of major concern to the Turks (cleanliness, social interaction, and timeliness) that were not in the American study; the Turkish study concluded by commenting that the SERVQUAL is not necessarily generic or universal.[11] Another study examined the service quality gaps in the Australian consulting engineering industry,[12] while one reviewed several industries in New Zealand;[13] neither could confirm the American dimensions.

Use of SERVQUAL to examine service quality differences cross-culturally, between two countries or two cultures, is even rarer. In one study,[14] comparisons were made between service quality concepts in developed countries versus developing countries:

Developed Countries	Developing Countries
emphasize technology	emphasize personnel
emphasize excellence	emphasize "merely good"
pursue continuous improvement	intermittent improvement
nonpersonal contacts	personal contacts
know customer intimately	know how customer uses service
timely response	substantial response
competence in individuals	competence in organizations
respect individual rights	stress social norms
detailed information	basic information
individual benefits	acceptance by public
company performance	company tradition
emotional security	physical security
stress core and noncore service	core only—noncore is less important

The concept of global service quality is further confused since cultural definitions of appropriate hospitality differ widely from one country to another, one example being the tolerable length of customer waiting time (time until service provided) (which is much longer in Brazil than in Germany) and the degree of personal service expected (not much in Scandinavia but lavish in Indonesia). Economics may play an important part in service quality: customers in undeveloped countries typically accept a lower level of service as adequate and expected since they cannot afford the costs involved in higher levels of service. When a country is bankrupt, the people eliminate everything that they know is not basic for their subsistence and base their decisions almost entirely on price, instead of other qualities such as quality and durability.[15] The most important decision in these markets becomes satisfying the most basic needs at the lowest possible price.

CROSS-CULTURAL VIEWS
OF SERVICE QUALITY

Service is the attempt of a person to fulfill the perceived needs of another within a particular social environment. Culture determines what service providers and consumers perceive as needs, what and how they will communicate, what they value, and how they will react to each other. A provider enters the service experience with a predisposition to certain behaviors based on his or her own national or ethnic culture, as well as the culture of the service organization he or she represents. A consumer also brings cultural baggage to the experience, a predisposition to expect and react in culturally prescribed ways.

Customer satisfaction is an overall postpurchase evaluation. One study defines customer satisfaction as general satisfaction, confirmation of expectations, and the distance from the customer's hypothetical ideal product. As the ideal point differs according to culture, the definition of customer satisfaction also should differ between cultures.[16] A desirable level of customer satisfaction results when the service consumer's expectations are met or exceeded. Those expectations are shaped by culture. Customers demand services on their own terms. If their expectations are met, they pronounce the service good. If the service delivered does not meet with customers culturally shaped expectations, they will be unimpressed by and dissatisfied with the service's experience and organization.

Companies marketing goods and services in many developing or undeveloped countries often benefit from the luxury of limited or no competition. As a result of such noncompetitive environment, few companies needed to focus on customer needs and little effort was made to find ways to improve satisfaction. Instead, the level of product or service quality offered to customers was often dictated by the company's existing capabilities, without much incentive to broaden or extend those capabilities.[17] Consumers in such countries are not accustomed to being asked for their opinions and suggestions on customer satisfaction issues.

The American service style can be described as extremely close and friendly; contact persons try to be attentive and friendly toward customers. An illustration is a waitress who comes up to the customer and says, "Hi, I'm Judy. I'm your waitress today. What can I do for you?" She will address her customers in the same manner throughout the entire service production process. Efficiency is important because, working in a market economy, she gets paid by results and she is usually rewarded for going beyond her nominal job description.[18]

The European style of service differs significantly across the continent. In general, the European service style is not as efficient as the American style, and is not as attentive as the East Asian style. It is also apparent that in Europe, north to south, attentiveness increases. In the Netherlands, consumers do not complain because they doubt its efficacy. In the Nordic countries, remoteness is more clearly present. The British tolerate bad service, which can be attributed to the remnants of the British class system under which only servants served: Waiters, busboys, and salesmen like to remind customers in a rude manner that they are not servants.[19]

Service in Germany can be best described as an oxymoron. Aversion to service is the flip side of a deeply rooted tradition: the centuries-old importance of craftsmanship, of making things well. Nothing else, including customers, seems to matter. The *Field of Dreams* theme appears to dominate in Germany: if we make it good, they will buy it. The slogan in Germany seems to be "shut up and pay." It took an American in Berlin fifteen months to get a new phone line installed in his office; and he was on a "priority first access list." A man tried to buy a loaf of bread; it was wrapped and ready to go, but because it was a few minutes before closing time and the cash in the register had already been counted, the woman behind the counter refused the customer's money, saying she could not make change and that he had to wait until the next day to buy bread. Because Germans generally do not take bad jobs and labor costs are so high, waiters and waitresses tend to be few and far between, even in popular restaurants. That they are surly is not surprising.[20]

The French have traditionally behaved similarly, believing in *Caveat Emptor*, let the buyer beware. Traditionally, the client was never king, and was usually considered wrong. The wind is turning and the phrase *le client est roi*, the client is king, is increasingly heard at French management seminars. The arrival of non-French companies in France and the loss of considerable market share to foreign companies that do provide superior service is the major reason for this turnaround in opinion.

Hospitality and service are part of the Arab culture, one part that honors those who serve others (as in the phrase, "The servant of the group is their master"). Nevertheless, in recent times, probably due to the rising affluence of Gulf citizens, the word "services" in Saudi Arabia has begun to connote demeaning work, and few Gulf citizens willingly engage in service-related jobs. The unevenness of service quality is due to high labor intensity, weak internal marketing, and the high turnover of foreign labor working in services. Despite huge investments in selecting and training customer contact personnel, they still refuse to smile or be courteous to the customers.[21] Employees regularly remind their superiors that they are government employees whose task is to process customers' papers, not to perform public relations work.

The Soviet Communist system was one in which the consumer counted for nothing and resulted in a consumer unfriendly system and indifferent attitudes by the service provider. In a Soviet hotel/motel, one did not check in but rather applied for a room. In a hotel where Western tourists normally stayed, a coachload of applicants (not guests) would line up for an appointment with the usual one receptionist at the check-in counter. On reaching the desk, every tourist would provide a written confirmation of a prepaid reservation which surprised the clerk. Every tourist was sent away with a ticket. On each floor, a keylady sat, ready to swap the ticket for a room key. Often the room key was missing, having accidentally been given to someone else. The tourist would then be asked to return to the reception desk and start the lengthy process all over again. Tourist staff members were neither helpful nor solicitous enough to provide tourists with the feeling of warmth and hospitality. Tourists usually had to pay high room rates for mediocre services. Sheets were not changed daily, bathroom floors were unclean, air conditioners did not function properly, and restaurants offered only limited choices of food and beverages.[22] During the Soviet era, many cafeterias and restaurants with empty tables refused to admit customers. The reason? Their quotas had been filled and the admitting of additional customers would mean extra work for the employees who would not get any extra pay for the extra work demanded by the additional customers. The Soviet service style could best be described as nonattentive, remote, and inefficient.[23]

This attitude of indifference to whether the Soviets sold anything or not occurred because in the Communist system pay was the same regardless of the level of sales and service performed. Thus, there was no incentive to provide good service. In almost all shops and convenience stores, a customer was required to stand in one line to place an order and obtain a ticket, stand in another line to pay for the order and obtain a receipt, then go stand in the first line again to pick up the order. This was implemented to prevent theft among employees. The procedure was in place to ensure control, not to elicit customer satisfaction.[24] This system dominated throughout Eastern Europe as well as Russia. (Customer service itself was not a term used in any communist country.) Many Eastern Europeans are still perplexed by Western expectations that unhappy workers put on a "happy face" when dealing with customers. (Such a requirement strikes many employees as artificial and insincere.)

Now that business is more commercialized, salespersons care more, but still typically do not do anything fancy. The major reason is lack of competition. The substandard nature of Socialist retailing can be seen by the populace preference for private shops over state-owned stores, even if the former have higher prices and are further away. Perceptions of stores in terms of layout, cleanliness, atmosphere, good service, quality foods, price, and good variety of merchandise favors private shops.[25] Many of these inefficiencies can be attributed to the former Communist government controls placed on these sectors and the low status which inhibited competition and innovation in the retail sectors. Remnants of Communist retailing remain: an average store's atmosphere is not pleasant, its layout is not especially convenient, and the staff are not typically helpful.

Customers in Eastern Europe and Russia are, nonetheless, getting acquainted with the concept of service and are beginning to expect higher levels of service. Elcint (an Israeli maker of medical equipment) had Eastern European customers who at first had little service expectations and would have been overjoyed to have seen a field technician within six weeks after a problem arose. Today, if the solution takes over a week, they get impatient and testy. Although still considerably behind the U.S. standard of same-day or next-day service, it is a major improvement within a few short years.[26]

The almost entire lack of customer service culture is one of Mexico's biggest problems. Mexicans may be friendly with each other, but little is thought about servicing a person's needs. People come for service and it is given with little thought about whether it is good or bad. Cynical customers are wise that their complaints are frequently futile and their expectations are, therefore, much lower. Prices do not necessarily correspond with the level of service as Americans have become used to; instead, prices correlate with masses of people who are substituting for service. In Mexico, as in most of Latin America, good service is denoted by numbers: if there are many people serving you, you are getting good service, the more people, the better the service.[27]

Mexico, although a developing country, is far from an impoverished country. A wide variety and flavor of consumer goods, in all categories, are available in Mexico. Yet, without fail, wealthier Mexicans still fly or drive to the United States to shop. Those Mexicans in border communities cross the border en masse to shop in American stores; retailing is a major industry in many American border towns. Why is this so? Isn't toilet paper still toilet paper? No. To many Mexicans, American products have a higher degree of quality than those of comparative Mexican products. Even when the same product is offered, that found in an American store is considered higher quality than the same product offered in a Mexican store. Mexicans, used to poorer quality domestic goods, are thus more demanding and have higher perceived quality needs than would a typical American.[28]

One study of complaint behavior by Mexican-Americans indicated Hispanics rated delayed or nondelivery of goods and services as the top complaint (32 percent) while national BBB (Better Business Bureau) statistics ranked unsatisfactory service the number one complaint area (which accounted for only 5 percent of the Hispanics complaints) followed by delivery and delay. Lower levels of Mexican-American complaints for unsatisfactory service may be due to lower expectations for resolution of service-related problems or due to the Hispanic perception of time. Delay and nondelivery may be more important to Mexican-Americans and determine their attitudes toward customer satisfaction than to the general population.[29]

In Africa, many small stores are open until late at night. Poor people go to the market where prices are negotiated. Salespeople will say anything to make you buy. They lie a lot about bad quality products and when a buyer tries to return such a product, the same salesman will deny that he sold it. Grocery stores called NTCs (National Trading Corporations), that are owned by the government are cheaper and provide better service.

The nature of Oriental service is empathetic, but remote. For example, most taxi drivers in Tokyo wear white gloves during working hours. They do not talk to their customers, but are very attentive and have even found a technical solution for opening the door for their customers automatically. In Japan, tour guides take extremely good care of their groups to prevent their getting into difficulties, but guides do not try to establish close contact with customers. They too wear uniform and gloves, distinguishing themselves from tourists. Workers tend to be better trained, more knowledgable, and not as pushy as those in the United States. The Japanese belief is that service is free, or should be. Tipping somebody means paying for a personal service, an insult in a culture still dominated by an emphasis on sacrifice for the common good. Taxis do not charge extra for luggage. This is achieved by burying the service costs in the relatively higher prices charged for the physical product. Service in Japan is still very much a matter of personal attention.[30]

Chinese tourists have often complained of the poor quality of service. Due to the small number of Chinese who have actually experienced living abroad, many Chinese tend to lack an understanding and appreciation of international service standards and visitors' expectations.[31] More important, service jobs have traditionally been considered demeaning and many individuals are assigned by the government to work in specific service positions (e.g., hotel worker, tour guide). Once assigned, minimal opportunity exists for advancement, and low wages do not permit increases in personal standards of living. The morale of Chinese service workers is further eroded by observing the special treatment provided the foreign tourists, the modern facilities, the services provided which are not available to an average worker.[32] Little tradition of hospitality exists among the Chinese.

In a Service Quality Center in Singapore that trains workers for Singapore, workers undergo basic training in a seven-day program, developing skills such as telephone manners, grooming, handling customer complaints, and keeping their tempers. Singapore is worried about losing its competitive edge. Since Singapore is basically a service town, it must offer excellent service to retain its comparative advantage over other enclaves. The problem is that young Singaporeans who work in services have grown up in relative prosperity, and their attitude to serving others often is casual and haphazard.[33]

Global Scan has classified global consumers into five distinct categories: Strivers (26 percent), Achievers (25 percent), Pressured (13 percent), Traditionalists (18 percent), and Adapters (18 percent). Segment sizes varied widely from country to country. The Strivers set highest priority on good service: yuppies, Gen Xers, young people on the go. The French have the highest proportion of Strivers (33 percent), followed by Achievers (22 percent) who are boomers, opinion leaders, and style setters. The Spanish are passionate about achievement; 60 percent are Achievers. Hong Kong Achievers are the most materialistic and most pressured. Germans dominate Traditionalists and Adapters. The traditionalists are the most conservative.[34]

SERVICE JAPANESE STYLE

Customer service, product quality, and after-sales service are the pillars of successful marketing in Japan. Consumers in Japan generally pay much more for the same item than do American consumers. Therefore, service quality has become a major component of the marketing mix, as the consumers' expectations are based on both the cost and the limited choices available. Customers expect prompt service and availability of a full line of parts for any major purchase.[35] Automobile firms have close relationships with their dealers, who carry only one brand and have exclusive territories. Building customer loyalty is a major goal for Japanese salesmen, and they go to enormous trouble and great effort to give their customers with fine service.

In Japan, personal banking service is more important than in the United States because Japan has traditionally been a cash- rather than a check-oriented society. It is not uncommon for a businessperson to visit a bank several times a day or an individual to visit a bank several times a week. A typical Japanese bank has a greeter (*annaigakari*) who greets everyone entering the bank and makes sure that they know where to go, handles inquiries, watches for suspicious people, and keeps track of complaints and problems. *Gaiko*, a Japanese personal banker, calls on customers at their offices or canvasses entire neighborhoods, in the process creating relationships and stimulating new business as well as helping current customers. The *gaiko* regularly go to such extremes as helping customers sell or buy homes, finding distributors for their merchandise, providing them with tax advice, and finding tenants for their buildings. These off-site activities of servicepeople in Japan are often intrusive. A *gaiko* in Japan is expected to know the investment portfolio of clients and to make suggestions as to how the bank's services could be employed.

Most service organizations in Japan have quality circles (QCs). These employee groups meet regularly (outside of business hours) to attempt to brainstorm and improve efficiency and service. Sanwa, one of the first Japanese banks to introduce QCs, had at one time well over 2,000 active groups. The QC group of doormen in one Japanese hotel collected names of important people so that they could greet them by name. Telephone operators' QC decided to place mirrors in front of the switchboard to improve their self awareness and combat boredom that may interfere with their responses.[36]

Japanese companies attach tremendous weight to customer feedback—complaints and comments. The consumer can return any item with a minimum of bother, since a store will be anxious to know if the item is being returned because of some perceived defect. Stores are required to make a detailed report to the manufacturer on any defects and to send the offending item back to the manufacturer's quality control center for careful analysis. Manufacturers listen to what users complain about most and then redesign their products to correct those features. Customer satisfaction in Japan is a highly quantified and driving force in the management process. Nissan and Toyota measure their dealers by regular surveys of customer satisfaction with sales and service.

Consumers expect a serious reaction from the provider because it is a measure of the company's sincerity and trustworthiness. JAL gives its cabin crews longer etiquette and politeness training than any other airline, so its customers rarely need to demand an apology or a refund. In department stores, executives and clerks alike line up to bow to the first customers in the store, setting the tone for how customers are to be treated.[37] Service must precede all products, regardless of how advanced or unique they are.

First-rate service is the standard by which all Japanese products/ services are judged. First-rate in Japan is a level of attentiveness and care for the customer's personal needs, as well as business needs, where the Japanese surpass the usual measurements of involvement. *Sabisu* is the Japanese word for "service": helpful, beneficial, or friendly action. The service-minded Japanese attach importance to promptness. The rare tip given in Japan is a token of appreciation for, rather than in anticipation of, good service and helps to establish a rapport between the guest and the host. Japanese firms deliver a much higher level of personal service than those in the United States, an estimated 60 percent higher. Most hotels in Japan employ hostesses to usher people into elevators. Long before you approach the elevator, they press the call button for you, they bow as you approach, and their gloved hands direct you into the open elevator, holding the door open until all their passengers have entered; similarly, all large department stores offer escalator hostess service.[38]

In Japanese retail stores, customers are treated as honored guests. When a customer enters an establishment, staff members nearby will greet the customer with a standardized call of *irasshai mase* (welcome). This will often be stated in a loud, vigorous tone, which becomes more decorous as the status of the establishment increases. When a customer leaves, there will be a chorus of *arigato gozai masu* (thank you very much) from all nearby staff.[39]

Japanese retailers compete fiercely in the area of sales service. Free home delivery is available even for small purchases. During the gift-giving season, sales personnel are sent to the houses of important customers to handle gift orders.

Service to a Japanese vendor means no effort will be spared to make a customer feel he or she is the center of everything. To a retail establishment, this means that there are enough salespeople so that no customer will have to wait long, and many assistant managers to see that everyone is looked after properly. A place is provided to leave a customer's children, and maybe exhibits to see while in the store. Having one employee to continuously wipe off the escalator railings is the typical high service level for a Japanese retail establishment.[40] Because consumers are paying a premium for the department store's name, they expect not just premium packaging, but overwhelming service. Not to do so would endanger the store's prestige, loyalty, and status.

Koichi Satoh, president and general manager of the Hotel Okura says, "The only thing we deliver or are trying to deliver to our guests is satisfaction . . . we have nothing else." The hotel has installed private fax and data lines with individual numbers. Detailed planning is the norm: "What if a mega earthquake hits you in the middle of the night damaging the kitchen: will you say 'I'm sorry guests, no breakfast?' In our business, no excuse is accepted when something goes wrong. We have provisions of food and water for three days." Service tops the list of a survey of Japanese guests, while American guests (on the same survey) gave priority to the physical amenities of the room and hotel security.

OKYAKASUMA WA KAMISAMA DESU— THE CUSTOMER IS GOD

For Japanese companies, the "customer is king" attitude is not good enough. In the United States, it is said that the customer is always right; in Japan, it is said that *okyakasuma wa kamisama desu*—the customer is God.[41] This attitude of respect permeates entire organizations. When a company loses face, each member of the organization accepts culpability and shame: It is not the company, but *my* company. *Anshin* is the Japanese word for "trust from the heart" or security and comfort. The object is to increase the comfort level of one's customers, to go far beyond providing quality products on time; typical Japanese customers want to be comfortable with their business partners and suppliers. *Anshin* is to understand the customers' needs; to be responsive to customer demands is an obligation, not a luxury.

The goals of attaining *anshin* are to enhance satisfaction and to give customers the assurance that one's company will be there for them. Even more important, good communications serve to mitigate the kinds of misunderstandings that can damage long-term relationships. Addressing key issues immediately reassures customers that they have a vendor that is committed to their success. This is done because, according to Japanese custom, the individual is at ease only when the spirit is "satisfied." *Ki ga susumanai* roughly means "my spirit is dissatisfied" and is used to describe feelings of incompleteness about any unfinished business.[42] Customer loyalty fosters repeat business and referrals. *Anshinkan* (peace of mind) is designed to reassure customers that a business is reliable and trustworthy. The vendors' motto is "spoil the customer and satisfy his whims or whatever is needed to hold his business."[43]

Hilton International launched its *Wa No Kutsurogi* service brand in Tokyo. This translates to "Comfort and Service, the Japanese

Way" and consists of distinctive features and amenities, such as Oriental restaurants on the premises and green tea service, targeted to both business and leisure travelers. Studies have indicated that the key requirements of Japanese travelers are to feel secure and comfortable, to be able to maximize limited time overseas, and to stay in hotels that maintain high standards of cleanliness and have a smart appearance.

To achieve the level of personalized service the Japanese market demands often requires considerable staffing: Hotel Okura in Tokyo has 1,600 full-time staffers for 880 rooms (nearly a 2:1 ratio), whereas New York's Helmsley Palace has about 1,000 people for 1,008 rooms (a 1:1 ratio). Much of the service level delivered in Japan is made possible by simply having more people. Japanese hotels often do not have reservation systems and automated checkout facilities. In the United States, added customer value does not typically justify the added costs and associated higher prices. Japanese firms would prefer to reduce labor input rather than increase it, but are inhibited by customer expectations and competitive pressures.[44]

CONCLUSIONS

Service quality is difficult to measure because it is often unclear what the consumer expects, yet quality is a matter of meeting customer expectations. It depends upon consumer perception, which is determined by the person doing the service, the technical outcome of the service, the image of the company, and the expectations of the customers.[45] Customer dissatisfaction may result from unrealistic expectations. In addition, service quality and customer satisfaction are heavily culture bound; these concepts differ considerably between cultures. What is acceptable in one society may be perceived as unacceptably over service or unacceptably under service by one from another society. In some parts of the world (for example, Eastern Europe and the former Soviet Union, with their history of shortages), the concept is nonexistent, and companies and customers alike are being forced to learn the concept of customer service in order to compete and survive.

An international manufacturer of construction products that emphasized the speedy service provided by a sales force in radio-equipped station wagons made the mistake of offering too much service in the United States. The company prided itself on the fact that that a maximum two hours elapsed between the receipt of a customer order from a construction site and the actual delivery by a salesperson. The cost of this extra service was included in the premium prices charged by the firm. The company discovered that in the United States, its products were at a serious competitive price disadvantage. Customers gave the company high marks for its service but they preferred to buy from lower-cost competitors. Price was more important than time utility to U.S. customers. In Europe, competition made speedy delivery a necessity and the company had prospered.[46] Likewise, in Belgium, home delivery of food is not as important as is found in the United States, consumers place less importance on time; to be successful, freshness or novelty would have to be emphasized instead. Japan might have what is considered the highest level of service anywhere; reliance on special regulatory conditions and country-specific conditions (Japanese language and cultural differences from the rest of the world) make Japanese service and Japanese services nonexportable.

Marketers should stress those particular service quality attributes specifically rated higher by specific cultural groups. Hispanics perceive product and service quality as being dependent on the level of service they receive from employees and the benefits they receive from a particular entity more than Anglos do. Therefore, these particular attributes should be emphasized (both in marketing/advertising and at the store/company level) if the entity either currently serves or wishes to target that consumer segment. In one study, Mexican respondents indicated higher perceptions of importance of service quality attributes compared to that reported by American respondents. This can be attributed to their perceived lack of availability of quality goods in Mexico. Businesses who cater to or intend to cater to Mexican consumers should enunciate the quality of their goods as well as to only offer higher quality goods, as Mexican consumers are more quality conscious than those found in the United States.[47] Whereas American respondents indicated personalized service and easily found products were the significant factors, Mexican respondents, however, indicated availability, full product line, function as advertised, and confidence in the support staff as the significant factors. The Mexican responses confirmed the perception of poorer quality goods by the factors of importance chosen. The American respondents, on the other hand, assumed these items and based their responses on higher order service items. Thus, the cultures are influenced by different service factors.

What should marketers do? Should they attempt to impose their cultural-bound definition of service upon another society? Or should they understand and replicate service levels as currently exists in the society? It may be cost prohibitive to provide an American-type service quality in an undeveloped country; a company may not be able to compete or provide a product which is affordable to the masses. The service provided may be unrecognizable by the host nationals. The local elite and businesspersons who are well traveled and have experienced such service elsewhere may or may not appreciate the efforts and partake of the product. If the endeavor is attempting to follow a standardized marketing mix (e.g., McDonald's or Hilton on a global basis), the domestic level of service quality then becomes part of the mix and must be offered to keep the product standardized and consistent. That is, for an "American" fast-foods franchise or "American" service establishment, "American" levels of service quality is expected to be present, regardless of the locale. If adaptation is the chosen strategy, the best action is to adapt to local levels and definitions of service quality.

Chapter 15

Green Marketing

Green marketing refers to the marketing of products and services considered environmentally friendly that make their marketers "environmentally responsible." The advent of green marketing was due to consumer demands. Polls show that 76 percent of Americans consider themselves environmentalists and would prefer to buy from a company that is "Green."[1] A survey conducted by *The Wall Street Journal* and NBC News indicated that more than 80 percent of Americans consider protecting the environment more important than keeping prices down. According to the same study, 46 percent said that they had bought products based on a manufacturer's or a product's environmental reputation within the last six months. An even larger percentage, 53 percent, said that they had purposely not bought a specific product because of environmental concerns.[2]

What makes a product Green? Green products and packages have one or more of the following characteristics: (1) are less toxic, (2) are more durable, (3) contain reusable materials, or (4) are made of recyclable materials. The U.S. Federal Trade Commission issued "Guides for the Use of Environmental Claims" (a set of advertising guidelines) that define a green product as one that (1) has reduced raw material, high recycled content (e.g., aluminum cans); (2) non-polluting manufacture/non-toxic material (e.g., de-inking solvents); (3) no unnecessary animal testing (e.g., cosmetics); (4) no impact on protected species (e.g., dolphin-safe tuna); (5) low energy consumption during production/use/disposal; (6) minimal or no packaging, reuse/refillability when possible (e.g., detergent bottles); (7) long useful life, upgrading capabilities; (8) post-consumer collection/disassembly system; remanufacturing capability.

These Green marketing guidelines were required after some companies began misusing Green marketing. For example, it became necessary to have guidelines for "recyclable" after some companies put the term on their packages when the product was actually recyclable only under certain conditions. Other possible misused terms include: (1) biodegradable (whether or not a product will be truly able to completely break down and return to the earth within a reasonable time); (2) environmentally safe; and (3) environmentally friendly. The Federal Trade Commission's guidelines were established to set national Green marketing standards, but it has received several criticisms. Many environmental marketers feel that the guidelines are loaded with oversights, omissions, opportunities for legal wrangling, and shortsightedness. The biggest problem is that the state guidelines are still different from the national guidelines: a company can put "ozone friendly" on a package label in California, but not in Rhode Island.[3] To overcome this federal-state labeling problem, a group of 11 state attorneys general issued its final environmental advertising recommendations called "Green Report II." The report requests the federal government to adopt standards with specific definitions for terms such as degradability, compostable, recycled, and recyclable.[4] The FTC further indicates any objective environmental claims must be substantiated by scientific evidence.

Green marketing encompasses efforts such as Proctor and Gamble's to develop disposable diapers that can be composted and detergents that are degradable concentrated to reduce packaging bulk in landfills. AT&T has substituted biodegradable cardboard for plastic foam packaging. Alberto-Culver markets "ozone friendly" hairspray containing no chlorofluorocarbons (CFCs). The Body Shop has over 700 boutiques worldwide selling its non-animal-tested, mostly natural product line with recycling/refilling policies. More and more companies are taking significant action to clean up, protect, and recycle the environment. Some even have found a business in the ecology: The Seventh Generation offers a large catalog of "green products." As DuPont chairman Edgar Woolard Jr. states, "Corporations that think they can drag their heels indefinitely on environmental problems should be advised society won't tolerate it. Companies with real sensitivity toward the environment will be there to supply your customers after you're gone."[5] Few companies can ignore the green consumers, green trade barriers, and high environmental standards that have been raised. Consumer pressure and government edict have combined to force sensitivity to environmental issues on corporations not only in the United States but for any foreign corporation that wishes to do business in the United States. This is true in other parts of the world as well; a Canadian survey of marketing executives from that country's 500 largest firms found that 47 percent had already altered their packaging to make their products more environmentally friendly.

Companies use Green marketing not only to increase consumer approval, but also to cut costs. McDonald's used recyclable materials for wrappers and reduced its environmental waste by 60 percent; their "give a tree away" day led the way for other fast-foods companies to follow suit. All of McDonald's napkins and tray liners in the restaurants are made from recycled paper, as are the carry-out drink trays, and even the stationery used at the headquarters. By making its drinking straws 20 percent lighter, McDonald's saved one million pounds of waste per year. Besides using Green marketing in its own products, McDonald's buys recycled materials for remodeling and building its restaurants. McDonald's also challenges its suppliers to supply and use recycled products and materials.[6] The effective use of Green marketing has made the public aware that McDonald's Corporation is an environmentally concerned company, and this has generated not only public consumer approval, but additional sales as well.

At DuPont's Richmond (Virginia) plant, through the use of new technology, process redesign and computerized process controls, the company reduced the hazardous waste generated by the plant by 80 percent, cut chlorofluorocarbon emissions by 70 percent, and eliminated 50 percent of its tetrachlorotethylene emissions, in the process saving $3 million per year. Some 250 companies have signed on to the EPA's new 33/50 program: voluntary emissions costs of 33 percent by 1992 and 50 percent by 1995, with further reductions to be negotiated later. Savings include disposal fees for hazardous wastes, costs of potential liabilities for wastes that may go astray. Disposal fees for hazardous wastes have risen as much as 300 percent over the past decade alone, approaching $2,000 per ton for some wastes. Anheuser-Busch recycles one used can for every one of the cans it produces, saving 95 percent of the energy needed to make new cans from raw ore.

The Chicago Board of Trade recently voted to create a commodities exchange that will trade in government permits to emit sulfur dioxide, rights that will be issued to electric utilities by the EPA under the Clean Air Act in an effort to reduce acid rain. To meet the demands of the Clean Air Act, companies are looking for ways to cut air pollution caused by automotive exhaust. Arco recently announced the development of an environmentally superior gasoline formula that will reduce auto emissions significantly without the need for new engines and fuels. Other companies as well are entering the fray for this potentially lucrative market.

Definite signs exist that environmental concerns have begun to influence American businesses in their international investment decisions, one example being the ecological nightmare that is Eastern Europe. The former East Germany and Leipzig in particular offers a splendid example that the "people's paradise" was not always so. Horrid air pollution which would make Los Angeles seem pure in comparison, dead rivers worse than the Cuyahoga ever was, and moonscapes from strip mines provide ever-mindful proof that it was not the capitalists but the communists who were the worst offenders. Chernobyl and its delayed autocratic response provides another example. The destruction of the once rich Aral Sea due to the Soviet Union's diverting water from two major river sources has devastated an entire region.

The destruction of the Brazilian and other tropical rain forests have caused companies such as Steelcase to eliminate rosewood and other hardwoods from the rain forest from their products in favor of more commonly available woods. American producers and distributors of tuna certify their products as "Dolphin-safe tuna" and take stringent measures to minimize dolphin deaths in the tuna fishing industry. The increased United States environmental concern over "dolphin-safe" tuna has forced foreign firms to follow the more stringent United States standards. Foreign tuna producers, whether they be from Mexico or Taiwan must take the pledge to secure access to the richest consumer market in the world. As a result of the domestic environmental pressures, many U.S. companies, regardless of looser environmental standards elsewhere, have proceeded with an environmentally conscious effort.

Some writers claim that marketing has been a prime contributor to the degradation of the environment. The successful satisfaction of consumer wants and needs in industrialized countries supposedly has led to materialistic and disposable societies. This line of thinking says the success of marketing efforts in industrialized countries has created a desire for comparable lifestyles among less developed and developing countries, encouraging the replacement of historic land management practices with urbanization and environmentally unsound industrial decision making.[7]

The issue of Green marketing presents a problem because so much attention has been given to environmental issues that if a company does not properly get "involved," it will lose out on many business opportunities. In addition, the company receives a poor company image from consumers by its failure to be environmentally involved. In the past few years, some companies have been boycotted by consumers and various environmental organizations. Boycotts can be detrimental to a company's image, especially if the boycott receives media attention. Companies that are not participating in Green marketing have received negative media attention and this further degrades the company's image. Exxon's oil spill is a good example of a company that suffered as a result of being environmentally irresponsible. Even though Exxon made all possible efforts to "clean up" its mess, its reputation suffered as did its pocketbook. Exxon had to spend billions of dollars in an effort to regain public approval, and even this tremendous effort did not reinstate full public approval.[8] Between the media and active environmental organizations, Exxon received so much negative attention that even today, the company is still trying to overcome the consequences of its mistake.

A firm cannot easily adopt a Green marketing philosophy. As noted earlier, federal agencies are often unable to agree on Green standards. Consumers in recessions may trade Green behaviors for more price-conscious responses, abandoning a Green marketer's products, which often are higher priced. Other consumers are cynical about Green marketing claims that turn out to be gimmicks. A lack of consensus exists about Green marketing actions: McDonald's switch from styrofoam to paper products, for example, is being criticized for contributing to deforestation. The obvious risk in dealing in Green marketing is violating some of the ambiguous legislation that exists.

CROSS-CULTURAL DIFFERENCES IN GREEN MARKETING

Internationally, Green marketing is an even larger issue than it is in the United States. Green marketing actually began in the early 1980s in Europe, when European companies began selling "green products"—new types of disposable diapers, detergents, batteries, aerosols, and other products that did not damage the environment. This manufacturing of new types of products grew quickly and soon caught on in the United States and other parts of the world. For the British, damage to the environment ranks with a world war as the most important threat to mankind. Air pollution in Athens has long been the subject of deep popular discontent and partly explains why the Greek government has aligned itself with hardline Northern EU countries' lead in the fight to impose strict new limits on automobile emissions. The growing political power of Green Parties in Scandinavia, the Benelux, and especially Germany has combined with public concern over such issues as the death of the forest from acid rain (*Waldsterben*) to force mainstream political parties to endorse tough environmental legislation. In Italy, public outcry over the waste imported from developing countries prompted the country to adopt a tough new hazardous waste bill.[9]

In Italy, Fiat leads the world in "Green" cars. Since the 1970s, Fiat has been recycling 80 percent of its factory waste; it was also one of the first European car manufacturers to produce cars which ran on lead-free fuel. Fiat has also established a huge recycling scheme called Fiat Auto Recycling (F.A.R.E.). This collects secondhand cars with the aim of recycling 100 percent of each car. Fiat is also the world leader in diesel car and electric vehicle technology. The electric car that was developed by Fiat is the first truly "Green" standard production car, a world first—one which will likely be the start of a new generation of cars designed to support the environment. BMW and Mercedes-Benz are examining clean technology for cars. Mazda, likewise, is examining hydrogen fuel as a possible alternative clean energy source. Detroit's big three are working hard on solar energy automobiles and more efficient batteries. Volkswagen has its "3V" policy (*vermedien, verringen, und Verworten*—prevention, reduction, recycling).

Germany has passed the strictest Green marketing laws. The German "Blue Angel" (first introduced in 1978) ecolabel is used as a symbol of environmental friendliness in Germany and by 1993, over 4,000 products in 58 categories carried the label. This Blue Angel logo originated because of the growing consumer demand in Germany for environmentally friendly products.[10] Eighty percent of German households are aware of the ecolabel and the label receives widespread support from manufacturers. On December 1, 1991 the German Packaging Order (called the "Topfer Law," after its environment minister) became law. The guiding objective of the order is waste avoidance; waste which cannot be avoided shall be recycled. Every three years beginning in 1992, the German government will publish the per capita amount of waste; these figures serve as a basis for the recycling quotas that each industry must achieve. The order imposed a duty on industry and retailers to make them take the packaging material back. It set an 80 percent waste collection target by 1995. The active role of the German Green party in German society was the direct cause for this new law.[11]

The law requires that packaging materials must be recycled or reused. Use of transit packaging in Germany means that consumers must take it back or belong to a recycling scheme. A parallel or dual waste collection system is part of the law. For a manufacturer's product to participate in direct collection and not have to be returned to the retailer for recycling, a manufacturer must guarantee financial support for curbside or central collection of all materials. For participating manufacturers, a green dot can be displayed on the package which signals the consumer that a product is eligible for pickup. Packaging without the green dot must be returned to the retailer for recycling. Although goods sold without the green dot are not illegal, retailers are reluctant to stock such products. Packaging used by fast-food outlets is not covered by the German green dot program. As a result, one German city has imposed a tax on all fast-food containers. The result has led to cream being served in reusable metal pitchers, jam and yogurt in glass jars, french fries in plates made of edible wafers and soft drinks offered in returnable bottles.[12]

Firms must often redesign products they sell in Germany to allow for easier disposal and recycling to meet the strict Green standards imposed there. Hewlett-Packard redesigned and reduced its office machine packaging worldwide to meet German packaging requirements. In addition, France, Belgium, and Denmark have set up regulations in order to deal with the solid waste problems that are much like those of Germany. An adverse effect of the law was that Germany made paper collection mandatory in the 1980s without setting up end uses for it. This, in conjunction with a collection surge in the United States, led to vast stocks of unwanted newsprint that resulted in a collapse of world prices as the market was flooded.

Since 1991, a new EU ecolabeling regulation has been discussed with the objectives to promote products with a reduced environmental impact throughout their entire life cycle and to provide better information to consumers on the environmental impacts of products.[13] The European Union threatens to utilize environmental standards to control internal and external trade in consumer products; marketers who do not conform may be restricted from participation. Those who do meet the requirements will enjoy reduced competition and a growing market share.[14] (This standard may also contradict WTO intentions.) Hoover was the first manufacturer to be awarded an EU ecolabel and claims that as a result, its sales in Germany have tripled and sales in the premium sector of the UK's washing machine market have doubled.[15] Other nations are also sponsoring ecolabeling programs: Canada has issued Environmental Choice, guidelines for products ranging from paints to reusable cloth diapers. Japan has its own Ecomark program; its symbol consists of two arms embracing the world. (The arms form the letter *e*, standing for environment, earth, or ecology.)[16]

European nations under intense pressure from environmentally correct lobbies created packaging regulations designed to reduce waste, primarily by promoting recycling. One result has been the phasing out of some packaging materials altogether. Nevertheless, recessions have a way to turn the most ardent Green into a consumer. The economic slowdown of the early 1990s has caused a reversal of the Green Movement in the EU. One major EU effort—the carbon dioxide tax—was voted down in the midst of economic downturns. Another EU task force called for new rules to be more market oriented and supported by cost-benefit analyses.[17]

In many Latin American countries, including Mexico, packaging requirements are less stringent and less sophisticated. As such, it is difficult to meet the standards of Europe. Although they may cry foul, proposing these are hidden protectionist requirements; GATT makes it clear that countries do have the right to impose stringent rules for environmental reasons.[18] Mexicans are more concerned with economic priorities (basic necessities of life) rather than societal or environmental concerns. An economically sound country such as the United States or a country in Western Europe has the luxury of putting environmental and societal issues at the top of their agendas. Not so in undeveloped countries or developing countries such as Mexico.

Colombia is one Latin American country that is developing an ecolabeling program. The objectives of the Colombian ecolabel are to promote environmental conservation in several sectors, addressing a variety of aspects, including polluting emissions, energy and natural resource use, as well as to provide the domestic industry with the means and incentives to increase its competitiveness through the implementation of environmental management strategies. This program also assists Colombian export firms in penetrating foreign markets, especially those such as the EU with considerable "green consumerism" interest.[19]

Sweden is one Scandinavian country with a passion for the environment; when the public utility offered urban customers a choice between nuclear and nonnuclear electricity in 1996, 40 percent of apartment dwellers chose nonnuclear, even though it costs 10 percent more. Even then, tradeoffs are necessary. Sweden has yet to close any of its 12 nuclear power plants since it still gets about half of its power from nuclear sources. With high unemployment in Sweden, Swedes are reluctant to do anything that would further reduce job possibilities in energy-intensive industries such as metalworking, mining, or paper. Another problem is that any replacement energy source will cost more or pose new environmental problems. Solar power does not work well in Sweden, where the sun shines only briefly in the winter, when electrical power demands are the greatest. Although scientists have developed a new fast-growing tree that could be burned for power, its use would contravene Sweden's commitments against energy forms that increase the emissions of greenhouse gases. Large windmills are unpopular with nearby residents because of the high noise level emitted. Sweden has four commercially viable rivers that have not been dammed, but the public insists on keeping them in a natural state.

Japan is ambiguous about the environment. Japanese government budget allocation to the environment has increased from $617 million in 1988 to $3.5 billion in 1991, doubling again through 1995. Japanese consumers are becoming more bargain conscious, frugal, and environmentally aware. Recycling of secondhand goods is flourishing. Consumers are leaning toward healthier, more ecologically sound products. Suntory, a Japanese beer company, sells a brand called "The Earth," with cans and bottles emblazoned with the slogan, "Suntory is thinking about the Earth." The can has stay-on rather than pull-off tabs. Orient Corporation linked up with the Wild Bird Society of Japan to offer an affinity card emblazoned with a painting of a bird, 0.5 percent of whose charges go to the conservation group. Major department stores such as Takeshimaya and Mitsukoshi have opened Earth-friendly corners selling environmentally sound products.[20] Dentsu has identified a trend in Japan called green spending, a long-term reappraisal of family values. Consumer resistance to expensive, ecologically harmful or unhealthy products resulted in a range of streamlined back-to-basics items including refillable containers and natural ingredients.[21]

The Japan's Economic Bureau found that consumers named Kao as the most environmentally conscious company in the country. Kao reduced its overall energy use by 40 percent in the last 17 years. Japan's Health Ministry's 1990 White Paper was dominated by environmental issues, but the Japanese Environmental Agency has far less enforcement power the EPA of the United States. Some 28,000 locally tailored environmental agreements in force between Japanese industry and local communities act as a nontariff barrier. By way of contrast, only three rivers in Japan flow freely over their entire length unharnessed in any way that would serve the interests of the Japanese people. Very few places exist that are wild or unshaped by humans in Japan. To Americans, nature is kind, benevolent, a source of infinite gifts, and is therefore something to be cherished and kept intact whenever possible. To the Japanese, nature is volcanic and stormy, exacting and difficult, something that is only kind when tamed, and only truly beautiful when sculptured or adorned.[22]

In Mediterranean countries, the ecological awareness of the average household is much less strongly developed than in countries further to the north, such as Germany, Holland, or Norway.[23] For example, in Italy, environmental issues are not nearly as important as in Germany. In Denmark, soft drinks may be sold only in glass bottles with refundable deposits. In the Netherlands, old or broken appliances must be returned to the manufacturer for recycling.[24] Green consumerism first appeared in the Netherlands with a boycott of aerosols containing CFCs and spread to Germany, thanks to consumer magazines which rated brands' green qualities through their own laboratories. (*The Green Consumer Guide*, first published in 1988 in the UK and quickly translated to German, was a best-seller and offered specific ratings for companies and products.) In 1992's Gallup's Health of the Planet Survey, Germans had the most concern for the environment (67 percent rated their national environmental problems as "very serious" versus 51 percent in the United States and 42 percent in Japan). Activism is almost nonexistent in Japan. Half as many Japanese as Germans actively avoid products perceived as harmful. In Denmark, a power plant, an enzyme plant, a refinery, and a wallboard factory all use one another's byproducts as source materials. Netherlands has effluent charges. Deposits are mandatory for bottles in Germany and for cans in Norway.

It is clear that Europe, especially northern Europe, is leading the way in Green marketing. (However, interest in Green marketing in the UK is considerably less than that found in German markets.) Europe adopted the "Polluter Pays principle" in 1972 and has since issued over 150 environmental directives. Meanwhile, in the United States, the Green Seal program initially tried a full life cycle approach while the Green Cross system merely verifies a company's claims.

ECOMARKETING/ECOTOURISM

Ecotourism is the responsible travel to natural areas which conserves the environment and improves the welfare of local people.

Ecotourism is a concept that describes a form of development that respects tradition and culture, protects and preserves the environment, and educates and welcomes visitors.[25] Ecotourism represents different concepts to conservationists, development assistance organizations, and travel agents. Ecotourism strives to mesh small-scale, low-impact development with the outdoor-oriented, adventure-minded travelers, to gently invade and preserve paradise, not spoil it. It can mean anything from a strenuous trek through an uncharted Brazilian jungle to a leisurely float down an unspoiled American urban river.

Ecotourism is the fastest growing segment of the tourism industry today. Worldwide, ecotourism accounts for perhaps one-third of the $416 billion tourists spent traveling abroad in 1994. Since 1990, 18 countries have opened ecotourism development offices; none existed before.[26] More and more destination countries are becoming interested in "green" tourism, cultural tourism and ecotours, and are considering ecotourism as part of their tourism strategy.[27] Many regions are aggressively marketing their attractions to ecotourists.[28] Some countries, such as Nicaragua, are slowly recognizing the importance of tourism as a positive income producer and one requiring minimal investment in infrastructure. By one estimate, nature tourism accounted for between $2 and $12 billion of the $55 billion tourism generated for developing countries in 1988. New Zealand's Ministry of the Environment recently reported that nature and culture visits to New Zealand are growing at a rate of 30 percent, or eight times faster than the growth rate of traditional tourism, at 4 percent. In South Africa, the leadership recognizes the importance of tourism in that country which targets to have one million tourists per year by the year 1996. This expected tourism will generate 6 percent of South Africa's gross domestic product and create more than 150,000 new jobs.[29]

The majority of international ecotourism consumers are from North America, Europe, and Japan. Almost one-third of all Americans travelers surveyed in 1995 indicated they had taken at least one trip to an ecotourism destination, up from only 7 percent as recent as 1992. The ecotourists are looking to get away from it all. Ecotourists are wealthier, better educated, more mature, and more environmentally focused in comparison with other tourists. They take longer trips and spend more money per day than travelers with less of an interest in nature.[30] Ecotourism is very tour intensive and mobile; ecotourists do not tend to stay in one place, they come to see nature. They spend two or three days at most in one place and tend to visit five or six places in a period of two weeks.

Further, many developing countries, perceiving ecotourism as a more environmentally benign and sustainable alternative to mass tourism, and a potentially lucrative industry, have developed institutions and programs to attract ecotourists. Costa Rica, Ecuador, and Kenya are usually mentioned as models of successful ecotourism. Costa Rica is distinguishing itself from the rest of Central America by becoming an ecotourism haven. Costa Rica has been aggressively protecting its natural heritage and has created a network of national parks, biological reserves, and refuges.[31] Currently, these areas cover 25 percent of the nation's territory and hold 4 percent of the world's total floral and fauna species which have been growing and remaining healthy in the protected areas. It cannot compete with Cancun, Acapulco, or Rio for resort tourism nor with Yucatan or Guatemala for archeology. Tourism is expected to overtake bananas as the number one producer of foreign exchange in Costa Rica by the year 2000.[32] These destinations, which offer unique environments and wildlife, earn much-needed foreign exchange through ecotourism.

Recently, Belize reassessed its tourism development plans and held an ecotourism conference in order to redirect its tourism efforts in the direction of greater environmental preservation.[33] Belize is a natural for ecotourism, having 65 percent of its land still in the wild state, with rain forest, pine savanna, and mangrove estuaries. Offshore, its barrier reef is second in size only to Australia's Great Barrier Reef. Resorts are limited to no more than 40 rooms. The Chan Chich Lodge has a maximum capacity of 24 people and was built with environmentally friendly construction techniques.[34]

At Tres Garantias Ejido in Southern Quintana Roo in Mexico, ecotourism has rustic cabins, hunting reserves, and was driven by Agenda 21, the blueprint for sustainable development drawn up at the 1992 UNCED Earth Summit in Rio.[35] Studies have shown that the number of animals locally have increased since hunting was banned in the area when the government initiated the Tres Garantias ecotourism project in the reserve. This is a positive advantage not only because of the increased numbers of animals, but also, the fact that these animals have been spilling over into areas where hunting is allowed, benefiting local hunters. Other countries such as Australia, New Zealand, and Canada are vigorously investing in and promoting ecotourism to diversify their tourism base. Sarawak (Borneo) in Malaysia, a major exporter of timber and oil, has begun to utilize its rich natural environment to promote ecotourism.

However, ecotourism is not always positive and sometimes causes negative impacts on the environment despite the best intentions. Tourism support facilities translate into hotels or lodges, airports, roads, and waste disposals. These facilities will inevitably affect the environment despite best efforts. In Nepal, an influx of tourists, including ecotourists, have caused ecological harm.[36] Ecotourists are inspired by a desire to have more authentic travel experiences. This desire has often taken a costly toll on the environment, especially in fragile coastal and mountain ecologies.

Ecotourism, it appears, only works on a small, specialized scale.[37] The fundamental principles that underlie the concept of ecotourism include the following:[38]

- It should not degrade the resource and should be developed in an environmentally sound manner.
- It should provide firsthand, participatory, and enlightening experiences.
- It should encourage all parties to recognize the intrinsic value of the resource.
- It should involve acceptance of the resource on its own terms and recognition of its limits.
- It should provide long-term benefits to resource, community, and industry.
- It should promote moral and ethical responsibilities and behaviors.

CONCLUSIONS

The four classical constituents for a corporation are its shareholders (stockholders), employees, customers, and its community (some also include suppliers as a fifth constituent). The priorities and weights given to each constituent vary among nations according to culture and business tradition. For example, in Japan, employees are the major concern, followed by customers, with shareholders having minimal influence and concern. In the United States, stockholders are the top priority, even to the point of legal fiat mandating it be so. The constituency "community" is usually defined to mean people and towns geographically contiguous to a corporation's facility, not the ecosystem. In fact, there are few if any cultures (outside of possibly Europe) that consider the ecosystem a viable constituency for a corporation to consider. Only in Europe, are there companies creating an ecoaudit, let alone making their ecoaudit report public as an addition to the normal annual reports.

The American view can be summed up by Milton Friedman, the Nobel Prize-winning economist, who once said, "If a social responsible action doesn't contribute to the bottom line, it shouldn't be done." In essence, he was making the statement that the only social responsibility a corporation has is to maximize its profits. Validity exists to his view: a corporation has a fiduciary responsibility to its stockholders to maximize returns within the legal bounds set by the local government and its regulating agencies. If publicly held, it can actually be sued by shareholders if it strays too far off its legally chartered path. With this legal mission of a corporation's existence in mind, to what extent does a private firm have fiduciary responsibility to indulge in nonbusiness aspects, such as Green marketing?

Yet, Green marketing can also provide significant international competitive advantages. Through a combination of stringent regulatory standards and generous incentives to its industry, Japan has succeeded in reducing air and water pollution to a greater extent than any other industrialized country. It has reduced the energy content of a unit of GDP by one-third and effected similar reductions in raw material use. Since 1973, Japan has cut the amount of energy needed to produce a given unit of gross national product by 33 percent.[39] Japan has hence gained a competitive advantage.

The twenty-first century has been dubbed "the century of environmental awareness." Mike Elux, group environment adviser of British chemical giant ICI, says that "The recent leap in concern over environmental issues is 'not a style change' but the natural evolution of a longtime upward trend. Nevertheless, there is plenty of evidence to suggest that the upward angle will grow far steeper than previously. In this public climate, Green companies will have an edge."[40] Consumer good marketers often wish to emphasize in advertisements the environmental friendliness of their products; such environmental claims may be received quite differently in a country where environmental issues are received differently. It may not be a competitive advantage by its presence; it is a distinct disadvantage by its absence in some markets.[41]

Patrick Carson, Vice President for Environmental Affairs at Loblaw International, Canada's largest food distributor, researched environmental issues and analyzed their impact on his firm. He provides four guidelines for firms to become environmentally sensitive:

1. Focus on environmental issues.
2. Keep tabs on the emerging Green consumer.
3. Keep ahead of government regulations.
4. Watch for emerging business opportunities.[42]

It is clear that economics and status of industrialized development of a nation/culture defines the level of interest and priority for environmental affairs and Green marketing. Although some of the worst environmental disasters are going on in the world's least developed countries (e.g., deforestation of the Himalayan foothills in Nepal have resulted in uncontrolled floods in Bangladesh, and the wholesale destruction of forests in sub-Saharan Africa which have extended the Sahara further south for hundreds of miles), these nations are far more worried about subsistence and survival to take an active environmental role. Any action that is taken must be the result of external activities (e.g., aid from Industrialized nations or from environmental groups such as the Nature Conservancy) and not to be expected from the poor nations themselves.

Although Green marketing appears to be the near-exclusive domain of companies and consumers in the industrialized world, it is clear that some cultures are more green than others (e.g., Germany, Scandinavia, and the Low countries), as Green issues have climbed to the top of their countries' social agendas. In these nations, strict environmental standards and Green political parties with political power are the norm. Yet, sufficient evidence exists to indicate that Green marketing, even in these countries, is dependent upon economic conditions. Green marketing may be thought of as a "fair weather friend:" when times are good and economic conditions allow, one will be Green; but in recessions, one tends to revert to one's prior set of beliefs. In the United States, Green is preached and many consumers spout their intentions to buy Green products. Nonetheless, even as shoppers increasingly want to know if what they are buying is the earth's friend or enemy, companies are having a hard time getting price-conscious consumers to pay more for Green products; when asked to pay premiums for Green products, these intentions do not turn into buying behavior.

Ongoing concerns about environmental issues have not made their way to the European consumers' shopping habits, as Euroconsumers reject ecofriendly products for their regular products. Most consumers do not want to pay extra for ecofriendly products while others simply believe Green products do not work as well. In the UK, sales of Green detergents fell 40 percent between 1993 and 1995, accounting for less than 1 percent of the detergent market. German sales volumes of ecofriendly kitchen towels and tissues have fallen by over 20 percent within the same time frame. The ecofriendly products appear to be a small, relatively unimportant niche market in Europe. As mainstream consumer products companies introduce environmentally responsible products, less incentives exist for pure Green products.[43]

Conclusion

Cultural differences abound. The risks of ignoring them are great, local failure if one is lucky, global disaster if not. Differences can be in something as mundane as language. The 15 nations of the European Union recognize 11 official languages! When Coca-Cola first entered China, the symbols for Coke translated as "bite the wax tadpole." After much research, another variation with approximately the same sound was found, one that meant "may the mouth rejoice." Differences may be as important yet less observable as nonverbal signals. While the French do greet each other with kisses on the cheek, one kiss is an unfinished greeting and is therefore an insult. Never touch the head of a Thai or pass an object over it; the head is considered sacred in Thailand. Symbols can vary in meaning (e.g., the Japanese revere the crane as being very lucky, for it is said to live for 1,000 years). Even seemingly innocent use of symbols can backfire: To commemorate Mexico's Flag Day, two local Mexico City McDonald's restaurants papered their serving trays with placemats embossed with a replica of the national emblem; authorities swooped down and confiscated the disrespectful placemats.

Even attitudes toward basic necessities are not uniform or universal: In the United States, T-shirts and jeans convey an informal attitude toward clothing and a lack of interest in any status that clothing may convey; Americans thus convey casualness and an interest in not standing out. In Russia, the opposite is true. Because real blue jeans and T-shirts are in short supply, those who wear such clothing signal to society that they are aware of current fashions and are status conscious; thus, they separate the individual from the rest of society. The rationale for buying is different for the two cultures, and is just as logical if viewed from each culture's perspective. Accumulation of jewelry in India is far less intended for display of social status than for security and accumulation of wealth.

Like the proverb of the elephant being described by the blind men, separate cultures can view the same item and yet see, feel, and believe different things. Two Kit Kat commercials were tested in six countries to determine the effectiveness of advertising approaches across cultures: the "Quackers" and the "Hitchhiker" commericals. The objective was to reinforce the link between Kit Kat and the act of taking a break. The main benefit perceived in the Quackers commercial is the idea of sharing a Kit Kat in Belgium, taking a break with a Kit Kat in England, but the quality of the product in Italy. The Hitchhiker commercial shows Germans how to relax with a Kit Kat, while for the French, it shows the magical effect of Kit Kat. The Belgians perceive Kit Kat as a crispy bar, while the English think of the product as a snack; the Italians think of Kit Kat as a good product, it is a relaxing product to the Germans, and is seen as a little product by the Dutch.[1] The Japanese consumers view products much more as valuable in and of themselves, not in the instrumental (utilitarian) manner of a Westerner. For a Japanese consumer, the beauty of a stereo set lies not only in the functional aspects, but also in the appearance, the size, and so on. Whether product features are ultimately functional or not is much less important than to a Westerner; to the Japanese, products have an intrinsic value and can thus be enjoyed in their own rights.[2]

Oftentimes, the values and beliefs present in different cultures can create interpretation problems over the simplest of ideas. A member of a collectivist culture viewing the classic *Twelve Angry Men* would be surprised that twelve ordinary men would pose a challenge to the authority of the professional, the judge. In addition, the single juror appears to have no loyalty to the group and disturbs its harmony by dissenting. Nepotism denotes favoritism and is thus an ill practice in the United States yet in Latin America and throughout the Arab world, to give special treatment to a relative is considered to be fulfilling an obligation; it only makes sense to hire someone you can trust.

Even the concept of conversation could differ significantly enough to create confusion and lay the groundwork for failure. In the Danish culture, the main purpose of interpersonal communication is maintenance of a familiar atmosphere and relation of affection . . .

it is impolite to explain things or to ask questions. In Sweden, the purpose of daily interpersonal communications is transmission of new information or frank feelings. One prefers to be silent unless one has an important message. In Denmark, one must keep talking. In Mexico, one should always inquire about another's wife and family; in Saudi Arabia, one should never do so.

Food and drink are especially culture bound and prone to mistakes if one is not careful. Different nationalities eat different things at different times of the day. The British eat a large, cooked breakfast. The Belgians traditionally eat soup with their supper. The French eat vegetables and potatoes as separate courses. The Japanese prefer their food fresh and eating it raw. The French have a locally known aversion to doing business over breakfast. Schweppes tonic water typically serves as a mixer in the United States and Britain, where drinks like gin and tonic are popular. The French drink it without alcohol. In Japan, perfume is rarely used, suntans are considered ugly, and bath oil is impractical in home showers or communal baths; thus, companies selling those products have an uphill battle. The concept of cooling and heating the body is important in Chinese thinking: malted milk is considered heating, fresh milk is cooling, brandy is sustaining, and whiskey is harmful. Even eating practices can differ: men and women eat separately in the Arab world.

Sometimes events are beyond control of a single company. Political tensions between Britain and Saudi Arabia are taking a toll on British business. The engineering company Babcock International blames a 1996 year-end $27 million loss on a big drop in Saudi orders. Other companies believe they, too, are being punished now that Saudi dissident Muhammad A.S. al-Mass'ari has overturned the British government's attempts to deport him. The Saudis, on April 22, 1996, said four people who confessed to the November 13, 1995 bomb blast that struck a Saudi National Guard installation in Riyadh admitted they were influenced by Islamic groups outside the kingdom, including al-Mass'ari's Committee for the Defense of Legitimate Rights. The Saudi government wants to stamp out any further unrest by gagging outside agitators, such as al-Mass'ari, whose group regularly lambastes the Saudi royal family as corrupt in widely photocopied faxes and Internet messages. The British government angered human rights groups by trying to deport al-Mass'ari, but an appeals court ruled the deportation order was invalid because it could endanger his life.

Other British companies have also been hit. Critical coverage of Saudi Arabia's human rights record by the BBC-led Rome-based Orbit Communications, directly led to a decision to stop transmitting the BBC's Arabic TV service. Share prices in British Aerospace, GKN, Rolls-Royce, and Vickers, which have or are seeking contracts worth billions of dollars, all declined on the news. The stakes in the dispute are especially high for British Aerospace, as nearly one-third of the company's $10 billion in revenues and almost all of its profits come from Saudi weapons sales.[3] What can a company do in such a situation? Go with the flow. Control what can be and accept what cannot be—and know the difference, as the Prayer of Serenity goes.

That progress is being made can be seen from Chrysler's invasion of the Japanese market. For years, the Big Three refused to sell cars with right-side steering wheels to the Japanese. Now, not only are they doing so but in a major way. To Americans, Chrysler Corporation's Neon subcompact is cute. But the Japanese press is calling the Neon a "Japan car killer." Whatever you call it, a right-side steering wheel Neon arrived in Japanese showrooms on June 15, 1996 after months of hype. The Neon launch shaped up as an important test case of U.S. car makers' ability to score in Japan. In the year since the controversial Japan-U.S. auto agreement, America's Big Three have been struggling, spending millions to establish organizations that will enable them to compete seriously in Japan. Neon's debut also marks Chrysler's first big step out of the Jeep niche and toward a wider product line in Japan.

Chrysler is making a serious effort to sell in Japan. America's number three automaker paid $100 million last summer for control of a small network of Japanese dealerships. In April, it opened a $10 million inspection center and parts depot in Kanagawa Prefecture, two hours from Tokyo. Chrysler has also invested $180 million in developing right-side-drive models for Japan and other international markets. By the end of 1996, the company plans to have five right-side-drive models available in Japan: three Jeeps, the Neon, and the Voyager minivan. The Japanese subsidiary is also pressing for a high-end right-side-drive model such as the Stratus or Cirrus to complete its lineup. In 1995, the Jeep Cherokee was the company's only product in Japan.

Neon is aimed at Japan's toughest market segment, the small sedan. The Japanese buy about 3 million such autos each year—almost half of Japan's car market—and competition is fierce. Neon goes wheel-to-wheel with such popular cars as the Toyota Corolla and the Honda Civic. Next to the 340,000 Corollas or 121,000 Civics sold in Japan last year, Chrysler's target of 8,000 Neons for 1997—eventually going to 20,000 units per year—looks insignificant. However, as yet, only four imported models have sold more than 10,000 units in a year: the Volkswagen Golf, the Mercedes C-Class, the Opel Astra, and Chrysler's Cherokee.

Before Chrysler can persuade Japanese consumers to buy, it must persuade more dealers to stock its cars. Chrysler has only about 125 outlets, compared to Honda Motor Company's 1,800. Adding dealers, says Osamu Nagata, Vice President of Marketing for Chrysler Japan Sales, is still the toughest task facing the Big Three. U.S. automakers must also persuade salespeople to actually sell the cars, especially in multibrand showrooms. Some 80 percent of the 15,000 Jeeps bought in Japan last year were sold through Honda, which has no plans to sell Neons. An education and incentive program for salespeople seems essential.[4]

Chrysler is spending $5 million on advertising in the initial three months of the launch, targeting first-time female buyers aged 24 to 36 and male buyers aged 30 to 49. Some 70 percent of the ad budget is for 30- and 50-second television spots. Just as in the United States, the car zooms up to the camera—only in Japan it says, "*Konnichi wa. Neon desu* (Hello. I'm Neon)."

The Neon should appeal to the Japanese consumer. The car has a distinctive front end, is basically the right size, and comes with standard features such as dual air bags, which are still expensive options on many Japanese models. Even the mighty Toyota Motor Corporation is taking notice. "We've seen a real improvement in the imports," says a Toyota spokesman. "It's definitely making things more interesting." If Chrysler's Neon can squeeze out just a fraction of the market share of Toyota, Nissan, or Honda, it will have widened the crack in the door to Japan.

Contrast the Neon's efforts to an already established success story: GM's Opel has been a hit in Japan's imported vehicle market in just three years of marketing in Japan. Opel's small size is well suited to Japanese roads and parking places, it has long made right-side drive versions for sale in Japan, and it has the European cachet Japanese consumers generally prefer. Japanese consumers are extremely finicky and care about a car's fit and finish, rather than the way it is sold or how it drives. Opel has played up to those desires.[5]

In summary, three major rules would start a company on the route to success in cross-cultural marketing:

1. Recognize that a foreign customer is different—in perceptions, motivation, beliefs, and outlook. Identify, understand, accept, and respect the other's culture. Be prepared to communicate and operate on two separate and different cultural wavelengths. Don't assume sameness. One should not fall into the Self-Reference Criterion fallacy and assume that anything that is acceptable in one's own culture is necessarily acceptable in all other cultures. Familiar behaviors may have different meanings. One must adjust the pace of business to that of the people with whom one is trying to do business. One must treat everybody with whom one deals with the greatest personal respect. Even the British, who the Americans typically treat as brothers and next of kin, have a separate and distinct business culture; thinking of them as Americans in spirit and treating them as such will only serve to worsen relations and possibly ruin a business deal. What one thinks of as normal or human behavior may only be cultural. Do not assume that what you meant is what was understood; do not assume that what you understood is what was meant

2. Be culturally neutral. Being different does not denote being better or inferior. Do not cast judgment on the other party's cultural mores any more than you would want them to judge your values. It may be true that from a moral point of view, some foreign customs may appear senseless, capricious, or even cruel and insane to you. But remember you are visiting the country as a businessperson—not as a missionary. You plan to do business there—not to convert the natives to American customs and practices. Recognize that they probably feel the same way about your culture as you do theirs. It

may not be necessary to adopt their values as part of your own personal value system. All that is necessary is that you accept and respect their norms as part of their culture. Market to their culture and their mores and norms as you would want them to market to your own sensitivities.

3. Be sensitive to their cultural norms, do's, and taboos. Try to understand what they are and how your behavior may impact them even if it causes you discomfort or emotional stress. Most people do behave rationally; you just have to discover the rationale. You do not have to like or accept different behavior, but you should try to understand where it comes from in order to make peace with that behavior, or at least not react so strongly to it. It is necessary to accept, and to proceed with the business without showing distress if one wishes to come home with an agreement that is beneficial to both parties and marks the start of a long-term, healthy relationship between two companies from two cultures. One way to bridge cultural differences is to demonstrate interest in, knowledge of, respect for, and appreciation of the other side's culture. Failure to do so can easily be interpreted as an act of cultural superiority and arrogance, a statement that the other side's culture is not significant or important. Questions about culture framed in an uncritical way show that you find the other side's culture to be interesting, important, and worth learning about. Therefore, international marketers should try to learn as much as possible about the other side's culture. Marketers should be tolerant and respectful of cultural differences. Once differences are understood, marketers should seek ways of accommodating them. Some islands of cultural commonality should be found and enjoyed together.

Notes

Foreword

1. Hans B. Thorelli, "Marketing, Open Markets and Political Democracy: The experience of the Pacrim countries." *Advances in International Marketing*, 7, 33-46, Greenwich, CT: JAI Press. (1996).

2. _____, "Swedish Consumer Policy, Its Transferability and Related Research Implications." *Advances in Consumer Research*, 8, (1981): 467-73.

3. _____, "The Multi-National Corporation As a Change Agent." *Southern Journal of Business*, (July 1996): 1-11.

4. _____, Helmut Becker, and Jack Engledow, *The Information Seeker: An International Study of Consumer Information and Advertising Image*. Cambridge, MA: Ballinger. (1975).

5. _____, "The Information Seekers: Multinational Strategy Target." *California Management Review*, 23, (1980): 46-52.

Introduction

1. Bill Saporito, "Where the Global Action Is." *Fortune*, (1993): 62-65.

2. Richard Turner and Peter Gumbel, "As Euro Disney Braces for Its Grand Opening, the French Go Goofy." *The Wall Street Journal*, (April 10, 1992): Al, A14.

3. Earl P. Spencer, "Euro Disney—What Happened? What Next?" *Journal of International Marketing*, 3/3 (1995): 103-114.

4. Manfred F.R. Kets De Vries, "Toppling the Cultural Tower of Babel." *Chief Executive*, 94 (May 1994): 68-71.

5. Peter Gumbel and Richard Turner, "Fans Like EuroDisney but Its Parent's Goofs Weigh the Park Down." *The Wall Street Journal*, (March 10, 1994): A1, A12.

6. Ibid.

7. Jolie Solomon, "Mickey's Trip to Trouble." *Newsweek*, (14 February, 1994), 34-38.

8. Jukka M. Laitamaki, "Is It Mickey Mouse or Senior Mickey? A Cross-Cultural Case Study of Disney Theme Park Business Plan in Latin America." Fordham University Working Paper, (1994).

9. Peter Curwen, "EuroDisney: The Mouse that Roared (Not!)" *European Business Review*, 95/5 (1995): 15-20.

10. Stewart Toy and Paul Dwyer, "Is Disney Headed for the Euro Trash Heap?" *Business Week*, (January 24, 1994): 52.

11. Peter Gumbel and David J. Jefferson, "Disney Continues Drive to Expand Worldwide." *The Wall Street Journal* (November 20, 1992): B2.

12. Anonymous, "The Not-so-Magic Kingdom." *The Economist*, (September 26, 1992): 87-88.

13. Toy and Dwyer, op. cit. (1994).

14. Spencer, op. cit. (1995).

Chapter 1

1. Gregory J. Trifonovitch, "Cultural Learning/Cultural Teaching." *Educational Perspectives: Journal of the College of Education: University of Hawaii*, 16/4 (December 1977): 1-5.

2. David K. Tse, Kam-hon Lee, Ilan Vertinsky, and Donald A. Wehrung, "Does Culture Matter? A Cross-Cultural Study of Executives' Choice, Decisiveness, and Risk Adjustment in International Marketing." *Journal of Marketing*, 52/4 (October 1988): 81-95.

3. Timothy Aeppel, "Will Wessis Learn to Dine on Broilers After a Subbortnik?" *The Wall Street Journal*, (October 5, 1990): A1.

4. Anne Michele Morice, "New French Law Strikes Sour Note for Radio Stations." *The Wall Street Journal*, (January 23, 1996): A8.

5. Paul Klebnikov, "Minister Toubon Meet General Gamelin." *Forbes*, (May 22, 1995): 292.

6. Anonymous, "Did We Say That?" *Playboy*, (September, 1995): 15.

7. Huberto Valencia, "Point of View: Avoiding Hispanic Market Blunders." *Journal of Advertising Research*, 23 (December/January 1984): 19-22.

8. Richard Alan Kustin, "A Cross-Cultural Study of a Global Product in Israel and Australia." *International Marketing Review* 10/5 (1994): 4-13.

9. Dirk Beveridge, "McDonald's, Coke Irk Muslims." *The Honolulu Advertiser*, (June 12, 1994): e5.

10. Eugene L. Mendonsa, "Coming to Terms with 'Rubber Time'." *Business Marketing*, (October 1989): 67-68.

11. David Ricks, *Blunders in International Business*, Cambridge, MA: Blackwell Publishers, 1983.

12. Michael S. Lelyveld, "Maine 'eggs-ports' Win Brownie Points in Hong Kong." *The Journal of Commercial*, (January 30, 1995): 1a, 10a.

13. Laurence Jacobs, Charles Keown, Reginald Worthley, and Kyung-Il Ghymn, "Cross-Cultural Colour Comparisons: Global Marketers Beware." *International Marketing Review*, 8/3 (1991): 21-30.

14. Wilhelm-Karl Weber, "International Commerce with Verbal Savoir Faire." *Business Marketing*, (May 1986): 85-92

15. Suman Dubey, "Kellogg Invites India's Middle Class to Breakfast of Ready to Eat Cereal." *The Wall Street Journal*, (August 30, 1994): B5.

16. Tara Parker Pope, "Will the British Warm Up to Iced Tea?" *The Wall Street Journal*, (August 22, 1994): B1, B4.

17. Norihiko Shirouzu, "Snapple in Japan: How a Splash Dried Up." *The Wall Street Journal*, (April 24, 1996): B1, B3.

Chapter 2

1. Theodore Levitt, "Globalization of Markets." *Harvard Business Review*, (May/June 1983): 92-102.

2. Howard V. Perlmutter, "The Tortuous Evolution of the Multinational Corporation." *Columbia Journal of World Business*, 4 (January/February 1969): 9-18.

3. Yoram Wind, Susan Douglas, and Howard V. Perlmutter, "Guidelines for Developing International Marketing Strategies." *Journal of Marketing*, 37 (April 1973): 14-23.

4. Peter Gumbel and Carla Anne Robbins, "Has the West Lost Russia? Probably Not, for Much Has Changed." *The Wall Street Journal*, (Tuesday May 28, 1996): A1.

5. Andrew Tanzer and Robert LaFranco, "Luring Asians from Their TV Sets." *Forbes*, (June 3, 1996): 40-41.

6. Kenichi Ohmae, "The Triad World View." *Journal of Business Strategy*, 7/4 (Spring 1986): 8-19.

7. David M. Szymanski, Sundar G. Bharadwaj, and P. Rajan Vardarajan, "Standardization versus Adaptation of International Marketing Strategy: An Empirical Investigation." *Journal of Marketing*, 57/4 (October 1993): 1-17.

8. Fara Warner, "Basketball Thrills Koreans as NBA Dribbles into Asia." *The Wall Street Journal*, (May 17, 1996): B8.

9. Michael Porter, *Competition in Global Industries*. Cambridge, MA: Harvard Business School Press (1986).

10. Susan Segal-Horn and Heather Davison, "Global Markets." *Journal of Global Marketing*, 5/3 (1992): 31-61.

11. Martin Van Mesdag, "Winging It in Foreign Markets." *Harvard Business Review*, (January/February 1987): 71-74.

12. Aviv Shoham, "Global Marketing Standardization." *Journal of Global Marketing*, 9/1, 2 (1995): 91-110.

13. George S. Yip, "Global Strategy . . . in a World of Nations." *Sloan Management Review*, (Fall 1989): 29-40.

14. Richard Alan Kustin, "A Special Theory of Globalization: A Review and Critical Evaluation of the Theoretical and Empirical Evidence." *Journal of Global Marketing*, 7/3 (1994): 79-95.

15. John A. Quelch and Edward J. Hoff, "Customizing Global Marketing." *Harvard Business Review*, (May/June, 1986): 59-68.

16. Yip, op. cit.

17. Yusuf Chourdrhy, "Pitfalls in International Marketing Research." *Akron Business and Economic Review*, (Winter 1986): 18-28.

18. A. Tansu Barker, "A Marketing Oriented Perspective of Standardized Global Marketing." *Journal of Global Marketing*, 7/2 (1993): 123-135.

19. Tanzer and LaFranco, op. cit., 1996.

20. Philip Cateora, *International Marketing*. Orlando, FL: Dryden Press. (1993).

21. J.J. Boddewyn, Robin Soehl, and Jacques Picard, "Standardization in International Marketing: Is Ted Levitt in Fact Right?" *Business Horizons*, (November/December 1986): 69-75.

22. Yumiko Ono, "Gillette Tries to Nick Schick in Japan." *The Wall Street Journal*, (February 4, 1991): B1, B6.

23. Gregory Miles, "Tailoring a Global Product." *International Business*, (March, 1995): 50-52.

24. Joseph M. Winski and Laurel Wentz, "Parker Pen: What Went Wrong?" *Advertising Age*, (June 2, 1986): 60-61, 71.

25. Geert Hofstede, *Culture's Consequences*. London: Sage. (1984).

26. Geert Hofstede, *Software of the Mind*. London: McGraw-Hill Europe. (1991).

27. Paul A. Herbig and Joseph A. Miller, "Culture and Innovation." *Journal of Global Marketing*, 6/3 (1992): 75-104.

28. John Naisbitt and Patricia Aburdene, *Megatrends 2000: Ten New Directions for the 1990s*. New York: Avon Books. (1990).

29. Czinkota and Ronkainen, *International Marketing*. Orlando, FL: Dryden Press. (1993).

30. Roger Blackwell, Riad Ajami, and Kristina Stehpan, "Winning the Global Advertisng Race: Planning Globally, Acting Locally," *Journal of International Consumer Marketing*, 3/2 (1991): 97-120.

31. Rita Martenson, "Is Standardization of Marketing Feasible in Culture Bound Industries? A European Case Study," *International Management Review*, (Autumn 1987): 7-17.

32. *Marketing News*, (October 13, 1988).

33. Anonymous, "Don't Leave Home Without It Wherever You Live." *Business Week*, (February 21, 1994): 76-77.

34. Joseph Weber, "Campbell: Now It's MMM . . . Global." *Business Week*, (March 15, 1993): 52-55.

35. Robert Frank, "Potato Chips To Go Global—or so Pepsi Bets." *The Wall Street Journal*, (March 14, 1996): B1, B10.

36. E.S. Browning, "In Pursuit of the Elusive Euroconsumer." *The Wall Street Journal*, (April 29, 1992): B1.

37. Regina F. Maruca, "The Right Way to Go Global." *Harvard Business Review*, (March-April 1994): 135-145.

38. Joanne Lapman, "Marketers Turn Sour on Global Sales Pitch Harvard Guru Makes." *The Wall Street Journal*, (May 12, 1988): 1, 13.

39. Richard A. Kustin, "Marketing Globalization: A Didactic Examination for Corporate Strategy." *The International Executive*, 36/1 (January/February 1994): 79-93.

40. John Child, "Culture, Contingency, and Capitalism in the Cross National Study of Organizations." In L.L. Cummings and B.M. Staw (eds.), *Research in Organizational Behavior*, Vol. 3. Greenwich, CT: JAI Press. (1981): 303-356.

41. Van Mesdag, op. cit. 1987.

42. Quelch and Hoff, op. cit. (1986).

43. Martenson, op. cit. (1987).

44. Quelch and Hoff, op. cit. (1986).

45. S. Guber, "The Teenage Mind." *American Demographics*, (August 1987): 42-44.

46. William B. Werther, "Toward Global Convergence." *Business Horizons*, (January/February 1996): 3-9.

47. P. Sellers, "The ABCs of Marketing to Kids." Fortune, (May 1989): 114-120.

48. Sala S. Hassan and Lea P. Katsanis, "Identification of Global Consumer Segments." *Journal of International Consumer Marketing*, 3/2 (1991): 15-25.

Chapter 3

1. Paul A. Herbig and Hugh Kramer, "Cross-Cultural Negotiations: Success Through Understanding." *Management Decisions*, 29/8 (1991): 19-31.

2. Robert T. Moran and William G. Stripp, *Successful International Business Negotations*. Houston: Gulf Publishing. (1991).

3. Paul A. Herbig and Hugh Kramer, "Do's and Dont's of Cross-Cultural Negotiations." *Industrial Marketing Management*, 21/4 (November 1992): 287-298.

4. Robert M. March, "No-Nos in Negotiating with the Japanese." *Across the Board*, 26/4 (April 1989): 44-51.

5. John L. Graham, "Across the Negotiating Table from the Japanese." *International Marketing Review*, 15/3 (Autumn 1986): 58-71.

6. _____, "A Comparison of Japanese and American Business Negotiations." *International Journal of Research in Marketing*, 1/2 (1984): 58-71.

7. Donald Hendon, Rebecca Hendon and Paul Herbig, *Cross-Cultural Business Negotiations*. Westport, CT: Quorum. (1996).

8. Graham, op. cit. (1986).

9. John L. Graham and Yoshihiro Sano, *Smart Bargaining: Doing Business with the Japanese*. New York: Harper Business. (1989).

10. Moran and Stripp, op. cit. (1991).

11. Carl. R. Ruthstrom and Ken Matejka, "The Meaning of Yes in the Far East." *Industrial Marketing Management*, 19/3 (August 1990): 191-192.

12. G. Kennedy, *Negotiate Anywhere!* London: Arrow Books (1987).

13. Tim Ambler, "Reflections in China: Reorienting Images of Marketing." *Marketing Management*, (Summer 1995): 23-30.

14. Rosalie L. Tung, "How to Negotiate with the Japanese." *California Management Review*, 26/4 (1983): 52-77.

15. Naoko Oikawa and John F. Tanner, Jr., "The Influence of Japanese Culture on Business Relationships and Negotiations." *Journal of Services Marketing,* (Summer 1992): 67-74.

16. Paul A. Herbig and Hugh E. Kramer, "The Role of Cross-Cultural Negotiations in International Marketing." *Marketing Planning and Intelligence,* 10/2 (1992): 10-13.

Chapter 4

1. David Kilburn, "Unilever Struggles with Surf in Japan." *Advertising Age,* (May 6, 1991): 22.

2. Michael R. Mullen, "Diagnosing Measurement Equivalence in Cross-National Research." *Journal of International Business Studies,* 26/3 (Third Quarter, 1995): 573-594.

3. Terry Clark, "International Marketing and National Character." *Journal of Marketing,* 54/4 (October 1990): 66-79.

4. Peter Waldman, "Lost in Translation: How to 'Empower Women' in Chinese." *The Wall Street Journal,* (September 13, 1994): A1.

5. Morten Broberg, "Marketing Research in Poland." *Journal of Euromarketing,* 4/1 (1994): 63-82.

6. Uma Sekaran, "Methodological and Theoretical Issues and Advancements in Cross-Cultural Research." *Journal of International Business Studies,* (Fall 1983): 61-71.

7. Alma T. Mintu, Roger J. Calantone, and Jule B. Gassenheimer, "International Mail Surveys." *Journal of International Consumer Marketing,* 5/1, (1993): 69-83.

8. Scott Dawson and Dave Dickinson, "Conducting International Mail Surveys." *Journal of International Business Studies,* 19 (Fall, 1988): 491-496.

9. Henry C. Steele, "Marketing Research in China: The Hong Kong Connection." *Marketing and Research Today,* (August 1995): 155-165.

10. Kazuaki Katori, "Recent Developments and Future Trends Research in Japan Using New Electronic Media." *Journal of Advertising Research,* 12/2 (April/May 1990): 53-57.

11. Gabriela Ruiz, "Marketing Research in Mexico." *Business Mexico,* (October 1994): 34.

12. Secil Tuncalp, "The Marketing Research Scene in Saudi Arabia." *International Marketing Review,* 7/2 (1990): 23-29.

13. Earl Naumann, Donald W. Jackson Jr., and William G. Wolfe, "Examining the Practices of United States and Japanese Market Research Firms." *California Managaement Review,* 36/4 (Summer 1994): 49-69.

14. Johny K. Johansson and Ikujiro Nonaka, "Market Research the Japanese Way." *Harvard Business Review,* 65 (May/June 1987): 16-22.

15. Paul A. Herbig, *Marketing Japanese Style.* Westport, CT: Quorum. (1995).

16. Lourdes L. Valeriano, "Western Firms Poll Eastern Europeans to Discern Tastes of Nascent Consumers." *The Wall Street Journal,* (April 27, 1992): B1, B2.

17. Thomas L. Greenbaum, "Understanding Focus Group Research Abroad." *Marketing News*, (June 3, 1996): H14.

18. Yusuf A. Choudhry, "Pitfalls in International Marketing Research: Are you Speaking French Like a Spanish Cow?" *Akron Business and Economic Review*, 17/4 (Winter 1986): 18-28.

19. Naghi Namakforoosh, "Data Collection Methods Hold Key to Research in Mexico." *Marketing News*, (August 29, 1994): 28.

20. Morten Broberg, "Marketing Research in Poland." *Journal of Euromarketing*, 4/1 (1994): 63-82.

21. Elizabeth Lokon, "Probing Japanese Buyers' Minds." *Business Marketing*, (November 1987): 85-87.

22. Edward T. Hall and Mildred Reed Hall, *Hidden Differences*. New York: Anchor Books. (1987).

23. G. Pascal Zachary, "Major U.S.Companies Expand Efforts to Sell to Consumers Abroad." *The Wall Street Journal*, (June 13, 1996): A1, A6.

24. Jagdip Singh, "Measurement Issues in Cross-National Research." *Journal of International Business Studies*, 26/3 (Third Quarter 1995): 597-620.

25. Neil Lynch, "Demystifying the Asian Consumer." *Appliance Manufacturer*, (February 1990): W25-W27.

26. George Fields, "Advertising Strategy in Japan." *Dentsu's Japan Marketing/Advertising*, (Fall/Winter 1990): 52-56.

27. Mullen, op. cit. (1995).

28. S.G. Redding, "Cultural Effects on the Marketing Process in Southeast Asia." *Journal of the Market Research Society*, 24/2 (1988): 98-114.

Chapter 5

1. Michael Czinkota and Masaaki Kotabe, "Product Development the Japanese Way." *Journal of Business Strategy*, 12/4 (November/December 1990): 31-36.

2. Johny K. Johansson, "Japanese Consumers: What Foreign Marketers Know." *International Marketing Review*, 16/2 (Summer 1986): 37-43.

3. Robert Frank, "Coca-Cola is Shedding Its Once-Stody Image with Swift Expansion." *The Wall Street Journal*, (August 22, 1995): A1, A6.

4. Stuart Livingston, "Marketing to the Hispanic American Community." *Journal of Business Strategy*, 11/2 (March/April 1992): 54-57.

5. Humberto Valencia, "Hispanic Purchasing Powers Keeps Growing Fast." *Hispanic Business*, (December 1989): 12.

6. Jeffrey D. Zbar, "In Diverse Hispanic World, Image Counts." *Advertising Age*, 66/14 (April 3, 1995): S18-S19.

7. Ben Levy, "How Would Michael Play in Monterrey." *Marketing News*, 29/16 (July 31, 1995): 27, 31.

8. Damon D. Coke, "Nestlé Launches First Coffee Drink." *The Wall Street Journal*, (October 1, 1991): B1.

9. Gabrielia Stern, "Heinz Aims to Export Taste for Ketchup." *The Wall Street Journal*, (November 20, 1992): B1, B10.

10. Susan Carey, "Nations Have Quirks That Trivial Pursuit Just Can't Ignore." *The Wall Street Journal*, (January 10, 1996): A1.

11. Sadarumi Nishima, "Japanese Consumers: Introducing Foreign Products/Brands into the Japanese Market." *Journal of Advertising Research*, 30/2 (April-May 1990): 35-45.

12. Jo Ann Lublin, "U.S. Food Firms Find Europe's Huge Market Hardly a Piece of Cake." *The Wall Street Journal*, (August 16, 1988): A1, A20.

13. Anonymous, "Brands." *The Economist* (2 July 1994): 9-10.

14. Diana Milbank, "Made in America Becomes a Boast in Europe." *The Wall Street Journal*, (January 19, 1994): B1, B6.

15. Sac Onvisit and John J. Shaw, "The International Dimension of Branding." *International Marketing Review*, 6/3 (1991): 24.

16. Dale Littler and Katrin Schlieper, "The Development of the Eurobrand." *International Marketing Review*, 12/2 (1995): 22-37.

17. Anonymous, "Brands." *Asian Advertising and Marketing*, (March 1992): 23.

18. Sadafumi Nishikawa, "New Product Development." *Journal of Advertising Research*, 20/2 (April/May 1990): 27-31.

19. George Fields, *From Bonsai to Levi's*. New York: Macmillan. (1984).

20. Joel Saegert, Robert J. Hoover, and Marye Tharpe Hilger, "Characteristics of Mexican-American Consumers." *Journal of Consumer Research*, 12 (June 1985): 104-109.

21. Chris Robinson, "Asian Culture: The Marketing Consequences." *Journal of the Market Research Society*, 38/1 (1995): 55-62.

22. Kamran Kashani, "Beware the Pitfalls of Global Marketing." *Harvard Business Review*, 67/5 (September/October 1989): 91-98.

23. J. Knutsen, S. Thrasher, and Y. Kathawala, "The Impact of Culture Upon Package Perception: An Experiment in Hong Kong and the U.S." *International Journal of Management*, (June 1988): 117-124.

24. Gael M. McDonald and C. J. Roberts, "The Brand Naming Engima in the Asia Pacific Context." *International Marketing Review*, 11/3 (1991): 6-13.

25. Robert Frank, "Seeing Red Abroad, Pepsi Rolls Out a New Blue Can." *The Wall Street Journal*, (April 2, 1996): B1, B6.

26. Nishina, op. cit. (1990).

27. Kenichi Ohmae, *The Borderless World*. New York: Macmillan. (1990).

28. John Harris, "Advantage Mitsubishi." *Forbes*, (March 18, 1991): 78.

29. Craig Smith, "Chinese Government Struggles to Rejuvenate National Brands." *The Wall Street Journal*, (June 19, 1996): B1, B6.

30. Edward Lincoln, *Japan's Unequal Trade Status*. Washington DC: Brookings Institute. (1990).

31. Nishina, op. cit. (1990).

32. Raju Narisetti, "Can Rubbermaid Crack Foreign Markets?" *The Wall Street Journal*, (June 16, 1996): B1, B4.

33. Sarah Tippit, "Tupperware." *Reuters News Service*, (June 27, 1996).

Chapter 6

1. Bob Cutler, Rajshekhar G. Javalgi, and M. Krishna Erramilli, "The Visual Components of Print Advertising: A Five-Country Cross-Cultural Analysis." *European Journal of Marketing*, 26/4 (1992): 7-20.

2. Barbara Mueller, "Reflections of Culture: An Analysis of Japanese and American Advertising Appeals." *Journal of Advertising Research*, 17/2 (June/July 1987): 51-59.

3. G.E. Miracle (ed.), "Communication with Foreign Consumers." In *Management of International Advertising*. Ann Arbor, MI: Bureau of Business Research, The University of Michigan Press. (1966): 6-29.

4. Roger Blackwell, Riad Ajami, and Kristina Stephan, "Winning the Global Advertising Race: Planning Globally, Acting Locally." *Journal of International Consumer Marketing*, 3/2 (1991): 97-120.

5. Rita Martenson, "Is Standardization of Marketing Feasible in Culture Bound Industries?" *International Management Review*, (Autumn 1987): 7-17.

6. C. Anthony di Benneticio, Mariko Tamake, and Rajan Chandran, "Developing Creative Advertising Strategy for the Japanese Marketplace." *Journal of Advertising Research*, (January/February 1992): 39-53.

7. Eun Y. Kim, *A Cross-Cultural Reference of Business Practices in a New Korea*. Westport, CT: Quorum. (1996): 90.

8. Dana L. Alden, Wayne D. Hoyer, and Choi Lee, "Identifying Global and Culture-Specific Dimensions of Humor in Advertising: A Multinational Analysis." *Journal of Marketing*, 57/2 (April 1993): 64-75.

9. Ken Wells, "Global Ad Campaigns After Many Missteps, Finally Pay Dividends." *The Wall Street Journal*, (August 27, 1992): A1, A8.

10. Jerome B. Kernan and Teresa J. Domzal, "International Advertising: To Globalize,Visualize." *Journal of International Consumer Marketing*, 5/4 (1993): 51-71.

11. Cutler, Javalgi, and Erramilli, op. cit. (1992).

12. Fred Zandpour, Veronica Campos, Joelle Catalano, and Cypress Chang, "Global Reach and Local Touch: Achieving Cultural Fitness in TV Advertising." *Journal of Advertising Research*, 34/5 (1994): 35-63.

13. Kernan and Domzal, op. cit. (1993).

14. Tara P. Pope, "Ad Agencies Are Stumbling in East Europe." *The Wall Street Journal*, (May 10, 1992): B1, B14.

15. Fred Zandpour, Cypress Chang, and Joelle Catalano, "Store Is a Symbols and Straight Talk: A Comparative Analysis of French, Taiwanese, and U.S. TV Commercials." *Journal of Advertising Research*, (January/February 1992): 21-44.

16. Terence Nevett, "Differences Between American and British Television Advertising: Explanations and Implications." *Journal of Advertising*, 22/4 (1992): 12-23.

17. David A. Hanni, John K. Ryans, Jr., and Ivan R. Vernon, "Executive Insights: Coordinating International Advertising." *Journal of International Marketing*, 3/2 (1995): 83-98.

18. Stuart Livingston, "Marketing to the Hispanic American Community." *Journal of Business Strategy*, 11/2 (March/April 1992): 54-57.

19. Humberto Valencia, "Hispanic Purchasing Powers Keeps Growing Fast." *Hispanic Business*, (December 1989): 12

20. Jeffrey D. Zbar, "In Diverse Hispanic World, Image Counts." *Advertising Age*, 66/14 (April 3, 1995): S18-S19.

21. Michael Minor, "Comparing the Hispanic and Non-Hispanic Markets." *Journal of Services Marketing*, 4/2 (Spring 1992): 29-32.

22. Edward T. Hall and Mildred R. Hall, *Hidden Differences*. New York: Anchor Books. (1987).

23. George Fields, *From Bonsai to Levi's*. New York: Macmillan. (1984).

24. Jack Burton, "Japan Backlash." *Advertising Age*, (April 22, 1985): 122.

25. Johny K. Johansson, "Japanese Marketing Failures." *International Marketing Review*, 16/3 (Autumn 1986): 33-40.

26. Boyd DeMente and Fred T. Perry, *The Japanese as Consumers*. New York: Walker/Weatherhill. (1968).

27. Yumiko Ono, "Pepsi Challenges Japanese Taboo with an Ad That Tweaks Coke." *The Wall Street Journal*, (March 6, 1991): B1, B3.

28. Anonymous, *Business International* (August 19, 1991): 279-284.

29. Katherine T. Frith, "The Social and Legal Constraints on Advertising in Malaysia." *Media Asia*, 14/2 (1987): 103.

30. Leslie De Chernatony, Chris Halliburton, and Ratna Bernath, "International Branding." *International Marketing Review*, 12/2 (1995): 9-21.

31. Gonzalo Soroco, "The Mobile Hispanic Market: New Challenges in the 1990s." *Marketing Research*, 5/1 (Winter 1993): 6-11.

32. Martin duBois and Tara Parker-Pope, "Philip Morris Campaign Stirs Uproar in Europe." *The Wall Street Journal*, (July 1, 1996): B1, B6.

33. Diana Putterman, "Three Examples of What Hispanic Marketing Can Do." *Brandweek*, 34/42 (October 18, 1993): 26.

34. Namju Cho, "South Korea Relaxes Ad Content Rules and Ends Locked Time System on TV." *The Wall Street Journal*, (October 26, 1995): B2.

35. Alan T. Shao, Lawrence P. Shao, and Dale H. Shao, "Are Global Markets with Standardized Advertising Campaigns Feasible?" *Journal of International Consumer Marketing*, 4/3 (1991): 15-26.

36. David O. Balikowa, "Media Marketing." *Media, Culture & Society*, 17 (1995): 603-613.

37. J.J. Boddewyn, "Barriers to Advertising." *International Advertiser*, (May/June 1989): 21, 22.

38. Hallie Mummert, "Tapping Hispanic America." *Target Marketing*, 17/6 (June 1994): 32-37.

39. Nancy Church, "Advertising in the Eastern Bloc: Current Practices and Anticipated Avenues of Development." *Journal of Global Marketing*, 5/3 (1992): 109-129.

40. Balikowa, op. cit. (1995).

41. Yasuhiro Eguchi, "The Japanese Consumer and Imported Products." *Dentsu's Japan Marketing/Advertising*, (July 1981): 19-22.

42. Nancy Church, "Advertising in the Eastern Bloc: Current Practices and Anticipated Avenues of Development." *Journal of Global Marketing*, 5/3 (1992): 109-125.

43. G. Pascal Zachary, "Major U.S. Companies Expand Efforts to Sell to Consumers Abroad." *The Wall Street Journal*, (June 13, 1996): A1, A6.

44. "Pepsi Aims for the Stars." *Marketing News*, (June 3, 1996): 1.

45. Darren McDermott, "All American Infomercials Sizzle in Asia." *The Wall Street Journal*, (June 25, 1996): B7.

46. Allyson L. Stewart-Allen, "Creative New Media in Europe Here to Stay?" *Marketing News*, (June 3, 1996): 15.

47. Erdener Kaynak, "The Development of Multinational Advertising Strategy." In *The Management of International Advertising*, Westport, CT: Quorum Books. (1989).

Chapter 7

1. Trade Show Bureau survey of exhibiting companies in 1987: McGraw-Hill.

2. Pat F. Reynen, "When in Europe, Do as the Europeans Do." *Convene*, (September 1992): 19.

3. Steven Golob, "Sell Overseas at Trade Fairs." *Nation's Business*, (March 1988): 57-59.

4. William F. Kane, "Trade Fairs, Shows: Good Tools to Build International Markets." *Business America*, (July 17, 1989): 5-6.

5. Henry W. Vanderleest, "Planning for International Trade Show Participation: A Practitioners Perspective." *SAM Advanced Management Journal*, (Autumn 1994): 39-44.

6. Suzanne Oliver, "Watch That Wastebasket." *Forbes*, 157/6 (March 26, 1996): 72-74.

7. Alexei Odintsov, "Russia's Expocentr Takes Its Show on the Road." *Journal of Commerce*, 407/28672 (March 1, 1996): 5A(1).

8. Andrew M. Rizzo, "Export Strategies for Small Business." *Business America*, (September 6, 1992): 2-6.

9. D.J. Weinrauch, "Role and Utilization of Trade Shows for International Trade." In Klein and Smith (eds.), *Marketing Comes of Age*. Southern Marketing Association. (1994).

10. Daniel C. Bello and Hiram C. Barksdale, Jr., "Exporting at Industrial Trade Shows." *Industrial Marketing Management*, 15 (1986): 197-206.

11. William E. Nothdurft, *Going Global*. Washington, DC: The Brookings Institution. (1992).

12. P. Shure, "Europe . . . Still the Mecca for International Shows." *Convene*, (July/August 1992): 54.

13. Joachim Schafer, "German Trade Fairs Open Foreign Markets for U.S. Products." *Marketing News*, (May 8, 1987): 13.

14. Allen Konopacki, "CEOs Attend Trade Shows to Grab Power Buyers." *Marketing News*, (October 15, 1990): 5, 18.

15. J. Friendlander, "Flexing the Marketing Muscle of European Trade Shows." *Journal of European Business*, (January/February 1992): 10-15.

16. Philip J. Rosson and F.H. Rolf Seringhaus, "Visitor and Exhibitor Interaction at Industrial Trade Fairs." *Journal of Business Research*, 32 (1995): 81-90.

17. Anonymous, "Trade Fairs." *Asian Advertising and Marketing*, (July 1991): 8.

18. Jeannine K. Swan, "International Exhibiting: Minefield or Goldmine." *Business Marketing*, (June 1996): T-5.

19. Thomas Nara, "Establishing a European Beachhead." *Journal of Small Business Management*, (February 1991): 14-15.

20. Emily McAuliffe, "Exhibitors at Telcom '95 Woo $60 Billion Industry." *Business Marketing*, (November, 1995): 3, 8.

21. Kevin Commins, "European Trade Fairs Seek U.S. Exhibitors." *The Journal of Commerce*, (August 21, 1990): 4A.

22. Kate Bertrand, "The Baksheesh Beat." *Business Marketing*, (June 1987): 107-109.

23. Jaideep Motwani, Gillan Rice, and Essam Mahmoud, "Promoting Exports Through International Trade Shows." *Review of Business*, 13/4 (1992): 38-42.

24. Joachim Schafer, "Finding That Competitive Edge for Your Company at an International Trade Fair." *American Salesman*, (August 1988): 16-22.

25. Trade Show Bureau, "A Guide to the U.S. Exposition Industry." (1994): 64.

26. R.P. Humbert, "Trade Fairs Are an Excellent Way to Take Advantage of the Growing Opportunities in Western Europe." *Business America*, (December 21, 1987): 3-5.

27. Gregory Sandler, "Fair Dealer." *The Journal of European Business*, (March/April 1994): 46-49.

Chapter 8

1. Leslie De Chernatony, Chris Halliburton, and Ratna Bernath, "International Branding." *International Marketing Review*, 12/2 (1995): 9-21.

2. R. Foxman, P.S. Tansuhaj, and J.K. Wong, "Evaluating Cross-National Sales Promotion Strategy: An Audit Approach." *International Marketing Review*, (Winter 1988): 11.

3. Corlliss L. Green, "Media Exposure's Impact on Perceived Availability and Redemption of Coupons by Ethnic Consumers." *Journal of Advertising Research*, 35/2 (March/April 1995): 56-64.

4. Allyson L. Stewart-Allen, "Below-the-Line Promotions Are Below Expectations." *Marketing News*, 29/19 (September 11, 1995): 9.

5. Anonymous, "Global Coupon Use up, UK, Belgium Tops in Europe." *Marketing News*, (August 5, 1991): 6.

6. Laura Reina, "Distribution, Redemption of Coupons down in Canada." *Editor & Publisher*, 128/47 (November 25, 1995): 22.

7. Paul A. Herbig, *Marketing Japanese Style*. Westport, CT: Quorum Press. (1995).

8. Leon E. Wynter, "Reaching Hispanics Across a Racial and Cultural Divide." *The Wall Street Journal*, (February 15, 1995): B1.

9. Donald A. Ball and Wendell H. McCulloch, Jr., *International Business: The Challenge of Global Competition*. Burr Ridge, IL: Irwin Publishers. (1995): 489.

10. Gregory Sandler, "Fair Dealer." *The Journal of European Business*, (March/April 1994): 46-49.

11. Herbig, op. cit. (1995).

12. Kamran Kashani and John A. Quelch, "Can Sales Promotion Go Global?" *Business Horizons*, (May/June 1990): 37-43.

13. Helmut Bester and Emmanuel Petrakis, "Coupons and Oligopolistic Price Discrimination." *International Journal of Industrial Organization*, 14/2 (1996): 227-242.

14. Joanne Lipman, "Amid Recession, Firms Clip Coupon Value." *The Wall Street Journal*, (May 9, 1991): B5.

15. Ryan Mathews, "A Farewell to Coupons?" *Progressive Grocer*, 75/3 (March 1996): 71-72.

16. Fiona Plant, "Smart Card Supersedes Coupons?" *International Journal of Retail & Distribution Management*, (Spring 1995): xi.

17. Sigfredo A. Hernandez, "An Exploratory Study of Coupon Use in Puerto Rico: Cultural versus Institutional Barriers to Coupon Use." *Journal of Advertising Research*, 28/5 (1988): 40-46.

18. Anonymous, "Opening Up the World of Coupon Redemption." *Marketing*, (June 3,1993): 30.

19. Anonymous, "Global Coupon Use up, UK, Belgium Tops in Europe." *Marketing News*, (August 5, 1991): 6.

20. Anonymous, "International Coupon Trends." *Direct Marketing*, 56/4 (August 1993): 47-49.

21. J. Dee Hill and David McQuaid, "The Money's in the Mail." *Business Eastern Europe*, 23/48 (November 28, 1994): 7.

22. Reina, op. cit. (1995).

23. Allyson L. Stewart-Allen, "Creative New Media in Europe Here to Stay?" *Marketing News*, (June 3, 1996): 15.

24. Marcus W. Brauchli, "China Has Surly Image but Part of the Reason Is Bad Public Relations." *The Wall Street Journal*, (June 18, 1996): A1, A6.

25. Sherri Prasso, "Protests Push Pepsi to Back out of Burma." *Business Week*, (April 24, 1996).

26. Marcel Mauss, *Die Gabe-Form und Funktion des Austauschs in archaischen*. Gesellschaften, Frankfurt: (1990).

27. Dan Remington, "International Gift Giving: It's Not Hard to Put Your Foot in Your Mouth." *Sales & Marketing Management in Canada*, 31/10 (October 1990): 12-15.

28. Donna Delia-Loyle, "Deal Making on the Eastern Front." *Global Trade*, 110/10 (October 1990): 36, 38.

29. Manfred Bruhn, "Business Gifts: A Form of Nonverbal and Symbolic Communication." *European Management Journal*, 14/1 (February 1996): 61-68.

30. Stuart Taylor, "To Give or Not To Give." *Global Trade & Transportation*, 113/3 (March 1993): 32-33.

31. Herbig, op. cit. (1995).

32. Sharon E. Beatty, Lynn R. Kahle, Marjorie Utsey, and Charles Keown, "Gift-giving Behaviors in the United States and Japan." *Journal of International Consumer Marketing*, 6/1 (1993): 49-66.

33. Anonymous, "The Christmas Business." *International Management*, 48/10 (December 1993): 41-43.

34. Wiboon Arunthanes, Patriya Tansuhaj, and David J. Lemak, "Cross-cultural Business Gift Giving." *International Marketing Review*, 11/4 (1994): 44-55.

35. Joseph Kahn, "P&G Viewed China as a National Market and Is Conquering It." *The Wall Street Journal*, (September 12, 1995): A1, A6.

Chapter 9

1. Fons Trompenaars, *Riding the Waves of Culture*. Chicago: Irwin. (1994).

2. Gerhard Gschwandter, "Now to Sell in Germany." *Personal Selling Power*, 11 (September 1991): 57.

3. Eugene L. Mendonsa, "Coming to Terms with Rubber Time." *Business Marketing*, (October 1989): 67-68.

4. Earl D. Honeycutt Jr. and John B. Ford, "Guidelines for Managing an International Sales Force." *Industrial Marketing Management*, 24 (1995): 135-144.

5. John S. Hill, Richard R. Still, and Unal O. Boya, "Managing the Multinational Sales Force." *International Marketing Review*, 8/1 (1991): 19-31.

6. Robert March, *Honoring the Customer*. New York: John Wiley & Sons. (1990).

7. Brian M. Hawrysh and Judith L. Zaichkowsky, "Cultural Approaches to Negotiations: Understanding the Japanese." *European Journal of Marketing*, 25/10 (1991): 40-55.

8. David Friedman, *The Misunderstood Miracle*. Ithaca, New York: Cornell University Press. (1988).

9. William C. Moncrief, "A Comparison of Sales Activities in an International Setting." *Journal of Global Marketing*, 1/1, 2 (Fall/Winter 1987).

10. Hill, Still, and Boya, op. cit. (1991).

11. Neela Banerjee, "Eli Lilly Enlists Russian Doctors to Lobby for Its Pharmaceuticals." *The Wall Street Journal*, (Monday, January 29, 1996): A7.

12. G. Pascal Zachary, "Major U.S. Companies Expand Efforts to Sell to Consumers Abroad." *The Wall Street Journal*, (June 13, 1996): A1, A6.

13. Brian H. Flynn, "Selling Internationally." *Business Marketing*, (June 1987): 91-94.

14. Kuochung Chang and Cherng G. Ding, "The Influence of Culture on Industrial Buying Selection Criteria in Taiwan and Mainland China." *Industrial Marketing Management*, 24, (1995): 277-284.

15. Michael R. Czinkota and Jon Woronoff, *Unlocking Japan's Markets*. Chicago: Probus Publishing Company. (1991).

16. Kenichi Ohmae, *Triad Power: The Coming Shape of Global Competition*. New York: Free Press. (1985).

17. Honeycutt and Ford, op. cit. (1995).

18. Yuao Apasu, Shigeru Ichikawa, and John L. Graham, "Corporate Culture and Sales Force Management in Japan and America." *Journal of Personal Selling & Sales Management*, 7 (November 1987): 51-62.

19. David W. Cravens, Ken Grant, Thomas N. Ingram, Raymond W. LaForge, and Clifford E. Young, "Comparison of Field Sales Management Activities in Australian and American Sales Organizations." *Journal of Global Marketing*, 5/4 (1992): 23-32.

20. Ralph Anderson and Bert Rosenbloom, "The World Class Sales Manager: Adapting to Global Megatrends." *Journal of Global Marketing*, 5/4 (1992): 11-21.

21. Richard Ralph Still, "Sales Management: Some Cross-Cultural Aspects." *Journal of Personal Selling & Sales Management*, (Spring/Summer 1991): 6-9.

22. Anonymous, "Dell: Mail Order Was Suppose to Fail." *Business Week*, (January 20, 1992): 89.

23. Jane Frank, "Selling by Mail in a Global Market." *Journal of Direct Marketing*, 8/1 (Winter 1994): 17-31.

24. Michael Golding, "International Marketing: Testing Japan." *Catalog Age*, 7/4 (April 1990): 71 -74.

25. Melissa Dowling, "Catching the Wave to Japan." *Catalog Age*, 13/2 (February 1996): 55-59.

26. Anonymous, "Lessons from the National Geographic." *Business Europe*, (May 9-15, 1994): 7.

27. Anonymous, "Novell's Successful Crossborder Campaign." *Business Europe*, (May 2-8, 1994): 7.

28. Arnold Fishman, "International Mail Order." *Direct Marketing*, 54/6 (October 1991): 36-41.

29. Tom Eisenhart, "Savvy Mailers Tap Foreign Markets." *Business Marketing*, (September 1988): 55-65.

30. Amy Wei, "U.S. Exporters Find New Paths to Profits in Spain." *Business America*, 114/17 (August 23, 1993): 8-10.

31. Boyd DeMente and Fred Thomas Perry, *The Japanese As Consumers*. New York: Walker/Weatherhill. (1968).

32. Anonymous, "Understanding the Japanese Market." *Direct Marketing*, 55/12 (April 1993): 39-42.

33. Michael R. Violanti, "International Telemarketing." *Direct Marketing*, 52/12 (April 1990): 24-26.

34. Robert E. Garrity, "Marketers with a Yen." *Direct Marketing*, 54/7 (November 1991): 46-51.

35. Valerie Reitman, "In Japan's Car Market, Big Three Face Rivals Who Go Door-to-Door." *The Wall Street Journal*, (September 28, 1994): A1, A6.

36. Ann Marsh, "Czechs get Capitalism Lesson the Amway Way." *Advertising Age*, (April 18, 1994): 1-2.

37. Anonymous, "The Avon Lady of the Amazon." *Business Week*, (October 24, 1994): 93.

38. Andrew Tanzer, "Ding-Dong Capitalism Calling." *Forbes*, (October 14, 1991): 184-186.

39. Paul Herbig and Rama Yelkur, "Multilevel Marketing." Working Paper, Texas A&M International University. (1996).

Chapter 10

1. Kim Howard, "Global Retailing 2000." *Business Credit*, (February 1994): 22-24.

2. Sudhir H. Kale and Roger P. McIntyre, "Distribution Channel Relationships in Diverse Cultures." *International Marketing Review*, 8/3 (1991): 31-45.

3. Soumava Bandyopadhyay, Robert A. Robicheaux, and John S. Hill, "Cross-Cultural Differences in Intrachannel Communications: The United States and India." *Journal of International Marketing*, 2/3 (1994): 83-100.

4. Thomas Sowell, *Migrations and Cultures: A World View*. New York: McGraw-Hill. (1996).

5. Rene D. Mueller and Amanda J. Broderick, "East European Retailing: A Consumer Perspective." *International Journal of Retail & Distribution Management*, 23/1 (1995): 32-40.

6. Sei Kuribayashi, "Present Situation and Future Prospect of Japan's Distribution System." *Japan and the World Economy*, 3 (1991): 39-60.

7. Taichi Sakaiya, *What is Japan?* Tokyo: Kodnsha International. (1993).

8. Arthur M. Whitehill, *Japanese Management*. London: Routledge. (1991).

9. Michael R. Czinkota, "Distribution in Japan." *Columbia Journal of World Business*, 20 (Fall 1995): 12-20.

10. Eun Y. Kim, *A Cross-Cultual Reference of Business Practices in a New Korea*. Westport CT: Quorum. (1996): 88.

11. John Fahy and Fuyuki Taguchi, "Reassessing the Japanese Distribution System." *Sloan Management Review*, (Winter 1995): 49-59.

12. Teri Agins, "Shrinkage of Stores and Customers in U.S. Causes Italy's Benneton to Alter Its Tactics." *The Wall Street Journal*, (September 14, 1988): B1, B12.

13. Laurie M. Grossman, "Hypermarkets A Sure-Fire Hit Bombs." *The Wall Street Journal*, (June 25, 1992).

14. Neil Herndon, "Hong Kong Shoppers Cool to Wal-Mart's Value Club." *Marketing News*, (November 20, 1995): 11.

15. Bob Ortega, "Wal-Mart Is Slowed by Problems of Price and Culture in Mexico." *The Wall Street Journal*, (July 29, 1994): A1.

16. Anonymous, "Food Shopping Trends in Mexico." *American Demographics*, 10 (December 1995): 17

17. Matt Moffett and Jonathan Friedland, "Wal-Mart Won't Discount Its Prospects in Brazil, Though Its Losses Pile Up." *The Wall Street Journal*, (June 4, 1996): A15.

18. Fred Reinstein, "Selling to Japan: We Did It Their Way." *Export Today*, 3/3 (September/October 1987): 19-24.

19. Pauline Yoshihashi, "Now a Glamourous Barbie Heads to Japan." *The Wall Street Journal*, (June 5, 1991): B1, B4.

20. Neil King Jr., "Kmart's Czech Invasion Lurches Along." *The Wall Street Journal*, (June 8, 1993): A11.

21. Bob Ortega, "Foreign Forays: Penney Pushes Abroad in Unusually Big Way as It Pursues Growth." *The Wall Street Journal*, (February 1, 1994): A1, A7.

22. Daniel C. Bello and Bronislaw J. Verhage, "Performing Export Tasks in Industrial Channels of Distribution." *European Journal of Marketing*, 23/2 (1994): 68-84.

23. Peng S. Chan and Robert T. Justis, "Franchise Management in East Asia." *Academy of Management Executive*, 4/2 (1990): 75-85.

24. James S. Bugg, "China: Franchising's New Frontier." *Franchising World*, 26/6 (November/December 1994): 8-10.

25. Charlotte Chow, "Franchising in China." *Franchising World*, 26/3 (May/June 1994): 33-34.

26. Bob Davis, Peter Gumbel, and David P. Hamilton, "To All U.S. Managers Upset by Regulations: Try Germany or Japan." *The Wall Street Journal*, (December 14, 1995): A1, A5.

27. Saeed Samiee, "Strategic Considerations in European Retailing." *Journal of International Marketing*, 3/3 (1995): 49-76.

28. James Pressley, "Sunday Shopping in England and Wales Is Liberalized but Rules Create a Maze." *The Wall Street Journal*, (August 30, 1994).

29. Davis, Gumbel, and Hamilton, op. cit. (1995).

30. Tony Walker and Richard Tomlinson, "In Search of Fresh Pastures." *Financial Times*, (December 8, 1995): 15.

31. Gale Eisenstodt, "Bull in the Japan Shop." *Forbes*, 153/3 (January 31, 1994): 41-42.

32. Thomas N. Ingram, Thomas R. Day, and George H. Lucas, Jr., "Dealing with Global Intermediaries: Guidelines for Sales Managers." *Journal of Global Marketing*, 5/4 (1991): 65-77.

33. Samiee, op. cit. (1995).

Chapter 11

1. Wolfgang Gaul and Ulrich Lutz, "Pricing in International Marketing and Western European Economic Integration." *Management International Review*, 34/2 (Second Quarter 1994): 101-124.

2. Hermann Simon, "Pricing Problems in a Global Setting." *Marketing News*, (October 9, 1995): 4, 8.

3. Robert Frank, "Coca-Cola Faces a Price War in Japan and the Enemy Is Itself." *The Wall Street Journal*, (July 7, 1994): A1.

4. Gert Assmus and Carsten Wiese, "How to Address the Gray Market Threat Using Price Coordination." *Sloan Management Review*, (Spring 1995): 31-41.

5. Mark Zimmerman, *How to Do Business with the Japanese*. New York: Random House. (1985).

6. Shigeru Hoshino, "For Quality-Conscious Japanese Consumers, Low Prices Also Matter." *Tokyo Business Today*, (September 1990): 50-52.

7. *Business Week*, (November 20, 1989): 50.

8. Jeffrey S. Arpan, "Multinational Firm Pricing in International Markets." *Sloan Management Review*, (Winter 1972-1973): 1-9.

9. Neil King Jr., "Kmart's Czech Invasion Lurches Along." *The Wall Street Journal*, (June 8, 1993): A11.

10. James C. Morgan and J. Jeffrey Morgan, *Cracking the Japanese Market*. New York: Free Press. (1991).

11. Carol Howard and Paul Herbig, "Japanese Pricing Policies." *Journal of Consumer Marketing*, 5/17 (1996): 5-17.

12. Raphael Elimelech, "Pricing Japanese Success." *Management Today*, (May 1990): 84-89.

13. Paul Herbig, *Marketing Japanese Style*. Westport, CT: Quorum. (1995).

14. W. Wossen Kassaye, "Using Haggling in the Marketing of Goods Internationally." *Journal of International Consumer Marketing*, 3/1 (1990): 85.

15. Hugh E. Kramer and Paul A. Herbig, "Suq Haggling." *International Journal of Consumer Marketing*, 5/2: 25-35.

16. V.C. Uchendu, "Some Principles of Haggling in Peasant Markets." *Economic Development and Cultural Change*, 16/1 (October 1968).

17. William B. Quandt, "Egypt: A Strong Sense of National Identity." In Hans Binnendijk (ed.), *National Negotiating Styles*. Washington, DC: Department of State, Foreign Service Institute. (1987).

18. Anonymous, "Europe's Telecom Monopolies Transform." *The Wall Street Journal*, (June 10, 1993): A5.

19. Pete Engardio and Robert Neff, "Asia: A New Front in the War on Smoking." *International Business Week*, (February 25, 1991): 68.

20. *Economist*, (January 5, 1991): 48.

21. *The Wall Street Journal*, (March 29, 1991): A1.

22. Alecia Swasy, "Foreign Formula: Procter & Gamble Fixes Aim on Tough Market: The Latin Americans." *The Wall Street Journal*, (June 15, 1990): A7.

23. Robert Howells, "How to Price Products Competitively in Europe." *Target Marketing*, 14/5 (May 1991): 32, 34.

24. Norihiko Shirouzu, "Luxury Prices for U.S. Goods No Longer Pass Muster in Japan." *The Wall Street Journal,* (April 15, 1996): B1, B4.

25. Edith H. Updike and Bill Vlasic, "Will Neon Be the Little Car That Could in Japan?" *Business Week*, (June 1996).

26. A. Coskun Samli and Laurence Jacobs, "Pricing Practices of American Multinational Firms: Standardization vs. Localization Dichotomy." *Journal of Global Marketing*, 8/2 (1994): 51-65.

27. Ian C. MacMillan and Rita G. McGrath, "Discover Your Product's Hidden Potential." *Harvard Business Review*, (May-June 1996): 58-73.

Chapter 12

1. Evert Gummesson, "Toward a Theory of Professional Service Marketing." *Industrial Marketing Management*, 7 (1978): 90.

2. Philip Kotler and Paul N. Bloom, *Marketing Professional Services*. Englewood Cliffs, New Jersey: Prentice-Hall. (1984).

3. Lee D. Dahringer, Charles D. Frame, Oliver Yau, and Janet McColl-Kennedy, "Consumer Involvement in Services: An International Evaluation." *Journal of International Consumer Marketing*, 3/2 (1991): 23-32.

4. David Friedman, *The Misunderstood Miracle*. Ithaca, New York: Cornell University Press. (1988).

5. Shintaro Hori, "Fixing Japan's White-Collar Economy: A Personal View." *Harvard Business Review*, 25/6 (November/December 1993): 157-168.

6. Paula Dwyer, Margaret Dawson, and Dexter Roberts, "The New Music Biz." *Business Week*, (January 15, 1996): 48-52.

7. Greg Steinmetz, "Germans Finally Open Their Wallets to Credit Cards but Aren't Hooked Yet." *The Wall Street Journal*, (April 1, 1996): B2.

8. Douglas Lavin, "French Smart Card Proves a Bright Idea." *The Wall Street Journal*, (April 7, 1996): B2.

9. Anonymous, "Visa, Chinese Bank Unveil Credit Card After Months of Tests." *The Wall Street Journal*, (June 28, 1996): A8.

10. Steven Lipin, Brian Coleman, and Jeremy Mark, "Pick a Card; Visa, American Express and Mastercard vie in Overseas Strategies." *The Wall Street Journal*, (February 15, 1994): A1.

11. Robert Guenther, "Citicorp Pushes Its Bank Cards Overseas." *The Wall Street Journal*, (August 20, 1990): B1, B3.

12. G. Pascal Zachary, "Major U.S. Companies Expand Efforts to Sell to Consumers Abroad." *The Wall Street Journal*, (June 13, 1996): A1, A6.

13. Eun Y. Kim, *A Cross-Cultural Reference of Business Practices in a New Korea*. Westport, CT: Quorum, (1996): 89.

14. Susan Carey, "World Travel Study Cites Restrictions in Some Nations for Limiting Tourism." *The Wall Street Journal*, (April 25, 1991): B2.

15. Ken Walls, "Its New ATMs in Place, a Bank Reaches Out to South Africa's Poor." *The Wall Street Journal,* (June 13, 1996): A1, A10.

16. Michael R. Sesis and Craig Forman, "As Competition Rises in Global Banking, Europeans Have Edge." *The Wall Street Journal*, (March 25, 1991): A1, A4.

17. Anonymous, "Innocents Abroad: Federal Express Finds Its Pioneering Formula Falls Flat Overseas." *The Wall Street Journal*, (March 15, 1991): B1.

18. Daniel Pearl, "Federal Express Pins Hope on New Strategy in Europe." *The Wall Street Journal*, (March 18, 1992): B1.

19. Scott McCartney, "Latin America Pays Big Dividends for American Airlines." *The Wall Street Journal*, (June 4, 1996): B4.

20. John Marcom Jr., "Dream Factory to the World." *Forbes*, (April 29, 1991): 98-102.

21. Dahlinger, Frame, Yau, and McColl-Kennedy, op. cit. (1991).

22. Michael T. Malloy, "America Go Home." *The Wall Street Journal*, (March 26, 1993): R7.

23. R. Hoskins and S. McFadyen, "International Marketing Strategies for a Cultural Service." *International Marketing Review*, 8/2 (1991): 40-52.

24. Richard L. Hudson, "Uncommon Market." *The Wall Street Journal*, (March 26, 1993): R7.

25. Ken Wells, "Global Ad Campaigns After Many Missteps, Finally Pay Dividends." *The Wall Street Journal*, (August 27, 1992): A1, A8.

26. World Travel and Tourism Council 1993.

27. Russell W. Belk and Janeen A. Costa, "International Tourism." *Journal of Macromarketing*, (Fall 1995): 33-49.

28. Adam J. Freedman, "EcoTopia." *National Review*, 47 (December 11, 1995): 38.

29. B. Nicoulaud, "Problems and Strategies in the International Marketing of Services." *European Journal of Marketing*, 23/6 (1991): 55-64.

30. Jill Jusko, "CHIC Addresses Threats to Tourism." *Hotel and Motel Management*, 209 (July 1994): 6/29.

31. Anonymous, "Fiji: A Comparison of Two Villages." *Focus*, (February 1995): 5-7.

32. Lawrence J. Speer, "Once Popular Tourist Mecca Looking to Bounce Back." *Hotel and Motel Management*, 208 (June 7, 1993): 27.

33. Richard L. Hudson, "Software Makers Are Developing Ways to Make Their Programs More Polyglot." *The Wall Street Journal*, (July 27, 1992): B1.

34. G. Pascal Zachary, "Major U.S. Companies Expand Efforts to Sell to Consumers Abroad." *The Wall Street Journal*, (June 13, 1996): A1, A6.

35. Leon E. Wynter, "Language Barriers As a Marketing Tool." *The Wall Street Journal*, (January 25, 1995): B1.

Chapter 13

1. Richard T. Hise and Terrance Gabel, "Customer Service As a Strategic Weapon in International Operations." *Journal of Global Marketing*, 8(3,4) (1995): 151-170.

2. William Dempsey and Richard A. Lancioni, "International Customer Service Demands a Total Effort." *International Journal of Physical Distribution and Materials*, 19/5 (1989): 6-9.

3. Hise and Gabel, op. cit. (1995).

4. Nilly Landau, "Hitting a Moving Target." *International Business*, (March 1995): 40.

5. Michael Rey, "Whiter than White." *Business Eastern Europe*, 24/45 (November 6, 1995): 5.

6. Larissa A. Kyj and Myrolslaw J. Kyj, "Customer Service: Product Differentiation in International Markets." *International Journal of Physical Distribution and Materials*, 19/1 (1989): 30-38.

7. Myroslaw J. Kyj and Larissa S. Kyj, "Customer Service Competition in Business to Business and Industrial Markets: Myths and Realities." *Journal of Business and Industrial Marketing*, 2/4 (Fall 1989): 45-55.

8. B. Nicoulaud, "Problems and Strategies in the International Marketing of Services." *European Journal of Marketing*, 23/6 (1991): 55-64.

9. Michael R. Czinkota, "Distribution in Japan: Problems and Changes." *Columbia Journal of World Business*, 20 (Fall 1985): 12-20.

10. Tina Misstry, "Nissan Opens Bidding for Pan-Euro Account." *Campaign-London*, (July 7, 1995): 2.

11. Marino Osami, "Trend Toward Choosiness." *Journal of Japanese Trade and Industry*, 9/3 (May/June 1990): 16-19.

12. Anonymous, "Will Your Web Page Fly in Japan?" *INC*, (June 1996): 20

13. Boyd DeMente and Fred T. Perry, *The Japanese as Consumers: Asia's First Great Mass Market*. New York: Walker/Weatherhill. (1968).

14. Donald F. Blumberg, *Managing Service As a Strategic Profit Center*. New York: McGraw-Hill. (1991).

15. Paul A. Herbig and Frederick Palumbo, "Serving the Aftermarket in Japan and the U.S." *Industrial Marketing Management*, 22/4 (November 1993): 339-346.

16. Diane L. Kastiel, "Service and Support: High-Tech's New Battleground." *Business Marketing*, (June 1987): 54-62.

17. Milind M. Lele, "Product Service: How to Protect Your Unguarded Battlefield." *Business Marketing*, (June 1983): 69-75.

18. William B. Wagner and Raymond LaGarce, "Customer Service As a Marketing Strategy." *Industrial Marketing Management*, 11/1 (February 1981): 31-41.

19. Kate Evans-Correia, "Manufacturer's Guarantee." *Purchasing*, 116/10 (June 16, 1994): 36-36.

20. Robert Farish, "Service with a Smile." *Business Eastern Europe*, 24/8 (February 20, 1995): 1.

21. Oliver H.M. Yau, "Chinese Cultural Values: Their Dimensions and Marketing Implications." *European Journal of Marketing*, 22/5 (1990): 44-52.

22. T.W. Kang, *GAISHA*. New York: McGraw-Hill. (1990).

23. James C. Morgan and J. Jeffrey Morgan, *Cracking the Japanese Market*. New York: Macmillan. (1991).

24. Anonymous, "Initiating a New Level of Consumer Satisfaction." *Business Korea*, 12/1 (July 1994): 61.

25. Jack Sweeny and Pedro Pereira, "IBM Seeks new International Partners." *Computer Reseller News*, 607 (November 28, 1994): 1254.

26. Michael E. Porter, *Competitive Advantage*. New York: Free Press. (1985).

27. Morgan and Morgan, op. cit. (1991).

28. Keitaro Hasegawa, *Japanese Style Management*. New York: Kodansha. (1986).

29. Irene Chew, Keng Howe, Anthony T. Tseng, and Adrian T. K. Hong, "The Role of Culture in Training in a Multinational Context." *Journal of Management Development*, 9/5 (1995): 51-56.

30. Pete Engardio and Dexter Roberts, "Microsoft's Long March." *Business Week*, (June 24, 1996): 52-56.

31. Sheila Melvin, "Off on the Right Foot." *China Business Review*, 23/2 (March/April 1996): 24

32. Linda M. Ament and Gene Deszca, "Service Challenge of the 1990s." *Industrial & Commercial Training*, 24/9 (1992): 18-21.

33. Amy W. Gatilan and Kenneth C. Gilbert, "The Central European Need for Management Training and Advisory Services." *Multinational Business Review*, 4/1 (Spring 1996): 69-76.

34. Anonymous, "Japan Eyes the Auto-Service Market." *World Business Weekly,* (June 22, 1981): 19.

35. Keith Naughton, Robert Horn, and Edith H. Updike, "GM Starts Up a Long Hill in Asia." *Business Week*, (June 3, 1996): 56.

36. Lee, op. cit. (1983).

37. Martin Christopher, Richard Lancioni, and John Gattorna, "Managing International Customer Service." *International Marketing Review*, (Spring 1985): 65-70.

38. Robert March, *Honoring the Customer*. New York: John Wiley & Sons. (1991).

39. Neill Denny, "Daewoo Pushes Care over Cars." *Marketing*, (March 30, 1995): 5.

40. Heidi Elliott, "U.S. Giants Extend Their Reach Worldwide." *Electronic Business Today*, 22/5 (May, 1996): 63-66.

41. Vivienne Kendall, "Product Guarantees and After-Sales Service." *European Trends*, 4 (Fourth Quarter 1994): 58-64.

42. Nilly Landau, "A Call Center To Call Your Own." *International Business*, 7/9 (September 1994): 22-26.

43. J.L. Lambin and T.B. Hiller, "Volvo Trucks Europe." In J.A. Quelch (ed.), *Marketing Challenge of 1992*. Reading, MA: Addison Wesley. (1990): 349ff.

44. Denny, op. cit. (1995).

45. Nilly Landau, "Are You Being Served?" *International Business*, (March 1995): 38-40.

Chapter 14

1. Philip B. Crosby, *Quality Is Free*. New York: McGraw-Hill. (1979).

2. David A. Garvin, *Managing Quality*. New York: The Free Press. (1988).

3. A. Parasuraman, Valarie A. Zeithaml, and Leonard L. Berry, "A Conceptual Model of Service Quality and Its Implications for Future Research." *Journal of Marketing*, 49 (Fall 1985): 41-50.

4. Christian Gronroos, "A Service Quality Model and Its Marketing Implications." *European Journal of Marketing*, 18/4 (1984): 36-44.

5. Parasuraman, Zeithaml, and Berry, op. cit. (1985).

6. A. Parasuraman, Valarie A. Zeithaml, and Leonard L. Berry, "SERVQUAL: A Multiple-Item Scale for Measuring Consumer Perceptions of Service Quality." *Journal of Retailing*, 64 /1 (Spring 1988): 12-40.

7. Marcel Bouman and Ton van der Wiele, "Measuring Service Quality in the Car Service Industry." *International Journal of Service Industry Management*, 3/4 (1992): 4.

8. Simon S.K. Lam, "Measuring Service Quality: An Empirical Analysis in Hong Kong." *International Journal of Management*, 12/1 (June 1995): 182-188.

9. Wayne Kwan and Tan J. Hee, "Measuring Service Quality in Singapore Retail Banking." *Singapore Management Review*, 16/2 (July 1994): 1-24.

10. R.F. Blanchard and R.L. Galloway, "Quality in Retail Banking." *International Journal of Service Industry Management*, 5/4 (1994): 5-23.

11. Perran Akan, "Dimensions of Service Quality: A Study in Istanbul." *Managing Service Quality*, 5/6 (1995): 39-43.

12. Danny Samson and Rod Parker, "Service Quality: Gaps in the Australian Consulting Engineering Industry." *International Journal of Quality and Reliability Management*, 11/7 (1994): 60-70.

13. Jan Mattson, "Using Service Process Models to Improve Service Quality: Examples from New Zealand." *Managing Service Quality*, 4/1 (1994): 47-52.

14. Naresh K. Malhotra, Francis M. Ulgado, James Agarwal, and Imad B. Baalbaki, "International Services Marketing: A Comparative Evaluation of the Dimension of Service Quality Between Developed and Developing Countries." *International Marketing Review*, 11/2 (1994): 5-15.

15. Salvador G. Linan, "Empresarios Perdedores." *El Financiero*, (March 18, 1996): 18.

16. Gaye Kaufman, "Customer Satisfaction Studies Overseas Can Be Frustrating." *Marketing News,* 28 (August 29, 1994): 34.

17. Claes Fornell, "A National Customer Satisfaction Barometer: The Swedish Experience." *Journal of Marketing*, 56/1 (January 1992): 6-21.

18. Jarmo Lehtinen, "Service Quality: Multidisciplinary and Multinational Perspectives." In Stephen Brown, *Service Quality: Multidisciplinary and Multinational Perspectives*. Lexington, MA: Lexington Books, (1991): 135-142.

19. Dana Milbank, "Service Economy Seems Rather Creaky in Britain Just Now." *The Wall Street Journal*, (December 7, 1993): A1, A12.

20. Bill Powell, "You Want Service? Try Japan." *Newsweek*, (March 18, 1996): 22.

21. Sudhir H. Kale and Roger P. McIntyre, "Distribution Channel Relationships in Diverse Cultures." *International Marketing Review*, 8/1 (1991): 38-45.

22. Anonymous, "Perestroika." *The Economist*, (April 28, 1990): 3-22.

23. Lehtinen, op. cit. (1991).

24. Amy W. Gatilan and Kenneth C. Gilbert, "The Central European Need for Management Training and Advisory Services." *Multinational Business Review*, 4/1 (Spring 1996): 69-76.

25. Rene Dentiste Mueller and Amanda J. Broderick, "East European Retailing: A Consumer Perspective." *International Journal of Retail and Distribution Management*, 23/1 (1995): 32-40.

26. Nilly Landau, "Are You Being Served?" *International Business*, (March 1995): 38-40.

27. James Blears, "Serve Them with Style Today." *Business Mexico*, (July 1994): 30-35.

28. Alan Genestre and Paul Herbig, "An Examination of the Cross-Cultural Differences in Service Quality: The Example of Mexico and the United States." *Journal of Consumer Marketing*, 13/3 (1996): 43-53.

29. T. Bettina Cornwell, Alan D. Bligh, and Emin Babakus, "Complaint Behavior of Mexican-American Consumers to a Third-Party Agency." *Journal of Consumer Affairs*, 25 (June 1, 1991): 1-14.

30. Johny K. Johansson, "Japanese Service Industries and Their Overseas Potential." *Services Industries Journal*, 10/1 (January 1990): 85-109.

31. Lu Wei, John L. Crompton, and Leslie M. Reid, "Cultural Conflicts: Experiences of U.S. Visitors to China." *Journal of Tourism Management*, 10/6 (December 1989): 322-332.

32. J.L. Dexter, Guan L. D. Choy, and Zhang Wen, "Tourism in P.R. China— Marketing Trends and Changing Policies." *Tourism Management*, 7/3, (September 1986): 200.

33. Susan Carey, "Service Companies Send Employees off to Boot Camp to Hone Their Social Skills." *The Asian Wall Street Journal Weekly*, (Nov. 11, 1991): 27.

34. Anonymous, "Service." *Business International*, (July 23, 1990): 237.

35. William Lazer, Shoji Murata, and Hiroshi Kosaka, "Japanese Marketing." *Journal of Marketing*, 49 (Sping 1985): 69-81.

36. Michael R. Czinkota and Jon Woronoff, *Unlocking Japan's Markets*. Chicago: Probus Publishing Company. (1991).

37. David A. Aaker, "How Will the Japanese Compete in Retail Services?" *California Management Review*, 33/1 (Fall 1990): 54-67.

38. Pat Borgstorff, Carol Howard, and Paul Herbig, "Cultural Rationale for Japanese Service Philosophy." *Journal of Services Marketing*, 12/1 (1996): 43-50.

39. Misako Kamamota, "Japanese Concept of Service." *Dentsu's Japan Marketing/Advertising*, (Summer 1990): 26-30.

40. James Williamson, "Department Stores in Japan: Where Customers Are Treated as Honored Guests." *Retail and Distribution Management*, 14/4 (1986): 14-17.

41. James C. Morgan and J. Jeffrey Morgan, *Cracking the Japanese Market*. New York: Free Press. (1991).

42. Larry J. Rosenberg, "Deciphering the Japanese Cultural Code." *International Marketing Review*, 16/3 (Autumn 1986): 46-56.

43. Pete Tasker, *Inside Japan*. London: Didgwick & Jackson. (1987).

44. Jon P. Alston, "Wa, Guanxi, and Inhwa: Managerial Principals in Japan, China, and Korea." *Business Horizons*, 32/2 (March/April 1989): 26-31.

45. Christian Gronos, *Service Management and Marketing*. Lexington, MA: Lexington Book. (1990).

46. Anonymous, "Service." *Business International*, (July 23, 1990): 237.

47. Genestre and Herbig, op. cit. (1996).

Chapter 15

1. Jacquelyn A. Ottman, *Green Marketing*. Chicago: NTC Publishing Group. (1993).

2. Carl Frankel, "Blueprint for Green Marketing." *American Demographics*, (April 1992): 36.

3. Howard Schlossberg, "Effect of FTC Green Guidelines Still Doubtful for Some Marketers." *Marketing News*, (1992): 6.

4. Jennifer Lawrence, "State Guides Define Green Terms." *Advertising Age*, (1993): 7.

5. Paul Herbig and Dan Butler, "The Greening of International Marketing." *Journal of Teaching in International Business*, 5/1, 2 (1993): 63-76.

6. Thomas F. P. Sullivan, *The Greening of American Business*. Rockville, MD: Government Institutes, Inc. (1992).

7. Carolyn F. Siegel, "Restoration of the Earth: An Environmental Reality." *Journal of Marketing Education*, (Fall 1992): 24-29.

8. Jaclyn Fierman, "The Big Muddle In Green Marketing." *Fortune*, (June 3, 1991): 101.

9. Leigh Bruce, "How Green Is Your Company?" *International Management*, (January 1989): 24.

10. "Green Marketing and Product Development." In *Developing Consumer Products for Global Markets*, Chapter 12.

11. Hans W. Micklitz, "The German Packaging Order." *Columbia Journal of World Business*, 27/3,4 (Fall/Winter 1992): 120-127.

12. Stephen Kinzer, "Germany Upholds Tax on Fast-Food Consumers." *The New York Times*, (August 22, 1994), C-2.

13. R. Welford, "A Guide to Eco-Labeling and the EC Eco-Labeling Scheme." *European Environment*, 2/6, (1992): 13-15.

14. Barry N. Rosen and George B. Sloane III, "Environmenal Product Standards, Trade and European Consumer Goods Marketing." *Columbia Journal of World Business*, 30/1 (Spring 1995): 74-86.

15. Anonymous, "Company & Industry." *EU Crossborder Monitor*, 3/22 (June 7, 1995): 3.

16. Walter Coddington, *Environmental Marketing*. New York: McGraw-Hill. (1993).

17. Bruce Barnard, "Does Business Want a Green Europe?" *Europe*, 355 (April 1996): 22-24.

18. Jeffrey Stoub, "It Isn't Easy Being Green." *Business Mexico*, (July 1994): 15-16.

19. Diana Gaviria, "Introducing the Ecolabelling Concept." *International Trade Forum*, 3 (1995): 8-11.

20. Robert Neff, "Now, Japan's Advertisers Are Nuts About Nature." *Business Week*, (September 27, 1990): 13-14.

21. Anonymous, "Back to Basics in 1992." *Focus Japan*, 20/4 (April 1993): 3.

22. Michael Silverstein, "What Does It Mean To Be Green." *Business and Society Review*, 93 (Spring 1995): 16-20.

23. F.L. Simon, "Marketing Green Products in the Triad." *Columbia Journal of World Business*, (Fall/Winter 1992): 269-285.

24. Otis Port, "'Green' Product Design." *Business Week*, (June 10, 1996): 109.

25. Sherry M. Bushnell, *The Ecotourism Planning Kit: A Business Planning Guide*. Honolulu, HI: Pacific Business Center. (1994).

26. Ken Wells, "Belize Offers an Adventure in Ecotourism." *The Wall Street Journal*, (April 16, 1996): B8.

27. Shari Caudron, "The Green Handshake: Partnerships Usher in a New Era of Market-Based Environmentalism." *Industry Week*, (April 3, 1995): 33-35.

28. Juanita Liu, *Pacific Islands Ecotourism: A Public Policy and Planning Guide*. Honolulu, HI: Pacific Business Center. (1994).

29. Elizabeth Sheridan, "Leaders Link South Africa's Prosperity to Tourism." *Hotel and Motel Management*, (July 25, 1994): 6, 28.

30. Paul F. J. Eagles, "The Travel Motivations of Canadian Ecotourists." *Journal of Travel Research*, (Fall 1992): 3-7.

31. Sally Deneen, "Like the Rich Plant Life in Its Forests, Costa Rica's Tourism Industry Keeps Growing and Growing." *Hotel and Motel Management*, (March 6, 1995): 13, 35.

32. Thomas A. Burke, "Ecological Tourism Scores Big Success." *Trade and Culture*, 1/2 (April 1995): 115-116.

33. Ottoman, op. cit. (1993).

34. Christine MacDonald, "Tourism: Striking a Balance with Nature." *Institutional Investor*, 28/3 (March 1994): SSS12.

35. Barbara MacKinnon, "Beauty & the Beasts of Ecotourism." *Business Mexico*, (April 1995): 5.

36. Louis J. D'Amore, "A Code of Ethics and Guidelines for Socially and Environmentally Responsible Tourism." *Journal of Travel Research*, (Winter 1993): 64-66.

37. Mary Farquharson, "Ecotourism: A Dream Diluted." *Business Mexico*, 2/6 (June 1992): 8-11.

38. Pamela Wight, "Ecotourism: Ethics or Eco-Sell?" *Journal of Travel Research*, (Winter 1993): 3-9.

39. Coddington, op. cit. (1993).

40. Lee M. Thomas, "The Business Community and the Environment: An Important Partnership." *Business Horizons*, (March/April 1992): 21.

41. Patrick Carson and Julia Moulden, "Green Is Gold." *Insider's Digest*, (December 1991): 12.

42. Robert J. Sutton and Jamal Al-Khatib, "Cross-National Comparisons of Consumers' Environmental Concerns." *Journal of Euromarketing*, 4/1 (1994): 45-60.

43. Tara Parker-Pope, "Europeans' Environmental Concerns Don't Make it to the Shopping Basket." *The Wall Street Journal*, (April 18, 1995): B1.

Conclusion

1. Andrew Davison and Erik Grab, "The Contribution of Advertising Testing to the Development of Effective International Advertising: The Kit Kat Case Study." *Marketing and Research Today*, (February, 1993): 12-17.

2. Johny K. Johansson, "Japanese Marketing Failures." *International Marketing Review*, 16/3 (Autumn 1986): 33-40.

3. Paula Dwyer, "A Saudi Backlash Against Britain?" *Business Week*, (June 17, 1996): 86.

4. Edith H. Updike and Bill Vlasic, "Will Neon Be the Little Car That Could in Japan?" *Business Week*, (June 10, 1996): 56.

5. Gabriella Stern and Valerie Reitman, "GM's Saturn to Unveil Japan Sales Plan." *The Wall Street Journal*, (July 8, 1996): A3.

Bibliography

Aaker, David A. (1990). "How Will the Japanese Compete in Retail Services?" *California Management Review*, 33/1 (Fall): 54-67.

Abegglen, James C. and George Stalk (1985). *Kaisha, the Japanese Corporation*. New York: McGraw-Hill.

Aeppel, Timothy (1990). "Will Wessis Learn to Dine on Broilers After a Subbortnik?" *The Wall Street Journal*, (October 5): A1.

Agins, Terri (1988). "Shrinkage of Stores and Customers in U.S. Causes Italy's Benneton to Alter Its Tactics." *The Wall Street Journal*, (September 14): B1, B12.

Agrawal, Madhu (1996). "Review of a 40 year Debate in International Advertising." *International Marketing Review*, 12/1: 26-48.

Akan, Perran (1995). "Dimensions of Service Quality: A Study in Istanbul." *Managing Service Quality*, 5/6: 39-43.

Alden, Dana L., Wayne D. Hoyer, and Choi Lee (1993). "Identifying Global and Culture-Specific Dimensions of Humor in Advertising: A Multinational Analysis." *Journal of Marketing*, 57/2 (April): 64-75.

Aldridge, David N. (1990). "Marketing Strategy: The Japanese Approach." *Marketing and Research Today*, 18/4 (November): 239-244.

Alexander, Nicholas (1990). "Retailers and International Markets: Motives for Expansion." *International Marketing Review*, 7/4: 75-85.

Allen, Bill and Maureen Johnson (1994). "Taking the English Apple to Spain: The Adams Experience." *Marketing and Research Today*, (February): 54-60.

Alston, Jon P. (1989). "Wa, Guanxi, and Inhwa: Managerial Principles in Japan, China, and Korea." *Business Horizons*, 32/2 (March/April): 26-31.

Ambler, Tim (1995). "Reflections in China: Reorienting Images of Marketing." *Marketing Management*, (Summer): 23-30.

Ament, Linda M. and Gene Deszca (1992). "Service Challenge of the 1990s." *Industrial & Commercial Training*, 24/9: 18-21.

Anderson, Ralph and Bert Rosenbloom (1992). "The World Class Sales Manager: Adapting to Global Megatrends." *Journal of Global Marketing*, 5/4: 11-21.

Anonymous (1981). "Japan Eyes the Auto-Service Market." *World Business Weekly*, (June 22): 19.

Anonymous (1990). "Service." *Business International*, (July 23): 237.

Anonymous (1991). "Global Coupon Use Up, UK Belgium Tops in Europe." *Marketing News*, (August 5): 6.

Anonymous (1991). "Innocents Abroad: Federal Express Finds Its Pioneering Formula Falls Flat Overseas." *The Wall Street Journal*, (March 15): B1.

Anonymous (1991). "Trade Fairs." *Asian Advertising and Marketing*, (July): 8.

Anonymous (1992). "Brands." *Asian Advertising and Marketing*, (March): 23.

Anonymous (1992). "Dell: Mail Order Was Supposed to Fail." *Business Week*, (January 20): 89.

Anonymous (1992). "The Not-so-Magic Kingdom." *The Economist*, (September 26): 87-88.

Anonymous (1993). "Back to Basics in 1992." *Focus Japan*, 20/4 (April): 3.

Anonymous (1993). "The Christmas Business." *International Management*, 48/10 (December): 41-43.

Anonymous (1993). "Europe's Telecom Monopolies Transform." *The Wall Street Journal*, (June 10): A5.

Anonymous (1993). "International Coupon Trends." *Direct Marketing*, 56/4 (August): 47-49.

Anonymous (1993). "Making Global Direct Marketing Work." *Target Marketing*, (November): 42-55.

Anonymous (1993). "Opening Up the World of Coupon Redemption." *Marketing*, (June 3): 30.

Anonymous (1993). "Understanding the Japanese Market." *Direct Marketing*, 55/12 (April): 39-42.

Anonymous (1994). "The Avon Lady of the Amazon." *Business Week*, (October 24): 93.

Anonymous (1994). "Brands." *The Economist*, (July 2): 9-10.

Anonymous (1994). "Don't Leave Home Without It Wherever You Live." *Business Week*, (February 21): 76-77.

Anonymous (1994). "Initiating a New Level of Consumer Satisfaction." *Business Korea*, 12/1 (July): 61.

Anonymous (1994). "Lessons from the National Geographic." *Business Europe*, (May 9-15): 7.

Anonymous (1994). "Novell's Successful Crossborder Campaign." *Business Europe*, (May 2-8): 7.

Anonymous (1995). "Company & Industry." *EU Crossborder Monitor*, 3/22, (June 7): 3.

Anonymous (1995). "Did We Say That?" *Playboy*, (September): 15.

Anonymous (1995). "EuroAds: Why Bother?" *Campaign*, (January 20): 28-29.

Anonymous (1995). "Fiji: A Comparison of Two Villages." *Focus*, (February): 5-7.

Anonymous (1995). "Food Shopping Trends in Mexico." *American Demographics*, 10 (December): 17.

Anonymous (1996). "Pepsi Aims for the Stars." *Marketing News*, (June 3): 1.

Anonymous (1996). "Visa, Chinese Bank Unveil Credit Card After Months of Tests." *The Wall Street Journal*, (June 28): A8.

Anonymous (1996). "Will Your Web Page Fly in Japan?" *INC*, (June): 20.

Aonuma, Yoshimatsu (1991). "A Japanese Explains Japan's Business Style." *Across the Board*, (February): 41-51.

Apasu, Yuao, Shigeru Ichikawa, and John L. Graham (1987). "Corporate Culture and Sales Force Management in Japan and America." *Journal of Personal Selling & Sales Management*, 7 (November): 51-62.

Appelbaum, Ullrich and Chris Halliburton (1993). "How to Develop International Advertising Campaigns that Work." *International Journal of Advertising*, 12: 223-241.

Arpan, Jeffrey S. (1972). "Multinational Firm Pricing in International Markets." *Sloan Management Review*, (Winter): 1-9.

Arunthanes, Wibbon, Patriya Tansuhaj, and David J. Lemak (1994). "Cross-cultural Business Gift-giving." *International Marketing Review*, 11/4: 44-55.

Assmus, Gert and Carsten Wiese (1995). "How to Address the Gray Market Threat Using Price Coordination." *Sloan Management Review*, (Spring): 31-41.

Ayal, I. and L. Nachum (1994). "A Fresh Look at the Standardization Problem." *Journal of International Marketing and Marketing Research*, 19/1: 17-35.

Balikowa, David Ouma (1995). "Media Marketing." *Media, Culture, & Society*, 17: 603-613.

Ball, Donald A. and Wendell H. McCulloch, Jr. (1995). *International Business: The Challenge of Global Competition*. Burr Ridge, IL: Irwin Publishers.

Bandyopadhyay, Soumava, Robert A. Robicheaux, and John S. Hill (1994). "Cross-Cultural Differences in Intrachannel Communications: The United States and India." *Journal of International Marketing*, 2/3: 83-100.

Banerjee, Neela (1996). "Eli Lilly Enlists Russian Doctors to Lobby for Its Pharmaceuticals." *The Wall Street Journal*, (January 29): A7.

Barker, A. Tansu (1993). "A Marketing Oriented Perspective of Standardized Global Marketing." *Journal of Global Marketing*, 7/2: 123-135.

Barnard, Bruce (1996). "Does Business Want a Green Europe?" *Europe*, 355 (April): 22-24.

Bartos, Rena (1989). "International Demographic Data? Incomparable!" *Marketing and Research Today*, (November): 205-215.

Bass, Bernard M. and Philip C. Burger (1979). *Assessment of Managers: An International Comparison*. New York: The Free Press.

Batzer, E. and H. Laumer. (1989). *Marketing Strategies and Distribution Channels of Foreign Companies in Japan*. Boulder, CO: Westview Press.

Beatty, Sharon E., Lynn R. Kahle, Marjorie Utsey, and Charles Keown (1993). "Gift-Giving Behaviors in the United States and Japan." *Journal of International Consumer Marketing*, 6/1: 49-66.

Belk, Russell W. and Janeen A. Costa (1995). "International Tourism." *Journal of MacroMarketing*, (Fall): 33-49.

Bello, Daniel C. and Hiram C. Barksdale, Jr. (1986). "Exporting at Industrial Trade Shows." *Industrial Marketing Management*, 15: 197-206.

Bello, Daniel C. and Bronislaw J. Verhage (1994). "Performing Export Tasks in Industrial Channels of Distribution." *European Journal of Marketing*, 23/2: 68-84.

Bertrand, Kate (1987). "The Baksheesh Beat." *Business Marketing*, (June): 107-109.

Bester, Helmut and Emmanuel Petrakis (1996). "Coupons and Oligopolistic Price Discrimination." *International Journal of Industrial Organization*, 14/2: 227-242.

Beveridge, Dirk (1994). "McDonald's, Coke Irk Muslims." *The Honolulu Advertiser*, (June 12): e5.

Binnendijk, Hans (ed.) (1987). *National Negotiating Styles*. Washington, DC: Department of State, Foreign Service Institute.

Black, J. Stewart and Mark Mendenhall. (1993). "Resolving Conflicts with the Japanese: Mission Impossible." *Sloan Management Review*, 25/2 (Spring): 49-59.

Blackwell, Roger, Riad Ajami, and Kristina Stephan (1991). "Winning the Global Advertising Race: Planning Globally, Acting Locally." *Journal of International Consumer Marketing*, 3/2: 97-120.

Blanchard, R.F. and R.L. Galloway (1994). "Quality in Retail Banking." *International Journal of Service Industry Management*, 5/4: 5-23.

Blears, James (1994). "Serve Them with Style Today." *Business Mexico*, (July): 30-35.

Blumberg, Donald F. (1991). *Managing Service as a Strategic Profit Center*. New York: McGraw-Hill.

Boddewyn, J.J. (1988). "The One and Many Worlds of Advertising." *International Journal of Advertising*, 7: 11-16.

Boddewyn, J.J. (1989). "Barriers to Advertising." *International Advertiser*, (May/June): 21, 22.

Boddewyn, J.J., Robin Soehl, and Jacques Picard (1986). "Standardization in International Marketing: Is Ted Levitt in Fact Right?" *Business Horizons*, (November/December): 69-75.

Bonvillian, Gary and William A. Nowlin (1994). "Cultural Awareness: An Essential Element of Doing Business Abroad." *Business Horizons*, (November/December): 44-50.

Borgstorff, Pat, Carol Howard, and Paul Herbig (1997). "Cultural Rationale for Japanese Service Philosophy." *Journal of Services Marketing*, 12/3: 41-47.

Bouman, Marcel and Ton van der Wiele (1992). "Measuring Service Quality in the Car Service Industry." *International Journal of Service Industry Management*, 3/4: 4-12.

Brauchli, Marcus W. (1996). "China Has Surly Image but Part of the Reason is Bad Public Relations." *The Wall Street Journal*, (June 18): A1, A6.

Broberg, Morten (1994). "Marketing Research in Poland." *Journal of Euromarketing*, 4/1: 63-82.

Brock, Sabra E. (1989). "Marketing Research in Asia: Problems, Opportunities, and Lessons." *Marketing Research*, (September): 44-49.

Brockhoff, Klaus (1991). "Competitor Technology Intelligence in German Companies." *Industrial Marketing Management*, 20: 91-98.

Brokaw, Stephen C. and C. Lakshman (1995). "Cross-Cultual Consumer Research in India." *Journal of International Consumer Marketing*, 7/3: 53-80.

Brown, Stephen W., Evert Gummesson, Bo Edvardsson, and Bengtove Gustavsson (1991). *Service Quality: Mulitidsciplinary and Multinational Perspectives.* Lexington, MA: Lexington Books.

Browning, E.S. (1992). "In Pursuit of the Elusive Euroconsumer." *The Wall Street Journal*, (April 29): B1.

Bruce, Leigh (1989). "How Green Is Your Company?" *International Management*, (January): 24.

Bruhn, Manfred (1996). "Business Gifts: A Form of Nonverbal and Symbolic Communication." *European Management Journal*, 14/1 (February): 61-68.

Bugg, James S. (1994). "China: Franchising's New Frontier." *Franchising World*, 26/6 (November/December): 8-10.

Burke, Thomas A. (1995). "Ecological Tourism Scores Big Success." *Trade and Culture*, 1/2 (April): 115-116.

Burton, Burton (1985). "Japan Backlash." *Advertising Age*, (April 22): 122.

Bushnell, Sherry M. (1994). *The Ecotourism Planning Kit: A Business Planning Guide*. Honolulu, HI: Pacific Business Center.

Byrne, Eileen (1994). "Getting the Message Across." *Business Mexico*, 4/5: 8-11.

Byrne, Eileen (1994). "Mexican Consumers and Their Appetites." *Business Mexico*, (May): 16-18.

Carey, Susan (1991a). "World Travel Study Cites Restrictions in Some Nations for Limiting Tourism." *The Wall Street Journal*, (April 25): B2.

Carey, Susan (1991b). "Service Companies Send Employees off to Boot Camp to Hone Their Social Skills." *The Asian Wall Street Journal Weekly*, (November 11): 27.

Carey, Susan (1996). "Nations Have Quirks that Trivial Pursuit just Can't Ignore." *The Wall Street Journal*, (January 10): A1.

Carree, M.A., J.C.A. Potjes, and A.R. Thurik (1993). "Small Store Presence in Japan." *Economic Letters*, 41: 329-334.

Carson, Patrick and Julia Moulden (1991). "Green Is Gold." *Insider's Digest*, (December): 12.

Cateora, Philip (1993). *International Marketing*. Orlando, FL: Dryden Press.

Caudron, Shari (1995). "The Green Handshake: Partnerships Usher in a New Era of Market-Based Environmentalism." *Industry Week*, (April 3): 33-35.

Chan, K.C. (1993). "World-Class Marketing." *Industrial Management and Data Systems*, 93/2: 13-23.

Chan, Peng S. and Robert T. Justis (1990). "Franchise Management in East Asia." *Academy of Management Executive*, 4/2: 75-85.

Chang, Kuochung and Cherng G. Ding (1995). "The Influence of Culture on Industrial Buying Selection Criteria in Taiwan and Mainland China." *Industrial Marketing Management*, 24: 277-284.

Chew, Irene, Keng Howe, Anthony Tsai-pen Tseng, and Adrian Teo Kim Hong (1995). "The Role of Culture in Training in a Multinational Context." *Journal of Management Development*, 9/5: 51-56.

Child, John (1981). "Culture, Contingency, and Capitalism in the Cross National Study of Organizations." In L.L. Cummings and B.M. Staw (eds.) *Research in Organizational Behavior*, Vol. 3. Greenwich, CT: JAI Press; 303-356.

Chinese Culture Connection (1987). "Chinese Values and the Search for Culture-Free Dimensions of Culture." *Journal of Cross-Cultural Psychology*, 18/2 (June): 143-164.

Cho, Namju (1995). "South Korea Relaxes Ad Content Rules and Ends Locked Time System on TV." *The Wall Street Journal*, (October 26): B2.

Chourdrhy, Yusuf (1986). "Pitfalls in International Marketing Research." *Akron Business and Economic Review*, (Winter): 18-28.

Chow, Charlotte (1994). "Franchising in China." *Franchising World*, 26/3 (May/June): 33-34.

Christian, Allan (1993). "Connecting with the Japanese Customer." *Business America*, (October 4): 23-24.

Christopher, Martin, Richard Lancioni, and John Gattorna (1985). "Managing International Customer Service." *International Marketing Review*, (Spring): 65-70.

Church, Nancy (1992). "Advertising in the Eastern Bloc: Current Practices and Anticipated Avenues of Development." *Journal of Global Marketing*, 5/3: 109-129.

Clark, Terry (1990). "International Marketing and National Character: A Review and Proposal for an Integrative Theory." *Journal of Marketing*, 54/4 (October): 66-79.

Coddington, Walter (1993). *Environmental Marketing*. New York: McGraw-Hill.

Coke, Damon D. (1991). "Nestle Launches First Coffee Drink." *The Wall Street Journal*, (October 1): B1.

Commins, Kevins (1990). "European Trade Fairs Seek U.S. Exhibitors." *The Journal of Commerce*, (August 21): 4A.

Copeland, Lennie (1984). "Foreign Markets: Not for the Amateur." *Business Marketing*, (July): 112-118.

Copeland, Lennie and Lewis Griggs (1985). *Going International*. New York: Random House.

Cornwell, T. Bettina, Alan David Bligh, and Emin Babakus (1991). "Complaint Behavior of Mexican-American Consumers to a Third Party Agency." *Journal of Consumer Affairs*, 25 (June 1): 1-14.

Cotter, Michael J. and James A. Henley, Jr. (1994). "Martial Arts Marketing." *Multinational Business Review*, 1/2: 79-85.

Cravens, David W., Ken Grant, Thomas N. Ingram, Raymond W. LaForge, and Clifford E. Young (1992). "Comparison of Field Sales Management Activities in Australian and American Sales Organizations." *Journal of Global Marketing*, 5/4: 23-32.

Crawford, John E. and William H. Motes (1993). "Toward a Better Understanding of Cross-Cultural Pricing Tactics." *International Journal of Management*, 10/3 (September): 332-341.

Crosby, Philip B. (1979). *Quality Is Free*. New York: McGraw-Hill.

Curwen, Peter (1995). "EuroDisney: The Mouse That Roared (Not!)" *European Business Review*, 95/5: 15-20.

Cutler, Blayne (1990). "Reaching the Real Europe." *American Demographics,* (October): 38-43.

Cutler, Bob D., Rajshekhar G. Javalgi, and M. Krishna Erramilli (1992). "The Visual Components of Print Advertising: A Five Country Cross-Cultural Analysis." *European Journal of Marketing*, 26/4: 7-20.

Cutler, Bob D., Rajshekhar G. Javalgi, and Dongdae Lee (1995). "The Portrayal of People in Magazine Advertisements: The United States and Korea." *Journal of International Consumer Marketing*, 8/2: 45-58.

Czinkota, Michael R. (1985). "Distribution in Japan: Problems and Changes." *Columbia Journal of World Business*, 20 (Fall): 12-20.

Czinkota, Michael R. and Masaaki Kotabe (1990). "Product Development the Japanese Way." *Journal of Business Strategy*, 12/4 (November/December): 31-36.

Czinkota, Michael and Ronkainen, Illa (1993). *International Marketing.* Orlando, FL: Dryden Press.

Czinkota, Michael R. and Jon Woronoff (1986). *Japan's Market: The Distribution System.* New York: Praeger.

Czinkota, Michael R. and Jon Woronoff (1991). *Unlocking Japan's Markets.* Chicago: Probus Publishing Company.

Dahringer, Lee D. (1991). "Marketing Services Internationally: Barriers and Management Strategies." *The Journal of Services Marketing*, 5/3 (Summer): 5-12.

Dahringer, Lee D., Charles D. Frame, Oliver Yau, and Janet McColl-Kennedy (1991). "Consumer Involvement in Services: An International Evaluation." *Journal of International Consumer Marketing*, 3/2: 13-21.

D'Amore, Louis J. (1993). "A Code of Ethics and Guidelines for Socially and Environmentally Responsible Tourism." *Journal of Travel Research*, (Winter): 64-66.

Darling, John R. and Van R. Wood. (1990). "A Longitudinal Study Comparing Perceptions of U.S. and Japanese Consumer Products in a Third/Neutral Country." *Journal of International Business Studies*, 21/3 (Third Quarter): 427-450.

Davis, Bob, Peter Gumbel, and David P. Hamilton (1995). "To All U.S. Managers Upset by Regulations: Try Germany or Japan." *The Wall Street Journal*, (December 14): A1, A5.

Davison, J. Andrew and Erick Grab (1993). "The Contributions of Advertising Testing to the Development of Effective International Advertising: The Kit Kat Case Study." *Marketing and Research Today*, (February): 15-25.

Dawson, Scott and Dave Dickinson (1988). "Conducting International Mail Surveys." *Journal of International Business Studies*, 19 (Fall): 491-496.

De Chernatony, Leslie, Chris Halliburton, and Ratna Bernath (1995). "International Branding." *International Marketing Review*, 12/2: 9-21.

DeMente, Boyd (1989). *Japanese Etiquette and Ethics in Business.* Chicago: NTC.

DeMente, Boyd and Fred T. Perry (1968). *The Japanese as Consumers: Asia's First Great Mass Market*. New York: Walker/Weatherhill.

De Mooij, Marieke (1994). *Advertising Worldwide*. Salisbury, England: Prentice Hall International.

Delia-Loyle, Donna (1990). "Dealmaking on the Eastern Front." *Global Trade*, 110/10 (October): 36, 38.

Dempsey, William and Richard A. Lancioni (1989). "International Customer Service Demands a Total Effort." *International Journal of Physical Distribution and Materials*, 19/5: 6-9.

Deneen, Sally (1995). "Like the Rich Plant Life in Its Forests, Costa Rica's Tourism Industry Keeps Growing and Growing." *Hotel and Motel Management*, (March 6): 13, 35.

Denny, Neill (1995). "Daewoo Pushes Care over Cars." *Marketing*, (March 30): 5.

Dexter, J.L., Guan Li Dong Choy, and Zhang Wen (1986). "Tourism in P.R. China—Marketing Trends and Changing Policies." *Tourism Management*, 7/3 (September): 200.

diBenedetto, C. Anthony, Mariko Tamate, and Rajan Chandran (1992). "Developing Creative Advertising Strategy for the Japanese Marketplace." *Journal of Advertising Research*, (January/February): 39-53.

Douglas, Susan P. and Yoram Wind (1987). "The Myth of Globalization." *Columbia Journal of World Business*, (Winter): 19-29.

Dowling, Melissa (1996). "Catching the Wave to Japan." *Catalog Age*, 13/2 (February): 55-59.

Drucker, Peter F. (1981). "Behind Japan's Success." *Harvard Business Review*, 25/1 (January/February): 83-92.

Drucker, Peter F. (1989). *The New Realities*. Oxford, England: Heinemann Professional Publishing Company.

Dubey, Suman (1994). "Kellogg Invites India's Middle Class to Breakfast of Ready to Eat Cereal." *The Wall Street Journal*, (August 30): B5.

Dulek, Ronald E., John S. Fielden, and Jon S. Hill (1991). "International Communications: An Executive Primer." *Business Horizons*, (January/February): 29-36.

Dunn, Dan T. Jr. (1979). "Agents and Distributors in the Middle East." *Business Horizons*, (October): 69-78.

Dwyer, Paula (1996). "A Saudi Backlash Against Britain?" *Business Week*, (June 17): 86.

Dwyer, Paula, Margaret Dawson, and Dexter Roberts (1996). "The New Music Biz." *Business Week*, (January 15): 48-52.

Eagles, Paul F. J. (1992). "The Travel Motivations of Canadian Ecotourists." *Journal of Travel Research*, (Fall): 3-7.

Eguchi, Yasuhiro (1981). "The Japanese Consumer and Imported Products." *Dentsu's Japan Marketing/Advertising*, (July): 19-22.

Eisenhart, Tom (1988). "Savvy Mailers Tap Foreign Markets." *Business Marketing*, (September): 55-65.

Eisenstodt, Gale (1988). "Bull in the Japan Shop." *Forbes*, 153/3 (January 31): 41-42.

Elimelech, Raphael (1990). "Pricing Japanese Success." *Management Today*, (May): 84-89.

Elliot, Heidi (1996). "U.S. Giants Extend Their Reach Worldwide." *Electronic Business Today*, 22/5 (May): 63-66.

Engardio, Pete and Robert Neff (1991). "Asia: A New Front in the War on Smoking." *International Business Week*, (February 25): 68.

Engardio, Pete and Dexter Roberts (1996). "Microsoft's Long March." *Business Week*, (June 24): 52-56.

Evans-Correia, Kate (1994). "Manufacturer's Guarantee." *Purchasing*, 116/10 (June 16): 36-36.

Fahy, John and Fuyuki Taguchi (1995). "Reassessing the Japanese Distribution System." *Sloan Mangement Review*, (Winter): 49-61.

Farish, Robert (1995). "Service with a Smile." *Business Eastern Europe*, 24/8 (February 20): 1.

Farquharson, Mary (1992). "Ecotourism: A Dream Diluted." *Business Mexico*, 2/6 (June): 8-11.

Fields, George (1984a). "Why Are the Japanese Consumers (Not) 'Westernized'?" *Dentsu's Japan Marketing/Advertising*, 11/3 (Summer): 25-29.

Fields, George (1984b). *From Bonsai to Levi's*. New York: Macmillan.

Fields, George (1989). *Gucci on the Ginza*. Tokyo: Kodansha International Limited.

Fields, George (1990). "Advertising Strategy in Japan." *Dentsu's Japan Marketing/Advertising*, (Fall/Winter): 52-56.

Fierman, Jaclyn (1991). "The Big Muddle in Green Marketing." *Fortune*, (June 3): 101.

Firoz, Nadeem M. and Ahmed S. Maghrabi (1994). "The Role of Service Marketing in Economic Development: An Analysis." *International Journal of Management*, 11/2: 641-647.

Fishman, Arnold (1991). "International Mail Order." *Direct Marketing*, 54/6 (October): 36-41.

Flath, D. (1989). "Vertical Restraints in Japan." *Japan and the World Economy*, 1: 187-203.

Flath, D. (1990). "Why Are There So Many Retail Stores in Japan?" *Japan and the World Economy*, 2: 365-386.

Flath, D. and T. Nariu (1988). "Returns Policy in the Japanese Marketing System." *Journal of Japanese and International Economies*, 3: 49-63.

Flynn, Brian H. (1987). "Selling Internationally." *Business Marketing*, (June): 91-94.

Ford, John B. and Earl D. Honeycutt, Jr. (1992). "Japanese National Culture as a Basis for Understanding Japanese Business Practices." *Business Horizons*, 25/6 (November/December): 27-34.

Fornell, Claes (1992). "A National Cuistomer Satisfaction Barometer: The Swedish Experience." *Journal of Marketing*, 56/1 (January): 6-21.

Foxman, R., P.S. Tansuhaj, and J.K. Wong (1988). "Evaluating Cross National Sales Promotion Strategy: An Audit Approach." *International Marketing Review*, (Winter): 11.

Frank, Jane (1994). "Selling by Mail in a Global Market." *Journal of Direct Marketing*, 8/1 (Winter): 17-31.

Frank, Robert (1994). "Coca-Cola Faces a Price War in Japan and the Enemy Is Itself." *The Wall Street Journal*, (July 7): A1.

Frank, Robert (1995). "Coca-Cola Is Shedding Its Once-Stodgy Image with Swift Expansion." *The Wall Street Journal*, (August 22): A1, A6.

Frank, Robert (1996). "Potato Chips to go Global—or so Pepsi Bets." *The Wall Street Journal*, (March 14): B1, B10.

Frank, Robert (1996). "Seeing Red Abroad, Pepsi Rolls Out a New Blue Can." *The Wall Street Journal* (April 2): B1, B6.

Frankel, Carl (1992). "Blueprint for Green Marketing." *American Demographics*, (April): 36.

Friedman, David (1988). *The Misunderstood Miracle*. Ithaca, N.Y.: Cornell University Press.

Friendlander, J. (1992). "Flexing the Marketing Muscle of European Trade Shows." *Journal of European Business*, (January/February): 10-15.

Frith, Katherine T. (1987). "The Social and Legal Constraints on Advertising in Malaysia." *Media Asia*, 14/2: 103.

Fujitak, Kikuharu (1990). "The Transition and Future of Marketing Research." *Journal of Advertising Research*, 12/2 (April/May): 58-62.

Garrity, Robert E. (1991). "Marketers With A Yen." *Direct Marketing*, 54/7 (November): 46-51.

Garvin, David A. (1988). *Managing Quality*. New York: The Free Press.

Gatilan, Amy W. and Kenneth C. Gilbert (1996). "The Central European Need for Management Training and Advisory Services." *Multinational Business Review*, 4/1 (Spring): 69-76.

Gaul, Wolfgang and Ulrich Lutz (1994). "Pricing in International Marketing and Western European Economic Integration." *Management International Review*, 34/2 (Second Quarter): 101-124.

Gaviria, Diana (1995). "Introducing the Ecolabelling Concept." *International Trade Forum*, 3: 8-11.

Gemmell, Arthur J. (1991). "Planning the Japanese Way in the United States." *Journal of Business Strategy*, 15/2 (March/April): 4-10.

Genestre, Alain and Paul Herbig (1996). "An Examination of the Cross-Cultural Differences in Service Quality: The Example of Mexico and the United States." *Journal of Consumer Marketing*, 13/3: 47-53.

Ghauri, Perdez N. (1986). "Guidelines for International Business Negotiations." *International Marketing Review*, 4 (Autumn): 72-82.

Gilmour, Peter (1977). "Customer Service: Differentiation by Market Segment." *International Journal of Physical Distribution and Materials Management*, 7/3: 141-148.

Golding, Michael (1990). "International Marketing: Testing Japan." *Catalog Age*, 7/4 (April): 71-74.

Golob, Steven (1988). "Sell Overseas at Trade Fairs." *Nation's Business*, (March): 57-59.

Goodnow, James D. and Rustan Kosenko (1992). "Strategies for Successful Penetration of the Japanese Market or How to Beat Japan at Its Own Game." *Journal of Business & Industrial Marketing*, 7/1 (Winter): 41-49.

Gordon, Craig C., Denise D. Schoenbachler, Geoffrey L. Gordon, and Thomas M. Rogers (1995). "Taking a 'Real-Time' Approach to International Marketing Research." *Journal of Professional Services Marketing*, 11/2: 189-205.

Graham, John L. (1984). "A Comparison of Japanese and American Business Negotiations." *International Journal of Research in Marketing*, 1/2: 51-68.

Graham, John L. (1986). "Across the Negotiating Table from the Japanese." *International Marketing Review*, 15/3 (Autumn): 58-71.

Graham, John L. and J. Douglas Andrews (1987). "A Holistic Analysis of Japanese and American Business Negotiations." *Journal of Business Communications*, 24/4: 63-77.

Graham, John L. and Yoshihiro Sano (1989). *Smart Bargaining: Doing Business with the Japanese*. New York: Harper Business.

Green, Corlliss L. (1995). "Media Exposure's Impact on Perceived Availability and Redemption of Coupons by Ethnic Consumers." *Journal of Advertising Research*, 35/2 (March/April): 56-64.

Green, Robert T. and Dana L. Alden (1988). "Functional Equivalence in Cross-Cultural Consumer Behavior: Gift Giving in Japan and the United States." *Psychology Marketing*, 5: 155-168.

Greenbaum, Thomas L. (1996). "Understanding Focus Group Research Abroad." *Marketing News*, (June 3): H14.

Griffin, Trenholme J. and W. Russell Daggatt (1990). *The Global Negotiator*. New York: Harper Business.

Gronroos, Christian (1984). "A Service Quality Model and Its Marketing Implications." *European Journal of Marketing*, 18/4: 36-44.

Gronroos, Christian (1990). *Service Management and Marketing*. Lexington, MA: Lexington Books.

Grossman, Laurie M. (1992). "Hypermarkets: A Sure-Fire Hit Bombs." *The Wall Street Journal*, (June 25).

Gschwandter, Gerhard (1991). "How to Sell in Germany." *Personal Selling Power*, 11 (September): 57.

Guber, S. (1987). "The Teenage Mind." *American Demographics*, (August): 42-44.

Guenther, Robert (1990). "Citicorp Pushes Its Bank Cards Overseas." *The Wall Street Journal*, (August 20): B1, B3.

Gumbel, Peter and David J. Jefferson (1992). "Disney Continues Drive to Expand World-Wide." *The Wall Street Journal*, (November 20): B2.

Gumbel, Peter and Carla Anne Robbins (1996). "Has the West Lost Russia? Probably Not, for Much Has Changed." *The Wall Street Journal*, (May 28): A1.

Gumbel, Peter and Richard Turner (1994). "Fans Like EuroDisney but Its Parent's Goofs Weigh the Park Down." *The Wall Street Journal*, (March 10): A1, A12.

Gummesson, Evert (1978). "Toward a Theory of Professional Service Marketing." *Industrial Marketing Management*, 7: 90.

Hall, Edward T. and Mildred R. Hall (1987). *Hidden Differences*. New York: Anchor Books.

Halliburton, Chris and Reinhard Hunerberg (1993). "Executive Insights: Pan European Marketing—Myth or Reality." *Journal of International Marketing*, 1/3: 77-92.

Han, C.M. (1989). "Country Image: Halo or Summary Construct." *Journal of Marketing Research*, 26 (May): 222-229.

Hanni, David A., John K. Ryans, Jr., and Ivan R. Vernon (1995). "Executive Insights: Coordinating International Advertising—the Goodyear Case Revisited for Latin America." *Journal of International Marketing*, 3/2: 83-98.

Harris, Greg (1994). "International Advertising Standardization: What Do the Multinationals Actually Standardize?" *Journal of International Marketing*, 2/4: 13-30.

Harris, John (1991). "Advantage Mitsubishi." *Forbes*, (March 18): 78.

Harris, Philip R. and Robert T. Moran (1996). *Managing Cultural Differences*, 4th edition. Houston, TX: Gulf Publishing Co.

Harvey, Michael G. (1993). "Point of View: A Model to Determine Standardization of the Advertising Process in International Markets." *Journal of Advertising Research*, (July/August): 57-64.

Hasegawa, Keitaro (1986). *Japanese Style Management*. New York: Kodansha.

Hassan, Sala S. and Lea P. Katsanis (1991). "Identification of Global Consumer Segments." *Journal of International Consumer Marketing*, 3/2.

Hawrysh, Brian M., and Judith L. Zaichkowsky (1991). "Cultural Approaches to Negotiations: Understanding the Japanese." *European Journal of Marketing*, 25/10: 40-55.

Hendon, Donald, Rebecca Hendon, and Paul Herbig (1996). *Cross Cultural Business Negotiations*. Westport, CT: Quorum.

Henry, Dee (1990). "Mailing the Mysterious East." *Catalog Age*, 7/6 (June): 15-20.

Herbig, Paul A. (1995). *Marketing Japanese Style*. Westport, CT: Quorum.

Herbig; Paul A. and Pat Borgstorff (1994). "The Japanese Consumer: Are They Really Different from U.S. Consumers." *Journal of International Marketing*, 2/1: 11-17.

Herbig, Paul A. and Dan Butler. (1993). "The Greening of International Marketing." *Journal of Teaching in International Business*, 5/1,2: 63-76.

Herbig, Paul A. and Hugh Kramer (1991). "International Product Rollout: A Cultural Cluster Approach." *Journal of International Consumer Marketing*, 4/1: 12-20.

Herbig, Paul A. and Hugh Kramer (1991). "Cross-Cultural Negotiations: Success Through Understanding." *Management Decisions*, 29/8: 19-31.

Herbig, Paul A. and Hugh Kramer (1992a). "Do's and Dont's of Cross-Cultural Negotiations." *Industrial Marketing Management*, 21/4 (November): 287-298.

Herbig, Paul A. and Hugh Kramer (1992b). "The Role of Cross-Cultural Negotiations in International Marketing." *Marketing Planning and Intelligence*, 10/2: 10-13.

Herbig, Paul A. and Joseph A. Miller (1992). "Culture and Innovation." 6/3: 75-104.

Herbig, Paul A. and Fred Palumbo (1993a). "Serving the Aftermarket in Japan and the U.S." *Industrial Marketing Management*, 22/4 (November): 339-346.

Herbig, Paul A. and Fred Palumbo (1993b). "The Japanese Philosophy of Service." *International Journal of Commerce and Management*, 4/1,2: 69-84.

Herbig, Paul A. and Fred Palumbo (1994). "Japanese Consumer Protection." *Journal of Consumer Marketing*, 11/1 (Spring/Summer): 5-14.

Herbig, Paul and Rama Yelkur (1996). "Multilevel Marketing." Working Paper, Texas A&M International University.

Hernandez, Sigfredo A. (1988). "An Exploratory Study of Coupon Use in Puerto Rico: Cultural versus Institutional Barriers to Coupon Use." *Journal of Advertising Research*, 28/5: 40-46.

Herndon, Neil (1995). "Hong Kong Shoppers Cool to Wal-Mart's Value Club." *Marketing News*, (November 20): 11.

Higgins, Susan and John Ryans (1991). "EC-92 and International Advertising Agencies." *International Journal of Advertising*, 10: 293-298.

Hill, J. Dee and David McQuaid (1994). "The Money's in the Mail." *Business Eastern Europe*, 23/48 (November 28): 7.

Hill, John S., Richard R. Still, and Unal O. Boya (1991). "Managing the Multinational Sales Force." *International Marketing Review*, 8/1: 19-31.

Hisatomi, Takashi (1991). "Global Marketing by the Nissan Motor Company Limited." *Marketing and Research Today*, 19/1 (February): 56-61.

Hise, Richard T. and Terrance Gabel (1995). "Customer Service As a Strategic Weapon in International Operations." *Journal of Global Marketing*, 8/3, 4: 151-170.

Hofstede, Geert (1983). "Dimensions of National Cultures in Fifty Countries and Three Regions." In *Expiscations in Cross-Cultural Psychology*. Lisse, Netherlands: Swets and Zeiltinger.

Hofstede, Geert (1984). *Culture's Consequences*. London: Sage.

Hofstede, Geert (1988)."The Confucius Connection: From Cultural Roots to Economic Growth." *Organizational Dynamics*, 16/4 (Spring): 4-21.

Hofstede, Geert (1991). *Software of the Mind*. London: Sage.

Holyoke, Larry and William Glasgall (1994). "A Bargain Basement Called Japan." *Business Week*, (June 27): 42-43.

Honeycutt Jr., Earl D., and John B. Ford (1995). "Guidelines for Managing an International Sales Force." *Industrial Marketing Management*, 24: 135-144.

Hong, Jae W., Aydin Muderrisoglu, and George M. Zinkhan (1987). "Cultural Differences and Advertising Expression: A Comparative Content Analysis of Japanese and U.S. Magazine Advertising." *Journal of Advertising*, 16/1: 55-62.

Hori, Shintaro (1993). "Fixing Japan's White-Collar Economy: A Personal View." *Harvard Business Review*, 25/6 (November/December): 157-168.

Hoshino, Shigeru (1990). "For Quality-Conscious Japanese Consumers, Low Prices Also Matter." *Tokyo Business Today*, (September): 50-52.

Hoskins, J. and S. McFadyen (1991). "International Marketing Strategies for a Cultural Service." *International Marketing Review*, 8/2: 40-52.

Hout, Thomas, Michael E. Porter, and Eileen Rudden (1982). "How Global Companies Win Out." *Harvard Business Review*, (September/October): 98-108.

Howard, Carol and Paul Herbig (1996). "Japanese Pricing Policies." *Journal of Consumer Marketing*, 13/4: 5-17.

Howard, Kim (1994). "Global Retailing 2000." *Business Credit*, (February): 22-24.

Howe, Irene Chrew Keng, Anthony Tsai-pen Tseng, and Adrian Teo Kim Hong (1995). "The Role of Culture in Training in a Multinational Context." *Journal of Management Development*, 9/5: 51-56.

Howells, Robert (1991). "How to Price Products Competitively in Europe." *Target Marketing*, 14/5 (May): 32, 34.

Hudson, Richard L. (1992). "Software Makers Are Developing Ways to Make Their Programs more Polyglot." *The Wall Street Journal*, (July 27): B1.

Humbert, R. P. (1987). "Trade Fairs Are an Excellent Way to Take Advantage of the Growing Opportunities in Western Europe." *Business America*, (December 21): 3-5.

Ingram, Thomas N., Thomas R. Day, and George H. Lucas, Jr. (1991). "Dealing with Global Intermediaries: Guidelines for Sales Managers." *Journal of Global Marketing*, 5/4: 65-77.

Inman, Robert P. (ed.) (1985). *Managing the Service Economy: Prospects and Problems*. Cambridge: Cambridge University Press.

Inuzuka, Toshikazu (1990). "Attitudes to Imports of the Japanese Consumer." *Journal of Japanese Trade and Industry*, 12/3 (May/June): 6-9.

Ishikawa, S. (1980). "Marketing of Imported Goods in Japan: Problems to Beat." *Dentsu's Japan Marketing/Advertising*, (January): 32-37.

Itoh, M. (1991). "The Japanese Distribution System and Access to the Japanese-Market." In P. Krugman, (ed.), *Trade with Japan*. Chicago: University of Chicago Press.

Itoh, M. and M. Maruyama (1991). "Is the Japanese Distribution System Really Inefficient?" In P. Krugman (ed.), *Trade with Japan*. Chicago: University of Chicago Press.

Jacobs, Laurence, Charles Keown, Reginald Worthley, and Kyung-II Ghymn (1991). "Cross-Cultural Color Comparisons: Global Marketers Beware." *International Marketing Review*, 8/3: 21-30.

Jain, Subhash C. and Lewis R. Tucker (1995). "The Influence of Culture on Strategic Constructs in the Process of Globalization: An Empirical Study of North Amerian and Japanese MNCs." *International Business Review*, 4/1: 19-37.

James, William L. and John S. Hill (1991). "International Advertising Messages: To Adapt or Not to Adapt." *Journal of Advertising Research*, (June/July): 65-75.

James, William L. and John S. Hill (1995). "Perceptions of Multinational Salespersons and Their Market Environments." *Journal of Global Marketing*, 8/3,4:67-84.

Jarvis, Susan S. and William W. Thompson (1995). "Making Sure Your Canadian Advertisement Does Not Sink Your Sale." *Journal of Consumer Marketing*, 12/2: 40-46.

Jastram, Roy W. (1974). "The Nakodo Negotiator." *California Management Review*, 17/2: 88-92.

Jatusripitak, Somkid, Liam Fahey, and Philip Kotler (1985). "Strategic Global Marketing: Lessons from the Japanese." *Columbia Journal of World Business*, 20/1 (Spring): 47-53.

Johansson, Johny K. (1986a). "Japanese Consumers: What Foreign Marketers Should Know." *International Marketing Review*, 16/2 (Summer): 37-43.

Johansson, Johny K. (1986b). "Japanese Marketing Failures." *International Marketing Review*, 16/3 (Autumn): 33-40.

Johansson, Johny K. (1990). "Japanese Service Industries and Their Overseas Potential." *Services Industries Journal*, 10/1 (January): 85-109.

Johansson, Johny K. and Ikujiro Nonaka (1987). "Market Research the Japanese Way." *Harvard Business Review*, 27/3 (May/June): 101-115.

Johansson, Johny K. and Masaaki Hirano (1996). "Japanese Marketing in the Post Bubble Era." *The International Executive*, 38/1 (January/February): 33-43.

Johnson, Jean L., Tomoaki Sakano, Joseph A. Cote, and Naota Onzo (1993). "The Exercise of Interfirm Power and Its Repercussions in U.S.-Japanese Channel Relationships." *Journal of Marketing*, 57/2 (April): 1-10.

Johnson, Jean L., Tomoaki Sakano, and Naoto Onzo (1990). "Behavioral Relations in Across-Culture Distribution Systems: Influence, Control, and Conflict in U.S.-Japanese Marketing Channels." *Journal of International Business Studies*, 21/4 (Fourth Quarter): 639-655.

Johnstone, Harvey, Erdener Kaynak, and Richard M. Sparkman, Jr. (1987). "A Cross-Cultural/Cross-National Study of the Information Content of Television Advertisements." *International Journal of Advertising*, 6/3: 223-236.

Jones, Barry and Roger Ramsden (1991). "The Global Brand Age." *Management Today*, (September): 78-80.

Jusko, Jill (1994). "CHIC Addresses Threats to Tourism." *Hotel and Motel Management*, 209 (July): 6-29.

Kaarel, Jan W. (1991). "Brand Strategy Positions Products Worldwide." *Journal of Business Strategy*, (May/June): 16-18.

Kahn, Joseph (1995). "P&G Viewed China as a National Market and Is Conquering It." *The Wall Street Journal*, (September 12): A1, A6.

Kaikati, Jack G. (1993). "Don't Crack the Japanese Distribution System, Just Circumvent It." *Columbia Journal of World Business*, 23/3 (Summer): 34-45.

Kale, Sudhir H. and Roger P. McIntyre (1991). "Distribution Channel Relationships in Diverse Cultures." *International Marketing Review*, 8/1: 38-45.

Kamamota, Misako (1990). "Japanese Concept of Service." *Dentsu's Japan Marketing/Advertising*, Summer: 26-30.

Kamath, Rajan and Jeffrey K. Liker (1994). "A Second Look at Japanese Product Development." *Harvard Business Review*, 26/5 (November/December): 154-170.

Kane, William F. (1989). "Trade Fairs, Shows: Good Tools to Build International Markets." *Business America*, (July 17): 5-6.

Kang, T.W. (1990). *GAISHA*. New York: McGraw-Hill.

Kashani, Kamran (1989). "Beware the Pitfalls of Global Marketing." *Harvard Business Review*, (September/October): 91-98.

Kashani, Kamran and John A. Quelch (1990). "Can Sales Promotion Go Global?" *Business Horizons*, (May/June): 37-43.

Kassaye, W. Wossen (1990). "Using Haggling in the Market of Goods Internationally." *Journal of International Consumer Marketing*, 3/1: 85.

Kastiel, Diane Lyn (1987). "Service and Support: High-Tech's New Battleground." *Business Marketing*, 27/6 (June): 54-62.

Katori, Kazuaki (1990). "Recent Developments and Future Trends in Marketing Research in Japan Using New Electronic Media." *Journal of Advertising Research*, 12/2 (April/May): 53-57.

Kaufman, Gaye (1994). "Customer Satisfaction Studies Overseas Can Be Frustrating." *Marketing News*, 28 (August 29): 34.

Kaynak, Erdener (1989). "The Development of Multinational Advertising Strategy." In *The Management of International Advertising*. Westport, CT: Quorum Books.

Kelley, Bill (1991). "Culture Clash: West Meets East." *Sales and Marketing Management*, 31/6 (July): 28-34.

Kendell, Vivienne (1994). "Product Guarantees and After-Sales Service." *European Trends*, 4 (Fourth Quarter): 58-64.

Kennedy, Eric Michael (1993). "The Japanese Distribution System." *Business America*, (May 17): 20-21.

Kennedy, G. (1987). *Negotiate Anywhere!* London: Arrow Books.

Kernan, Jerome B. and Teresa J. Domzal (1993). "International Advertising: To Globalize, Visualize." *Journal of International Consumer Marketing*, 5/4: 51-71.

Kiiyama, Masaru (1994). "Bargain Basements Move Up." *Japan Update*, 29 (February): 13-15.

Kilburn, David (1986). "How Japanese Products Succeed in Japan." *Journal of the American Chamber of Commerce in Japan*, 26/6 (June): 24-27.

Kilburn, David (1991). "Unilever Struggles with Surf in Japan." *Advertising Age*, (May 6): 22.

Kim, Eun Y. (1996). *A Cross-Cultural Reference of Business Practices in a New Korea*. Westport, CT: Quorum.

King Jr., Neil (1993). "K Mart's Czech Invasion Lurches Along." *The Wall Street Journal*, (June 8): A11.

Kinzer, Stephen (1994). "Germany Upholds Tax on Fast-food Consumers." *The New York Times*, (August 22): C-2.

Kirpalani, V.H. (1985). *International Marketing*. New York: Random House.

Klebnikov, Paul (1995). "Minister Toubon, Meet General Gamelin." *Forbes*, (May 22): 292.

Knotts, Rose (1989). "Cross Cultural Management: Transformations and Adaptations." *Business Horizons*, (January/February): 31-34.

Knutsen, J., S. Thrasher, and Y. Kathawala (1988). "The Impact of Culture Upon Package Perception: An Experiment in Hong Kong and the U.S." *International Journal of Management*, (June): 117-124.

Kogut, Bruce and Harbin Singh (1988). "The Effect of National Culture on the Choice of Entry Mode." *Journal of International Business Studies*, 19 (Fall): 411-432.

Konopacki, Allen (1990). "CEOs Attend Trade Shows to Grab Power Buyers." *Marketing News*, (October 15): 5, 18.

Koseki, Kelichi (1990). "Marketing Strategies as Adopted by Ajinomoto in Southeast Asia." *Journal of Advertising Research*, 10/2 (April/May): 31-35.

Kotler, Philip (1994). "Reconceptualizing Marketing." *European Management Journal*, 12/4 (December): 353-361.

Kotler, Philip and Paul N. Bloom (1984). *Marketing Professional Services*. Englewood Cliffs, NJ: Prentice Hall.

Kotler, Philip and Liam Fahey (1982). "The World's Champion Marketers: The Japanese." *Journal of Business Strategy*, 2 (Summer): 3-13.

Kotler, Philip, Lam Fahey, and Somkid Jatusripitak (1985). *The New Competition*. Englewood Cliffs, NJ: Prentice-Hall.

Kramer, Hugh E. (1989). "Cross-Cultural Negotiations: The Western Japanese Interface." *Singapore Marketing Review*, 4: 21-34.

Kramer, Hugh E. and Paul A. Herbig (1992). "Suq Haggling." *International Journal of Consumer Marketing*, 5/2: 25-35.

Kuribayashi, Sei (1991). "Present Situation and Future Prospect of Japan's Distribution System." *Japan and the World Economy*, 3: 39-60.

Kusa, Masaru (1990). "Kao's Marketing Strategy and Marketing Intelligence System." *Journal of Advertising Research*, 10/2 (April/May): 20-25.

Kustin, Richard A. (1994a). "Marketing Globalization: A Didactic Examination for Corporate Strategy." *The International Executive*, 36/1 (January/February): 79-93.

Kustin, Richard A. (1994b). "A Cross-Cultural Study of a Global Product in Israel and Australia." *International Marketing Review*, 10/5: 4-13.

Kustin, Richard A. (1994c). "A Special Theory of Globalization: A Review and Critical Evaluation of the Theoretical and Empirical Evidence." *Journal of Global Marketing*, 7/3: 79-95.

Kwan, Wayne and Tan Jing Hee (1994). "Measuring Service Quality in Singapore Retail Banking." *Singapore Management Review*, 16/2 (July): 1-24.

Kyj, Larissa S. and Myrolslaw J. Kyj (1989). "Customer Service: Product Differentiation in International Markets." *International Journal of Physical Distribution and Materials*, 19/1: 30-38.

Kyj, Myroslaw J. and Larissa S. Kyj (1987). "Customer Service as a Competitive Tool." *Industrial Marketing Management*, 16 (August): 225-230.

Kyj, Myroslaw J. and Larissa S. Kyj (1989). "Customer Service Competition in Business to Business and Industrial Markets: Myths and Realities." *Journal of Business and Industrial Marketing*, 2/4 (Fall): 45-55.

Laitamaki, Jukka M. (1994). "Is It Mickey Mouse or Senior Mickey? A Cross-Cultural Case Study of Disney Theme Park Business Plan in Latin America." Working Paper, Fordham University.

Lam, Simon S.K. (1995a). "Measuring Service Quality: An Empirical Analysis in Hong Kong." *International Journal of Management*, 12/1 (June): 182-188.

Lam, Simon S.K. (1995b). "Assessing the Validity of SERVQUAL: An Empirical Analysis in Hong Kong." *Asia Pacific Journal of Quality Management*, 4/4: 33-40.

Lambin, J.L. and T.B. Hiller (1990). "Volvo Trucks Europe." In J.A. Quelch (ed.), *Marketing Challenge of 1992*. Reading, MA: Addison Welsey: 349ff.

Lancioni, Richard A. (1991). "Pricing for International Business Development." *Management Decison*, 29/1: 39-41.

Landau, Nilly (1994). "A Call Center to Call Your Own." *International Business*, 7/9 (September): 22-26.

Landau, Nilly (1995a). "Hitting a Moving Target." *International Business*, (March): 40.

Landau, Nilly (1995b). "Are You Being Served?" *International Business*, (March): 38-40.

Lapman, Joanne (1988). "Marketers Turn Sour on Global Sales Pitch Harvard Guru Makes." *The Wall Street Journal*, (May 12): 1, 13.

Larke, Roy (1992). "Japanese Retailing: Fascinating, but Little Understood." *International Journal of Retail & Distribution Management*, 20/1 (January/February): 3-15.

Lavin, Douglas (1996). "French Smart Card Proves a Bright Idea." *The Wall Street Journal*, (April 7): B2.

Lawrence, Jennifer (1993). "State Guides Define Green Terms." *Advertising Age*, 7.

Lazer, William, Shoji Murata, and Hiroshi Kosaka (1985). "Japanese Marketing." *Journal of Marketing*, 49 (Spring): 69-81.

Lecraw, Donald J. (1984). "Pricing Strategies of Transnational Corporations." *Asia Pacific Jounal of Management*, (January): 112-120.

Lehtinen, Jarmo (1991). "Service Quality: Multidisciplinary and Multinational Perspectives." In Stephen Brown, *Service Quality: Multidisciplinary and Multinational Perpectives*. Lexington, MA: Lexington Books: 135-142.

Leigh, Bruce (1989). "How Green Is Your Company?" *International Management*, (January): 24.

Lele, Milind M. (1983). "Product Service: How to Protect Your Unguarded Battlefield." *Business Marketing*, 23/6 (June): 69-75.

Lele, Milind M. (1986). "How Service Needs Influence Product Strategy." *Sloan Management Review*, 16/3 (Fall): 63-70.

Lele, Milind M. and U.S. Karmarkar (1983). "Good Product Support Is Smart Marketing." *Harvard Business Review*, 33/6 (November/December): 124-132.

Lelyveld, Michael S. (1995). "Maine 'Eggs-Ports' Win Brownie Points in Hong Kong." *The Journal of Commercial*, (January 30): 1a, 10a.

Levitt, Theodore (1983). "Globalization of Markets." *Harvard Business Review*, (May/June), 92-102.

Levy, Ben (1995). "How would Michael play in Monterrey." *Marketing News*, 29/16 (July 31): 27, 31.

Lin, Huang (1992). "Marketing Strategy of BMW in Japan." *Management Japan*, 25/1 (Spring): 27-31.

Linan, Salvador G. (1996). "Empresarios Perdedores." *El Financiero*, (March 18): 18.

Lincoln, Edward (1990). *Japan's Unequal Trade Status*. Washington, DC: Brookings Institute.

Lipin, Steven, Brian Coleman, and Jeremy Mark (1994). "Pick a Card: Visa, American Express, and Mastercard Vie in Overseas Strategies." *The Wall Street Journal*, (February 15): A1.

Lipman, Joanne (1991). "Amid Recession, Firms Clip Coupon Value." *The Wall Street Journal*, (May 9): B5.

Littler, Dale and Katrin Schlieper (1995). "The Development of the Eurobrand." *International Marketing Review*, 12/2: 22-37.

Liu, Juanita (1994). *Pacific Islands Ecotourism: A Public Policy and Planning Guide*. Honolulu: Pacific Business Center, University of Hawaii.

Livingston, Stuart (1992). "Marketing to the Hispanic American Community." *Journal of Business Strategy*, 11/2 (March/April): 54-57.

Lohtia, Ritu, Wesley J. Johnson, and Linda Aab (1994). "Creating an Effective Print Advertisement for the China Market: Analysis and Advice." *Journal of Global Marketing*, 8/2: 7-22.

Lokon, Elizabeth (1987). "Probing Japanese Buyers' Minds." *Business Marketing*, (November): 85-89.

Lublin, Jo Ann (1988). "U.S. Food Firms Find Europe's Huge Market Hardly a Piece of Cake." *The Wall Street Journal*, (August 16): A1, A20.

Luthans, Fred, Richard R. Patrick, and Brett C. Luthans (1995). "Doing Business in Central and Eastern Europe." *Business Horizons*, (September/October): 10-16.

Lynch, Neil (1995). "Demystifying the Asian Consumer." *Appliance Manufacturer*, (February): W25-W27.

Lynch, Richard (1993). *European Marketing*. Chicago: Irwin.

Maaruyama, M. (1989). *Distribution System and Practices in Japan*. Tokyo: Economic Planning Agency.

MacDonald, Christine (1994). "Tourism: Striking a Balance with Nature." *Institutional Investor*, 28/3 (March): SSS12.

MacKinnon, Barbara (1995). "Beauty & the Beasts of Ecotourism." *Business Mexico*, (April): 5.

MacMillan, Ian C. and Rita G. McGrath (1996). "Discover Your Products' Hidden Potential." *Harvard Business Review*, (May/June): 58-73.

Maddox, Robert C. (1993). *Cross-Cultural Problems in International Business*. Westport, CT: Quorum Press.

Maggs, John (1991). "U.S. Paper Car Parts Makers Decry Japan Business Tactic." *Journal of Commerce and Commercial Activities in Japan*, 390 (October 17): 3A.

Malhotra, Naresh K., Francis M. Ulgado, James Agarwal, and Imad B. Baalbaki (1994). "International Services Marketing: A Comparative Evaluation of the Dimension of Service Quality Between Developed and Developing Countries." *International Marketing Review*, 11/2: 5-15.

March, Robert M. (1977). "Some Constraints on Adaptive Marketing by Foreign Consumer Goods Firms in Japan." *European Journal of Marketing*, 11/7: 14-19.

March, Robert M. (1983). *Japanese Negotiations*. New York: Kodansha International.

March, Robert M. (1989). "No-Nos in Negotiating with the Japanese." *Across the Board*, 26/4 (April): 44-51.

March, Robert M. (1991). *Honoring the Customer*. New York: John Wiley & Sons.

Marsh, Ann (1994). "Czechs Get Capitalism Lesson the Amway Way." *Advertising Age*, (April 18): 2.

Martenson, Rita (1987). "Is Standardization of Marketing Feasible in Culture-Bound Industries?: A European Case Study." *International Management Review*, (Autumn): 7-17.

Martenson, Rita (1989). "International Advertising in Cross-Cultural Environments." *Journal of International Consumer Marketing*, 2/1: 7-17.

Martin, Justin (1991). "Still a Distant Second." *Across the Board*, 28/11 (November): 42-47.

Maruca, Regina F. (1994). "The Right Way to Go Global." *Harvard Business Review*, (March/April): 135-145.

Mathews, Ryan (1996). "A Farewell to Coupons?" *Progressive Grocer*, 75/3 (March): 71-72.

Mattson, Jan (1994). "Using Service Process Models to Improve Service Quality: Examples from New Zealand." *Managing Service Quality*, 4/1: 47-52.

Mauss, Marcel (1990). *Die Gabe-Form und Funktion des Austauschs in Archaischen*. Gesellschaften, Frankfurt.

McAuliffe, Emily (1995). "Exhibitors at Telecom '95 Woo $60 Billion Industry." *Business Marketing*, (November): 3, 8.

McDermott, Darren (1996). "All American Infomercials Sizzle in Asia." *The Wall Street Journal*, (June 25): B7.

McDonald, Gael M. and C.J. Roberts (1991). "The Brand Naming Enigma in the Asia Pacific Context." *International Marketing Review*, 11/2: 6-13.

McDonald, William J. (1995). "Home Shopping Channel Customer Segments: A Cross-Cultural Perspective." *Journal of Direct Marketing*, 9/4 (Autumn): 57-67.

Melvin, Sheila (1996). "Off on the Right Foot." *China Business Review*, 23/2 (March/April): 24.

Mendenez, Teresa and John Yow (1989). "The Hispanic Target: An Overview of the Major Markets." *Marketing Research*, 1 (June): 11-15.

Mendonsa, Eugene L. (1989). "Coming to Terms With 'Rubber Time'." *Business Marketing* (October): 67-68.

Micklitz, Hans W. (1992). "The German Packaging Order." *Columbia Journal of World Business*, 27/3 and 4 (Fall/Winter): 120-127.

Milbank, Dana (1993). "Service Economy Seems Rather Creaky in Britain just Now." *The Wall Street Journal*, (December 7): A1, A12.

Milbank, Diana (1994). "Made in America Becomes a Boast in Europe." *The Wall Street Journal*, (January 19): B1, B6.

Miles, Gregory L. (1995). "Tailoring a Global Product." *International Business*, (March): 50-52.

Miller, Richard N. (1995). *Multinational Direct Marketing: The Methods and the Markets*. New York: McGraw-Hill.

Minor, Michael (1992). "Comparising the Hispanic and Non-Hispanic Markets: How Different Are They?" *Journal of Services Marketing*, 6/2: 29-35.

Mintu, Alma T., Roger J. Calantone, and Jule B. Gassenheimer (1993). "International Mail Surveys." *Journal of International Consumer Marketing*, 5/1: 69-83

Miracle, G.E. (ed.) (1966). "Communication with Foreign Consumers." In *Management of International Advertising*. Ann Arbor, MI: Bureau of Business Research, The University of Michigan Press: 6-29.

Misstry, Tina (1995). "Nissan Opens Bidding for Pan-Euro Account." *Campaign-London*, (July 7): 2.

Moffett, Matt and Jonathan Friedland (1996). "Wal-Mart Won't Discount Its Prospects in Brazil, Though Its Losses Pile Up." *The Wall Street Journal*, (June 4): A15.

Moncrief, William C. (1987). "A Comparison of Sales Activities in an International Setting." *Journal of Global Marketing*, 1/1,2 (Fall/Winter).

Moran, Robert T. and William G. Stripp (1991). *Successful International Business Negotiations*. Houston: Gulf Publishing.

Morgan, James C. and J. Jeffrey Morgan (1991). *Cracking the Japanese Market*. New York: Free Press.

Morice, Anne Michele (1996). "New French Law Strikes Sour Note for Radio Stations." *The Wall Street Journal*, (January 23): A8.

Motwani, Jaideep, Gillan Rice, and Essam Mahmoud (1992). "Promoting Exports Through International Trade Shows." *Review of Business*, 13/4: 38-42.

Mueller, Barbara (1987)."Reflections of Culture: An Analysis of Japanese and American Advertising Appeals." *Journal of Advertising Research*, 17/2 (June/July): 51-59.

Mueller, Barbara (1996). *International Advertising: Communicating Across Cultures*. Belmont, CA: Wadsworth Publishing.

Mueller, Rene D. and Amanda J. Broderick (1995). "East European Retailing: A Consumer Perspective." *International Journal of Retail & DistributionManagement*, 23/1: 32-40.

Mullen, Michael R. (1995). "Diagnosing Measurment Equivalence in Cross-National Research." *Journal of International Business Studies*, 26/3 (third quarter): 573-596.

Mummert, Hallie (1994). "Tapping Hispanic America." *Target Marketing*, 17/6 (June): 32-37.

Nakata, Cheryl and K. Sivakumar (1996). "National Culture and New Product Development: An Integrative Review." *Journal of Marketing*, 60/1 (January): 61-72.

Naisbitt, John and Patricia Aburdene (1990). *Megatrends 2000: Ten New Directions for the 1990s*. Avon Books: New York.

Namakforoosh, Naghi (1994). "Data Collection Methods Hold Key to Research in Mexico." *Marketing News*, (August 29): 28.

Nara, Thomas (1991). "Establishing a European Beachhead." *Journal of Small Business Management*, (February): 14-15.

Narisetti, Raju (1996). "Can Rubbermaid Crack Foreign Markets." *The Wall Street Journal*, (June 16): B1, B4.

Naughton, Keith, Robert Horn, and Edith H. Updike (1996). "GM Starts Up a Long Hill in Asia." *Business Week,* (June 3): 56.

Naumann, Earl, Donald W. Jackson, Jr., and William G. Wolfe (1994). "Examining the Practices of United States and Japanese Market Research Firms." *California Management Review*, 36/4 (Summer): 49-69.

Neff, Robert (1990). "Now, Japan's Advertisers Are Nuts about Nature." *Business Week*.

Nevett, Terence (1992). "Differences Between American and British Television Advertising: Explanations and Implications." *Journal of Advertising*, 21/4: 61-80.

Nicoulaud, B. (1991). "Problems and Strategies in the International Marketing of Services." *European Journal of Marketing*, 23/6: 55-64.

Nishikawa, Sadafumi (1990). "New Product Development." *Journal of Advertising Research*, 20/2 (April/May): 27-31.

Nishimura, K.G. (1994). "The Distribution System of Japan and the United States: A Comparative Study from the Viewpoint of Buyers." *Japan and the World Economy*, 5:265-268.

Nishina, Sadafumi (1990). "Japanese Consumers: Introducing Foreign Products/Brands into the Japanese Markets." *Journal of Advertising Research*, 30/2 (April/May): 35-45.

Nothdurft, William E. (1992). *Going Global*. Washington, DC: The Brookings Institution.

Odintsov, Alexei (1996). "Russia's Expocenter Takes Its Show on the Road." *Journal of Commerce*, 407/28676 (March): 5A.

Ohmae, Kenichi (1985). *Triad Power: The Coming Shape of Global Competition*. New York: Free Press.

Ohmae, Kenichi (1986). "The Triad World View." *Journal of Business Strategy*, 7/4 (Spring): 8-19.

Ohmae, Kenichi (1990). *The Borderless World*. New York: Macmillan.

Oikawa, Naoko and John F. Tanner, Jr. (1992). "The Influence of Japanese Culture on Business Relationships and Negotiations." *Journal of Services Marketing*, 6/3 (Summer): 67-74.

Oliver, Suzanne (1996). "Watch That Wastebasket." *Forbes*, 157/6 (March 26): 72-74.

Ono, Yumiko (1991). "Gillette Tries to Nick Schick in Japan." *The Wall Street Journal*, (February 4): B1, B6.

Ono, Yumiko (1991). "Pepsi Challenges Japanese Taboo with an Ad that Tweaks Coke." *The Wall Street Journal*, (March 6): B1, B3.

Onvisit, Sac and John J. Shaw (1991). "The International Dimension of Branding." *International Marketing Review*, 6/3:24.

Ortega, Bob (1994). "Foreign Forays: Penney Pushes Abroad in Unusually Big Way as It Pursues Growth." *The Wall Street Journal*, (February 1): A1, A7.

Ortega, Bob (1994). "Wal-Mart is Slowed by Problems of Price and Culture in Mexico." *The Wall Street Journal*, (July 29): A1.

Osami, Marino (1990). "Trend Toward Choosiness." *Journal of Japanese Trade and Industry*, 9/3 (May/June): 16-19.

Ottman, Jacquelyn A. (1993). *Green Marketing*. Chicago: NTC Publishing Group.

Parasuraman, A., Valarie A. Zeithaml, and Leonard L. Berry (1985). "A Conceptual Model of Service Quality and Its Implications for Future Research." *Journal of Marketing*, 49 (Fall): 41-50.

Parasuraman, A., Valarie A. Zeithaml, and Leonard L. Berry (1988). "SERVQUAL: A Multiple-Item Scale for Measuring Consumer Perceptions of Service Quality." *Journal of Retailing*, 64/1 (Spring): 12-40.

Peak, Herschel (1985). "Conquering Cross-Cultural Challenges." *Business Marketing*, 35/10 (October): 138-146.

Pearl, Daniel (1992). "Federal Express Pins Hope on New Strategy in Europe." *The Wall Street Journal*, (March 18): B1.

Perlmutter, Howard V. (1969), "The Tortuous Evolution of the Multinational Corporation." *Columbia Journal of World Business*, 4 (January/February): 9-18.

Petrison, Lisa A. and Paul Wang (1995). "Exploring the Dimensions of Consumer Privacy: An Analysis of Coverage in British and American Media." *Journal of Direct Marketing*, 9/4 (Autumn): 19-37.

Pitcher, A.E. (1985). "The Role of Branding in International Advertising." *International Journal of Advertising*, 4: 241-246.

Plant, Fiona (1995). "Smart Card Supersedes Coupons?" *International Journal of Retail & Distribution Management*, (Spring): xi.

Pope, Tara P. (1992). "Ad Agencies Are Stumbling in East Europe." *The Wall Street Journal*, (May 10): B1, B14.

Pope, Tara P. (1994). "Will the British Warm Up to Iced Tea?" *The Wall Street Journal*, (August 22): B1, B4.

Pope, Tara P. (1995). "Europeans' Environmental Concerns Don't Make It to the Shopping Basket." *The Wall Street Journal*, (April 18): B1.

Port, Otis (1996). " 'Green' Product Design." *Business Week*, (June 10): 109.

Porter, Michael E. (1985). *Competitive Advantage*. New York: Free Press.

Porter, Michael E. (1986). *Competition in Global Industries*. Cambridge, MA: Harvard Business School Press.

Potjes, Jeroen C.A. and A. Roy Thurik (1993). "Profit Margins in Japanese Retailing." *Japan and the World Economy*, 5/4: 337-362.

Powell, Bill (1996). "You Want Service, Try Japan." *Newsweek*, (March 18): 22.

Prasso, Sherri (1996). "Protests Push Pepsi to Back out of Burma." *Business Week*, (April 24).

Pressley, James (1994). "Sunday Shopping in England and Wales is Liberalized, but Rules Create a Maze." *The Wall Street Journal*, (August 30).

Putterman, Diana (1993). "Three Examples of What Hispanic Marketing Can Do." *Brandweek*, 34/42 (October 18): 26.

Quelch, John A. and Edward J. Hoff (1986). "Customizing Global Marketing." *Harvard Business Review*, (May/June): 59-68.

Quelch, John A., Erich Joachimsthaler, and Jose Luis Nueno (1991). "After the Wall: Marketing Guidelines for Eastern Europe." *Sloan Management Review*, (Winter): 82-95.

Redding, S.G. (1988). "Cultural Effects on the Marketing Process in Southeast Asia." *Journal of the Market Research Society*, 24/2: 98-114.

Reeder, John A. (1987). "When West Meets East: Cultural Aspects of Doing Business in Asia." *Business Horizons*, (January/February): 69-75.

Reina, Laura (1995). "Distribution, Redemption of Coupons down in Canada." *Editor & Publisher*, 128/47 (November 25): 22.

Reinstein, Fred (1987). "Selling to Japan: We Did It Their Way." *Export Today*, 3/3 (September/October): 19-24.

Reitman, Valerie (1994). "In Japan's Car Market, Big Three Face Rivals Who Go Door-to-Door." *The Wall Street Journal*, (September 28): A1, A6.

Remington, Dan (1990). "International Gift Giving: It Is Not Hard." *Sales and Marketing Management in Canada*, 31/10 (October): 12-15.

Rey, Michael (1995). "Whiter than White." *Business Eastern Europe*, 24/45 (November 6): 5.

Reynen, Pat F. (1992). "When in Europe, Do as the Europeans Do." *Convene*, (September): 19.

Ricks, David A. (1983). *Blunders in International Business*. Cambridge, MA: Blackwell Publishers.

Ricks, David A. (1984). "How to Avoid Business Blunders Abroad." *Business*, (April/June): 25-32.

Ricks, David A. (1988). "International Business Blunders: An Update." *D&B Review*, (January/March): 11-15.

Rizzo, Andrew M. (1992). "Export Strategies for Small Business." *Business America*, (September 6): 2-6.

Robinson, Chris (1995). "Asian Culture: The Marketing Consequences." *The Journal of the Market Research Society*, 38/1: 55-62.

Rosen, Barry N. and Jean J. Boddewyn (1988). "U.S. Brands Abroad: An Empirical Study of Global Branding." *International Marketing Review*, 16/1: 7-19.

Rosen, Barry N. and George B. Sloane III (1995). "Environmenal Product Standards, Trade, and European Consumer Goods Marketing." *Columbia Journal of World Business*, 30/1 (Spring): 74-86.

Rosenberg, Larry J. (1986). "Deciphering the Japanese Cultural Code." *International Marketing Review*, 16/3 (Autumn): 46-56.

Ross, Randolph (1983). "Understanding the Japanese Distribution System: An Exploratory Framework." *European Journal of Marketing*, 17 (Winter): 5-15.

Rosson, Philip J. and F.H. Rolf Seringhaus (1995). "Visitor and Exhibitor Interaction at Industrial Trade Fairs." *Journal of Business Research*, 32: 81-90.

Roth, Robert F. (1992). *International Marketing Communications*. Chicago: Crain Books.

Ruiz, Gabriel (1994). "Marketing Research in Mexico." *Business Mexico*, (October): 34

Ruthstrom, Carl R. and Ken Matejka (1990). "The Meanings of Yes in the Far East." *Industrial Marketing Management*, 19: 191-192.

Sadarumi, Nishima. (1990). "Japanese Consumers: Introducing Foreign Products/Brands into the Japanese Market." *Journal of Advertising Research*, 30/2 (April/May): 35-45.

Saegert, Joel, Robert J. Hoover, and Marye Tharpe Hilger (1985). "Characteristics of Mexican-American Consumers." *Journal of Consumer Research*, 12 (June): 104-109.

Sakaiya, Taichi (1993). *What is Japan?* Tokyo: Kodnsha International.

Samiee, Saeed (1995). "Strategic Considerations in European Retailing." *Journal of International Marketing*, 3/3: 49-76.

Samiee, Saeed and Insik Jeong (1994). "Cross-Cultural Research in Advertising: An Assessment of Methodologies." *Journal of the Academy of Marketing Sciences*, 22/3: 205-217.

Samli, A. Coskun and Laurence Jacobs (1994). "Pricing Practices of American Multinational Firms: Standardization verus Localization Dichotomy." *Journal of Global Marketing*, 8/2: 51-74.

Samson, Danny and Rod Parker (1994). "Service Quality: Gaps in the Australian Consulting Engineering Industry." *International Journal of Quality and Reliability Management*, 11/7: 60-70.

Sandler, Dennis M. and David Shani (1992). "Brand Globally but Advertise Locally? An empirical investigation." *International Marketing Review*, 9/4: 18-31.

Sandler, Gregory (1994). "Fair Dealer." *The Journal of European Business*, (March/April): 46-49.

Saporito, Bill (1993). "Where the Global Action Is." *Fortune*, 62-65.

Schafer, Joachim (1987). "German Trade Fairs Open Foreign Markets for U.S. Products." *Marketing News*, (May 8): 13.

Schafer, Joachim (1988). "Finding That Competitive Edge for Your Company at an International Trade Fair." *American Salesman*, (August): 16-22.

Schlossberg, Howard (1992). "Effect of FTC Green Guidelines Still Doubtful for Some Marketers." *Marketing News*, 6.

Segal-Horn, Susan and Heather Davison (1992). "Global Markets." *Journal of Global Marketing*, 5/3: 31-61.

Sekaran, Uma (1983). "Methodological and Theoretical Issues and Advancements in Cross-Cultural Research." *Journal of International Business Studies*, (Fall): 61-71.

Sellers, P. (1989). "The ABCs of Marketing to Kids." *Fortune*, (May): 114-120.

Sesis, Michael R. and Craig Forman (1991). "As Competition Rises in Global Banking, Europeans Have Edge." *The Wall Street Journal*, (March 25): A1, A4.

Shames, Germaine W. and W. Gerald Glover (1989). *World Class Service*. Yarmouth, ME: Intercultural Press.

Shao, Alan T., Lawrence P. Shao, and Dale H. Shao (1991). "Are Global Markets with Standardized Advertising Campaigns Feasible." *Journal of International Consumer Marketing*, 4/3: 15-25.

Shepherd, C. David, Marilyn M. Helms, and Rodney C. Tillotson (1992). "Japanese Marketing: A Review." *Marketing Intelligence and Planning*, 10/9: 35-40.

Sheridan, Elizabeth (1994). "Leaders Link South Africa's Prosperity to Tourism." *Hotel and Motel Management*, (July 25): 6, 28.

Shimaguchi, Mitsuaki and William Lazer (1979). "Japanese Distribution Channels: Invisible Barriers to Market Entry." *MSU Business Topics*, 15/3 (Winter): 49-62.

Shirouzu, Norihiko (1996). "Luxury Prices for U.S. Goods no Longer Pass Muster in Japan." *The Wall Street Journal*, (April 15): B1, B4.

Shirouzu, Norihiko (1996). "Snapple in Japan: How a Splash Dried Up." *The Wall Street Journal*, (April 24): B1, B3.

Shoham, Aviv (1995). "Global Marketing Standardization." *Journal of Global Marketing*, 9/1,2: 91-110.

Shure, P. (1992). "Europe . . . Still the Mecca for International Shows." *Convene*, (July/August): 54.

Siegel, Carolyn F. (1992). "Restoration of the Earth: An Environmental Reality." *Journal of Marketing Education*, (Fall): 24-29.

Silverstein, Michael (1995). "What Does It Mean to be Green?" *Business and Society Review*, 93 (Spring): 16-20.

Simon, F.L. (1992). "Marketing Green Products in the Triad." *Columbia Journal of World Business*, (Fall/Winter): 269-285.

Simon, Hermann (1995). "Pricing Problems in a Global Setting." *Marketing News*, (October 9): 4, 8.

Singh, Jagdip (1995). "Measurement Issues in Crossnational Research." *Journal of International Business*, 26/3 (Third Quarter): 597-620.

Singhapakdi, Anusorn, Scott J. Vitell, and Orose Leelakulthanit (1994). "A Crosscultural Study of Moral Philosophies, Ethical Perceptions, and Judgements: A Comparaison of American and Thai Marketers." *International Marketing Review*, 11/6: 65-78.

Smith, Smith (1996). "Chinese Government Struggles to Rejuvenate National Brands." *The Wall Street Journal*, (June 19): B1, B6.

Solomon, Jolie (1994). "Mickey's Trip to Trouble." *Newsweek*, (February 14): 34-38.

Soroco, Gonzalo (1993). "The Mobile Hispanic Market: New Challenges in the 1990s." *Marketing Research*, 5/1 (Winter): 6-11.

Sowell, Thomas (1996). *Migrations and Cultures: A World View.* New York: McGraw-Hill.

Speer, Lawrence J. (1993). "Once Popular Tourist Mecca Looking to Bounce Back." *Hotel and Motel Management*, 208 (June 7): 27.

Spencer, Earl P. (1995). "Euro Disney-What Happened? What Next?" *Journal of International Marketing*, 3/3: 103-114.

Spiller, Lisa D. and Alexandra J. Campbell (1994). "The Use of International Direct Marketing by Small Businesses in Canada, Mexico, and the United States." *Journal of Direct Marketing*, 8/1 (Winter): 7-16.

Steele, Henry C. (1990). "Marketing Research in China: The Hong Kong Connection." *Marketing and Research Today*, (August): 155-165.

Steinmetz, Greg (1996). "Germans Finally Open Their Wallets to Credit Cards but Aren't Hooked Yet." *The Wall Street Journal*, (April 1): B2.

Stern, Gabriella (1992). "Heinz Aims to Export Taste for Ketchup." *The Wall Street Journal*, (November 20): B1, B10.

Stern, Gabriella and Valerie Reitman (1996). "GM's Saturn to Unveil Japan Sales Plan." *The Wall Street Journal*, (July 8): A3.

Stewart-Allen, Allyson L. (1995). "Below-The-Line Promotions Are Below Expectations." *Marketing News*, 29/19 (September 11): 9

Stewart-Allen, Allyson L. (1996). "Creative New Media in Europe Here to Stay?" *Marketing News*, (June 3): 15.

Still, Richard Ralph (1991). "Sales Management: Some Cross-Cultural Aspects." *Journal of Personal Selling & Sales Management*, (Spring/Summer): 6-9.

Stoub, Jeffrey (1994). "It Isn't Easy Being Green." *Business Mexico*, (July): 15-16.

Sullivan, Jerry, Naoki Kameda, and Tatsuo Nobu (1991). "Bypassing in Managerial Communication." *Business Horizons*, 34/1 (January/February): 71-80.

Sullivan, Thomas F. P. (1992). *The Greening of American Business.* Rockville, MD: Government Institutes, Inc.

Sutton, Robert J. and Jamal Al-Khatib (1994). "Cross-National Comparisons of Consumers' Environmental Concerns." *Journal of Euromarketing*, 4/1: 45-60.

Swan, Jeannine K. (1996). "International Exhibiting: Minefield or Goldmine." *Business Marketing*, (June): T-5.

Swasy, Alecia (1990). "Foreign Formula: Procter & Gamble Fixes Aim on Tough Market: The Latin Americans." *The Wall Street Journal*, (June 15): A7.

Sweeny, Jack and Pedro Pereira (1994). "IBM Seeks New International Partners." *Computer Reseller News*, 607 (November 28): 1254.

Szymanski, David M., Sundar G. Bharadwj, and P. Rajan Varadarajan (1993). "Standardization versus Adaptation of International Marketing Strategy: An Empirical Investigation." *Journal of Marketing*, 57/4 (October): 1-17.

Tanzer, Andrew (1991). "Ding-Dong Capitalism Calling." *Forbes*, (October 14): 184-186.

Tanzer, Andrew and Robert LaFranco (1996). "Luring Asians from Their TV Sets." *Forbes*, (June 3): 40-41.

Tasker, Pete (1987). *Inside Japan.* London: Didgwick & Jackson.

Taylor, Stuart (1993). "To Give or not To Give." *Global Trade & Transportation*, 113/3 (March): 32-33.

Thomas, Lee M. (1992). "The Business Community and the Environment: An Important Partnership." *Business Horizons*, (March/April): 21.

Thorelli, Hans B. (1980). "The Information Seekers: Multinational Strategy Target." *California Management Review*, 23: 46-52.

Thorelli, Hans B. (1981). "Swedish Consumer Policy, Its Transferability, and Related Research Implications." *Advances in Consumer Research*, 8: 467-473.

Thorelli, Hans B. (1996). "The Multinational Corporation As a Change Agent." *Southern Journal of Business*, (July): 1-11.

Thorelli, Hans B. (1996). "Marketing, Open Markets, and Political Democracy: The Experience of the Pacrim Countries." *Advances in International Marketing*, 7, 33-46, Greenwich, CT: JAI Press.

Thorelli, Hans B., Helmut Becker, and Jack Engledow (1975). *The Information Seeker: An International Study of Consumer Information and Advertising Image.* Cambridge, MA: Ballinger.

Tippit, Sarah (1996). "Tupperware." *Reuter News Service*, (June 27).

Topol, Martin T. and Elaine Sherman (1994). "Trends and Challenges of Expanding Internationally via Direct Marketing." *Journal of Direct Marketing*, 8/1 (Winter): 32-42.

Toy, Stewart and Paul Dwyer (1994). "Is Disney Headed for the Euro Trash Heap?" *Business Week*, (January 24): 52.

Trifonovitch, Gregory J. (1977). "Cultural Learning/Cultural Teaching." *Educational Perspectives: Journal of the College of Education: University of Hawaii*, 16/4 (December): 1-5.

Trompenaars, Fons (1994). *Riding the Waves of Culture.* Chicago: Irwin.

Tse, David K., Kam-hon Lee, Ilan Vertinsky, and Donald A. Wehrung (1988). "Does Culture Matter? A Cross-Cultural Study of Executives' Choice, Decisiveness, and Risk Adjustment in International Marketing." *Journal of Marketing*, 52/4 (October): 81-95.

Tuncalp, Secil (1990). "The Marketing Research Scene in Saudi Arabia." *International Marketing Review*, 23-29.

Tung, Rosalie L. (1982). *Business Negotiations with the Japanese*. Lexington, MA: Lexington Books.

Tung, Rosalie L. (1983). "How to Negotiate with the Japanese." *California Management Review*, 26/4: 52-77.

Turner, Richard and Peter Gumbel (1992). "As Euro Disney Braces for Its Grand Opening, The French Go Goofy." *The Wall Street Journal*, (April 10): A1, A14.

Uchendu, V.C. (1968). "Some Principles of Haggling in Peasant Markets." *Economic Development and Cultural Change*, 16/1 (October).

Updike, Edith H. and Bill Vlasic (1996). "Will Neon be the Little Car that Could in Japan?" *Business Week*, (June): 56.

Valencia, Humberto (1984). "Point of View: Avoiding Hispanic Market Blunders." *Journal of Advertising Research*, 23 (December/January): 19-22.

Valencia, Humberto (1989). "Hispanic Purchasing Power Keeps Growing Fast." *Hispanic Business*, (December): 12.

Valeriano, Lourdes Lee (1992). "Western Firms Poll Eastern Europeans to Discern Tastes of Nascent Consumers." *The Wall Street Journal*, (April 27): B1, B2.

Vanderleest, Henry W. (1994). "Planning for International Trade Show Participation: A Practitioner's Perspective." *SAM Advanced Management Journal*, (Autumn): 39-44.

Van Mesdag, Martin (1987). "Winging It in Foreign Markets." *Harvard Business Review*, (January/February): 71-75.

Violanti, Michael R. (1990). "International Telemarketing." *Direct Marketing*, 52/12 (April): 24-26.

de Vries, Manfred F.R. Kets (1994). "Toppling the Cultural Tower of Babel." *Chief Executive*, 94 (May): 68-71.

Wagner, William B. and Raymond LaGarce (1981). "Customer Service As a Marketing Strategy." *Industrial Marketing Management*, 11/1 (February): 31-41.

Waldman, Peter (1994). "Lost in Translation: How to 'Empower Women' in Chinese." *The Wall Street Journal*, (September 13): A1.

Walker, Tony and Richard Tomlinson (1995). "In Search of Fresh Pastures." *Financial Times* (December 8): 15.

Walls, Ken (1996). "Its New ATMs In Place, A Bank Reaches Out to South Africa's Poor." *The Wall Street Journal*, (June 13): A1, A10.

Warner, Warner (1996). "Basketball Thrills Koreans as NBA Dribbles into Asia." *The Wall Street Journal*, (May 17): B8.

Weber, Joseph (1993). "Campbell: Now It's MMM . . . Global." *Business Week*, (March 15): 52-55.

Weber, Wilhelm-Karl (1986). "International Commerce with Verbal Savoir Faire." *Business Marketing*, (May): 85-92.

Weekly, James K. (1992). "Pricing in Foreign Markets Pitfalls and Opportunities." *Industrial Marketing Management*, 21: 173-179.

Wei, Amy (1993). "U.S. Exporters Find New Paths to Profits in Spain." *Business America*, 114/17 (August 23): 8-10.

Wei, Lu, John L. Crompton, and Leslie M. Reid (1989). "Cultural Conflicts: Experiences of U.S. Visitors to China." *Journal of Tourism Management*, 10/6 (December): 322-332.

Weihrich, Heinz (1990). "Management Practices in the United States, Japan, and the People's Republic of China." *Industrial Management*, 10/2 (March/April): 3-7.

Weinrauch, D.J. (1994). "Role and Utilization of Trade Shows for International Trade." In Klein and Smith (eds.), *Marketing Comes of Age*. Southern Marketing Association.

Welford, R. (1992). "A Guide to Eco-Labeling and the EC Eco-Labeling Scheme." *European Environment*, 2/6: 13-15.

Wells, Ken (1992). "Global Ad Campaigns, After Many Missteps, Finally Pay Dividends." *The Wall Street Journal*, (August 27): A1, A8.

Wells, Ken (1996). "Belize Offers an Adventure in Ecotourism." *The Wall Street Journal*, (April 16): B8.

Weltz, Richard (1987). "A Not-So Funny Thing Happened on the Way to the Printer." *Business Marketing*, (February): 113-116.

Werther, William B. Jr. (1996). "Toward Global Convergence." *Business Horizons*, (January/February): 3-9.

Whitehill, Arthur M. (1991). *Japanese Management*. London: Routledge.

Wight, Pamela (1993). "Ecotourism: Ethics or Eco-Sell?" *Journal of Travel Research*, (Winter): 3-9.

Wilk, Robert J. (1991). "The New Rich." *Marketing and Research Today*, 19/1 (February): 62-67.

Williamson, James (1986). "Department Stores in Japan: Where Customers Are Treated as Honoured Guests." *Retail and Distribution Management*, 14/4 (July/August): 14-17.

Wind, Yoram, Susan Douglas, and Howard V. Perlmutter (1973), "Guidelines for Developing International Marketing Strategies." *Journal of Marketing*, 37 (April): 14-23.

Winski, Joseph M. and Laurel Wentz (1986). "Parker Pen: What Went Wrong?" *Advertising Age*, (June 2): 60-61, 71.

Wynter, Leon E. (1995). "Language Barriers as a Marketing Tool." *The Wall Street Journal*, (January 25): B1.

Wynter, Leon E. (1995). "Reaching Hispanics Across a Racial and Culture Divide." *The Wall Street Journal*, (February 15): B1.

Yau, Oliver H.M. (1990). "Chinese Cultural Values: Their Dimensions and Marketing Implications." *European Journal of Marketing*, 22/5: 44-52.

Yip, George S. (1989). "Global Strategy . . . in a World of Nations." *Sloan Management Review*, (Fall): 29-40

Yip, George S. (1995). *Total Global Strategy*. Englewood Cliffs, NJ: Prentice-Hall.

Yoshihashi, Pauline (1991). "Now a Glamorous Barbie Heads to Japan." *The Wall Street Journal*, (June 5): B1, B4.

Zachary, G. Pascal (1996). "Major U.S. Companies Expand Efforts to Sell to Consumers Abroad." *The Wall Street Journal*, (June 13): A1, A6.

Zandpour, Fred, Veronica Campos, Joelle Catalano, and Cypress Chang (1994). "Global Reach and Local Touch: Achieving Cultural Fitness in TV Advertising." *Journal of Advertising Research*, 34/5: 35-63.

Zandpour, Fred, Cypress Chang and Joelle Catalano (1992). "Store Is a Symbols and Straight Talk: A Comparative Analysis of French, Taiwanese, and U.S. TV Commercials." *Journal of Advertising Research*, (January/February): 21-44.

Zbar, Jeffrey D. (1995). "In Diverse Hispanic World, Image Counts." *Advertising Age*, 66/14 (April): S18-S19.

Zimmerman, Mark (1985). *How to Do Business with the Japanese*. New York: Random House.

Index

Order Your Own Copy of
This Important Book for Your Personal Library!

HANDBOOK OF CROSS-CULTURAL MARKETING

_____ in hardbound at $59.95 (ISBN: 0-7890-0154-3)

_____ in softbound at $29.95 (ISBN: 0-7890-0285-X)

COST OF BOOKS_____

OUTSIDE USA/CANADA/
MEXICO: ADD 20%_____

POSTAGE & HANDLING_____
(US: $3.00 for first book & $1.25
for each additional book)
Outside US: $4.75 for first book
& $1.75 for each additional book)

SUBTOTAL_____

IN CANADA: ADD 7% GST_____

STATE TAX_____
(NY, OH & MN residents, please
add appropriate local sales tax)

FINAL TOTAL_____
(If paying in Canadian funds,
convert using the current
exchange rate. UNESCO
coupons welcome.)

☐ **BILL ME LATER:** ($5 service charge will be added)
(Bill-me option is good on US/Canada/Mexico orders only;
not good to jobbers, wholesalers, or subscription agencies.)

☐ Check here if billing address is different from
shipping address and attach purchase order and
billing address information.

Signature_____

☐ **PAYMENT ENCLOSED: $**_____

☐ **PLEASE CHARGE TO MY CREDIT CARD.**

☐ Visa   ☐ MasterCard   ☐ AmEx   ☐ Discover
☐ Diners Club
Account # _____

Exp. Date _____

Signature _____

Prices in US dollars and subject to change without notice.

NAME _____

INSTITUTION _____

ADDRESS _____

CITY _____

STATE/ZIP _____

COUNTRY _____ COUNTY (NY residents only) _____

TEL _____ FAX _____

E-MAIL_____
May we use your e-mail address for confirmations and other types of information? ☐ Yes   ☐ No

Order From Your Local Bookstore or Directly From
The Haworth Press, Inc.
10 Alice Street, Binghamton, New York 13904-1580 • USA
TELEPHONE: 1-800-HAWORTH (1-800-429-6784) / Outside US/Canada: (607) 722-5857
FAX: 1-800-895-0582 / Outside US/Canada: (607) 772-6362
E-mail: getinfo@haworth.com
PLEASE PHOTOCOPY THIS FORM FOR YOUR PERSONAL USE.

BOF96

examples of cross-cultural marketing gaffes: 2, 3, 17, 36-7, 69-70, 102, 114-15

Knorr mistake (didn't factor in cooking time) 70
cross-cultural advertising flops: 113-14
use of symbol backfires : 297; 20 (coke putting Saudi flag w/ Koranic words on it for
                                           world cup ✓)

excellent e.g. of adaptation vs standardization: Schick vs Gillette in Japan 39-40
                                                  Parker 40-41

Hofstede shows that value indexes are not collapsing toward a common mean. If anything, value
are diverging, even among countries in the same culture cluster : 41

262-63: SERVQUAL model dev in US not applicable cross-culturally
cross-cultural concepts of service : 265-66

promotional problems: 144

60 horagai   56 tatemae   54 shokaisha   52 kisho, senryaku, iran   66 ringi

Note: many sources outdated